IMAGE AND IDEOLOGY IN

MODERN/POSTMODERN DISCOURSE

IMAGE AND IDEOLOGY IN

MODERN/POSTMODERN DISCOURSE

Edited and with an Introduction by

David B. Downing

and

Susan Bazargan

STATE UNIVERSITY OF NEW YORK PRESS

Published by
State University of New York Press, Albany

© 1991   State University of New York

For information, address the State University of New York Press,
State University Plaza, Albany, NY 12246

Production by Christine M. Lynch
Marketing by Theresa A. Swierzowski

Library of Congress Cataloging-in-Publication Data

Image and ideology in modern/postmodern discourse / edited and with an
    introduction by David B. Downing and Susan Bazargan.
        p.   cm.
    Includes bibliographical references (p.   ) and index.
    ISBN 0-7914-0715-2 (cloth : alk. paper). — ISBN 0-7914-0716-0
(paper : alk. paper)
        1. Literature, Modern—20th century—History and criticism.
    2. Imagery (Psychology) in literature. 3. Ideology in literature.
    4. Modernism (Literature) 5. Postmodernism (Literature)
    6. Postmodernism. I. Downing, David B., 1947-   . II. Bazargan,
    Susan.
    PN771.I45   1991
    809'.04—dc20
                                                                    90-10284
                                                                    CIP

10 9 8 7 6 5 4 3 2 1

Contents

Preface

"Dear Glaucon, I said, you will not be
able to follow me here, though I
would do my best, and you should
behold not an image only but the
absolute truth."
—Plato, Book VII, *The Republic*

"Behind the baroque of images hides
the grey eminence of politics."
—Jean Baudrillard, *Simulations*

The historical leap from Plato to Baudrillard over the status of the image may suggest the "two sides" in the contemporary debates between the essentialist philosophical discourse concerned with "truth" and the critique of all such foundationalist beliefs in the name of "politics." No matter which side one leans toward, it is becoming increasingly apparent that, more than ever, the production, replication, and distribution of verbal and visual images complicate, to say the least, any critical effort to analyze the "image" within the constraints of a formalist aesthetic. Yet, as we began this study, it became apparent that few writers have specifically addressed the connections between image and ideology. In other words, while considerable groundwork has been laid, there is a significant need to address the multiple, trans-disciplinary problems arising from the ways cultures, authors, and texts mobilize particular images to confront, conceal, work through, or resolve contradictory ideological conditions.

This project began in 1987 when we solicited papers for an MMLA Session on "Image and Ideology in Modernist Literature." We sought papers exploring the ways both verbal and pictorial imagery in modernist texts served as forms of "privileged representations," inextricably bound by systems of power and value. Earlier versions of the essays by Caraher, Pearce, and Seyhan thus initiated what became a much larger project. The very problematic terms themselves, *image* and *ideology*, tended to diverge rather than converge in critical discussion. This may partly reflect the general historical battles between formalism and Marxism, but we find that it also reflects a deeper discursive separation of imagery and ideology in contemporary disciplinary study of the arts and literature. In the following two years, we planned and produced a special double issue of the journal *Works and Days* which included eight more articles and provided the experimental format by which we could theoretically formulate a set of issues no longer contained by the terms *modernist* and *literature*. It became necessary to trace some of the lost historical connections between image and ideology, to articulate a position within the modernist/postmodernist debates, and to provide evidence for the need for a sociohistorical study of the image which has yet to be written. In Part I of this book, we therefore elaborate these issues and use the essays that follow as the material for formulating such a rationale. Parts II and III ostensibly divide themselves by content over the historical division between representative modernist texts and the postmodernist cultural moment, but, as we argue in the introduction, this convenient division is generally displaced by the arguments of the essays themselves. Part IV provides more broad-ranging theoretical interventions in the study of iconology and ideology.

Acknowledgments

This project would not have come to completion without the help of many individuals and institutions. Our greatest debt of thanks must go to the contributors to this volume: it has been a collaborative effort from its beginnings in many discussions, phone conversations, and letters leading to friendships as well as this collection of essays.

Susan Bazargan's work at the School of Criticism and Theory during summer 1986 provided the initial impetus for this book; her participation in Tom Mitchell's NEH Summer Seminar on "Verbal and Visual Representation" at the University of Chicago in 1988 helped develop the project further. She wishes to express her gratitude to SCT, NEH, and Eastern Illinois University for intellectual and financial support, and the English Department for providing her with release time as well as encouragement and moral support. Special thanks goes to Jan Marquardt-Cherry of the Art Department for her helpful suggestions on Byzantine icons and images.

David Downing would like to thank the Faculty Professional Development Council of the Pennsylvania State System of Higher Education for a Fall, 1989 research grant that provided much needed release time to complete the first draft of the manuscript. He would also like to thank Ernest Gilman for his invitation to speak on this topic before the Literature and Visual Arts Program of New York University, and for his encouraging response to an early draft of the introduction. Brian Caraher and David Raybin also offered valuable suggestions on revising the introduction. Patrick McLaughlin carefully proofread the entire manuscript, and he painstakingly compiled the index.

Susan wishes to thank her children Mahta, Mehrdad, and Mojgone for their love and good humor, their tolerance and support, their varying perspectives on what matters. David wishes to thank Joan, Peter, and Jordan for their many different ways of making so much so worthwhile.

PART I

Introduction

Chapter 1

Image and Ideology:
Some Preliminary Histories and Polemics

David B. Downing and Susan Bazargan

The story of "image" is a long one. The story of ideology is a relatively short one. At least that is the case if we are looking at etymological time lines: image has its roots in the Greek word *icon*, (εικῶν), likeness, imitation, translated as *imago* in Latin and image in English.[1] Accordingly, the word played a central role in Plato's metaphysics and thus in the establishment of Western systems of representation. Ideology, on the other hand, did not appear in English until 1796 "as a direct translation of the new French word *idéologie* which had been proposed in that year by the rationalist philosopher Destutt de Tracy" (Williams 126). Although originating in the French revolution, de Tracy's use of the term was distinctly nonrevolutionary: indeed, de Tracy wished to establish a philosophical discipline that would provide the foundation for all the sciences; it signified "the science of ideas," and its task was to observe and describe the human mind in the "same way as a natural object" (Barth 1). However, it is Napoleon Bonaparte, himself first sympathetic to the ideologues, who may be largely responsible for the devaluation of ideology, which he called "that sinister metaphysics," into a derogatory term of political denunciation.[2]

But it was not until the young Karl Marx read de Tracy's *Elements d'Idéologie* during his 1844-45 exile in Paris that the term began to assume its modern significance as a name for ideas and beliefs which were blind to the material conditions which produced them, and thus Marx and Engels came to see ideology as "illusion, false consciousness, upside-down reality" (Williams 128).[3] Evolving out of the strictly Marxist meaning, there has also arisen a less dualistic, less pejorative sense of ideology as a name for any given system of ideas and their connection to particular social classes, values, institutions, and power relations. The unresolvable debates between the two uses (and, of course, there are many variations of each) led W. J. T. Mitchell in his *Iconology* to deploy both meanings in the effort to stage a critical encounter between the divergent discourses of iconology and ideology. Despite these differences, however, what needs to be pointed out as a starting point for this volume is that the two terms *image* and *ideology* have often constituted the very system of oppositions called "Western metaphysics." That is, if "image" followed the lead of Aristotelian poetics towards a formalistic, ahistorical "image" of truth and beauty, "ideology" most often named the historical configurations and particular beliefs which the "truth" of abstract images had to overcome in the move toward a transcendent reality. Or, conversely, the abstract sciences of philosophy (logos) provided the dialectical procedures to transcend the historically contingent (ideological) status of particular images. Either way, that the deconstruction of such idealized oppositions has become one of the main critical projects of the past few decades does not conceal the fact that the ideological status of the visual as well as verbal image has received far less attention than one might suspect. Throughout the intricately complex evolution of the term *image*, its benign use in literary, artistic, and historical studies often conceals its ideological history laden as it is with conflict, war, and bloodshed. The rationale, therefore, of this book arises precisely from a need to explore critically the social, political, and cultural critique of the status of images in contemporary critical discourse.

We begin in Section I with two brief stories which we feel are paradigmatic of significant historical moments when the very relations between images and their sociohistorical and political consequences (i.e., their ideology) were crucial yet often ignored or obscured by contemporary critical studies. Two traditions, the Hellenic and the Judeo-Christian, each nurtured the term *image*, each contributed to the ambiguity of the word, and thus to the controversial views of its status, value, and significance. Our first story, therefore, is from ancient Greece and our second from the Byzantine Christian Empire. Our intention is not to outline a consistent historical trajectory nor to provide a general overview, which would be far beyond the scope of this introduction. Rather, we see these examples as critical fragments, narratives reconstructed from our own postmodernist perspective, which we feel have relevance, however indirectly, to the studies of modernist and postmodernist discourse offered by the contributors to this volume. In section II we likewise offer not an objective and descriptive overview of the articles that follow, but rather our own critical articulation of those issues and intertextual relations that we felt significantly stage the encounter between image and ideology.

I

The word *icon* (image) in the Platonic dialogues is never free of ideological contexts. Indeed, Plato's infamous indictment of the poet in *The Republic* follows clearly enough from his perception that the uncertain status of poetic images threatens the truth and order of the ideal state: the poet is a mere "manufacturer of images and is very far removed from the truth" (Book X 300). In Book II the argument seems equally simple if equally repressive: poets often present images of evil behavior which youths will imitate; since the young can't distinguish between true and false images, the poets must be censored so that the gods will be presented only in images of unchanging goodness which the young will imitate in a model education system. Indeed, Plato's position seems clear enough if we read the text alone. And that's the problem. As a consequence of interpretive methods based strictly on primary texts, Plato's banishment of the poet has been accommodated within variations of two basic interpretive histories. The first is, crudely stated, that Plato was wrong. He didn't understand poetry, and his fear of images derives from an irrational intuition of their power and omniscience; or at least Plato's rational dialectic is viewed as so totalitarian as simply not to tolerate any such irrational powers. The second, and perhaps more pervasive, pattern of interpretation has been called by Eric Havelock the "method of reduction," which basically maintains that Plato didn't quite "mean" what he actually says.[4] This long history of interpretive reductions has played an important role in the effort to save Plato by making his outrageous pronouncements more palatable to modern tastes, but none of the answers seems to hold up to close scrutiny. For most students as well as scholars, the text-based interpretations leave a sense of mystery and dissatisfaction. Why, after all, when Plato constructs the model curriculum, essentially the first university curriculum in the West with the disciplines of mathematics, physics, metaphysics, politics, and ethics, did he find the poet so "undisciplinary"?[5] Why do poetry and poetic images seem such a terrible psychic poison to him? Why does Plato seem to attack the very form and substance of the poetized statement, with its verbal images, its rhythmic cadences, its choice of poetic language? Why this tremendous range of hostility?

The felt need for something more, some other texts, some other cultural documents, suggests a crucial gap or lack in the history of the reception of the great works and "images" of Western culture. It has been only in the last few decades that those cultural gaps have received some attention in the pioneering work of Eric Havelock and, preceding him, Milman Parry. As cultural historians, these scholars open the study of Plato and Homer to the wide-ranging social and political power relations sustaining the dominant institutions of Greek culture. As such, these sources reveal that what Plato means by poetry and what we mean by poetry have very little in common. In fact, what Havelock suggests is that the *The Republic* should be viewed not as a political treatise on ideal forms of government, but rather as an attack on the whole existing educational system of Greece. The sociopolitical impact of such an attack arises from the sense that Plato is inaugurating a cultural revolution in the whole way the society organizes its knowledge, knowing, learning, power, technology in a broad-based shift from oral to literate culture.[6]

While it is of course beyond the scope of this brief sketch to elaborate on the cultural shift from oral to literate modes as Walter Ong has done,[7] we can provide evidence to suggest that poetry and poetic images were central to the

ancient Greek educational apparatus and, furthermore, central to the maintenance of the state and the established patterns of dominance and social hierarchies. In this light, Plato's attack on the poet begins to make sense. Poetry is in
its oral performance an entire technology for the preservation of useful knowledge, cultural history, and traditional practices and values as conveyed by the
examples, indeed images, memorized and recited by not only the poets and
rhetors but also the fathers, legislators, artisans, soldiers—virtually all
significant male members of the society. Plato's attack now takes on a more
radical ideological force lost by the assumption of Plato's reactionary and
repressive doctrines of censorship as gleaned from the text "itself." In general,
we are forced to realize that Plato assumes among his contemporaries a view of
the poet and his poetic images which is wholly unfamiliar to our post-romantic
ways of thinking. As Havelock explains:

> In fact, it is not too much to say that the notion of the aesthetic as a system of
> values which might apply to artistic composition never once enters the argu-
> ment. Plato writes as though he had never heard of aesthetics or even of art.
> Instead he insists on discussing the poets as though their job was to supply
> metrical encyclopedias. The poet is a source on the one hand of essential
> information and on the other of essential moral training. (*Preface* 29)

As such, the actual performance of poetry was far more central to the Greek
cultural pattern than we can easily conceive to be the case. Performance means
oral performance, and the work of Milman Parry supplies the crucial evidence
here. In the 1920s Parry documented the fact that the Homeric poems were
actually heavily rhythmic, repetitious textual fragments woven together
between 700 and 650 B.C. from oral narratives. The hexameter dithyrambs were
actually repetitious and didactic clichés and common stereotypical images.
They had to be: otherwise it would be extremely difficult, if not impossible, to
memorize such lengthy narratives. As opposed then to our notions of poetic
images as unique imaginative creations, Homer's verse was primarily constituted by the stereotypes and clichés which would later be seen as defeating the
originality and creativity valued by romantic aesthetic theory.[8]

A new dimension of Plato's attack on the image now opens up to us: to
attack iconic mimesis and imitation can be seen as an attack on blind memorization and identification with dominant cultural images. As Xiao-mei Chen
explains, "Plato's 'frontal attack' on poetry was in fact a 'frontal attack' on the
prevailing cultural tradition and its claims to truth . . . . The Platonic corpus can
then be read as a representation or record of Plato's struggles to invent his own
anti-canonical theory" (41).

As a way of illustrating the ideological consequences for Greek culture of
this mnemonic rhetoric of images, Hesiod provides an example of the early
signs of a shift from concrete oral images to abstract, literate categories.

Whereas the Homeric narratives provided no abstract system of meanings apart from the particular images and examples of the good ways and acceptable customs of the traditional culture, Hesiod in his introduction to the *Theogony* begins to identify the source and justification for such memorization. As Eric Havelock explains:

> Homer simply invoked the Muse who is figuratively responsible for anything he says. Hesiod in effect asks, Who is the Muse? What precisely does she do? What am I doing, and how do I do it? As he asks and answers this question he begins himself to transcend the epic purpose and conception. He marks the beginning of a great transition. He has moved to define that context and purpose of poetry which for the wholly oral minstrel had been unconscious. (*Preface* 99)

As Hesiod hymns his invocation to the muses he "commemorates their birth and identifies them as the daughters of Mnemosune" (100), or memory. The Greek notion of memory suggests as well "the notions of recall and of record and of memorization. Through this allegorical parentage Hesiod identifies the technological reasons for poetry's existence: it describes the muses' function" (100). And they are not the daughters of romantic inspiration and creative invention, but rather the offspring of a far more traditional and static process of memorization of the cultural record: "their central task is not to create but to preserve" (100). And since their other parent is Zeus, their songs memorize and commemorate the order of Zeus the father as patriarchal origin of the social and political order. Poetry thus justifies the traditional phallocratic order. And Hesiod's allegory in turn suggests "for poetry precisely that central role in the maintenance of Greek culture which Plato would reject" (102).

The contrast with Homer is subtle but significant and thus worth being precise about. Whereas the Homeric epics display very little self-reflexive verse, very little interest in examining the sociocultural role of the narrator, the poet, and the rhetor, Hesiod's allegory begins at least a quest to name the sources, reasons, and roles of the poet and the Muse. In other words, in Homer's case, the presentation of the culturally acceptable "custom ways" (ethos) and laws (nomos) always proceeds by way of specific, concrete examples of such behavior. The narrative therefore serves as a model for specific practices and behaviors. Rarely does Homer reflect in more general or abstract terms upon the poet's relationship to the dominant laws and customs. In contrast, Hesiod begins just such a reflection, but he of course does not challenge the order and source which he identifies: that role falls to Plato. And since Plato is now so generally credited as the father of the dominant metaphysic called "phallogocentrism," it is a necessary corrective to see Plato within the newly emerging discursive formations of ancient Greece as playing a critical, anticanonical, and less repressive function with respect to the poet than the more ahistorical generalizations may suggest. It is, indeed, as Chen points out from a Foucauldian perspective, primarily a consequence of "the will to power and the will to truth on the part of the dominating culture itself that has changed Platonism—a previously subversive discourse of the earlier official Homeric culture—into the subsequent orthodox discourse of the post-Platonic era" (42).

To return to the cultural circumstances of Plato's life, Homeric verse was being used as a didactic instrument so that the poetic and rhetorical performance sustained the culture through memorization of (primarily, even in Plato's life) orally transmitted information. One aspect of the cultural crisis of Plato's day was that the content of the knowledge "reposited" in the Homeric poems was no longer very adequate or useful; basically, it was outdated. For example, the famous catalogue of ships in Book II of the *Iliad* no longer served to describe the kinds of ships necessary for expeditions and shipbuilders: technological changes in the production of ships called for new knowledge, new directions in kind, method, and materials unfamiliar in Homer's day. Moreover, even the social function of the poet of Plato's day was primarily to serve as an instrument of the state, the official discourse whereby the poet (as, for example, Pindar) wrote odes to commemorate athletic and military heroes by ascribing to their feats the images of a heroic and godly genealogy: that is, to relate them to the same dominant genealogical past as was assumed to be the heritage of the rulers of the state. One of the basic problems for Plato was that there was no system of abstractions, no vocabulary or syntax even, with which to begin the process of criticism.[9] So Plato's attack on traditional static images can be seen as an effort to foster the creation of a grammar and syntax of abstract terms with which to break from the mnemonic, mimetic, imagistic mode of learning, and thus to inaugurate a "philosophical rhetoric." As Havelock explains, in Plato's move from concrete images and examples to abstract ones, Plato understood that there was a kind of "psychic pathology" enacted by didactic forms of mimesis since the best method for memorization was identification with a character in an oral story: to feel like, to "become" Achilles in the heat of battle. That is, in the Homeric *Paedeia* students invested immense psychic energy in memorizing vast amounts of verse. In order to do this, it was best if the verse were rhythmic and repetitious and the images were stereotypical clichés so as to be easily memorized. Under these conditions, there was, of course, no time or energy to stand back, to think about, to distance oneself from and criticize that which one was memorizing. In order to abstract, one must refrain from such immediacy of identification: one must separate the knower from the known, the self from the received images of the self (Havelock, *Preface* 197-233).

In the specific context of *The Republic,* then, one of Plato's first tasks was to create a sense of the self or subject independent of the object. The language that he had historically available is that of the psyche and the soul; thus, as

Havelock explains, Plato's dialogues are instrumental in redefining the term psyche and moving it away from concrete images of "breath," "life-cloud," and "ghosts" towards a notion for signifying the autonomous self or soul. In Plato's words: "our argument shows that the power and capacity of learning exists in the soul already" (Book VII 209). Such autonomy requires a transcendental soul and thus a whole system of terms seeking abstraction, divestment of particular images, in a turn toward, ultimately, universal essence, Being, and so forth. This assertion of the thoughtful, critical psyche had to be theoretical because one had to stand back from action and doing and become a "spectator," as indeed one of the root words of theory is "theoros" which literally means "spectator." Under the conditions fostered by such theoretical distance, one could sustain the sheer activity of thinking in order to break the habit of self-identification with the memorized images of the oral tradition. The ideological contradiction is that in his effort to break with the conservative oral tradition and the dominance of poetic images, Plato deployed images: that is, at the very heart of his logical argument, the figurative allegory of the cave must become an image of the transcendence of imagery: the literal light that the freed prisoners perceive is not the truth but merely an image of the invisible light of Being. Thus, at the very heart of Plato's doctrine of forms is a central contradiction: the forms are invisible, but the very term *form* derives from idea, *eidos*, which in turn derives from the Proto-Indo-European *weid*. The participial form of *weid-to* became *videre* in Latin, to see, to look. To see in poetic terms was "iconic," a visible image. Conversely, ideology (the supposed opposite) of Platonic forms and ideas also finds a common etymological source as it derives from *ideo* and is also linked to *weid*, and thus, however indirectly, to icon and image.[10]

Such ideological as well as etymological ambivalence in Platonic thought and Greek culture helps explain Plato's own ambivalence in the *Phaedrus* to the main tool of abstraction central to his own accomplishment: writing. Indeed, it sustains Derrida's critique of Plato's *pharmakon*—the ambivalent and polyvalent drug, remedy, poison of writing as the very instrument of Platonic thought. *Phaedrus* was composed towards the end of Plato's life when Greek culture had dramatically begun the shift from the stages of craft literacy to a more general literacy, and it is then that Plato objects to the very instruments of literate abstraction which inaugurated the more radical critique of the traditional oral modes. The irony is that Plato's own pedagogical system, the philosophical rhetoric of the dialectic, was based on spoken discourse, on dialogues. Only the invisible "soul writing" could be acceptable in that system.

With the changes in the discursive formation of Greek culture, Aristotle was more easily able to shift attention away from the critique of the dominant cultural role of the poet (indeed, the poet was far less dominant even by the end of Plato's life).[11] Accordingly, Aristotle simply converted the poem and the image and the drama into more kinds, types, "genres" of formal objects to be known by the inquiring subject. Thus, to end this sketch on a more polemical note, we can say that when in the *Poetics* Aristotle isolated the formal elements of Plot, Character, Diction, Thought, Spectacle, and Melody as part of the "natural order" of things, it was easy enough to see that the formal order of poetic images was an obvious improvement upon the chaos of historical events.[12] The anticanonical and subversive force of the Platonic corpus thereby began to acquire canonized status within the newly emerging discourse of Western metaphysics. Indeed, the poet's mimesis, now reconsidered apart from its pedagogical and cultural function in an oral culture, improves upon nature. Such improvement of the image upon the original could be partly accomplished by "ennobling" the character, raising as it were the listener/viewer's own soul, since all great poetry and tragedy is "an imitation of persons who are above the common level" (Adams 57) in which the "common level" can be read as a synecdoche for the dust of historical realities. Aristotle had thus set the stage for two thousand years of the fetishism of the autotelic image over the suffering of historical "selves."

Only a few hundred years later, we find that, even in its earliest expressions, Christianity sustained a tortuous ambivalence toward the status of the image or icon. On the one hand, Christian doctrine followed Plato in linking the verbal with the intelligible and the spiritual and thus fell at odds with the worship of "graven images," associated with the sensible, the worldly, and the corrupt. Early Christianity resisted what its patrician saints perceived as the sensual and aesthetic culture of antiquity and prohibited "pagan" rituals of venerating corporeal images. But on the other hand, Christianity followed Aristotle in valuing the divine image over the historical reality insofar as man's supreme position on earth could be justified by virtue of his having been made "in the image of God." More importantly, Christ's Incarnation was interpreted as the affirmation and celebration of image making *par excellence*, since Christ was the *Logos* having become flesh—the visible imaging the invisible, just as the light outside Plato's cave was an image of the invisible reality. Thus, for example, through the merging of Christian and Hellenic doctrine, Philo, the eminent Jewish Biblical scholar of the first century A.D., could expound his influential doctrine that the Logos was "the first Image of God" or "God's shadow," the "archetype of all other things." What followed logically was the conjoining of word and image, hence the "image-quality" of the Word, as Ladner explains, and the identification of "[sacred] ideas with [incorporeal] images" ("Concept of the Image" 79-80).[13]

Our story, however, focuses on one of the great historical battles of iconoclasm: the Byzantine Iconoclastic Controversy of the eighth and ninth centuries. The problem, if not the moral of this story, gained literal currency during this era on the face of Byzantine coins: the emblematic authorizing of the system of economic exchange had a twofold (or two-faced) structure represented by images of Christ and the emperor on the coins (Ladner, "Concept of the Image" 111). Indeed, the concept of the ruler as an image of God had entered patristic thought by way of the Greek Pythagoras's early formulation of the political content of the religious image. That influence was so pervasive that despite their fundamental differences, the Byzantine iconoclasts and iconophiles both agreed on one point: they did not question the use of imperial images and their adoration. And in neo-Pythagorean political treatises, the concept of man's similitude to God was transformed into a practical political model whereby the emperor was the imitator of God and the ordinary man was subjugated to the position of "the image of the royal archetype." In defining the nature and purpose of religious images, theologians repeatedly made connections between imperial images and those of Christ.[14]

The iconoclastic battle, however, can be seen as a battle of the opposing sides of the coin: the church and the state.[15] Despite being waged in a theological vocabulary, the social and political consequences of these debates precisely determined the range of the emperor's dominion. Indeed, ambitious rulers consolidated and justified their political designs under the banner of iconoclasm. The problem as perceived by the Byzantine emperors was that they felt threatened by the power of the church, specifically monks and monasteries—the owners of holy images. The emperors tried to assert imperial authority through the suppression of icons and the encouragement of "non-religious art," that is, imperial imagery, to substitute for "the sacred images of Christian tradition" (Ladner "The Byzantine Iconoclastic Controversy" 43). Such holy images were powerful means of propaganda, since they generated that magic aura attracting pilgrims and their endowments to monasteries and to the monks, the guardians of the magic spell of icons,[16] the "custodians of images," as Arnold Hauser calls them (140). The political and ideological issues also had a rudimentary economic dimension: since monasteries were free of taxation, they deprived the emperor of revenue and public support.

It was Leo III, then, who during his reign from 717 to 741, began the iconoclastic campaigns which became more vigorous and systematic during the reign of his son, Constantine V. The first Iconoclastic Synod of Hiereia met in 754 during Constantine's reign (741-775) with the task of formulating rigorous conservative measures against the worship of images: in short, they outlawed all religious "images."[17] This first phase of the Iconoclastic Controversy culminated in the Second Council of Nicea in 787, whose deliberations led to an edict which temporarily restored the worship of holy images. The ideological victory of the Second Council can be largely attributed to the *Orations* of St. John of Damascus. Although St. John was dead by 753, when he was anathematized by the Iconoclastic Council, his eloquent analysis and defense of images became the major text forming the crux of the arguments put forth by the Second Council. For our purposes, the significance of St. John is that he encapsulates in germinal form the heart of the ideological controversies over the crisis of representation in the twentieth century.[18]

What St. John provided was a far more theoretically self-conscious and elaborate critique and defense of the image than had hitherto existed. What St. John's orations emphasize, first and foremost, is the notion of representation as a hierarchical system which privileges some forms of imaging over others, the supreme kind being the "natural" image identical to the prototype. He thereby ties image to divine power in the very definition of the image as "a likeness, example, effigy of that which it represents" (Earl 31), and as such it is an emanation of that thing represented, sharing its power and glory:

> If power is not divided nor glory distributed, honouring the image becomes honouring the one who is depicted in the image . . . . Material things in themselves demand no veneration, but if the person who is represented is full of grace, the material becomes partaker of grace metaphorically, by faith. (qtd. in Barnard 96)

Thus the visible, as image of the invisible, is in some measure "endowed sacramentally" with the virtue of the invisible (Martin 119). The political consequences of this definition emerge when we consider that St. John provided a practical model whereby one could "measure" the relative status of subjects and images. That is, he devised an elaborate neo-Platonic ladder of revelation with six gradations of types of images extending from the visible to the invisible. At the top of the hierarchy was the "natural" image which is identical to its prototype as, for example, Christ is the "actual self-existent image" of God.[19] This kind of image had to be differentiated from man as the "artificial" or "potential" image of God. At the second highest stage, an image may be a prophecy, a "plan of future undertaking, like the foreknowledge in the mind of God." Thirdly, an image could be an "imitation" in the sense of man being made in the image of God, but the "created cannot be strictly an image of the uncreated" Divine power. Fourth, an image could be an analogy or allegory. The examples St. John offers in the third *Oration* are those instances when the sun, the rose, the tree, the flower, the scent can be conceived as "images of the Holy Trinity." The fifth kind of image is the "type" or *figura*, a foreshadowing of something else: "the bush and the fleece, the rod and the urn foreshadow the Virginal Mother of God." Finally, the sixth and the lowest form of image is that which is made by man such as a "pictorial book or record" or a history as the "recollection of past events" (Martin 118-19).

Our reasons for briefly explicating this hierarchy is to demonstrate that St. John has inscribed within a discourse on images many of the issues that later on became fundamental to Renaissance, Enlightenment, and modern aesthetic theory: imitation, analogy, allegory, metaphor, type, *figura*. But in the case of St. John, the ideological consequences are more self-evident: when a church father "measured" a man's behavior against the hierarchy of images, he could be excluded from the community if his evil acts/images fell below the lowest, sixth level. Moreover, artistic performance (painting, sculpture, drama) was often described metaphorically to designate those acts and images through which human beings, mostly male, could assimilate to God, and thus, practically speaking, find themselves placed within the socioreligious hierarchies of the community.[20] It is as if the terms for an aesthetic theory are emerging in a cultural context in which there is as yet no separate aesthetic realm so that the social and ideological consequences of the theory are more self-evident.[21] Moreover, St. John's *Orations* are significant in that they extend the term *imago* in ways that include not only visual representations but also verbal ones.[22] Drawing upon these conceptions of St. John, it was possible for the Second Council to plead that if images were to be banned then so would be their literary as well as political counterparts. St. John's defense, as James Earl points out, "rested upon this *reductio ad absurdum,* and also upon the mystical nature of the *imago* in all its physical, literary, and spiritual manifestations" (30).

What remains perhaps an even more significant legacy of St. John's influential discourse on images is that underlying the hierarchical ladder of revelation was a paradigmatic image of time and history that was, ironically, ahistorical. In at least three of the six kinds of images, the dynamics of representation at work is that of typology, a basic principle of the repetition of dominant images which informs the logic of icons. In typological interpretation, the Old Testament is seen as a "prefiguration of the New Testament and its history of salvation" (Auerbach 30). Thus the original event or persona is often called the "type" or *figura* (from which "figures" of speech are derived) and its "fulfillment," the antitype. Figural interpretation, as Erich Auerbach puts it, "establishes a connection between two events or persons, the first of which signifies not only itself but also the second, while the second encompasses or fulfills the first" (53). The "logic" sustaining this causal relation between "first" and "second" order images requires that the first "event" or image cannot be a mere accidental or random historical action. Any version of contextualized or fragmentary history is therefore effaced in the name of a formalistic cycle of imaginary types both authorized and fulfilled by the requirements of its own ethnocentric system of images. As a privileged form of Truth, the image becomes a vehicle for annihilating time and transcending history; thus the study of Byzantine iconography reveals the shift from an historical interest in representation to a purely speculative one.[23] For example, in St. John's definition, images or icons can be regarded, according to James Earl, as "typological structures" (16). The extension of this basic dynamics of "figure and fulfillment" offered then a conceptual framework which was applied to individual Christian moral behavior as well as to historical explanation and justification. In celebrating the Mass, for example, the individual Christian participated in "a cosmic drama, a re-enactment of the life and passion of Christ, and at the same time all salvation history—a re-enactment which parallels, fulfills, and participates in these larger aspects of history" (Earl 18). Thus, in the adoration of an icon or *imago,* the individual would "remember" the martyr and so close the temporal gap separating him and the new saint just as in partaking of the Body and Blood of Christ, the Christian would transcend time and place and politics and history. Beginning with St. John's iconological definition of the human being as a *potential* image of God—a "disposition still to be fulfilled" (Ladner *Ad Imaginem Dei* 12-13)—we find not only those justifications which have propelled reformation movements but also those justifications for acts of persecution, exploitation, and conquest in the name of man's *homoiosis*, likeness or similitude to God.[24] The paradigmatic nature of this medieval iconology has thus been carried forward most obviously in the Puritan's typological conversion of the New World[25] as well as the Jewish conversion of the Exodus story into the typological justification for the settlement of Israel. But in general (to once again conclude on a polemical note) typological interpretations of human history have played a larger if unconscious role in the colonialism and imperialism which have given shape to Western culture of the twentieth century.

II

While the etymological ties between image and ideology suggest the dissolution of any clear opposition between autotelic images and sociopolitical ideologies, the essays that follow likewise suggest the impossibility of any clear opposition between modernism and postmodernism. The designation of "modern/postmodern discourse" reflects our general sense that neither term by itself adequately refers to an historical/ideological period or mode.[26] As the essays illustrate, literary and cultural modernism is not nearly so monological as it is often conceived to be by postmodernist definitions. According to such definitions, the modernist literary revolution against the positivist epistemology of bourgeois humanism ended in an apolitical reification of an artistic/aesthetic order and form ranging from Arnold's "the best that is known and thought," to Eliot's "ideal order," to what Joseph Frank called "spatial form" as epitomized by the New Critics' intrinsic formalism. The ahistorical consequences of these modernist doctrines occurred in spite of their own intended political value as a resistance to a massively corrupt and materialistic culture. The postmodern then allegedly follows as a fracturing, dispersal, and dissemination of any such idealized order. Thus the ideological and political valence of postmodern discourse is most often seen to emerge from the fracturing and rupturing of dominant images, meanings, authorities, and subjectivities.

The specific focus of our volume, "image and ideology," provides a tactical site for an entry into such debates over the political and ideological work of critical practice as it emerges from the status accorded modern/postmodern discourse. Our central focus is crucial in that it is precisely the valorizing of the autonomy of the image, whether as the "spatial form" represented by the "verbal icon" of New Critical texts, or the Imagists' "art for art's sake" aestheticism, or in the general humanist images of the paternal "Sameness" of the human nature of "Man" as a source of cultural stability, that has dictated the terms for the reception of the texts of the modernist era into the classroom as well as the scholarly enterprise. Moreover, the focus on image and ideology in these chapters draws out the central role that the "image" has played in the West as a mode of representing "truth" as a transcendence of the specifically ideological and historically contingent.

Another centrally related claim of this book is that implicit in all the familiar epistemological, historical, or psychological accounts of what Fredric Jameson has called the "crisis in representation" is, perforce, a crisis in the status of the visual and verbal image, a crisis with deep historical roots, nonetheless foregrounded by postmodernism.27 As W. J. T. Mitchell argues, "the cliché of postmodernism is that it is an epoch of the absorption of all language into images and 'simulacra'" ("Iconology and Ideology" 326). Jameson's description of postmodernism likewise focuses on the status of the image: "In the form of the logic of the image or the spectacle of the simulacrum, everything has become 'cultural' in some sense. A whole new house of mirrors of visual replication and of textual reproduction has replaced the older stability of reference and of the non-cultural 'real'" (Jameson, "Hans Haacke" 42). Jameson's "images" suggest that the older, stable "mirror theory" of correspondence, objectivity, reference, and reality has been culturally displaced by a destabilizing "house of mirrors," or horrors, that leave us exasperated, as Jameson often seems to be, with the unending powers of postcapitalist appropriation, commercialization, and complicity.

On the one hand, a view of the postmodern as an aesthetic and cultural period displacing modernism has its clear social gains if we concur that postmodernist politics is "a politics of difference, wherein many of the voices of color, gender, and sexual orientation, newly liberated from the margins, have found representation under conditions that are not exclusively tailored to the hitherto heroicized needs and interests of white, male intellectuals and/or white, male workers" (Ross xvi). But despite such significant gains, we should remain wary of the implications of postmodernism as a strictly linear displacement of modernism: a metanarrative that totalizes a particular view of history within a plotted, linear series of events. Such a metanarrative informs Jameson's influential "cognitive mapping" of the chronological shift from modernism to postmodernism by reference to the mode of production. In his often-cited 1984 essay, "Postmodernism, or the Cultural Logic of Late Capitalism," he draws on Ernest Mandel's socioeconomic analysis in *Late Capitalism*. In short, this model enables him to map the sequence whereby market capitalism (roughly,

1700-1850) produced realism, monopoly capitalism in the age of imperialism produced modernism, and multinational capitalism produced postmodernism. According to such a totalizing model, as Douglas Kellner has remarked, "the era of high modernism is over, its great individual authors have vanished, its styles are exhausted, and its monumental works are no longer possible" (*Postmodernism* 32). But however true the diachronic historical assessment of the "exhaustion" of the modernist idiom, the postmodernist mode is neither total nor dominant except with respect to particular cultural sectors and audiences. As Kellner has argued: "In fact, both processes [modernism and postmodernism] are conceivably happening at once making it questionable to affirm unambiguously that postmodernism is a new cultural dominant" (30-31).[28]

The contributors to this book question such totalizing metanarratives. Nevertheless, these critical interrogations do not always condemn the effort to conceptualize in more general and systematic (if fallible) ways so long as such broader perspectives do not negate or efface marginalized peoples. In this light, Linda Nicholson proposes a view of a "carefully constructed postmodernism" that recognizes both the problems of foundationalism and of fragmentation: "postmodernism must reject a description of itself as embodying a set of timeless ideals contrary to those of modernism; it must insist on being recognized as a set of viewpoints of a time, justifiable only within its own time" (11). Read in this way, the wide-ranging and cross-cultural terms of image and ideology, for example, may remain justifiably general categories "for our time" despite the inevitable differences in the way such categories may be interpreted. Moreover, even the referential multiplicity inscribed in most uses of the words *our* and *time* need not efface all efforts to construct models of historical continuities between, say, the nineteenth-century culture of Marx's "time" and our postmodernist moment.

The anti-foundationalist stance advocated by the contributors to this book therefore entails a twofold critical view: on the one hand, they recognize the increased bricolage of postmodernist and modernist images, but they also wish to resist a passive acquiescence to the unfocused and nebulous play of indeterminacy. The authors enact such critical resistance while also avoiding the latent nostalgia that accompanies the loss of any widespread, socially sanctioned belief in the sufficiency of the mirror image of representation.[29] The provisionality of postmodern cultural criticism leads, then, to the important ideological questions of power and politics: whose images, whose history, whose interests are being served?

Indeed, the politically self-conscious practice of postmodern iconology as recommended by the contributors helps us realize that we must struggle as well against the etymology of the very word insofar as it reinscribes the mirror theory: the proper *icon* must mirror/reflect the true *logos*. That we can no longer safely refer to such metanarratives of transcendence signals the sociopolitical conditions of postmodern critical practice which acknowledges the fact that, as Norman Bryson says, "the image is not obliged to go out of its way to 'meet' the social formation . . . . since it is always already there at its destination; it has never been in a state of disarticulation from the society" (152). Furthermore, the enormous proliferation of both verbal and visual images in postmodern culture, and the infusion of the image with the social and the political, call for an interrogation of any separation of the visual and verbal domains.[30]

Such a politically self-conscious critique of disciplinary boundaries suggests the terrain of what Linda Hutcheon calls the "complicitous critique" of postmodern critical practice.[31] In the sociopolitical conditions of postmodern culture, oppositional practice often satirizes, critiques, and attacks in local and historical ways various forms of domination, exclusion, oppression, and nonreciprocal relations. But such critique recognizes its own complicitous status: as producers and receivers of images, we are, in Hutcheon's words, "all implicated in the legitimation of our culture" (*Politics* 15). In abdicating the rhetoric of science, totality, and transcendence, we may find ourselves with no position outside the culture from which to judge a culture's image-making practices. Rather, only differences within the social system allow for positions of rhetorical critique. In this sense, emancipatory images and rhetorics need constantly to be historically and situationally evaluated, especially with respect to marginalized and oppressed peoples, if we are to determine how we may "de-doxify" the systems of meaning, images, and representations by which we know our culture and our selves. As Steven Connor remarks: "cultural analysis always risks falling into complicity with the increasingly globalized forms which seek to harness, exploit, and administer—and therefore violently to curtail—" (244) the diversity and radical differences in the global political scene. Thus, "the task for a theoretical postmodernity of the future must be . . . to forge new and more inclusive forms of ethical collectivity . . . common frames of assent" that would simultaneously acknowledge "a global diversity of voices" (244). Or, as Nancy Fraser and Linda Nicholson have cast the hope for such critical alliances: "such commonalities are by no means universal; rather, they are interlaced with differences, even with conflicts. This, then, is a practice made up of a patchwork of overlapping alliances, not one circumscribed by an essential definition" (35).

The common frame of an "ethical collectivity" in this book derives from the diverse commitments of the contributors who nevertheless jointly ally themselves with the need to articulate modern/postmodern critical practices that lead to active resistance of the oppression and domination which Paulo Freire would call the "generative theme" for our era. Thus, while the organization of this book initially seems to highlight a chronological displacement between the "modernist" texts addressed in Part II and the "postmodernist" discourses of Part III, the superficial chronology is displaced by the thematic, methodological, and political commitments of the contributors themselves. Thus, the essays that follow all tend to share an appraisal that, to restate a major premise, the postmodernist resistance to high modernist aestheticism has institutionalized itself within English Department curriculums as an idealized opposition, a false duality between modernist totality and postmodernist fragmentation. One of the consequences of such institutional incorporation of modernists and postmodernists has often been, as Linda Hutcheon explains, "to forget the lesson of postmodernism's complex relation to modernism: its retention of modernism's initial oppositional impulses, both ideological and aesthetic, and its equally strong rejection of its founding notion of formalist autonomy" (*Politics* 26). Such forgetting leads to the depletion of the actual oppositional political work that needs to be done. Indeed, the contributors to this volume deploy such postmodernist idioms as Foucault's genealogy of power, Bakhtin's dialogism, Kristeva's semiotic, or Baudrillard's simulations to emphasize the activity of a critical practice which mediates between the idealized poles of modernist tradition and aestheticism and postmodernist multiplicity and dispersion. In the end, the contributors are less concerned with academic definitions of what modernism or postmodernism *is* than with what the critique of the images and ideologies that sustain and surround those debates can *do*. This book thereby situates ideological articulations of images within the social and cultural codes of modern/postmodern practices. As such, postmodernist disruption emerges as a counter-dominant discourse within the modernist period and indeed within modernist texts themselves.[32]

The opening essay by Brian Caraher can thus be seen as an effort to articulate the ways in which such a traditionally modernist text as Conrad's "Youth: A Narrative" dramatizes a play of image and ideology that prefigures various modes of postmodern discourse.[33] The critical difference between modernist and postmodernist narratives "appears already contained within the discursive range of modernity." There are two interrelated dimensions to this project. The first is the recognition that the chronological displacement of modernism by postmodernism replays the modernist condition of displacing and differing "from what is regarded as ancient, classical, traditional." To conceive of modernity "as itself already over, behind, past, classic, intellectually completed" reifies the historical period as a representable discursive object that has been displaced. But that very effort entails the second recognition: such periodized objectivity "assumes or projects an ideology of representation still in need of postmodern debunking." As Caraher argues, "literary modernism at least has actually already performed a major task of the postmodern project."

"Under the pressure of postmodern concerns," Caraher thereby reads Conrad's "Youth" as a critique of the romance narrative which, insofar as it derives from an "ill-founded, egocentric, illusory" image of an idealized "East," provides an implicit justification of imperialist adventure and quest. Caraher

derives from his specific analysis the more general claim that modernist literature itself reveals the illusions by which image structures narrative. Readers
who uncritically accept the traditional plot as a relatively unproblematic
"romantic quest for an image of the East and of fulfillment" thereby participate
in sustaining the patriarchal and imperial ideologies that nourish those images
in the first place. In contrast, a second, allegorical or "metanarrational narrative" insistently intrudes in a kind of multiple or postmodernist critique of the
"ideological assumptions upon which the tale of romance is founded and structured." This second, destabilizing metanarrative highlights a more general theoretical contention: numerous modernist writers have revealed the ideological
foundations of narrative structure to be colonial images. In other words, the
very art of consistent storytelling itself depends upon "a covert ideology and
pivotal valuation" of patriarchal and monological images of those desired others, the East, Youth, Woman, etc., that sustain the colonizing plots of white,
Western men.

Caraher's formulation echoes Richard Pearce's argument with respect to
Virginia Woolf. Pearce enables us to appreciate the extent to which Woolf's narratives also engage a powerful critique of those patriarchal narratives of adventure, romance, and dominance that affect not only issues of gender but also of
race, class, and nationality. In particular, Pearce argues, Woolf shifted patriarchy
by rejecting the monological male sentence which, as described by Gilbert and
Gubar, is "the sentence-as-definitive-judgment." Woolf creates another mode of
reading in another syntax which is not a monologic judgment but a dialogical
breaking up of coherent images into a field of continually shifting relationships,
images, points of view, a destabilizing effect similar to what is often attributed
to postmodern art and literature.

And yet, as Pearce remarks, the "lady writing" must continually struggle
against traditional structures of male authority. In *Mrs. Dalloway,* for example,
Woolf's narrative, while throughout "open to images of relationship denied by
the male hierarchy of thought," nonetheless has the ostensible structure of "an
old-fashioned romance plot: the courtship of Peter Walsh." Just back from
India, Peter "reflects the mentality—and authority of imperialism" and he
"imposes his frame, his order, his image of unity, on the multiple, even contradictory, strands of the novel."

Such a unity of images, concluding many of Woolf's novels, is in fact a
source of delight for many of her readers. But as Pearce reminds us, such readings "are not wrong." They reflect "the residual power of traditional authority"
in the community of readers. So what we find is that Pearce's dialogical reading
reveals a textual innovation that calls in turn for a readerly innovation. On the
one hand, Woolf's textual innovation is to deploy a "new kind of authorial figure," that is, a mode of authorizing narratives without an omniscient, monologic
point of view to unify the narrative flow of semiotic images. Such a mode has

often been described as a characteristic of postmodern narrative which Pearce
locates in Woolf's modernist text. The "em-bodying," as Pearce describes it,
undermines the final images of unity. But to engage that undermining as postmodernist readers, we must actively participate in the dialogical play of voices,
images, relationships that intersect this text with our own.

Pearce describes this embodying-disembodying play of interpretations in
The Waves where Woolf positions Bernard so that "he literally takes on the
paternalistic role of an omniscient narrator." Pearce's observation here is that
Woolf makes visible the image of omniscience as one of many possibilities for
readerly interaction with the text whereas in most conventional narratives the
image of omniscience remains concealed. The political consequences of such a
critique of dominance avoids as well what Pearce sees as "the misleading distinction between a totalizing modernism and a revolutionary postmodernism."

In the effort to avoid similar misleading distinctions, Norman Wacker
opens a new way to read Pound that has explicitly political implications without
simply bemoaning his connections to Mussolini and fascism on the one hand or
his elite aesthetic obscurity on the other. As Wacker explains, "Pound documents the passing from one representational 'regime of truth' to a new mechanics of image and ideology which anticipates both the modernity of the cold war
and the postmodernity which has decentered it." Pound's poetics becomes an
act and process of articulating images so as to place "our categories of representation before our eyes" not as a neutral, theoretical position, but as a constructive archive, a "medium for rethinking of tradition" and society at moments of
historical disruption. Poetic articulations can thus be read as "a celebration of
improvised objects, fortuitous insight, and disruptions of fascist ideology." The
articulation of images, whether of Chinese philosophers, World War II battles,
or Homeric episodes, is seen not within the idiom of an allusive formalism but
as the construction of a cross-cultural genealogy which, as a poem-in-process
for the reader as well as the poet, breaks the hold on the dominant Western
models of representing truth in images that are monological and thus in the
hands of a powerful elite.[34]

Poetic images are now "charged" with "the greatest possible breadth of
those normally submerged determinations which condition [their] use." That is,
in Wacker's view, a reconstructive articulation of Pound's poetics reveals the
ways that images are not autonomous, isolated forms, but sites for interpretation
whose active political charge is an ideological construction. In thus implicating
Pound's own ideological complicities within his poetics, Wacker demonstrates
that we are not led, as many critics have been, to a disabling of his entire poetics
as evidenced in *The Cantos* by pointing out his own failures, whether in his
anti-Semitism or his political reactionism in the *Pisan Cantos*. Indeed, Wacker
locates patriarchy at the very heart of Pound's *ethos* in his central image of "old
men's voices" as a historical residue of a renewed tradition. As Wacker

explains, Pound didn't recognize "sexism, racism, and imperialism in his source materials," but his poetics of disruption calls for the readerly construction of images which fracture the oppressions of the source materials and thus reject those dominant "representations of truth" which conceal their own ideological interests.

Moreover, Wacker's reading of Pound specifically marks the postmodern tendencies of his work: the tension between the verbal and the visual revealed in Pound's use of "cinematic logics" and the "semiotics of the film" registers the dramatic, *performative* potential of his socio-poetics. Thus in Pound the modernist urge to "make it new" takes on postmodern traces of "doubleness of construction in action" in that his composition reflects upon both the act of articulation and the revelation of the cultural determinants of that act. The duplicity, along with the cinematic blendings of sight and sound—"the visual echo of the aural movement"—enables Pound to fuse the ideological connotations of images and their visual impact on the reader. The intrusion of the visual upon the verbal in Pound—his efforts to "write to paint"—also identifies with the abstractionism of paintings which defy representation as reproduction, and instead create new cognitive and political spaces by isolating "expressive qualities of objects and deploy[ing] them in new constructions."

The political implications of such a revised poetics derive from the very assumptions that the meaning of images are never discretely in the text, nor ideally in the author's intention, nor merely in the reader, but rather in a dialogic engagement of many voices and positions which implicate each other. Such implications resist the apolitical status of what Jameson calls "nostalgia art," that which "gives us the image of various generations of the past as fashion-plate images that entertain no determinable ideological relationship to other moments of time: they are not the outcome of anything, nor are they the antecedents of our present; they are simply images" (Stephanson 18). In other words, even textual readings of such canonized texts are never merely "textual" or preserved within isolated academic sites such as the classroom or the scholarly journal but are implicated within a cultural system of signs and discourses. Failure to recognize those intertextual politics tends precisely to facilitate the "culture of surveillance" which ranges all the way from United States colonialism in Nicaragua to the material systems for hiring, firing, and evaluation within the academy.

Indeed, such racism and sexism sustain well the regressive force behind the use of the images, plots, and stereotypes of the "southern gothic" as a literary and social "genre" which conceals and mystifies the underlying images of misogynistic violence and horror by displacing them to "southern gothic" rhetorics of black humor and farce. As Margie Burns explains, "any awareness stimulated by the hint of very real violence . . . is displaced—trivialized—into typically 'gothic suspense' and a (feminine) morbid curiosity." Like the fate of the unwanted and despised spinsters that surface in many literary texts of the twentieth century, the relative spinsterhoods of Faulkner's Emily and O'Connor's grandmother serve as paradigmatic instances whereby the fates of these marginalized, elderly women emerge from narratives which construct a series of images of houses, walls, facades, barriers which "simultaneously blazon and conceal" the sites of sexual and political injustice. In Burns's words, the use of southern gothic images "transforms 'history' into an intimidation serving the interests of a privileged class." For example, gothic images of interiors actually signify "an *exteriorization*—a shunning, in which the pain and horror of real events are dislocated into imaginary gardens." In these imaginary gardens, the ideological force charges the spinstered "lady," "the old flowers of decayed femininity," with the total demoralization of social values and "good taste," charges which in turn justify her extermination under conditions not radically at odds with the more obvious forms of colonialist violence documented by Conrad's "Youth." Burns reminds us, such "imaginary gardens provide no escape from real oppression and pain, because they offer no real change."

Such change may be possible, however, if we recognize the images that sustain the ideological force of the metanarratives that justify systems of authority and oppression. Thus the essays in Part III explore the ways in which postmodern artists, like their modernist predecessors, have engaged and responded to authorial images and voices. In exploring the works of John Fowles, Gian Balsamo brings into focus the Bakhtinian point made earlier in Part II by Richard Pearce, that "the novel is revolutionary because of the variety of voices that contend ideologically with the authorial voice." Balsamo's essay also adumbrates Walter Benjamin's articulation of "historical configuration," as explored by Azade Seyhan in Part IV. Bakhtin's notion of heteroglossia finds added complexity in Balsamo's reading of Fowles in that the dissonance of the "polyphonic chant" of his narrators—in *A Maggot,* for example—is related not only to the multiple levels of fictionality, but also to the dialogic modulations between "the writer's discourse" and the "social dialogue" revolving around the object of narration. Furthermore, such an interaction, transgressing those boundaries that separate aesthetic from social, political, and institutional practices, implicates the readers also, who have to ponder "the *questions* which justify [the book's] existence as a work of art." The "social dialogue" in Fowles's novels draws upon a plethora of pictorial and verbal images and their implied ideologies. Fowles, Balsamo argues, aggregates such images, but in a "congeries of disconcerting art arrangements" to disrupt, in postmodern fashion, the homogeneity between historical sources and modes of emplotment.[35]

In particular, Balsamo focuses on the politics of genre and gender in Fowles. In his displacement of the writer by the scribe in *A Maggot*, Fowles, not unlike Woolf in *The Waves,* immolates the "conventional image of the writer," an immolation that parallels that of "most of the male protagonists in [his] novels and stories." In response to Fowles's critics who detect a "phallocentric view" in his fiction, Balsamo argues that if Fowles incorporates feminine archetypes cast by the male characters as "frozen images of timeless magic and mystery," he aims to reveal them ultimately as "images of exclusion," as "fetishistic aberrations" affecting the dominating, frustrated male as well as the victimized female. In his use—and disruption—of such genres as the "Victorian novel" or the "medieval *contes d'aventure et d'amour*," Fowles invites the reader to question the "very rhetoric of images" imposed by "the history of the systems of power and the history of the canon of value." Thus the reader's inquiry leads to an awareness of the ruling patriarchal ideology and consequently to a sense of freedom, a possibility for an individual, "existential" emancipation.

And yet, Balsamo reminds us, the reader, like King Phillip in Velasquez's *Las Meniñas*, is never free from his/her own "reflection": "We cannot look without seeing ourselves mirrored in the picture." The entanglement of the "subject" with images and mirrors is one main focus of James Buzard's essay on John le Carré. In particular, the role of a photographic image in representing for a Western spy the obsessively longed-for reality of a hated Russian enemy leads to "questions about the condition of a postimperial England whose degraded marginality in the international alignment grows ever more apparent to its secret servants." While le Carré's fiction is usually placed within the traditional mode of the espionage or spy novel genre with its assumptions of realistic character and consistent motive, Buzard offers a new interpretation by placing his fiction within the postmodern problematic of dispersal and critique. What happens, then, is that the superficially stable "image of the potent opponent" becomes a sign for the unraveling of any stable identity or clear motive. As Buzard explains, "the looming presence of Karla's image reminds the British spy of the threatening object against which his own function and identity are measured." But interpretation and explanation of motive runs aground on the unknowability of motive for a "coherent volitional subject." Buzard draws on the Althusserian notion of the interpellated subject in order to articulate the ways that the photographic image serves to interpellate, to "hail," to name the subject within a socially recognizable category. Le Carré's fiction then reveals a central ideological battle to maintain "the illusion of a coherent Western (liberal humanist) subject in the face of a considerable evidence of that subject's dispersal, corruption, or loss." But Buzard pushes his critique further in the effort to demonstrate that "le Carré's fiction can be read . . . as problematizing both liberal-humanist and strict Althusserian interpretations of subjectivity." The monolithic but polarized global politics of East/West relations "robs political choice of its specificity," so Buzard proposes "a different politics, one . . . more attentive to the ways ideology is reproduced and resisted within Western societies." Such resistance then takes the form of a critique of all those spectral images of a terrifying Other which serves to galvanize the structures of oppression as they operate within what Harry Polkinhorn terms the "gyroscopic" model of Western history.

One of the most important phases of such a postmodern critique is the necessary engagement with Latin American and Third World political dimensions as in the essays by Harry Polkinhorn and Michael Messmer. In the case of Polkinhorn's study of Latin American experimentalism, the subversive and transgressive properties of, for example, Chicano art, disrupt any one-dimensional image of history and culture in the relations between Third World and superpower nations. Polkinhorn characterizes the dominant, monological versions of historical change as perpetuated in Western discourse on the model of a "gyroscope," a spinning machine which stabilizes all images along a single, dominant axis. In Polkinhorn's version of the gyroscope, the dominant historical axis has often concealed the originating sources and powers of its own structures of mediation through an objectifying epistemology. In contrast, "Latin American art forms propose themselves as a critique of just such ideological control and 'objectifying' distance characteristic of dominant Western modes of historical representation." Polkinhorn offers a new way to situate the Latin American avant-garde within the discussions of a politically self-conscious postmodernism by demonstrating that the art forms he discusses resist the very gyroscopic, chronological models of history that would see the postmodern as merely the most recent stage in a series of stylistic innovations that have "surpassed" the historical avant-garde. In this way, Polkinhorn develops a critical understanding of Latin American art that reaffirms Andrew Ross's position that: "The debate about the culture of postmodernism is very much a debate about the *instability* of these ideological processes. And it is precisely because this instability is most palpably felt at the level of everyday life that a postmodernist politics must complete the Gramscian move to extend the political into all spheres, domains and practices of our culture" (xv). Thus, for the Latin American experimentalists "the ideological array of images, institutions, and representations that drive forward gyroscopic history" is smashed into the "junk heap" of an historical archive "which becomes an irreverent source for the recycling of particular cultural artifacts" in local, communal efforts of coping with "image/power" systems that have so materially fostered the conditions of oppression.

In general, then, the possibilities for emancipation from dominant images of oppression and victimization lie in the struggles of individuals to create and sustain alternative images of particular and local histories which may compete with the one-sidedness of monological History. The ways in which such alternative images can be created to represent the Other—in this case the effaced European peasant life—is the locus of Michael Messmer's essay on John

Berger whose "hybrid texts" draw upon the dialogical play of photographic image and verbal text. Photographs, with their extraordinary proliferation and appropriation as the "visual language" of advertising, are the icons *par excellence* of the twentieth century, and Messmer's study of Berger brings into focus not only their highly political valence in capitalist societies, but also their problematic status as a mode of representation, as a "mediator" between "reality and the viewer." Messmer locates the crux of Berger's arguments on photographic images in the author's comparisons between painting and photography. Unlike painting, which begins on an empty canvas, photographs begin with "appearances in the world" so that photographs, according to Berger, are "weak in intentionality." As Messmer puts it, "It [the camera] quotes from . . . the language of appearances, as opposed to a painting, which *translates* from that language." Weak in meaning and intentionality, photographs can be easily subjected to "manipulation and simplification and can be used to hide rather than reveal the truth . . . As mere traces of experience rather than re-creations or representations of them, photographs (especially . . . in their myriad public uses . . .) are curiously mute with regard to their subjects." Although photographs are records of the past, their public use in the modern world, unlike their private use, does not rejoin the past with the present. In its public uses, photography "conforms to the needs of capitalism to deny sensitivity, to negate the past."

In his alternative use of photographs, however, Berger has shown how they can be treated as "a vast inchoate memory of collective experience," parts of which can be mobilized "to present images as belonging to 'a *living* memory'" rather than as "perfect nostalgic objects." Whether it is in his presentation of peasant life or that of the migrant worker, Berger merges photographs with verbal texts, but not as a way of subjecting the visual image to the "dogmatic assertion" of words; photographs are not "illustrations" of texts, nor are words "captions" or "titles" to photos. Instead the interplay between them is such that "two different, but mutually reinforcing channels of communication are opened." As such, Berger's visual/verbal texts place new demands on the reader who has to engage in "an oscillating reader maneuver." Instead of the conventional linear reading process, the reading experience is fractured "into a series of back and forth movements, from oral text to commentary or from image to written text, or from one image to another . . . . Thus the organization of the texts themselves helps pull the reader into the text and hence into the lives of the peoples represented therein."

Berger's specific commitment to the peasant in his cultural politics and his artistic praxis clearly distances him from those "modernist" attitudes that separate high and mass culture. Rather, his "experimental texts," standing "at the junction of modernism and postmodernism," serve "as appropriate vehicles for enabling the ethnographer to grapple with the problem of situating lives lived at the local level within the broader framework of the global economy." Berger's cultural politics arise from his perception of "an ideal of equality based upon the necessity of work in a world of scarcity" which reflects a deeply ecological concern for the future with a radical scepticism towards the technological "progress" of the West. The value of Berger's textual practices emerges from his engagement with the postmodern struggles to confront the lives of the French peasantry in an effort "to undo, to unwrite, the false axioms" of the dominant patriarchal North Atlantic system. Thus our own status as techno-peasants challenges the exploitations of late capitalist intellectuals as well as economic programs.

Part IV of this book includes essays of general theoretical significance that traverse the distinctions between modernism and postmodernism. To cross these boundaries, we begin with Azade Seyhan's study of Walter Benjamin. As one of the most influential critical theorists of the modernist period, Benjamin situates the "crisis in representation" as it operates through the interrelations of image and ideology within his conception of allegory. Seyhan first follows Heidegger in suggesting the crucial role of the image in the very construction of the notion of modernity: "The fundamental event in the modern age is the conquest of the world as picture," or "structured image." Seyhan argues that "Benjamin's examination of representation and his radical restoration and diversification of allegory map the critical path from the modern to the postmodern." Benjamin's allegorical vision "reads time as iconized history" so that his "concept of historical materialism operates by recalling and arresting moments of history that are then reconfigured in new narratives in such a way as to release their liberating potential."

As one illustration of the allegory as "the trope of interlinkage" between the modern and the postmodern, we can note the remarkable similarities, described by Seyhan, between Benjamin's concept of allegory and Baudrillard's notion of the image as simulacrum: allegory is an "image that replaces the real or 'masks' the *absence* of a basic reality." Seyhan claims that the "emblem of modernity" reveals no unified, totalizing image of an underlying historical reality as presence, or spirit in the Hegelian sense, or as the traditional male view of progressive order in the Western march of civilization. But Seyhan also clearly documents the significant differences between these two thinkers: whereas Baudrillard's simulational pervasiveness of images abdicates ideological critique in favor of seduction and play, Benjamin's historical allegories do "not yield to this inevitability without a fight" for liberation from all the oppressive conditions perpetuated by the dominating classes. Like Polkinhorn's assessment of the "junkheap" of civilization as a multicultural resource and challenge to the linear historical model, Benjamin's "allegorical moment" "does not sanction a peaceful synthesis." Rather, Benjamin sees the allegorical "image of ruins" characterizing the twentieth century as a catastrophe, but one analogous "to the images of the kaleidoscope which go from chaos to order." The image of a male hand (the often-concealed image of authority) turns the kaleidoscope to provide a momentary image of order as a stay against the confusion and chaos of history. But since "the hand that shakes the kaleidoscope belongs to the dominant powers," it must be smashed: Benjamin's allegorical "act of violence" thereby "destroys the stability of the image embedded in social time and deconstructs the ideology . . . maintained by the dominant systems of representation." Through such a critical praxis, Benjamin, according to Seyhan, ends up deploying, "though inconclusively, a dialectic of salvation." Her final reference to "the eternal recurrence of the new" provides a "moment of salvation" for the marginalized women, Third World cultures, working-class people, and the dispossessed others of modern history who remain oppressed by the dominant images of progress and glamour in the West. The "corrosive job" of allegorical criticism serves as a "heuristic fiction" which "provides the alert reader with access to the complex social operations that construct image and ideology."

Brian Macaskill likewise focuses his study on the ideological force of the "rupture" of ostensibly static and autonomous images. Just as Polkinhorn focused on the "border equation" by which the Latin American avant-garde transgresses the political, linguistic, and visual borders of containment, Macaskill provides a general theoretical framework in which to articulate the importance to a politically self-conscious critical practice of the rupture of stable artistic and literary borders. Macaskill's starting point is the general acknowledgment that "the image is crucially a site of power . . . where it serves to illuminate the nationalistic stories that cultures tell themselves about who they are." Macaskill thus opens an interrogation into all those dominant forms of Western criticism that have sought to contain and to "police the domain of the aesthetic image" within the borders of the "specifically literary" realm.

His study of the rupture of the image involves what might be called a "politics of the gap" ruling verbal as well as pictorial images. The gap situates itself between the "cultural sign-system exterior to the frame (which we know and inhabit as the world) and the stylistically framed interior of the various artistic media used to represent or to address that world." Despite the "barrier" quality of any gap, often used to establish binary distinctions ("art and life" or "modern and postmodern"), Macaskill instead draws attention to the "complicities and continuities that division negotiates." Like John Berger, whose work advocates mutual reenforcement and dialogue between verbal texts and photographs, Macaskill also recognizes "the continuity that iconic, narrative and cinematographic images can evoke among themselves and the referents they denote." Thus from the medieval miniature of Otto II to the "rupturing potential of images in a French new wave film," *Hiroshima Mon Amour*, to "the politics of a verbally constructed image from a novel by Nadine Gordimer," Macaskill develops a politically effective version of postmodern critique which avoids the recurrent retreat to the "protopolitical" forms of cultural and artistic innovation. He contrasts, that is, the recontainment of the disruptive effects of *Hiroshima* within "the recuperative ideology on which the film's intelligibility is based" with the more potentially effective critique found in Gordimer's *The Conservationist*.

Similar to Berger's project of articulating peasant subjectivity within postmodern cultural politics, Kristina Straub's work addresses the "project of articulating feminine subjectivity" both within and against the relatively privileged status accorded postmodern theoretical discourse. In particular, Straub perceives a disturbing "drift in feminist theory that might be seen to be at odds with the populist potential of feminist criticism—the drift towards postmodern, especially deconstructionist, theory." Here we find a specific site where the protopolitical version of postmodernism is registered by the institutionalization of academic feminism in elite circles where it joins hands with a postmodernist phallocratic theory. Such institutionalized critical practice need not necessarily lead to a divorce from the broader, populist, and activist causes of the American left, but, practically speaking, it often has had just such consequences. Straub's starting point thus reflects Paul Smith's concluding remarks in his essay in *Men In Feminism*: "In American academia, poststructuralist theory—feminist or not—is by and large ingrown, with no public sphere to which to belong or through which to be effective" (Jardine and Smith 40).[36] Straub therefore offers a feminist strategy which "may provide much of the subversive energy needed to work against the erection of postmodernism as yet another phallic monument." Her basic assumptions in articulating such an oppositional strategy are similar to Berger's claim that "all theories are metaphors": as Straub argues, "theory itself is a form of self-imaging," thus draining "theory" of its essentializing male mode of "spectatoring," viewing omnisciently. Her feminist emphasis, moreover, engages the styles, fashions, and images of postmodernist theory at precisely those sites, both narrowly academic and broadly cultural, where it is necessary for feminists "to re-image themselves as women both oppressed and articulated by that imagery" of oppression. Indeed, the very image of fashion manifest in the production of a *chic haute couture* realm of high postmodernist theory suggests "postmodernism's own subjection to historical process." And that historical process often materializes as a set of binary oppositions between feminism and postmodernism which artificially sustain the alienating conditions of patriarchal culture.

By investigating "the process of image making implicit in theory itself," Straub questions the essentialism underlying the definitions and the boundaries of any such disabling binary opposition. She thereby advocates an openness "to leftist political strategies" and the political realities of class and race as well as gender. Moreover, she advocates a resistance to the postmodernist tendency to reify a fragmented, "decentered," deconstructed subject, the consequences of which often mean that feminist subject positions then lose their oppositional force within and outside the academy. She thus joins with Alice Jardine in resisting institutional isolation and recalling a global/macro level as well as micro/political level for feminist work: "feminism can no longer be *only* about women or men as objects of study, but needs to be also about forming, encouraging, and protecting a certain shape of subjectivity that will be able to address the massive and urgent issues facing the entire planet" (Jardine and Smith 263). Straub cites as an example of such an effective juncture between feminism and deconstruction "Doane and Hodges's *Nostalgia and Sexual Difference* for its resistance to the boundaries that separate theory from politics, the academic from the popular." The consequences of such efforts to articulate a postmodern feminism, one not curtailed by a narrowly conceived association of postmodernism as merely stylistic innovation, leads finally to the position Nancy Fraser and Linda Nicholson have advocated: "postmodern feminists need not abandon the large theoretical tools needed to address large political problems."

When we turn to Jean Baudrillard, however, we find that he has relinquished such anguish over the plight of the "merely stylistic" because, for him, the very question of the "real" and the ideological comes undone. As Baudrillard explains in *Simulations*, "it is dangerous to unmask images, since they dissimulate the fact that there is nothing behind them." Moreover, since "it is always the aim of ideological analysis to restore the objective process, it is always a false problem to want to restore the truth beneath the simulacrum." Given these assumptions, Baudrillard directly challenges those strains of the feminist liberation movement which, as he explains in the interview with Dianne Hunter, "stay on the side of an exacerbation of sexual difference." Seduction for Baudrillard becomes a mode "apart from ideology": "seduction *plays* with sexual difference" but "does not believe in it." In this way the feminist shame of the artifice of male production and consumption leads to efforts of opposing "phallocratic structure," but, for Baudrillard, such opposition plays into the binary oppositions inscribed by male dualism—a metaphysics of power and resistance. For Baudrillard, "the feminine is not what opposes itself to the masculine, but what *seduces* the masculine." In his attack on essentialism, Baudrillard thereby claims that "masculinity does not exist" and that conversely, through the modes of seduction, "power is on the side of the feminine and of simulation."

Many will undoubtedly object that the very notion of "feminine seduction" is just another essentializing category,[37] but Baudrillard, nevertheless, represents one of the most influential versions of postmodernist doctrines which challenge all leftist, oppositional political theories as naive and nostalgic to the extent that they depend on any traces of essential qualities, universal values, or objective realities.[38] As Douglas Kellner explains, Baudrillard's 1979 publication of "*De la séduction* is an important text, which marks Baudrillard's move to his current theoretical matrix. Henceforth, *seduction* will replace symbolic exchange as the privileged oppositional term to the world of production and utility . . ."(*Jean Baudrillard* 143). Baudrillard's version of postmodernism names the end of the "mirror of the bourgeois sign" as it is inscribed within traditional models of representation and reference: yet "still today the nostalgia for a natural referent of the sign is still alive" despite the postmodern occasion "where the signs refer no longer to any nature, but only to the law of exchange, and come under the commercial law of value" (*Simulations* 86). Baudrillard thus signals the abandonment of the bourgeois devotion to the production of images of nature as objective reality and moves to the deployment of images in seductive play which is always already "of the order of artifice" and "of sign and ritual." In short, as Michael Walsh explains, for Baudrillard, "the image is everywhere victorious." His recent work thereby challenges contemporary forms of oppositional practice which conceive of ideology in a traditional way as "a betrayal of reality by signs," a false consciousness that needs to destroy the ideological surface to uncover the underlying "truth" or "reality." For Baudrillard, "it is always the aim of ideological analysis to restore the objective process; it is always a false problem to want to restore the truth beneath the simulacrum" (*Simulations* 48). In contrast, "behind the baroque of images hides the grey eminence of politics" (*Simulations* 10). Baudrillard thus extends the Foucauldian notion of power to its own "alogical" consequences so that he leaves us with no doubt that for him "ideology is fatal." Nevertheless, many of the contributors to this book conceive ideology in less essentialized idioms: as Michael Walsh argues, Baudrillard's reductive characterization of ideology as a mask for naive realism "is hardly an exhaustive definition." Ideological analysis may reveal not the "objective process" but the very "grey eminence of politics" which has provided the critical focus for most of the essays in this book.

The challenges to the ideological critique of systems of imagery are precisely where we are led in W. J. T. Mitchell's influential study *Iconology*. Once Mitchell's study breaks completely from the traditional effort to separate visual from verbal imagery, iconology from ideology, we are pushed close to Baudrillard's postmodernism where there is likewise no image/reality dualism, but only image as simulacrum. This is precisely the point Timothy Erwin draws out in concluding his critical review of *Iconology* when he asks Mitchell what his response would be "to the postmodern claim of Baudrillard that in the multiplicity of simulacra the opposing ideologies of iconoclast and iconophile amount to the same thing, the disappearance of God?" In his article in this book, Mitchell acknowledges that Baudrillard's "argument for the intertwining of iconoclasm and idolatry struck me . . . as very close to my own work on the Marxist discourse of fetishism and ideology." But what Mitchell opens up is a new direction or possibility for what he calls "a postmodern iconology" or "*critical* iconology." The key move for such a revived iconology would be "a mutually critical encounter with the discourse of ideology." In other words, the point "is not simply to make iconology 'ideologically aware' or self-critical, but to make the ideological critique iconologically aware." As such, if as we suggested at the beginning of this introduction, the terms *image* and *ideology* often constitute the binary hierarchies sustained by Western metaphysical dualism, then Mitchell's call for a "postmodern iconology" in which the two terms are now thoroughly imbricated opens strategic possibilities for intervention in the dominant Platonic/Kantian epistemology. And the institutional consequences of such interventions challenge not only the traditional surveillance of disciplinary borders but also the broader sociocultural hierarchies sustained by the production and consumption of images and ideologies in the popular media. No longer can the ideological dominance of the word over the image be uncritically assumed by the rationalist epistemologies whose advocates often claim to uphold the "representations of truth" in the great works of Western culture. In the face of the conservative programs recently popularized by Alan Bloom, William Bennett, and others, this is no small task. But we may "acknowledge" with Mitchell that even if postmodern critical practices do not simply "get us out of the problem," they may at least "help us to recognize it when we see it." All the contributors to this volume would agree with this assessment: misrecognition is no answer; oppositional critical practice must recognize the ideological substrata of its own images of opposition.

Notes

1. The history of the image has yet to be written. Various critical efforts have focused on the definition of the term. For the most recent see Mitchell, "What Is an Image?" in *Iconology*. In "The Origin of the Term 'Image'," Ray Frazer mentions that during the Renaissance, the word *image* as a literary term was unknown. The current words, he says, were still *icon*, which meant "a picture of something" and *Enargia*, which indicated the "process of making the reader seem to see something" (149). But according to P. N. Furbank, Thomas Wilson, as early as 1562, briefly mentions "image" in his *Arte of Rhetorique* (Furbank 26). The term *figure of speech* comes from the Latin *figurae*, and *figura*—which was sometimes equated with *imago*. On the association between *figura* and *imago*, see Auerbach 48. For the distinction between figures and tropes, also see Auerbach 25-26. For a useful introduction to the term *ideology*, see James Kavanagh.

2. See Barth's discussion of the French ideologues in *Truth and Ideology*. The ideologues' demand for increasing involvement in education and politics led to their confrontation with Napoleon, who was initially eager to be associated with them. In 1797, Napoleon declared himself a "hero of liberal ideas," but his growing imperialistic ambitions had no use for political liberty, so that he turned against the ideologues and used them as scapegoats: ideology was then indeed a "sinister metaphysics."

3. The term "false consciousness" was first used by Engels in a letter to Franz Mehring on 14 July 1893 (Barth 49).

4. Havelock describes several important variations of this argument. One common variation would be the argument that the project is utopian, so Plato's censorship only applies under ideal conditions: since *The Republic* is a book of political theory, poetry is not charged with a political offense but an intellectual one in an ideal world. Another example would be that Plato doesn't mean all poetry, just the bad stuff, so his criticism is directed against a passing fashion in literary criticism where the sophists are using the poets artificially as a source of instruction. See Havelock 7-11.

5. Since "disciplines" in the sense we are intending here refers to the relatively abstract "disciplines of knowledge," the categories and names of the newly evolving disciplines of ontology, ethics, etc., require the instrument of writing to organize and manage. Thus the oral poetic tradition cannot be conceived as a discipline in this sense. Indeed, as Havelock explains, Plato equates *mimesis* with *doxa* or "opinion" (or belief) (248). "*Doxa* is therefore well chosen as a label not only of the poet's image of reality but of that general image of reality which constituted the content of the Greek mind before Plato" (251). The poet is "undisciplinary" precisely in the sense that the traditional doxa could not easily be broken down into discrete and abstract categories, although that was exactly a central part of Plato's educational program.

6. In a fine assimilation of the cultural criticism of Derrida and Foucault, Xiao-mei Chen focuses her critical articulation on precisely the issues raised by Havelock's work. She argues succinctly for the position we have taken. In her own words: "Havelock proposes that we read *The Republic* as a 'frontal attack upon the core of Greek literature' . . . , that is, that we see it as a document revolutionary to its culture and its orders of discourse" (40).

7. Ong provides a useful overview of the history of literacy ranging from the oral period prior to the invention of the alphabet in 1500 B.C. to the invention of the Greek alphabet, 720-700 B.C., to the period of craft literacy, 650-421 B.C., to the period of semi-literacy during Plato's lifetime, 421-357 B.C. to the advent of a more general literacy beginning about 357 B.C. See Ong, Chapter 2, "The Modern Discovery of Primary Oral Cultures."

8. A necessary caution is in order here since in our brief sketch we seem to imply a sudden "great leap" from orality to literacy. As Jan Swearingen has persuasively argued: "Ong and Havelock, among others, continue to revise and perfect their analysis and their models, giving increased precision to distinctions which are hypotheses and heuristics. It is a great irony that they are regarded as proponents of a 'great leap' and of a monolithic, literal-minded dichotomy when instead their emphasis has increasingly been on gradualness and diversity" (155). See the entire special issue of *Pre/Text* (7:3-4, Fall/Winter 1980) for an extended discussion of the literacy/orality debates including an article and interview with Havelock.

9. As Havelock explains: "The Presocratics themselves were essentially oral thinkers, prophets of the concrete linked by long habit to the past, and to forms of expression which were also forms of experience, but they were trying to devise a vocabulary and syntax for a new future, when thought should be expressed in categories organized in a syntax suitable to abstract statement" (*Preface* x). As Havelock explains in a

recent interview: "the platonic writings as a corpus are devoted to introducing a new syntax of speech—a syntax of definition—of categorization—in which the verb *to be* is to be used as a predicate connecting a subject with an attribute, and I realized that that sort of language was not available to the Greek dramatists" ("Discussion" 138).

10. See *The American Heritage Dictionary of the English Language* (College Ed.) New York: American Heritage Publishing Co., Inc., 1969, p. 1548.

11. Such a remark may seem glib if not wholly inaccurate to many Aristotelian scholars especially, but so far as we can determine, it is in fact the case that we are looking at a dramatic cultural revolution. There are of course no statistics available, but it seems that prior to Plato, during what Ong calls the period of "craft literacy," those who could read and write were a select group, often scribes (often themselves slaves), most poets and some aristocrats. But during this period most writing had to do with economic and legal concerns: how much land one owned, how many fields had been plowed, etc. During Plato's lifetime there was a remarkable proliferation of writing and documents on paper and tablets in the general public ranging from the early rudimentary schooling as well as in social and legislative uses and the rhetorical training provided by tutors to the sons of aristocratic families. Thus, the need for strictly oral memorization had been dramatically reduced by the time Aristotle was writing the *Poetics*.

12. By this cursory treatment of Aristotle, we do not mean to imply that he was ignorant of the cultural role of the poet or with the socio-historical function of images and rhetoric. On the contrary, Aristotle's concern in *Rhetoric, Politics,* and elsewhere is with the social and cultural force of argument and persuasion. Our point is simply to focus on the key conceptual move in the *Poetics* by which poetry could be objectified and thus subjected to formal analysis. Likewise, that the poem or drama could be treated as an object in the "natural order" of classifications does not suggest Aristotle's ignorance of the pure artifice of those formal elements. Rather the artifice could be treated like an isolated object to be analyzed whether that object were a human artifact, such as a building or a poem, or a natural object, such as an animal or a plant. Our general point is that modernist formalism with its slighting of the cultural/political significance of the poet can be traced to Aristotle even if the "formalist Aristotle" is in many ways a reductive yet dominant production of subsequent Western cultural history. This interpretation is consistent with Herbert Marcuse's position in *Negations* where he argues: "In Aristotelian philosophy, ancient theory is precisely at the point where idealism retreats in the face of social contradictions and expresses them as ontological conditions. Platonic philosophy still contended with the social order of commercial Athens. Plato's idealism is interlaced with motifs of social criticism" (91).

13. The evolution of the status of "image" is obviously more complicated than suggested here. In Hellenic and Early Christian thought, the transitions from Plato to Philo and St. Paul, from Plotinus and Proculus to Pseudo-Dionysius and St. John of Damascus, need to be traced. See Ladner, "The Concept of the Image" 77-79.

14. As Kenneth Setton notes, in patristic thought of the fourth century, attempts to explain the divine unity between the Father and the Son often drew upon comparisons involving the Emperor's image. See Setton, especially Chapt. VIII, "Imperial Images."

15. The controversy over images was propelled by not only leaders of church and state but also collective mass efforts. That iconoclastic activities often synthesized and expressed public antipathy, discontent, and suffering is witnessed by iconoclastic occurrences in both ancient and modern history. One prime example comes from seventh century B.C., the Deuteronomic Reformation in Judah. Joseph Gutmann, who has analyzed the economic and sociopolitical causes of the movement, first focuses on the Hebrew prophets as the "products of the increasing social fragmentation and disequilibrium of their society" who stirred up the oppressed, "the small landowners and landless laborers in the backward Judea countryside" to call attention to the inequalities and injustices. But prophetic preaching, Gutmann writes, "was iconoclastic for political reasons. It was not, as commonly assumed, a return to the demand for antiiconic worship in so-called 'official normative Yahwism.'" "The prophets were not concerned with the use or non-use of idols of worship as such . . . . They were deliberately mocking what people worshipped as gods/God precisely because these images symbolized the values of the hated upper classes in their *most sacred form.*" In the sixth century B.C., when after a century of Hebrew domination by Assyrians, the boy Josiah became King—thanks to the "peasant army," the "impoverished, rootless, and frustrated elements of Judean society,"—the revolutionaries went on a rampage of smashing idols, those detested symbols of "foreign . . . influence and oppression" (8). Some twenty years later, Josiah, proclaiming himself a "new Moses," after canonizing the Deuteronomy, began his own sweeping iconoclastic programs, a reformation with deliberate political and economic intentions. The Deuteronomic Reformation established for later monarchies with similar ambitions a record to be emulated. Thus Archbishop Cranmer in 1547, addressing the boy Edward VI at his coronation, compared the king to his "predecessor Josias" and urged him to "seek . . . God truly worshipped and idolatry destroyed, the tyranny of the Bishops of Rome banished from [his] subjects, and images removed" (qtd. in Gutmann 5).

In modern history, we may refer to the French Revolution, in which iconoclastic activities allowed the public to give vent to its suppressed rage against the ruling classes. But in France such ambitions were complicated by concerns about the "artistic" value of the monuments and effigies. The revolutionaries, on the one hand, wished to annihilate all the signs of the detested *ancient régime*, but on the other hand, feared that France would lose its great artistic heritage. One solution to this dilemma was the institution of the Louvre Museum and the Museum of French Monuments to provide an alternate cultural setting in which the same symbols could take on "artistic" value and would thus be protected from destructive urges. As Stanley Idzerda writes, "The Louvre was first opened to the public in August 1793, and while many *sans-culottes* admired symbols of 'royalty, feudalism, and superstitions' inside the museum, they continued to engage in iconoclastic activities outside of it" (24).

16. To appreciate the strong influence of icons on medieval popular imagination, we need to remember that the medieval beholder most likely believed in the theory of vision introduced by Plato (see *Timaeus* 45b-c) and propounded by Augustine. According to this theory, the fire warming and animating the human body was collected with great intensity behind the eye and projected as a ray from the viewer to the object, whose representation was then returned to the eye. As Margaret Miles writes, "This strong visual experience was formulated negatively as the fear of contamination by a dangerous or 'unsightly'

visual object (or by a person with the 'evil eye') or positively as belief in the miraculous power of an icon, when assiduously gazed upon to heal one's disease" (7).

17. The Council, as Stephen Gero writes, "supported by a battery of scriptural and patristic texts, . . . decreed that the making and veneration of religious images is against ecclesiastical tradition, transgresses Christological orthodoxy, and insults the heavenly glory of the Mother of God and the departed saints" (54). On the Council of Hiereia, see also Martin, especially Chapt. VII.

18. St. John (c. 675-c. 749) was born in a Christian family, who held important offices under the Arab governors of Damascus. John's Arabic name was Mansur (the Ransomed). During 726-733, he wrote his Three Discourses (or Orations) against Iconoclasm. He then entered a monastery near Jerusalem and was ordained to priesthood (c. 735) (Martin 116-117). As E. J. Martin has noted, "the whole question of idolatrous worship . . . and the exact nature of images, is examined by St. John of Damascus so thoroughly and so finally that the argument about idolatry was felt by the Iconoclasts themselves to lack conviction and practically replaced by a new one based on Christology" (116). For an English translation of his *Orations on the Images*, see M. H. Allies, *St. John Damscene on Holy Images* (1898). See also Ladner, Barnard, and Earl.

19. The repercussions of St. John's privileging of the "natural" image over the "imitative" (the *physis-thesis* distinction) can be felt in later eras, in the valorization of forms of realism and naturalism in the arts. In the twentieth century, it is the photographic image more than any other form of representation that enjoys the highly privileged position of being a natural image, in that it is often perceived as being virtually identical with its prototype. When commercialized, photographic images can easily present illusions of reality as "how things naturally are"; that is, ideology as false consciousness. In its ability to mask its own artifices and minimize the role of its creator, the photograph—say in comparison with a painted portrait—is the modern equivalent of the acheiropoietic image, the acheiropoietoi being images that were considered truly miraculous since they had been made not by human hands, such as the impression of the Holy Face on the veil of St. Veronica (Ladner "Images and Ideas" 66). With their potential to share in the glory and power of their prototypes to the utmost degree, photographs (and their deployment in commercial arts and films) are the most venerable icons in the modern era, possessing the same kind of magic that lured the medieval populace to bestow endowments upon the owners of the holy images. But these "natural" images of the twentieth century can also act as a corrective to our vision in that they can make visible the invisible, forgotten, or misrepresented segments of the global community (witness the Palestinians in Said's *After the Last Sky* or migrant workers in Europe in Berger's *A Seventh Man*) (see also in this context Messmer's essay in this volume). These texts, encouraging "another way of seeing," not only employ the familiar juxtaposition of visual and verbal representation, but require a way of reading in which the intervention of words upon images—and vice versa—is imagined in new configurations; the postmodernist reader's hermeneutics, then, involve not only the act of interpreting words, but also the investigation of the boundary (or "parergon" in Derrida's words) of verbal and visual representation. In this context, see also Macaskill's essay in this volume.

20. The performance of the liturgy, for example, was seen as "a process of spiritual painting or repainting by the hands of Christ, and through the priest who is His pen"; if "wrong colors" were used or if dirt accumulated, man's image would be tarnished, and yet it was possible to restore that image to its original splendor. Man's soul was seen as "a sculpture the form of which had to be separated from the rock of brute matter." The act of carving would make it possible for man to achieve *similitude* to God. (See Ladner, "The Concept of the Image" 87-90.)

21. In his recent *Power of Images,* David Freedberg also considers a few of St. John's arguments. Freedberg's focus, however, sharply diverges from ours. Freedberg draws attention to St. John's articulation of two fundamental—and indeed familiar—precepts of the iconodules: the priority of sight; the defense of the Incarnation (401, 402). Freedberg's interest in these two tenets is to highlight, in the case of sight, the ontological problem of arousal; and in the matter of Incarnation, the emotional fusion of image and prototype. Nowhere does Freedberg mention St. John's hierarchy of images or the ideological consequences of the Damascene's arguments. This evasion is typical of Freedberg's overall approach to the issue of representation, despite his claim that "we can renounce neither history nor context" (439). Indeed, one can claim that *The Power of Images* is torn between an acknowledgment of the sociohistorical components of human cognition, on the one hand, and the overriding desire, on the other, to dissociate this very understanding from cultural conditioning, in order to reach the so-called raw and primitive human response. We "rigorously historicize the work, because we are afraid to come to terms with our responses," asserts Freedberg (429-30), who wishes to "reinstate emotion as part of cognition"(430). But ironically, in his dichotomizing of culture and nature, the "culturally conditioned" and the "psychological processes" (47), Freedberg himself dissociates cognition from emotion. Furthermore, Freedberg's effort to sustain a model of ontological cognition and response bears with it a nostalgia for the autotelic image as a representative of the "real." Witness, for example, his reading of this excerpt from St. John: "when the invisible becomes visible in flesh you may then draw a *likeness* of his visible form . . . . When he who is without form or limitation . . . takes upon himself the *form* of a servant in substance and stature, and a body of flesh, then you may draw his *likeness* and show it to anyone willing to contemplate it" (qtd. in Freedberg 404; italics ours). As Freedberg himself acknowledges (405), St. John insisted on the distinction between the image and the prototype; he also made it clear that he did not "worship matter but the creator of matter" (qtd. in Freedberg 403). Yet, in his commentary on the above excerpt, Freedberg says: "the image declares and makes present that which is absent, hidden, and which we cannot possibly know—but then do"(404); or "The *real*, apparently graspable image pictures the inconceivable" (404; our italics). What is missing from Freedberg's careful analysis of representation, then, is not only the ideological implications of images, but also what constitutes another main focus of this collection of essays—a sense of a postmodern "crisis in representation."

22. The familiar argument regarding images as the "Bible" of the illiterate, had already established an association between *imago* and *littera* so that *imago* came to be applied not only to pictorial representations of saints but also their verbal ones in *sermones* and in hagiography, the relation between the verbal and the visual being explained by "the central mystery of the faith," the notion of Incarnation (see Earl 28-

29). Not only conceptually but also stylistically the verbal representation of saints tried to imitate iconography. The main stylistic features of an icon are "its absolute stasis," its denial of earthly realism, and its conventionality (van der Leeuw, qtd. in Earl 21). The same principles govern the aesthetics of hagiography or "literary iconography." The lack of realism and psychological insight are coupled with a stasis brought about by a lack of narrative progression. Icons of religious figures were celebrated also in poetry. As an example, we may refer to the poetry of Manuel Philes (c. 1275-c. 1345). In his ekphrastic poem "To a Steatite Icon of the Mother of God," the medium (steatite) is as much the focus of attention as its iconic significance. See Kalaverezou-Maxeiner 80-82.

23. As Ladner notes, "From the seventh century onward the iconography of the *martyria*, which had been dominated by the memory and evocation of the Holy Places of Palestine and their pictorial decoration, was being replaced in Byzantium by iconographic programs of a different kind . . . . The Byzantine approach to religion and art changed from the historic to the speculative . . . and therefore, also the problem of the similarity of images was treated more in a philosophical than in a practical way" (106).

24. Another associated concept related to typology is the notion of the "type," a somewhat corrupted extension of figura in its original sense. As Paul Korchin mentions, the word *character* has Greek origins while *type* has Christian ones (112-13). The representation of character as a type (whose behavior is always "prefigured") might seem too outmoded to warrant much attention. And yet it is the tacit acceptance of this notion that encourages illusions of racial homogeneity and chauvinistic enterprises. In her recent study of pictorial (mostly photographic) representation of women, Martha Banta examines the concept of the "type" in relation to the "idea" of the American Girl during the period between 1876 and the end of World War I. One of the era's dominant cultural obsessions, Banta reveals, is "the woman as image of a type" (xxviii). The Girl, Banta says, "was expected to be young, pretty, white, Protestant, and 'American' if she were to aid observers (both native-based and visitors from abroad) in the understanding of the nation's unique destiny." That the woman as type needed to be protected from foreign adulteration is shown in Banta's investigation of the influence of the pseudoscience of physiognomy "upon the racists' need to keep the pure bloodstock of the American Girl inviolate" (xxxii).

25. As Sacvan Bercovitch points out, "From John Cotton's slightly unwarranted application of typical symbolism to New England events to Jonathan Edwards's adaptation of the analogic character of typology to this imagistic views of nature, the structure of the type-antitype construct pervades nearly all aspects of Puritan thought" (13).

26. William Spanos, in his study of postmodernism, recognizes his own change in the valence of the terms. As he explains, he first conceived of the postmodern as "an essentially chronological—a post-modern—event. In the later essays, however, I come to realize that the post-modern impulse has, in fact existed throughout the history of Western literature" (7). "I came to understand the postmodern occasion not merely as a chronological but also as an ontological phenomenon" (8). "The word *postmodern*, then, obscures the fact that the impulse informing the postmodern occasion is not fundamentally a chronological event in a developing plot but rather an inherent mode of human

understanding that has become prominent in the present (de-centered) historical conjuncture" (194). Spanos's view is representative of the group of writers involved with *boundary 2: a journal of postmodern literature.* The special issue on "Postmodernism and Politics" led to the University of Minnesota book of the same title with an important introduction and overview of this debate by Jonathan Arac. As Arac remarks: "the 'postmodern' thus proved not straightforwardly chronological. It partook of a more complex hermeneutical temporality, which proved confusing to some observers . . . as the journal uncovered an ever-receding history of postmodernism through unsettling received New-Critical interpretations over the whole of Western literature" (x-xi). Despite the confusion, the *boundary 2* view of postmodernism, which we have in general adopted, does avoid the common objection, voiced by Andreas Huyssen, that "Too many discussions of postmodernism" get "bogged down in the futile attempt to define the postmodern in terms of style alone" (viii). Such a stylistic definition characterizes, for example, Brian McHale's efforts to articulate a "descriptive poetic" of postmodern fiction distinct from its modernist precursors. Our sense is that virtually any of the characteristics McHale describes could as well be found, if only marginally, in many modernist texts. McHale acknowledges this point by referring to a shift in emphasis from the modernist "epistemological dominant" to the postmodernist "ontological dominant." As Steven Connor suggests: "the postmodernist transformation, or advance, can be seen as a selective intensification of certain tendencies within modernism itself" (109). For an opposite shift in critical perspectives, see Ihab Hassan's 1982 edition *The Dismemberment of Orpheus* where his earlier sense (in the 1971 edition) that there is no absolute break between modernism and postmodernism is replaced by a binary list of contrasting properties of modernism and postmodernism. Connor explains that for Hassan "modernism now becomes the name for the purblind logocentric past, expressive as it is of a totalitarian will to absolute power" (112). For a view of the place of irony in these debates see Alan Wilde's *Horizons of Assent.*

27. Catharine Stimpson describes the "crisis in representation" in terms that lead directly to the issues of image and ideology: "like every great word, 'representation/s' is a stew. A scrambled menu, it serves up several meanings at once. For a representation can be an image—visual, verbal, or aural . . . . A representation can also be a narrative, a sequence of images and ideas . . . . Or, a representation can be the product of ideology, that vast scheme for showing forth the world and justifying its dealings" (223). As Linda Hutcheon comments on this passage, "postmodern representation is self-consciously all of these—image, narrative, product of (and producer of) ideology" (*Politics* 31). Consequently, "if images, like words, are seen as signs, then it is possible to look beyond what W. J. T. Mitchell calls the 'deceptive appearance of naturalness and transparence concealing an opaque, distorting, arbitrary mechanism of representation, a process of ideological mystification'" (121).

28. David Shumway likewise argues that "a longer historical view of the phenomena Jameson calls postmodern will surely not see them as terribly distant from other twentieth century productions" (202).

29. At times, Jameson wishes to combat such "protopolitical" relativity with reference to the "untranscendable horizon" of History, the "absent cause" (*Political Uncon-*

scious 35). While there are clear differences between the positions of Jameson and Baudrillard, they both often tend to cast their arguments in the form of a socially descriptive narrative in which we have passed from a previous reality to a now pervasive "loss of reality" as signaled by the simulacra or simulation quality of contemporary cultural life. The implication, therefore, is that we have somehow left behind, regrettably, an unrecoverable real. But the contributors to this book tend to agree more with Michael Ryan's recent critique of Baudrillard when he asserts that "society is not a real that can become simulational (as Baudrillard and Jameson imply), but an arrangement of rhetorical forms and materialized tropes (images) that has never been anything but simulational. And it is precisely at that point, with that insight, that a postmodern politics should begin" (Ryan 576).

30. Linda Hutcheon describes the central question that then arises: "More than ever, the question must be asked: what interests and powers does the traditional separation of the visual and the verbal serve in both consumer mass culture and high art? . . . The ideological dimension implied here is inextricably a part of the theoretical dimension" and thus inextricably a part of the reading and interpretation of images.

31. With respect to such "complicitous" forms of postmodernism, Steven Connor warns: "There is nothing in such rhetorical ultra-leftism to suggest the likelihood of any shift or complication in the institutional-economic structures of academic research, communication and publication, or the massively powerful apparatus of exclusion, hierarchy and certification which is higher education in advanced Western countries" (218). This is a particularly sensitive issue for most of us who are academics and therefore serve so obviously within a dominant institutional setting. In other words, as Richard Ohmann acknowledges: "since we offer our services either on the market or through institutions like colleges that express social inequality, we tend generally to serve those who pay. Willy-nilly, most of us spend at least part of our energies reproducing the injustices of the social order" (252).

32. According to Spanos such postmodern modes of disruption are necessary to "'overcome' the master codes of the Western literary tradition" (3). This version of a resistant postmodernism aligns itself with Andreas Huyssen's argument "that a postmodernist culture emerging from these political, social, and cultural constellations will have to be a postmodernism of resistance, including resistance to that easy postmodernism of the 'anything goes' variety. Resistance will always have to be specific and contingent upon the cultural field within which it operates. It cannot be defined simply in terms of negativity or non-identity a la Adorno, nor will the litanies of a totalizing, collective project suffice" (220-21). Consider also in this context Linda Hutcheon's claim that "postmodernist art and theory have self-consciously acknowledged their ideological positioning in the world and they have been incited to do so, not only in reaction to that provocative accusation of triviality, but also by those previously silenced ex-centrics, both outside (post-colonial) and within (women, gays) our supposedly monolithic western culture" (179).

33. The position Caraher stakes out is similar to Henry Sussman's recent assessment that "the postmodern . . . does not transcend or leave behind the modern. It is always already inscribed within the modern" (176).

34. In this sense, Wacker's reading of Pound aligns itself with the oppositional practice of William Spanos who claims that "it was paradoxically, Ezra Pound, who, however problematically, provided the essential metaphor for this errant, eccentric, or deviant (de-)creative process in his interesting, interminably long poem *The Cantos*" (Spanos 236).

35. See Linda Hutcheon's discussion of *A Maggot* as a postmodern novel in *Politics*, Ch. 3, "Re-presenting the Past," 62-92.

36. Smith elaborates on this point earlier in his paper: "Feminist theory of this sort—and however ' feminist' it may be, and howsoever 'feminist' is construed—does not exist outside the academy and, more specifically, is in many ways not easily separable from the general 'theory' that has worked its way into studies in the humanities over the last ten or twenty years." He thus precisely expresses Straub's fears: "this theory, as feminist theory itself has taught us to know, is implicated fully into the phallocracy: it helps invent, legitimate, and reproduce the male order" (Jardine and Smith 34).

37. For example, Kellner argues that "Baudrillard utilizes an essentialist discourse of a 'feminine nature'" (*Jean Baudrillard* 146). For a feminist critique of the logical contradictions in Baudrillard's arguments regarding "seduction," see Jane Gallop.

38. As Baudrillard explains, the dissimulation of Western metaphysics in all guises of Platonic idealism has often led, for traditional liberal humanists, to "metaphysical despair" which "came from the idea that the images concealed nothing at all, and that in fact they were not images, such as the original model would have made them, but actually perfect simulacra forever radiant with their own fascination" (*Simulations* 9). David Shumway offers a poststructuralist critique of the entire notion of "simulation": "The claims for the simulational society are themselves based on a nostalgia for origins and the assumption that there was a time when most people had a deep understanding of their own place in history . . . . That the entire notion of the simulacrum is Platonic should have warned poststructuralists away from it. To call something a simulacrum makes sense only in an essentialist context" (197).

Works Cited

Adams, Hazard, ed. *Critical Theory Since Plato*. New York: Harcourt Brace Jovanovich, 1977.

Arac, Jonathan, ed. *Postmodernism and Politics*. Minneapolis: U of Minnesota P, 1986.

Auerbach, Erich. "Figura." *Scenes from the Drama of European Literature*. New York: Meridian Books, 1959.

Banta, Martha. *Imaging American Women: Idea and Ideals in Cultural History*. New York: Columbia UP, 1987.

Barnard, L. W. *The Graeco-Roman and Oriental Background of the Iconoclastic Controversy*. Leiden: E. J. Brill, 1974.

Barth, Hans. *Truth and Ideology*. Trans. Frederic Lilge. Berkeley and Los Angeles: U of California P, 1961.

Baudrillard, Jean. *De la séduction*. Paris: Denoel-Gonthier, 1979.

————. *Simulations*. Trans. Paul Foss, Paul Patton, and Phillip Bertchman. New York: Semiotext(e), 1983.

Bercovitch, Sacvan, ed. *Typology and Early American Literature*. Amherst: U of Massachusetts P, 1972.

Bryson, Norman. *Vistion and Painting: The Logic of the Gaze*. New Haven: Yale UP, 1983.

Chen, Xiao-mei. "Derrida's Pharmacy: Towards a Foucauldian Reading of 'La Pharmacie de Platon.'" *Works and Days* 8. 4.2 (Fall 1986): 33-50.

Connor, Steven. *Postmodernist Culture: An Introduction to Theories of the Contemporary*. Oxford: Basil Blackwell, 1989.

Derrida, Jacques. *Dissemination*. Trans. Barbara Johnson. Chicago: U of Chicago P, 1981.

Earl, James W. "Typology and Iconographic Style in Early Medieval Hagiography." *Studies in the Literary Imagination* 1 (1975): 15-46.

Frank, Joseph. "Spatial Form in Modern Literature, Part I." *Sewanee Review*. 53 (Spring 1945): 229-35.

Fraser, Nancy and Linda Nicholson. "Social Criticism without Philosophy: An Encounter between Feminism and Post-modernism." Nicholson 19-38.

Frazer, Ray. "The Origin of the Term 'Image'." *English Literary History* 2 (1960): 149-161.

Freedberg, David. *The Power of Images: Studies in the History and Theory of Response*. Chicago: U of Chicago P, 1989.

Furbank, P. N. *Reflections on the Word "Image."* London: Secker and Warburg, 1970.

Gallop, Jane. "French Theory and the Seduction of Feminism." Jardine and Smith 111-15.

Gero, Stephen. "Byzantine Iconoclasm and the Failure of a Medieval Reformation." *The Image and the Word*. Ed. Joseph Gutmann. Missoula: Scholars P, 1977.

Gilman, Ernest B. *Iconoclasm and Poetry in the English Reformation*. Chicago: U of Chicago P, 1986.

Gutmann, Joseph. "Deuteronomy: Religious Reformation or Iconoclastic Revolution?" *The Image and the Word*. Ed. Joseph Gutmann. Missoula: Scholars P, 1977.

Hassan, Ihab. *The Dismemberment of Orpheus: Toward a Postmodern Literature.* 2nd ed. Madison: U of Wisconsin P, 1982.

Hauser, Arnold. *The Social History of Art.* Vol. I. New York: Vintage Books, 1957. 4 vols.

Havelock, Eric A. *Preface to Plato.* Cambridge: Harvard UP, 1963.

———. "Orality, Literacy, and Star Wars." *Pre/Text: An Interdisciplinary Journal of Rhetoric.* 7.3-4 (Fall/Winter 1986): 123-132.

Hutcheon, Linda. *A Poetics of Postmodernism.* New York: Routledge, 1988.

———. *The Politics of Postmodernism.* New York: Routledge, 1989.

Huyssen, Andreas. *After the Great Divide: Modernism, Mass Culture, Postmodernism.* Bloomington: Indiana UP, 1986.

Idzerda, Stanley. "Iconoclasm during the French Revolution." *The American Historical Review* 1 (1954): 13-26.

Jameson, Fredric. "Foreword" in Jean-Francois Lyotard *The Postmodern Condition: A Report on Knowledge.* Trans. Geoff Bennington and Brian Massumi. Minneapolis: U of Minnesota P, 1984.

———. "Hans Haacke and the Cultural Logic of Postmodernism." Wallis 38-50.

———. *The Ideologies of Theory: Essays 1971-86.* Minneapolis: U of Minnesota P, 1988. 2 vols.

———. *The Political Unconscious: Narrative as a Socially Symbolic Act.* Ithaca: Cornell UP, 1981.

———. "Postmodernism, or the Cultural Logic of Late Capitalism." *New Left Review* 146 (1984): 53-92.

Jardine, Alice, and Paul Smith. *Men in Feminism.* New York: Methuen, 1987.

Kalavrezou-Maxeiner, Ioli. *Byzantine Icons in Steatite.* Wien: Österreichischen Akademie der Wissenschaften, 1985.

Kaufmann, Walter., ed. and trans. *The Portable Nietzsche.* New York: Penguin, 1968.

Kavanagh, James H. "Ideology." *Critical Terms for Literary Study.* Eds. Frank Lentricchia and Thomas McLaughlin. Chicago: U of Chicago P, 1990. 306-20.

Kellner, Douglas. *Jean Baudrillard: From Marxism to Postmodernism and Beyond.* Stanford: Stanford UP, 1989.

———, ed. *Postmodernism/Jameson/Critique.* Washington, D.C.: Maisonneuve P, 1989.

Korchin, Paul. *Typologies in England, 1650-1820.* Princeton: Princeton UP, 1982.

Ladner, Gerhart. *Ad Imaginem Dei: The Image of Man in Medieval Art.* Latrobe, Pa.: The Archabbey P, 1965.

———. "The Concept of the Image in the Greek Fathers and the Byzantine Iconoclastic Controversy." *Images and Ideas in the Middle Ages.* Vol. 1. Los Angeles: U of California Center for Medieval and Renaissance Studies, 1983. 35-72.

Marcuse, Herbert. *Negations: Essays in Critical Theory.* Trans. Jeremy J. Shapiro. Boston: Beacon P, 1968.

Martin, Edward J. *A History of the Iconoclastic Controversy.* New York: AMS P, 1978.

McHale, Brian. *Postmodernist Fiction.* New York: Methuen, 1987.

Miles, Margaret. *Image as Insight: Visual Understanding in Western Christianity and Secular Culture.* Boston: Beacon, 1985.

Mitchell, W. J. T. *Iconology: Image, Text, Ideology.* Chicago: U of Chicago P, 1986.

Nicholson, Linda J., Ed. *Feminism/Postmodernism.* New York: Routledge, 1990.

Ohmann, Richard. "Graduate Students, Professionals, Intellectuals." *College English* 52.3 (March 1990): 247-257.

Ong, Walter J. *Orality and Literacy.* New York: Methuen, 1982.

Parry, Milman. *The Making of Homeric Verse.* Ed. Adam Parry. Oxford: Clarendon P, 1971.

Plato. *The Republic and Other Works.* Trans. B. Jowett. New York: Doubleday, 1973.

Ross, Andrew. *Universal Abandon? The Politics of Postmodernism.* Minneapolis: U of Minnesota P, 1988.

Ryan, Michael. "Postmodern Politics." *Theory, Culture & Society.* 5 (June 1988): 559-76.

Setton, Kenneth. *Christian Attitude Towards the Emperor in the Fourth Century.* New York: AMS, 1967.

Spanos, William V. *Repetitions: The Postmodern Occasion in Literature and Culture.* Baton Rouge: Louisiana State UP, 1987.

Stephanson, Anders. "Regarding Postmodernism—A Conversation with Fredric Jameson." Ross 3-30.

Stimpson, Catharine R. *Where the Meanings Are: Feminism and Cultural Spaces.* New York: Methuen, 1988.

Sussman, Henry. *Afterimages of Modernity: Structure and Indifference in Twentieth Century Literature.* Baltimore: Johns Hopkins UP, 1990.

Swearingen, C. Jan. "Literate Rhetors and Their Illiterate Audiences: The Orality of Early Literacy." *Pre/Text: An Inter-Disciplinary Journal of Rhetoric*. 7.3-4 (Fall/Winter 1986): 145-62.

Wallis, Brian, ed. *Hans Haacke: Unfinished Business*. Cambridge: MIT P, 1987.

Williams, Raymond. *Keywords: A Vocabulary of Culture and Society*. New York: Oxford UP, 1976.

PART II

Postmodern Revisions of Modernist Images

Chapter 2

A Modernist Allegory of Narration: Joseph Conrad's "Youth" and the Ideology of the Image

Brian G. Caraher

> The value of a sentence is in the
> personality which utters it, for nothing
> new can be said by man or woman.
> —Joseph Conrad (Korzeniowski)
> and/or Ford Madox Ford (Hueffer),
> *Nostromo* (157)[1]

> In more ways than one Mr. Conrad is
> something of a law unto himself, and
> creates his own forms, as he certainly
> has created his own methods.
> —Anonymous review of
> *"Youth: A Narrative" and
> Two Other Stories, Athenaeum*
> 20 December 1902: 824

At the beginning of *A Genealogy of Modernism* Michael Levenson evokes the figure of Joseph Conrad as the powerful craftsman of the self-conscious, self-questioning "modernist narrator on the Victorian sailing ship" (1). For Levenson, Conrad helps initiate English modernity and the literary and cultural crisis of modernism by problematizing the authority of omniscient narration. The modernist narrator aboard the late Victorian ship of moral dilemmas exhibits, in Levenson's words, "the disintegration of stable balanced relations between subject and object and the consequent enshrining of consciousness as the repository of meaning and value" (22). The crisis of modernist narrative and narration is thus a crisis in epistemology: fact or *physis* becomes cloven from subjective experience or *psyche*, and Conrad's ship of state in *The Nigger of the "Narcissus"* dramatizes the segregation of the individual realm of meaning and value from the world of facts and social acts (19-22, 31-36). Yet this epistemological crisis reverberates primarily at the level of form, according to Levenson. The emerging dissociation between subjective consciousness and worldly fact, the enduring "*agon* of modernism," registers as "the instability in the forms themselves" (36). Narrative form thus undergoes crisis, instability, and self-conscious questioning on the part of authors and their narrators alike.

Conrad's tale "Youth: A Narrative" might seem to countermand this portrayal of English literary modernism's genetic heritage. This first narrative employment of Charlie Marlow appeared the year after the publication of *The Nigger of the "Narcissus"* and has far more often than not been taken as a relatively slight yet entertaining tale of the endurance and strength of youthful impulse and yearning. However, Conrad's initial development of a first-person narrative persona aboard a Victorian sailing ship can yield not only another narrative example in which Levenson's divorce between *physis* and *psyche* appears underway in the early work of Joseph Conrad but also the deployment of what will become an increasingly important modernist narrative strategy—what I choose to call here, an allegory of narration.[2]

"Youth" can be recognized as an allegory of narration basically because there appear to be at least two ways of reading Conrad's narrative. These two ways, moreover, are not exclusive but are intimately dependent upon one another. One involves a romance, a narrative of a romantic quest for an image of the East and of youthful fulfillment. The second involves a metanarrational narrative, a plot that reveals insistently the narrational and ideological assumptions upon which the tale of romance is founded and structured. The second way of reading depends upon the first as analysis depends upon an analysand, and the first way of reading depends upon the second as an ideal or allegorical precept depends upon an image or an illustrative emblem.

I

To illustrate what I mean, let me briefly narrate these two interdependent ways of reading Conrad's "Youth." The first way of reading the tale attends upon it as the sentimental and nostalgic evocation by an older Marlow of his younger, romantically adventuresome self. Marlow's sense of his own experience is sincere and worthy of winning the reader's—especially a male reader's—sympathy and emotional camaraderie. The four men who share a table and a bottle of wine with Marlow listen to his tale and nod in agreement at the end; they would seem to exemplify an implied reader's perspective that Marlow's assessment of the nature of youth, romance, and the trials of strength that men undergo at sea merits credence, if not acceptance. In the story, then, we have an older Marlow (forty-two and just retired from active sea life) who looks back longingly on his younger self ("just twenty," as he says) ("Youth" 4). The older Marlow celebrates the days of his first voyage to the Far East, his first assignment as second mate, and his first command of his own boat. He endures unfortunate circumstances, disasters, even being blown up; but he triumphs in the end as he pays homage to his "youth" and his youthful "strength" as that which carries him through such difficult times. The older Marlow feels that such moments of glory are fleeting and sadly past, yet this older self—now somewhat wiser with age—still idolizes and idealizes that more impetuous, foolhardy, and romantic version of himself, twenty-two years earlier in time. As Marlow expounds just before his small cockle-shell of a lifeboat reaches the shores of the East,

> I need not tell you what it is to be knocking about in an open boat. I remember nights and days of calm, when we pulled, we pulled, and the boat seemed to stand still, as if bewitched within the circle of the sea horizon. I remember the heat, the deluge of rain-squalls that kept us baling for dear life (but filled our water-cask), and I remember sixteen hours on end with a mouth dry as a cinder and a steering-oar over the stern to keep my first command head on to a breaking sea. I did not know how good a man I was till then. I remember the drawn faces, the dejected figures of my two men, and I remember my youth and the feeling that will never come back any more—the feeling that I could last for ever, outlast the sea, the earth, and all men; the *deceitful feeling* that lures us on to joys, to perils, to love, to vain effort—to death; the triumphant conviction of strength, the heat of life in the handful of dust, the glow in the heart that with every year grows dim, grows cold, grows small, and expires—and expires, too soon, too soon—before life itself. (36-37; italics mine)

This beautiful passage lyrically evokes not only the dramatic contrast between an older, nostalgic Marlow and a younger, triumphantly active one but also the romantic ethos that permeates both versions of Marlow's character. However, the same passage cannot suppress at least one symptomatic disclosure of that which founds and structures Marlow's romantic idealizations: "the deceitful feeling," the older Marlow calls it, "that lures us [both young and old] on to joys, to perils, to love, to vain effort—to death." The older Marlow recounts much vain effort and the slow death by fiery self-consumption of a Victorian ship of unseaworthy shape named the *Judea* in his nostalgic tale of his younger self. Too many of the facts of the younger Marlow's journey coincide with the sense that an idealizing deception subtly pervades the older Marlow's tale of youthful romance. In other words, an epistemologically as well as narratologically curious divorce insinuates itself between the facts of the younger Marlow's voyage towards the East and the psychic idealization of those facts in the narrative articulated by the older Marlow. The narrative possibilities of the tale are not fully accounted for by the first way of reading the narrative.[3]

Indeed, a fuller understanding of the tale must be rooted in a reading experience of the story as an adventure tale gone awry. "Youth" appears to be a relatively simple adolescent or youthful romance of the seas and of exotic names and places. It also seems to promote a wistful nostalgia for lost youth. However, the narrative is structured as a repeated series of delays and disasters interlinked by sudden and equally repetitive effusions of sentimental rhetoric. Delay, deferral, and discontinuity underlie and perpetually threaten to undermine Marlow's insistent romantic quest adventure.

Indeed both the older *and* the younger Marlow gloss over how vain, futile, and comically absurd the whole adventure appears to be from the very start. Marlow tells a tale of youth, but everything about the vehicle of his adventure is morbidly old. The older Marlow recollects the ship, the *Judea*, as "a ruined cottage" and that its owner "has been bankrupt and dead these twenty years or more" (5). Both comments should give the attentive listener pause to wonder about both Marlow the narrator and Marlow the narrated. Furthermore, the first crew that signs onto the ancient, ominously doomed ship becomes promptly caught up in "gravedigger's work" in the gloomy hold of the vessel on the way from the Thames to Newcastle to fetch coals. A storm has shifted the ballast of damp sand severely leeward, and the incapacitated ship demands that all available hands engage in the Sisyphean task of trying to set her right (6). Months later after the damaged and leaking ship has been towed back to Falmouth harbor for the second time, the younger Marlow hears but doesn't heed the jeers of the locals that the intended voyage of a hapless, leaky sailing barque to Bangkok amounts to sheer futility.

Marlow prefers to remain loyal to the immobilized vehicle of his romantic quest and to spend a good deal of his pay on "a complete set of Byron's works and a new railway rug" (16). When the old ship is eventually recaulked and newly coppered, her load of now well-broken coal is reshipped. On a moonlit evening before embarking yet again, Marlow and the first mate observe that all the shipboard rats leave. Both mates ponder the highly unusual scene and "agree[ ] that the wisdom of rats has been grossly overrated, being in fact no greater than that of men" (17). Of course, the rather self-satisfied Marlow does not even suspect the eventual spontaneous combustion that is being prepared just below deck, though rather ironically (Marlow's word is "irrelevantly") he remembers the rats' desertion later on once the disaster is well under way (21). This comic touch underscores the ill-founded nature of Marlow's faith and loyalty in the ship and its goal of Bangkok. Later, when the ship is smoking badly, Marlow must be fished ignominiously out of the hold with a chain-hook because he has leaped below "to show how easily" the fire could be contained after several of his crew had already been overcome by the noxious fumes (21). Moreover, and perhaps most absurdly, after the ship has blown up, Marlow aloft with some of the crew orders them to "drop the bunt of the foresail twice" in order to put a neater harbor furl upon the sails (28). It is a "ship doomed to arrive nowhere," but Marlow persistently participates in rationalizing and romanticizing the absurdly comic facts and circumstances of the voyage.

Indeed, the young Marlow's character and the older Marlow's narrative are both driven forward by a single-minded romantic ideal, to possess a vision of the East regardless of the facts that insistently and comically resist Marlow's conscious desire and intentions. In Michael Levenson's terms, *psyche* becomes cloven from *physis*. Subjective consciousness, that is to say, disjoins itself and what it seeks to value from the arena of physical and social events that will no longer securely support it. Narratively speaking, of course, the desire for romance must endlessly, even absurdly, compensate for a world of circumstances that would delay, detour, deny, or simply stand in strange silence before any such romantic idealizations. Romantic narrative—Marlow's narrative of his youthful romance of and for the East, for example—is founded upon and structured by this perpetual and comic impossibility.[4]

This doubled pattern of reading "Youth," or the two interdependent ways of reading the tale that I have just been tracing, can be rather closely related to what Cedric Watts has described as the relation between narrative and covert plot in many of Conrad's novels and short stories. Watts contends that "a covert plot [is] another purposeful sequence, but one which is partly hidden . . . . When it is eventually seen, the covert plot proves to organize and explain those elements of the text which at first may have seemed odd or anomalous, obscure or redundant; and the whole text is in various ways transformed" (*Deceptive Text* 30). In general for Watts the relation between overt narrative and covert plot is retrospective, ironic, and dialectical. The reader or critic searches for another, more subtle, sometimes deceptive way in which Conrad's narratives may be (organically) unified. What I am suggesting here with the notion of Conrad's allegory of narration is that two ways of reading or attending to "Youth: A Narrative" articulate two contradictory, deceptively interdependent, and nondialectical plots set to work against one another in the telling of Marlow's tale. Romance wars against the very sequence of narrative events that it must appropriate and idealize in order to become articulated as a narrative of romantic quest.[5]

As Robert Foulke noticed a few years ago, there appears to be a moment of ambivalence with regard to the rhetoric of romance at the very conclusion to Conrad's *The Nigger of the "Narcissus."* Foulke maintains that

> the reader is left with two impulses at the end of the narrative. One leads him to doubt the celebration of a seaman narrator, to wonder whether the question buried in the middle of this last paragraph is in fact rhetorical. The other leads him to follow the narrating voice as it becomes excited to the pitch of high rhetoric—to share a vision appropriate to pure romance in which characters are noble and actions heroic within a surrealistic seascape. Both impulses are valid; to deny either distorts the text. (319)[6]

This concluding moment of ambivalence regarding skepticism or belief in a visionary rhetoric of romance would appear to be projected at length and more subtly into the structure of Marlow's romance in "Youth." The moment of ambivalence felt on the pulses of the attentive reader at the end of Conrad's novel of 1897, I would argue, is the sort of moment that can and may occur with considerable regularity as one negotiates the rhetorical effusions of Marlow striving to keep his foundering ship of romance headed boldly and blindly into the strong crosswinds of subversive, skeptical weather. However, both impulses that together prompt such ambivalence are "valid": the articulation and progress of Marlow's narrative depend upon the mutual conflict set to work between the romancer and the events he must strive to romance.

This approach to Conrad's allegory of narration in "Youth" may afford a way to realign Terry Eagleton's very suggestive remarks on the ideological contradictions purportedly at play in the author's choice and execution of plots. Eagleton has maintained that Conrad's predilection for "the *genre* of the adventure story" helps to generate "his own ideology in a determinate form" (139). However, Conrad does not so much express an ideology through the conventional form of the adventure tale as use that form to "produce" a peculiarly Conradian set of "ideological contradictions." As Eagleton phrases this situation,

> The characteristic Conradian work is an exotic tale of *action*, richly and concretely rendered, on whose margins play a set of skeptical questions about the very reality of action itself. The tale or yarn "foregrounds" action as solid and unproblematic; it assumes the unimpeachable realities of history, character, the objective world. Yet these assumptions are simultaneously thrown into radical doubt by the penumbra of spectral meanings which surround the narrative, crossing and blurring its contours. If the narrative is reduced to a yarn, those crucial meanings dissolve; if the meanings are directly probed, it is the narrative which evaporates . . . . The adventure story gives rise to a simple, solid specificity of action, which is in turn confronted with its corrosive negation—haunted like the ship *Narcissus* or *The Secret Sharer* with the ghost it must exorcise if the narrative is to survive. Such survival is for Conrad ideologically as well as artistically essential: faith, work and duty must not be allowed to yield to skepticism if the supreme fiction of social order is to be sustained. (139)

The separation of *physis* and *psyche* that Michael Levenson has charted as a fundamental, originary strategy of English literary modernism appears here in strongly drawn contours. The action-oriented plots of Conrad's tales of adventure at sea provide "a simple, solid specificity of action" along with "the unimpeachable realities of history, character, the objective world." However, there are significant dimensions of subjective experience, often localized in the narratorial consciousness, that move from the margins of textual narration into polarized relations with the purportedly "solid and unproblematic" level of locale, event and action. This counterposing of *physis* and *psyche* in Terry Eagleton's account of Conradian plots, moreover, draws out a significant dimension of what is at stake ideologically—not only aesthetically and formally. The Conradian world of action for Eagleton supports "the supreme fiction of social order" that must be preserved against the "corrosive negation" of skepticism and even "radical doubt" that haunt the spectral dimensions of meaning that circumambulate the narrated tales of adventure.

However, in the doubled pattern of reading "Youth" that I have already sketched above, it is not the arena of action that supports the supreme fiction of romance that Marlow narrates. Rather such motives toward fiction derive from Marlow's desire to project a plot of romantic adventure and quest onto circumstances of character and event that otherwise insistently resist and undermine his idealizations. Facts themselves occasion skepticism or doubt concerning the fictions of the social order. Accordingly, a critical understanding of the ideology of romance and the structure of romance narrative in Conrad needs to attend closely to the allegory of narration that can be articulated within the very language and perspective of the participant-narrator Marlow. At least in the case of "Youth" Marlow attempts a "supreme fiction" of Western "social order"—the quest for a vision of the East on the part of a young romancer journeying in the dual capacity of commerce and visionary idealism. Quite ironically, though, the narrated details of his insistent plot—the solid, action-driven events of his local history—exhibit the comic impossibility of his fiction's major terms of value and meaning.7

II

Several finer points of analysis can help bear out this doubled pattern of reading Conrad's narrative. For instance, Conrad's narrative opening helps to frame audience expectations. From the outset he uses conventions of Victorian romance and adventure fiction *a la* Frederick Marryat, Rider Haggard, Robert L. Stevenson, Rudyard Kipling, Arthur Conan Doyle, and the like in order to set up expectations of a certain sort of romance or adventure narrative in the offing.8 This connection between Conrad's work and both earlier and contemporaneous adventure fiction has been noted by many of the first reviewers of "Youth" as well as by Conrad himself. John Masefield, for example, who was an ardent admirer of Conrad's writings, singled out the story "Youth" in 1903 as being, "without doubt, the best thing Mr. Conrad has done" and strove to measure the qualities of its narrative against the standards of Kipling and Stevenson (442). Arthur Quiller-Couch reviewed "Youth" the month it first appeared in periodical form and remarked that the tale "might be one of the ordinary stories told by ordinary writers for ordinary boys at Christmas" (343). Conrad appears to have remembered this remark nearly four years later in a letter to the man who was responsible for the story's publication—William Blackwood. Indeed, Conrad concurs with Quiller-Couch's observation: "Exactly. Out of the material of a boy's story I've made *Youth* by the force of the idea expressed in accordance with a strict conception of my method" (*Collected Letters* 2: 417). Of course, this comment indicates that Conrad does not believe he began and ended with the material of boyish adventure; he has deliberately appropriated it toward some other end. Yet the attractions and the narrative conventions of such a popular adventure writer as Captain Frederick Marryat are available and active for Conrad; they help to shape the general, overt structure of Marlow's sea yarn as well as the expectations and predispositions of readers.[9]

Of special note in the conception of the narrative opening of "Youth," it can be said, are the conventions that reinforce opening an adventure narrative with an assumption or an overt assertion of what constitutes national and individual British identity, that subscribe to the celebration of the bond of men and the sea, and that assume the desirability of male-bonding behavior. Drinking, telling tales of daring and ambition, sentimentalizing adventure and courage, and extolling the glamour of one's youth constitute the sort of popular and boyish material that can be encoded telegraphically in succinctly phrased and thoroughly conventional sentences. As the primary narrator commences the tale, his sentences invoke the familiar conventions of a Marryat, or a Kipling, or a Stevenson:

> This could have occurred nowhere but in England, where men and sea interpenetrate, so to speak—the sea entering into the life of most men, and the men knowing something or everything about the sea, in the way of amusement, of travel, or of bread-winning.
>
> We were sitting round a mahogany table that reflected the bottle, the claret-glasses, and our faces as we leaned on our elbows . . . . We all began life in the merchant service. Between the five of us there was the strong bond of the sea, and also the fellowship of the craft. (3)

The five retired seamen were all once birthed into the maternal arms of the merchant marine and have come to maturity in respectable occupations: "a director of companies, an accountant, a lawyer"—the latter, "a fine crusted Tory, High Churchman, the best of old fellows, the soul of honour" (3). The other two men, Marlow and the anonymous narrator who introduces him, are tellers of tales, would-be praisers of their own past exploits. The first two paragraphs of the narrative thus quickly establish the assumption and transparency of shared British and Tory values and ideals, just as the easy transparency of the drinking table's reflection mirrors the five faces of the male comrades and former high adventurers.

Indeed the narrative conventions for adventure tales that shape the opening of "Youth" were quite popular among the readership of *Blackwood's Edinburgh Magazine (Maga)* where Conrad's tale was first published in September 1898.[10] Edward Garnett had advised Conrad's literary agent to begin submitting stories to *Maga* because the writer's work seemed well suited to the general interests of the magazine—namely, as Cedric Watts has phrased it, "fictional and factual material on 'outposts of empire,' travels and explorations" (*Joseph Conrad* 74). Ian Watt has also noted that Conrad's clear awareness of the kind of audience *Maga* afforded him "no doubt accounts for the bluff heartiness which occasionally injects a jarring note into Marlow's storytelling" (131, 130-34). Moreover, a few critics and scholars have intimated that the conception of Marlow's character and function may be directly linked to Conrad's understanding of the formulas for acceptance and success in such popular venues as *Maga*.[11] Walter Allen, for example, noticed the connection and its major implications many years ago:

> Is Marlow merely a device? In origin almost certainly. To gather a number of men of the world round a dinner table and have one of them relate a strange personal experience is one of the oldest, and now one of the stalest, contrivances in English magazine fiction, and perhaps it is especially associated with *Blackwood's Magazine*. Conrad early wrote for that periodical—*Lord Jim* was serialized there—and it may be that at first he was merely conforming to a way of storytelling traditional to *Blackwood's*. (365)

Even Marlow's rather excessively Dickensian character descriptions of Captain Beard and the North Sea pilot Jermyn in the opening pages of his own narrative nicely play along with the conventional expectations of a romance-adventure appearing in the popular pages of *Blackwood's* ("Youth" 4, 6). The setting for Marlow's tale and the narrative that he then begins to unfold can be quite plausibly situated within an intertextual matrix of generic conventions and readerly expectations of a certain type of romance involving British character and value on the road to exotic encounters, trials of personal mettle, and conviction in the destiny of one's birth and progress in the world.

The character and narrative voice of Marlow also play along with the type of expectations set up in the first few paragraphs of the narrative. Indeed Marlow begins his own tale of appealing to shared values concerning adventures at sea:

> You fellows know there are those voyages that seem ordered for the illustration of life, that might stand for a symbol of existence. You fight, work, sweat, nearly kill yourself, sometimes do kill yourself, trying to accomplish something—and you can't. You simply can do nothing, neither great nor little—not a thing in the world. (3-4)

Marlow affirms the human and symbolic value of adventure, but he also ironically foreshadows his romantic idealization of and enduring loyalty to the motto of the *Judea*—"Do or Die." Marlow's narrative, though, continues to insist upon a linear progression toward its desired end regardless of the delays, deferrals, or halting disruptions forced upon it by facts and circumstances. As I have already argued, it is based upon illusions or idealizations that fly insistently in the face of facts. Only Marlow's egocentric desire, voice, and values keep his narrative linear, coherent, and apparently moving toward an object. He knits the narrative together (a sea "yarn," after all) with his insistent illusions and his repeated incantations: "Bangkok," "the East," "youth," "glamour," "adventure," "trial of life," "pass the bottle," and "Do or Die." The persistence of his illusions and the narrative voice that reiterates them when they seem most challenged and open to doubt tend to exhibit something metanarrational about the vatic structure of romance narrative. The voice of romance, even the would-be hero of his own tale of romance, thrives upon the insistent idealization of facts and social acts that otherwise problematize, even immobilize, a desired progression.

Marlow himself, though, gives the lie to the object and to the naive view of the structure of his narrative. Well into the story, as the older Marlow recounts the extremely slow progress of the smoking *Judea* across the Indian Ocean, he discloses a moment of utter disaster that so discomposes the younger Marlow that the work of illusory idealization is abandoned in anger. The moment involves the sudden internal combustion of the coal fumes and smoldering fires that the old ship has brought with her into the blue calm of an alien ocean. At this moment the younger Marlow suffers his greatest personal injury—being blown up and burned, moustaches, eyebrows, and all. Shocked, he transfers the idealizing function of romance to the old captain of the *Judea* and distances himself in disbelief:

> And, mark, [Captain Beard] noticed directly the wheel deserted and his barque off her course—and his only thought was to get that miserable, stripped, undecked, smoldering shell of a ship back again with her head pointing at her port of destination. Bangkok! That's what he was after. I tell you this quiet, bowed, bandy-legged, almost deformed little man was immense in the single-ness of his idea and in his placid ignorance of our agitation. (25)

The Marlow of "Youth" accuses his otherwise rather Dickensian captain of the kind of hubristic egoism and "singleness" of "idea" that later Marlows in *Heart of Darkness* and *Lord Jim* will find lurking in the strange and disturbing willful-ness of Kurtz and Jim. This absurdly comic version of a Mr. Kurtz or a Lord Jim now becomes in the eyes of his Marlow the vehicle of single-minded ide-alization, as Marlow himself stands catastrophically and comically denuded of all the outward signs of his youth—"no hair, no eyebrows, no eyelashes, . . . my young moustache was burnt off, . . . my face was black, one cheek laid open, my nose cut, and my chin bleeding" (23). For the moment, with the *Judea* a "smoldering destruction" in the midst of an otherwise serene and peaceful Indian Ocean (24, 29), Marlow abandons the singleness of his own idea in the manner counselled by the citizens of Falmouth harbor or the mate of the *Somerville*—"O boys—you had better quit" (27).

Marlow, however, soon returns to his romance. He merely surrenders the ideal of "Bangkok" for the new, rather easily substituted one of "Java". The name of this lesser Bangkok still serves to elicit the reiterated promise of a "vision" of "the East". However, it is now virtually impossible to keep the comic dimension of Marlow's tale and his quest under restraint. In the rhetoric of youthful heroics Marlow intimates unwittingly just how illusional his version of the grail appears:

> Next day I sat steering my cockle-shell—my first command—with nothing but water and sky around me. I did sight in the afternoon the upper sails of a ship far away, but said nothing, and my men did not notice her. You see I was afraid she might be homeward bound, and I had no mind to turn back from the portals of the East. I was steering for Java—another blessed name—like Bangkok, you know. I steered for many days. (36)

Romance has been reinstated and singleness of idea recalled. Marlow constructs a humorously incongruous "first command" and commits himself and his small, well deceived crew to a course toward a vision, toward some semblance of what he has imagined from afar.

III

Marlow's vision of the East at the end of his narrative offers a stunning image, one which also appears curiously ambivalent and reversible. At first he evokes the soft outlines of distant mountains, a smooth bay, a warm night, and "a whispered promise of mysterious delight"; "mute and fantastic shapes" seem to welcome the exhausted Marlow and his crew (37). Marlow, now "exulting like a conqueror," comes face to face with the "mysterious East" that appears "perfumed like a flower, silent like death, dark like a grave" (38). The outlines of the East thus pathetically take on the attitudes of the exhausted seamen who glide into its accidental circumstances: "We were blind with fatigue. My men dropped the oars and fell off the thwart as if dead" (37). And then alone Marlow hears the East speaking to him "in a Western voice"; a volley of angry abuse in English and another unnamed language falls upon Marlow's ears from the commander of the *Celestial* who has mistaken him for a local (39). Marlow's vision of the East, mysterious from a distance, grows pathetic and then absurdly comic as Marlow attains his desired harbor and "hear[s] some of its language" (40). Finally, when Marlow sees "the men of the East," they have reversed the line of vision; they stare upon "three boats with the tired men from the West sleeping, unconscious of the land and the people and of the violence of sunshine" (40-41). Instead of Marlow gazing rapturously upon the idealized object of his romantic and narrative quest, the object—massed and silent and with eyes of its own—looks upon him and the sad detritus of his quest.

> But for me all the East is contained in that vision of my youth. It is all in that moment when I opened my young eyes on it. I came upon it from a tussle with the sea—and I was young—and I saw it looking at me. And this is all

that is left of it! Only a moment; a moment of strength, of romance, of glamour—of youth! . . . A flick of sunshine upon a strange shore, the time to
remember, the time for a sigh, and—good-bye!—Night—Good-bye . . . ! (42)

Marlow momentarily recognizes this unexpected reversal but then reasserts his
romantic illusions in the face of the silence of the East. Marlow appropriates
unsettling difference once again. Contrary circumstances and resistant facts and
conditions are overcome and the illusions of the egocentric and the romantic,
though stutteringly espoused in broken syntax, are yet again affirmed.

The doubled or reversible image offered near the end of Marlow's narrative,
moreover, poses itself as crucial to the structure of his narrative. It embodies the
idealized object or vision for which he has quested, but its doubled aspect ironically counterpoints the disconcerting facts that Marlow's idealizations and
effusive rhetoric have been striving to efface or overcome all along. To have his
vision of the East as he desires it, Marlow must efface the massed and collective
look of the silent Eastern men with the rhetoric of his ideal image of them. They
must present the illustrative emblem that he has come so far and so insistently
to see. Marlow resists recognizing the fact that "the East" has glimpsed an
unexpected vision of him and his exhausted fellow seamen slumped in their little boats "in the careless attitudes of death" (41). This vision of the West must
be resisted, reversed, effaced, because to fail to do so risks too great an exposure of the illusory motives that have driven the quest. Thus the ambivalent
content of the idealized image can be said to govern the very structure of the
romance and the romantic narrative that goes in quest of it. "The romance of
illusions," as the last words of the tale have it, is itself "a narrative" produced by
a desired and idealized image that still disturbingly and subtly exhibits the
structure of the romance and reveals it to be a narrative founded on
illusion—ill-founded, egocentric, illusory.

The final paragraph as well as the opening two paragraphs of "Youth," paragraphs in which the anonymous primary narrator speaks, offer another version
of the doubled or reversible image that Marlow has won for his efforts. The
mahogany table, around which the five Englishmen sit, reflects clearly all five
faces who gaze into it at the beginning of the narrative. Another, unsettling and
certainly more ambivalent idea-content appears readable in that reflection by
the end of the story:

And we all nodded at him: the man of finance, the man of accounts, the man
of law, we all nodded at him over the polished table that like a still sheet of
brown water reflected our faces, lined, wrinkled; our faces marked by toil, by
deceptions, by success, by love; our weary eyes looking still, looking always,
looking anxiously for something out of life, that while it is expected is already
gone—has passed unseen, in a sigh, in a flash. (42)

The loss of youth and strength and "the romance of illusions" darkly color the aging, weary, and anxious faces and eyes of those who still look for a vision that will not be ill-founded or illusory. However, "the sheet of brown water" in which the faces of the West are now reflected harbors the color and the unassimilated difference that romance desires yet also desires to efface. The East, as Marlow confides to his fellow countrymen, holds "the lands of brown nations, where a stealthy Nemesis lies in wait, pursues, overtakes so many of the conquering race, who are proud of their wisdom, of their knowledge, of their strength" (41-42). The desired image of the East structures and drives the romance adventure that goes in quest of it, but it also simultaneously reveals the insistent structure of illusions upon which romance narrative predicates itself. The ability to read the ideology of Marlow's and the primary narrator's potent images brings Conrad's allegory of narration full circle: the narrative of romantic illusions is founded upon and structured by a deceptive, ethnocentric idealization of a desired image. The romance of illusions, that is to say, remains ungrounded in anything save its insistent desire to read its plot, motives, and psychic idealizations into the resisting forms of otherness—whether those forms of resistance be leaking ships, smoldering coals from Newcastle, aging bodies, or the brown faces of the East. Conrad romances as well as allegorizes this alluring and anxious predicament; and he leaves it to the reader who can laugh at the deeds rationalized in the name of "youth," "glamour," "*Judea*," or "Do or Die" to see that Conradian romance depends upon an ideologically suspicious valorization of the image that summons romance to perform an allegory of its own production, an allegory of its own narration.

IV

However, it can remain all too easy to read "Youth: A Narrative" as a relatively simple tale of romance, replete with wistful nostalgia for youth and lost moments of visionary gleam. Perhaps another sort of evidence to warrant the explanatory power of the notion of allegories of narration in comprehending the structural dynamics of Conradian romance can be called to witness. The first version of "Youth" appeared as the lead item in the September 1898 issue of *Blackwood's Edinburgh Magazine*, and a regular column—often written but not signed by William Blackwood—called "The Looker-on" appeared as the final entry in the same issue.[12] The last three pages of this column in September 1898 featured a piece subtitled "Delicate Debate by Gentlefolk for Gentlefolk" and offered a rather high-toned Tory or Conservative scolding of four female contributors to a recent book called *The Modern Marriage Market*. The admonitory review does not actually strike any new or unexpected claim, but it does prove intriguing when read in conjunction with its issue-mate, "Youth." Blackwood, or whatever assistant or subeditor in his office who may have written or collaborated in it, appears to have appropriated many of Charlie Marlow's most favored terms of value—for instance, "illusions," "glamour," "romance," "mys-

tery," and "ideal of life." He uses them as major tokens in a discourse that chas-
tises women writers to be proper and reserved and not to engage in "the assas-
sination of romance" (451). The (presumably) male author warns: "It is not as
if we poor mortals could do without illusion, or that our lives could spare the
glamour of which every beggar has a share"—that is, we "could not afford to
part with" "the way of illusion," and this caution applies directly to relations
between "the more innocent sex" and "the sterner sex" (450). The writer essentially contends that the glamour and illusion of romance and its presumably stable network of roles and relations governing the two sexes must be kept intact
or we risk "destroying the illusions which have so long made man happy and
woman comfortable" (450). I venture that the anonymous, though rather Black-
woodian, author of this cautionary tract has in good measure transferred a nostalgic reading of Conrad's story away from the *facts* of Marlow's tale and has
used it to project a psychosocial paradigm concerning the conduct of the sexes.
Indeed this author would appear to use the very terms he refuses to read ironically and allegorically in Marlow's narrative. Conradian romance always
appears to run this risk. The only recourse is careful representation of this ideologically suspect tendency to idealize and rationalize illusionary modes of conduct. Such representation can reveal this tendency as itself constituting yet
another version of the structure of romance that Marlow narrates and that Conrad allegorizes in "Youth."

Conrad's "Youth" pioneers a major narrative strategy that quite arguably can
be recognized at work for Conrad in such later writings as *Heart of Darkness,
Lord Jim* and *Nostromo*. The tragic-romantic plots of these works feature the
corrosive effect of facts and events upon a narratorial desire to maintain some
insistent form of idealism or the romance of ideals. In the case of *Heart of
Darkness*, Marlow strives to maintain in the face of facts a romantic modeling
of European work and ideals in Africa. This Marlow articulates the work and
the rhetoric of "civilization" amidst conditions that severely undermine his
desire and his capacity to idealize in any convincing way. A later version of
Marlow in *Lord Jim* attempts to explore the unspoken motives and unarticu-
lated ideals that may guide the conduct of Jim at sea, at court, as well as in
Patusan. This Marlow struggles to rationalize Jim's conduct in terms of shadowy romantic ideals to which Jim has purportedly remained faithful since his
boyhood. However, Marlow's own motives and desires in telling Jim's
tale—and reading the facts of it the way he does—may signal the overriding
importance of the tale-teller's need to interpret facts and idealize conduct in a
manner consonant with his vision of the conduct of English seamen in the
Indian Ocean and the Far East. Moreover, in the massive narrative fabric of
Nostromo the English Captain Mitchell glamorizes the egocentric "value" of the
personal character of his captain of the Italian dockworkers, Nostromo. Mitchell
has no inkling of the facts that underlie the conduct of his would-be hero of the

newly formed Republic of Sulaco. The enormously corrosive effect of material interests and personal betrayal lurk beneath the idealizations of Mitchell in order to compromise and to deflate the interpretive value of the Englishman's romantic valorizations. In each of these three instances, Conrad's narratives problematize, immobilize, indeed render disjunctive, romantic quest adventures within the terms of their own narrative unfolding. The allegorical thrust of the narrative renders the desired unity and solidarity of character, motives, and psychic idealizations problematic for Charlie Marlow in Africa and in Far East Asia and for Captain Mitchell in Central and South America.

Conrad's "Youth" also signals the advent of a major modernist predilection—namely, the enormously formative presence and power of images in narrative discourse. *Images*—whether derived from a psychologically more sophisticated sense of the self or from culturally empowered conventions and desires—*structure narrative*.[13] Conrad as well as numerous modernist writers in his wake explore and problematize the nature of narrative and the motives of storytelling by dramatizing the covert ideology and pivotal valuation of the image.

In *Heart of Darkness*, for instance, Marlow strives to imagine the figure of Kurtz; but it takes Kurtz's sketch in oils of a blindfolded woman carrying a torch into darkness to begin to focus Marlow's interest. In many respects that visually precise but morally ambiguous image provides the base-image upon which at least two refigurations are superimposed palimpsest-like during the course of the narrative: the riverside image of the tall black woman stretching out her arms in longing and despair after Kurtz, and the cloistered image of the Intended at dusk in the sepulchral city also stretching out her arms in an eerily similar gesture of longing and despair. This complex palimpsest of an image structures a great deal of Marlow's level of interest and response. However, it also helps constitute a sense that the jungles of equatorial Africa are not themselves the "heart of darkness." Rather the jungles constitute a horror-stricken arena for the playing out of cultural and ideological contradictions articulated by and within a Western psyche. Through imperial agents like Mr. Kurtz, such psychic projections of thoroughly dichotomized cultural valuations can graphically become imaged upon the contours of an alien topography: dark/light, savage/civilized, black/white, African/European, evil/good, ignorance/knowledge, horror/ivory, whore/Intended, lust/love, jungle/city, brutish/eloquent, and willful damnation/saving illusion. All twelve of these binary pairs are pushed toward contradictory tension as the drama of Marlow's narrative plays itself out, but all twelve oppositions can be glimpsed as already operative in the complex image that motivates and torments Marlow's commitment to Kurtz's story. In other words, the specific, arresting image of white European influence in the heart of Africa allows, indeed encourages, Marlow and his most attentive listeners to trace the implications of its covert ideology through the horrors of the Inner Station back to the sheltered parlors of Brussels. Kurtz's portrait of European ideals that enter blindly into the midst of "darkness" operates artistically and ideologically like the vision of the East that Marlow paints in his own mind and the minds of his listeners in "Youth." The narrative complexity and formal execution of the image in *Heart of Darkness* goes well beyond Conrad's efforts in the earlier story. However, the structuring presence and power of psychically, ideologically, and culturally potent images in Conradian narrative would appear to be unmistakable. Indeed, quite generally considered, Conrad initiates a particularly modernist valuation of the image in fictional discourse. Modernist narrative, I would claim, both derives from and puts into question the ideology of the image, or images, that summon narrators and narratives now and again to rehearse their illusions.

V

Of course, the relation of modernist to postmodern discourse begs to be addressed. The discursive status and ideology of the image has been of tantamount interest in certain articulations of postmodernism, the postmodern, and postmodernist critical practice.[14] I would like to suggest briefly, by way of conclusion, that postmodernist narrative and postmodern discourse in general do seem to treat the image in a manner that differs from the paradigm that I have just sketched above for Conrad and modernist literary narrative. However, that difference appears already contained within the discursive range of modernity.

Postmodern discourse relishes the play of images. The markedly diverse work of Samuel Beckett, William Burroughs, Italo Calvino, John Fowles, Salman Rushdie, Roland Barthes, Jean Baudrillard, Ridley Scott, David Lynch, and Jim Jarmusch certainly lends some credence to this assertion. Even the global spread of music videos, of visually subliminal and evocative techniques in commercial advertising, of electronic video games, and of Steven Jobs-inspired word-and-text-processing software augur the pivotal importance of the play of images in postmodern social conditions. Indeed postmodern discourse releases literary, cultural, and even commercial activity toward a purported free play of images that foreground, even argue, their displacement and difference from an ideology of representation, an ideology of reflection. As Richard Kearney has recently argued in *The Wake of Imagination: Toward a Postmodern Culture*, postmodern discourse generally abandons the classical conception of imagination and the image. The image for postmodern culture precedes anything regarded as real, as original, as a fact or event in the world. Images displace the "original" realities that traditionally they are taken to reflect or represent. The postmodern maker poses simulacra or simulations without certain ground or secure epistemological base. He or she articulates "the omnipresence of self-destructing images which simulate each other in a limitless play of mirrors" (5). Simulated images thus make it impossible to test, or even to assume, a distinction between the factually real and the psychically projected or imaginary. In certain respects, this postmodern release into the play of images instates a distinctly ironic, antiessentialist, and post-romantic conception of what Frank Kermode some years ago called the "Romantic Image" (1-29, 43-48, 162-66). Instead of Kermode's aesthetic formalism and rather Kantian conception of the image as an autotelic symbol rapt out of time and space and the contingencies of historical production, postmodern practice tends to regard images as autotelic signs rapt out of any communicatively coherent system for their construction and interpretation. Such simulacra may be regarded as autotelic because they offer themselves as their own justification, and as bearing their own reality. A premium seems placed upon sheer, insistent immanence. Any foundational, metaphysical, or even utopian content becomes sharply disputed, indeed disclaimed or dismissed.

However, this postmodern discourse on the decentered, hyperreal status of the image bears with it a key problematic of modernity—namely, that "the modern" encounters the conditions and the experience of being displaced and different from what is regarded as ancient, classical, traditional, as differing from the already conventionally represented and objectified. Indeed, the postmodern might be characterized as the impulse to think of oneself and of culture as already *after* modernity and the condition of the modern. The postmodern might be posited as that state of modernity in which one feels the need to treat modernity as itself already over, behind, past, classic, intellectually completed, fully represented, and reified. Postmodern discourse replays in a new register, then, a formative dilemma of the discourse of modernity.

As Jean-François Lyotard has argued, the discourse of "modernity, in whatever age it appears, cannot exist without a shattering of belief and without discovery of the 'lack of reality' of reality, together with the invention of other realities" (77).[15] Postmodern discourse would disclose the "lack of reality" behind the play of representations and simulations and shift focus to the new or "other realities" of the postmodern imaginary. This discursive and cultural dynamic, however, recycles the problematic relation of modernity to what is regarded as "classical". In other words, postmodern discourse must read modernity as a historically completed and reified discourse. It must treat modernity as a classical discourse, one which assumes or projects an ideology of representation still in need of postmodern debunking. However, as I have tried to argue in the case of Joseph Conrad's early modernist narrative, literary modernism at least has actually already performed a major task of the postmodern project. The pivotal use of the image in Conrad's modernist narrative discloses an epistemological divorce between the world of the imaginary (the Western narrator's quest for a vision of the East) and the world of local and historical facts (the real localities and events appropriated and effaced by the rhetoric of romance). What is significant, indeed different, about Conrad's and modernism's regard for the image is that the dual, problematic status of the image and its ideological ramifications seem never to be lost to a postmodern sirens' song of simulation.

Conrad's allegory of narration can thus be read under postmodern cultural conditions as an allegory of representation, an allegory of imaginary production. It discloses subtly yet insistently the material conditions involved in Charlie Marlow's production of his romance narrative and its alluring image of the East. That is to say, Conrad's modernist allegory of narration dramatizes a narrator's and an audience's romancing of a simulacrum of youthful "reality" and at the same time exposes the illusion that such a simulated reality has neither an ironic nor an ideological relation to real, sociohistorical facts and conditions. Read under the pressure of postmodern concerns, then, Conrad's "Youth: A Narrative" yields an allegory of postmodern discursive production: postmodern discourse both derives from and puts into question the ideology of the image as simulacrum without sociohistorical conditions of production.

Notes

1. As it is fairly well known in Conrad scholarship, the sentence quoted occurs in a passage that quite likely was ghostwritten by Conrad's friend and collaborator Ford Madox Ford.

2. The presence of Charlie Marlow and the framing device of the primary narrator are usually recognized as significant advances upon Conrad's earlier uses of anonymous first-person narrative consciousnesses in such tales as *The Nigger of the "Narcissus"* (1897) and "Karain: A Memory" (1897). I would argue that Conrad's development of an allegory of narration is another significant advancement upon these earlier tales.

3. A host of relevant writings may be cited here as pursuing various aspects of this first general way of reading Conrad's tale. William York Tindall and Leo Gurko (79-82) have set the basic terms for the romantic and nostalgic reading of "Youth." C. B. Cox (viii-xi) and Ian Watt (133-34) generally accede to and perhaps even simplify the pattern of reading exemplified in Tindall and Gurko. John Howard Wills, David Thorburn (135-37), and Adam Gillon (63-68) provide somewhat more probing readings of the character of Marlow and of ambiguous features of the tale's narration, yet all three critics stress Marlow's triumphant victory in the face of recalcitrant facts and romantic illusions. More recently Daniel Schwarz, Kenneth Simons, Gail Fraser, and Robert Kimbrough all underscore the romanticizing and sentimentalizing function of both the younger and the older Marlow of the tale. Indeed Simons helps put this mode of reading simply: "The atmosphere Marlow creates rests finally on the sense that the episode retains the same appeal in the present as it had in the past, that youthful illusions are not undercut, but romanticized in retrospect" (8).

4. This way of reading "Youth" is somewhat related to William W. Bonney's remarks on the tale. Bonney contends that "Marlow's journey to Java is ultimately an impetuous, irresponsible lark," an "egoistic quest for adventure" that "draw[s] upon the most rampant of Western illusions" (24-25). Bonney underplays the comic dimensions

of Marlow's narrative and, instead, stresses how Conrad "figure[s] forth the demise of Judeo-Christian metaphysics" (25). The name of the ship *Judea* does help to foster speculation regarding theological and metaphysical undercurrents for Marlow's quest and his illusions regarding a vision of the East, yet the comedic and ironic complications of romance narrative should not be occluded.

In a reading that otherwise much resembles those cited in note three, Murray Krieger briefly but eloquently hits upon the "comic direction" of Conrad's "Youth": "The romanticism of the young Marlow is undercut by more than the ironic skepticism of the older Marlow who reconstructs him. It is undercut most immediately by the objective facts of the situation, by what is undeniably the triviality—indeed the farcicality, the sense of the ridiculous—that characterizes the ship, its captain, its cargo, the difficulties in getting under way: in short, the entire adventure" (279).

5. This approach to the structural and generic status of romance in Conrad's "Youth" is in consonance with Northrop Frye's structural accounts of romance in *Anatomy of Criticism* (186-203) and *The Secular Scripture: A Study of the Structure of Romance*. One major qualification, however, must be added. My allegorically narrative account of the structure of romance in "Youth" provides a distinctively *ironic* version of the structural and generic status of romantic narrative—that is, it recognizes the humorous potential and the comic impossibility of romance's idealizations of the narrated facts.

It is worth noting that Kenneth A. Bruffee offers a different account of Conrad's interest in romance narrative. Bruffee traces the generation of a new genre—"elegiac romance"—to Conrad's early fiction and maintains that Conrad first explored the formal convergence of three thematic concerns—namely, the tradition of quest romance, the cultural and intellectual discrediting of heroism and the cult of the hero, and the experience of cultural loss and change (15-132). Bruffee's account presents a rather Arnoldian image of Conrad, a persuasive account regarding general lineaments of Conrad's romantic heritage but deficient with regards to exploring the comic and ironic possibilities of Conrad's narrative strategies in such strange evocations of romance as "Youth."

6. Foulke's essay, included in Kimbrough (1979), first appeared in 1971.

7. Two markedly different but nevertheless very interesting arguments concerning the mode of Conrad's narrational presentation can be seen in Edward Said (90-110) and Jakob Lothe (1-44, 294-305). Said dwells upon the problem of writing and voice in Conrad in order to pursue a poststructuralist "psychology of Conrad's writing" (107). Lothe inventories the formal features of narrational perspective and textual structure throughout the canon of Conrad's major stories and novels.

8. This important connection between Conrad and Victorian writers of adventure has been noted in a number of contexts, usually in connection with *Heart of Darkness*. See especially David Thorburn (24-60), Frederick R. Karl (438), David H. Stewart (195-205), Murray Pittock (206-8), and Patrick Brantlinger (19-70, 227-74).

9. See Conrad's fascinating essay on Frederick Marryat and James Fenimore Cooper, originally published in the *Outlook* for 4 June 1898 and reprinted in *Joseph Conrad on Fiction*, ed. Walter F. Wright (47-50). The essay appears to have been composed just before or coextensively with "Youth" and contains numerous echoes of the

tale—for instance, Marryat "is the enslaver of youth, not by the literary artifices of presentation [Conrad's forte!], but by the natural glamour of his own temperament" (47).

10. See Karl (393-94). On the final page of the original manuscript of "Youth," completed in May 1898, Conrad wrote and circled the phrase "for B'woods." This notation primarily indicates his intention to send the tale to *Blackwood's* for publication. The magazine had accepted and paid rather handsomely for his story "Karain: A Memory" the previous year. However, the notation may also indicate Conrad's awareness that his tale was eminently appropriate for the audience of *Maga*, an audience that Conrad may very well have had in mind in contriving the narrative. See also Conrad's revealing letters to David Meldrum (7 Jan. 1902) and William Blackwood (31 May 1902), *Collected Letters*, 2: 367-69, 415-18.

11. Watt (130-32), Hugh Kenner (50), and Fraser (49).

12. The issue in question is *Blackwood's Edinburgh Magazine*, Vol. 164, No. 995 (September 1898). Conrad's story appears on pages 309-30, though the 1902 text shows slight alterations in punctuation and a few added lines on the last page. The anonymous review occurs on pages 450-52.

13. For an example of the psychological and textual complexity of images of self-composition in the structuring of modernist writing, see Brian G. Caraher.

14. See, for example, Roland Barthes, Jean Baudrillard, and W. J. T. Mitchell.

15. See also Jürgen Habermas for a comparable sociohistorical and philosophical argument.

Works Cited

Allen, Walter. *The English Novel.* New York: E. P. Dutton, 1954.

Barthes, Roland. *Image, Music, Text.* Trans. Stephen Heath. New York: Hill & Wang, 1973.

———. *Mythologies.* Trans. Annette Lavers. New York: Hill & Wang, 1973.

Baudrillard, Jean. *Simulations.* New York: Semiotexte, 1983.

Bonney, William H. *Thorns and Arabesques: Contexts for Conrad's Fiction.* Baltimore: Johns Hopkins UP, 1980.

Brantlinger, Patrick. *Rule of Darkness: British Literature and Imperialism, 1830-1914.* Ithaca: Cornell UP, 1988.

Bruffee, Kenneth A. *Elegiac Romance: Cultural Change and Loss of the Hero in Modern Fiction.* Ithaca: Cornell UP, 1983.

Caraher, Brian G. "A Question of Genre: Generic Experimentation, Self-Composition, and the Problem of Egoism in *Ulysses*." *ELH* 54 (1987): 183-214.

Conrad, Joseph. *The Collected Letters of Joseph Conrad.* Vol. 2, 1898-1902. Eds. Frederick R. Karl and Laurence Davies. Cambridge: Cambridge UP, 1986.

————. *Nostromo.* New York: Penguin, 1963.

————. "Tales of the Sea." *Joseph Conrad on Fiction.* Ed. Walter F. Wright. Lincoln: U of Nebraska P, 1964, 47-50.

————. "Youth: A Narrative." *"Youth," "Heart of Darkness," and "The End of the Tether".* Ed. C. B. Cox. London: Dent, 1974, 3-42.

Cox, C. B. "Introduction" to *Youth," "Heart of Darkness," and "The End of the Tether".* Ed. C. B. Cox. London: Dent, 1974, vii-xxii.

Eagleton, Terry. *Criticism and Ideology.* London: New Left Books, 1976.

Foulke, Robert. "Postures of Belief in *The Nigger of the "Narcissus".* In *The Nigger of the "Narcissus":* An Authoritative Text. Ed. Robert Kimbrough. New York: Norton, 1979, 308-21.

Fraser, Gail. *Interweaving Patterns in the Works of Joseph Conrad.* Ann Arbor: UMI Research P, 1988.

Frye, Northrop. *Anatomy of Criticism.* Princeton: Princeton UP, 1957.

————. *The Secular Scripture: A Study of the Structure of Romance.* Cambridge: Harvard UP, 1976.

Gillon, Adam. *Joseph Conrad.* Boston: Twayne, 1982.

Gurko, Leo. *Joseph Conrad: Giant in Exile.* New York: Macmillan, 1962.

Habermas, Jürgen. "Modernity versus Postmodernity." *New German Critique* 22 (Winter 1981): 3-14.

Karl, Frederick R. *Joseph Conrad: The Three Lives.* New York: Farrar, Straus and Giroux, 1979.

Kearney, Richard. *The Wake of the Imagination: Toward a Postmodern Culture.* Minneapolis: U of Minnesota P, 1989.

Kenner, Hugh. *A Sinking Island: The Modern English Writers.* Baltimore: Johns Hopkins UP, 1987.

Kermode, Frank. *Romantic Image.* London: Routledge & Kegan Paul, 1957.

Kimbrough, Robert. "Conrad's *Youth* (1902): An Introduction." *Heart of Darkness,* Norton Critical Edition. 3rd Ed. Ed. R. Kimbrough. New York: Norton, 1988, 406-18.

Krieger, Murray. "Conrad's *Youth*: A Naive Opening to Art and Life." *College English,* 20.6 (March 1959): 275-80.

Levenson, Michael H. *A Genealogy of Modernism: A Study of English Literary Doc-*

trine, 1908-1922. Cambridge: Cambridge UP, 1984.

"The Looker-on: Delicate Debate by Gentlefolk for Gentlefolk." *Blackwood's Edinburgh Magazine,* 164.995 (September 1898): 450-52.

Lothe, Jakob. *Conrad's Narrative Method.* Oxford: Clarendon P, 1989.

Lyotard, Jean-François. "Answering the Question: What is Postmodernism?" Trans. Regis Durand. *The Postmodern Condition: A Report on Knowledge.* Trans. Geoff Bennington and Brian Massumi. Minneapolis: U of Minnesota P, 1984, 71-82.

Masefield, John. Review of *"Youth: A Narrative" and Two Other Stories. Speaker,* 31 January 1903: 442.

Mitchell, W. J. T. *Iconology: Image, Text, Ideology.* Chicago: U of Chicago P, 1986.

Pittock, Murray. "Rider Haggard and *Heart of Darkness." Conradiana,* 19.3 (1987): 206-8.

Quiller-Couch, Arthur. Review of "Youth: A Narrative." *Speaker,* 17 September 1898: 343.

Said, Edward. "Conrad: The Presentation of Narrative," *The World, the Text, and the Critic.* Cambridge: Harvard UP, 1983, 90-110.

Schwarz, Daniel. *Conrad: "Almayer's Folly" to "Under Western Eyes."* Ithaca: Cornell UP, 1980.

Simons, Kenneth. *The Ludic Imagination: A Reading of Joseph Conrad.* Ann Arbor: UMI Research P, 1985.

Stewart, David H. "Kipling, Conrad and the Dark Heart." *Conradiana,* 19.3 (1987): 195-205.

Thorburn, David. *Conrad's Romanticism.* New Haven: Yale UP, 1974.

Tindall, William York. "Apology for Marlow," *From Jane Austen to Joseph Conrad.* Eds. R. C. Rathburn and M. Steinman. Minneapolis: U of Minnesota P, 1959.

Watt, Ian. *Conrad in the Nineteenth Century.* Berkeley and Los Angeles: U of California P, 1979.

Watts, Cedric. *The Deceptive Text: An Introduction to Covert Plots.* Sussex: Harvester P, 1984.

———. *Joseph Conrad: A Literary Life.* London: Macmillan, 1989.

Wills, John Howard. "A Neglected Masterpiece: Conrad's 'Youth'." *Texas Studies in Literature and Language* 4 (1962): 591-601.

Wright, Walter F., ed. *Joseph Conrad on Fiction.* Lincoln: U of Nebraska P, 1964.

Chapter 3

Virginia Woolf's Struggle with *Author-ity*[1]

Richard Pearce

"On or about December, 1910, Virginia Woolf declared, "human nature changed." "All human relations have shifted—those between masters and servants, husbands and wives, parents and children. And when human relations change there is at the same time a change in religion, conduct, politics, and literature. Let us agree to place one of these changes about the year 1910" ("Mr. Bennett and Mrs. Brown" 96-97). December 1910, Harvena Richter points out, was when the Post-Impressionist Exhibition opened in London. Artists pictured reality in a new way. "Time, space, and motion had been split. Human figures were reduced to essence or outline, or given multiple personality. . . . Yet it showed a wholeness of vision, a view of things in the totality of their appearance" (4).

Novelists too would begin to explore this paradox—of destroying the unity, fracturing the whole, disrupting the continuity, breaking the frame, decentering the subject, and shifting the point of view—to picture a new totality. Images on canvas and in the reader's mind would lose coherence. But they would gain new dimensions, new points of view, new centers of attention, a new sense of inclusiveness, and a new sense of complex and shifting interrelationships. Unity, that is, would give way to relationship.

This was the aesthetic and epistemological revolution that came to be known as modernism. Its disruptive power has been domesticated by critics, teachers, and readers, driven by the needs for mastery and order—and by the misleading distinction between a totalizing modernism and a revolutionary postmodernism.[2] Nor was the modernist revolution just aesthetic and epistemological; it was also political. For artists and writers were beginning to discover that coherence and unity were not just matters of solving aesthetic or epistemological problems or of reflecting visions of reality. Unity was imposed by forms of traditional author-ity. In fiction it was the author-ity of the omniscient narrator with his hierarchical view, his plotline leading step by step to a final goal, and his author-itative language.

Virginia Woolf struggled against male author-ity. Though she began by opposing the mixture of literature and politics, she came to recognize that language—or the way words are organized (ordered) in sentences and then "laid end to end"—is not natural or neutral (*Room* 80). Discourse is largely shaped by cultural forces, specifically by institutions (governments, churches, schools and the great books they promulgate, the family, the press, and the publishing industry). It is shaped, more specifically, by those who have the power to govern (we listen to them with special attention), the power to preach (we listen to them with reverence), the power to teach (we listen to them with respect for their knowledge), the power to rule the family (we obey them with love and respect), the power to report the news (we read them with the desire to know what happened), and the power to publish what we accept as important or interesting.

Even more specifically, Woolf recognized that down through history, those who had the power to govern, preach, teach, rule, report, and publish were men. And inevitably language—indeed the very structure of the English sentence—was shaped to fit their perspectives, capture their experiences, reflect their values, suit their needs. In *A Room of One's Own* she says,

> All the great novelists like Thackery and Dickens and Balzac have written a natural prose . . . taking their own tint without ceasing to be common property. They have based it on the sentence that was current at the time. The sentence that was current at the beginning of the nineteenth century ran something like this perhaps: "The grandeur of their works was an argument with them, not to stop short, but to proceed. They could have no higher excitement or satisfaction than in the exercise of their art and endless generations of truth and beauty. Success prompts exertion; and habit facilitates success." That is a man's sentence; behind it one can see Johnson, Gibbon and the rest. It was a sentence that was unsuited for a woman's use. (79-80)

According to Gilbert and Gubar the male sentence is not just a grammatical form, but "the sentence-as-definitive-judgment, the sentence-as-decree-or-interdiction, by which woman has been kept from feeling that she can be in full command of language" (230).

Virginia Woolf rejected traditional male sentences and the way they were "laid end to end." She developed a new author-ial voice—what Bernard in *The Waves* would call "the lady writing." She stretched the traditional sentence to achieve a new sense of inclusiveness and relationship. And, rather than a coherent image, she created a field of continually shifting relationships. Yet her major novels climax with images of unity: Peter Walsh's vision of Mrs. Dalloway, Lily Briscoe's completed painting, and the image of Bernard riding against death "with my spear couched and my hair flying back like a young man's, like Percival's when he galloped in India" (297).

I want to interrogate this unity, show it to be an assertion of the patriarchal, indeed imperialist, author-ity that the novels reject and undermine. But I also hope to show that unified readings of Woolf's novels are not misreadings. They reflect the residual power of the traditional author-ial voice. For she evokes a dialogic of power relations—where the "lady writing" becomes a source of new narrative power but must continually struggle against the author-ity of the male sentence.

Mrs. Dalloway opens in London, as Clarissa prepares for her party. "What a morning—fresh as if issued on a beach. What a lark! What a plunge!" And suddenly the clarity and coherence of this image is destroyed, for it is twenty years earlier. Nor is the new image so stable, for it shifts mid-sentence from the open window in Bourton to the terrace. And then we are back in the present. And then, with no warning, we are no longer in the drawing room but out on the street. Or were we there all along?

> For so it had always seemed to her, when, with a little squeak of the hinges, which she could hear now, she had burst open the French windows and plunged at Bourton into the open air. How fresh, how calm, stiller than this of course, the air was in the early morning; like the flap of a wave; the kiss of a wave; chill and sharp and yet (for a girl of eighteen as she was then) solemn, feeling as she did standing there at the open window, that something awful was about to happen; looking at the flowers, at the trees with the smoke winding off them and the rooks rising, falling; standing and looking until Peter Walsh said, "Musing among the vegetables?"—was that it?—"I prefer men to cauliflowers"—was that it? He must have said it at breakfast one morning when she had gone out on the terrace—Peter Walsh. He would be back from India one of these days, June or July, she forgot which, for his letters were awfully dull; it was his sayings one remembered; his eyes, his pocket-knife, his smile, his grumpiness and, when millions of things had utterly vanished—how strange it was!—a few sayings like this about cabbages.
> She stiffened a little on the kerb. (3-4)

In *Mrs. Dalloway*, Woolf fractures the image created in our minds; she undermines the author-ity of the traditional plotline and indeed the traditional male sentence, which lead us with logical and grammatical assurance from one point to the next. The narrator shifts between the present and past, London and Bourton, one character's point of view and another's—with connectives that are ambiguous, incongruous, illogical, even ungrammatical. She stretches the sentence, or the basic narrative unit, to include grammatical gaps, physical gaps, narrative intrusions, conflations of experiences and possible experiences, leaps in time and space, leaps from the mental to the physical world—and individual images that suddenly transform themselves, succeed one another helter skelter, fail to coalesce.

When Clarissa returns with her flowers the hall is "as cool as a vault." She feels "like a nun who has left the world. . . . blessed and purified." But she experiences the next moment as one of the "buds on the tree of life, flowers of darkness . . . (as if some lovely rose had blossomed for her eyes only)" (42-43). The cloistered vault has become a garden, the tree a rose bush, and the feeling of blessed purity an experience of lovely darkness. Then Lucy tells her that Mr. Dalloway will be having lunch at Lady Bruton's and takes the parasol "like a sacred weapon" (43). Clarissa shivers like a "plant on a river bed" (44). She fears "time itself" and reads it "on Lady Bruton's face, as if it had been a dial cut in impassive stone," and then experiences the hesitation, "the exquisite suspense, such as might stay a diver before plunging while the sea darkens and brightens beneath him, and the waves which threaten to break, but only gently split their surface, roll and conceal and encrust as they just turn over the weeds with pearl" (44). In the next moment "the appalling night" is seen more accurately as "this matter-of-fact June morning; soft with the glow of rose petals." And in a few lines she feels "like a nun withdrawing, or"—and now a final leap—"a child exploring a tower" (45). The narrator may be picturing the subtle shifts in mood in these three pages, but she does so through a galloping incongruity of the images.

We encounter an even greater incongruity in her portrayal of Clarissa and Peter's reunion. At the most poignant moment Peter's grief rises "like a moon looked at from a terrace, ghastly beautiful with light from the sunken day." But the moon is soon reduced to two dimensions, looking more like a disk hanging against the painted canvas of a stage set:

> as if in truth he were sitting there on the terrace he edged a little towards Clarissa; put his hand out; raised it; let it fall. There above them it hung, that moon . . . . Then, just as happens on a terrace in the moonlight, when one person begins to feel ashamed that he is already bored, and yet as the other sits silent, very quiet, sadly looking at the moon, does not like to speak, moves his foot, clears his throat, notices some iron scroll on a table leg, stirs a leaf, but says nothing—so Peter Walsh did now. For why go back to the past? he thought. (62-63)

Of course we have encountered a flashback to the past, for the terrace is like the terrace at Bourton. But we are also taken out of Clarissa's sitting room and faced with a second-rate romantic set that upstages the actors, who register their feelings in a series of delicate movements.

The incongruities multiply in the scene where Peter and Clarissa, who have been fencing with pocket-knife and knitting needles on the blue sofa, suddenly become two horses, pawing the ground and tossing their heads before a battle begins (66); and in the scene where Septimus and Evans, attracted to one another in the trenches of France, become "two dogs playing on a hearth rug; one worrying a paper screw, snarling, snapping, giving a pinch now and then, at the old dog's ear; the other lying somnolent, blinking at the fire, raising a paw, turning and growling good-temperedly" (130).

In her early work Virginia Woolf implies (and later she articulates) the connections between language and power. In *Mrs. Dalloway* she transgresses, undermines, or topples their structures, sometimes tentatively, sometimes boldly, sometimes playfully, sometimes defiantly. She creates a basic narrative unit open to images of relationship denied by the male hierarchy of thought. Her new unit of expression breaks hierarchic order of grammar, space, time, logic, and literary convention—and strives for ultimate inclusion.

But running through this revolutionary novel with the regularity of Big Ben, and drawing the various strands into a coherent picture, is an old-fashioned romance plot: the courtship of Peter Walsh. Granted Peter does not get Clarissa physically, emotionally, or dramatically. Indeed, their meeting after all those years is a failure. Still, he appears first in Clarissa's thoughts on that splendid spring morning, and he forms a major, coherent path through the novel. He intrudes into her bedroom and causes her to "hide her dress, like a virgin protecting her chastity" (59), he walks through the park past Septimus and Rezia, he takes us through the London streets first away from Clarissa and then back, he becomes a major focal point at her party. And he has the culminating vision, indeed the last word, "It is Clarissa, he said." And then the narrator author-izes his sentence: "For there she was." So Peter Walsh literally gets Mrs. Dalloway into his sentence, which—being the final sentence in the diagesis, or story proper, and then being author-ized by the narrator—becomes the unifying image toward which a strong narrative line has been leading.

But Peter has proven himself unreliable—continually imposing his views on others. "Star-gazing?" he asks, coming upon Clarissa and Sally after their ecstatic kiss (53). "Lovers squabbling under a tree," he thinks, as he passes Septimus picturing "legions of men prostrate behind him" and Rezia feeling so alone and unhappy (106-7). And, when he hears the siren of the ambulance taking Septimus to the hospital, he marvels at the wonders of civilization.

Indeed, Peter is not just unreliable: just back from India, he reflects the mentality—and author-ity—of imperialism. Clarissa Dalloway is independent and elusive. She flits from place to place, time to time, and indeed self to self. She escapes the hierarchy and logic of not only the plotline but the traditional English sentence. But (to use Gilbert and Gubar's phrase) she is finally "sentenced"—by the hero of the romance plot and a civil servant of the empire, as he imposes his frame, his order, his image of unity, on the multiple, even contradictory, strands of the novel.

Peter Walsh was able to establish his author-ity, in Mrs. Dalloway's story if not in her life, because the romance plot was so deeply inscribed in the form of the novel. That he was also a civil servant of the empire reflects the power of the ideology that the narrator blatantly condemns. It may also lead us to relate the ideology of imperialism to the conventions of romance—which included not only the conquest of a lady but the journey of adventure. Remember that Peter pictured himself as "an adventurer, reckless . . . swift, daring, indeed (landed as he was last night from India) a romantic buccaneer" (80)—as he followed a young woman down the street. And Mr. Ramsay will picture himself as a soldier leading his family on an expedition to a mountain across "the icy solitudes of the Polar region" (54).

According to Martin Green "the adventure tales that formed the light reading of Englishmen for two hundred years and more after *Robinson Crusoe* were, in fact, the energizing myth of English imperialism. They were, collectively, the story England told itself as it went to sleep at night; and, in the form of its dreams, they charged England's will with the energy to go out into the world and explore, conquer, and rule" (3).

Patrick Brantlinger shows that journeys of adventure dominate "'serious' domestic realism," as well as the light reading, the two being "seemingly opposite poles of a single system of discourse, the literary equivalents of imperialist domination abroad and liberal reform at home" (12). Imperialism was "a pervasive set of attitudes and ideas" that "influenced all aspects of Victorian and Edwardian culture" (8-12). And, Brantlinger demonstrates, it was closely interwoven with racism and sexism.

The journey of adventure is undermined in *To the Lighthouse*, where Woolf traces the journey of a father and son to the lighthouse—from its inception to its undertaking and completion ten years later. But we are hardly aware of the journey until the last chapter. For Woolf devotes the long opening section to the evening when Mrs. Ramsay sits in front of the drawing-room window with her little son James, while Lily Briscoe paints their picture. An argument begins between the mother who tells her son that "of course" he'll be able to go to the lighthouse, "if it's fine tomorrow," and the father who insists that "it won't be fine" (9-10). But Woolf's story encompasses much more than a journey to the lighthouse. It includes a whole set of relationships—in a household of seven other children and the house guests, Lily Briscoe, Charles Tansley, Augustus Carmichael, William Bankes, Minta Doyle, and Paul Rayley—over which Mrs. Ramsay presides. And the point of view shifts from character to character so we can never see any one of them as a unified self, but only as she or he sees or is seen by another character at a particular moment in a particular situation.

Moreover, at the very center of the story is a hole—an absence—that interrupts the journey, denies it its power to achieve control and unity, and gives form and meaning to what it leaves out. In the short chapter called "Time Passes," the characters we have come to know are absent. The summer house is seen from the point of view of eternity, or, more precisely, (Mother) Nature and the cleaning lady. And all the "important" events in the story occur elsewhere, indeed in square brackets. The death of Mrs. Ramsay, the death of her daughter in childbirth, a world war, a change in fortune and public taste—are evoked not as events but as absences, as holes in a chapter that while itself parenthetical is the most powerful chapter Virginia Woolf ever wrote.

In "Time Passes," Woolf disrupts and deconstructs the traditional journey with an untraditional view of its logical conclusion: loss, absence, waste. She connects the violence of war with the death of a woman who has struggled in a role of "the angel in the house"—or mother, nurturer, and unifier—and of a daughter who, like so many young women, died giving birth to her child. Perhaps we can now understand why, in the central section (or central hole in the novel), the authorial voice gives way to (Mother) Nature and the cleaning woman. This is a woman's vision that is suppressed by the traditional journey.

The final section does focus on the voyage to the lighthouse, where the father is reconciled to his children and passes his authority down to his son. But the narrator cuts back and forth between the voyage and Lily Briscoe, as she finishes the painting she began on the same day the journey was conceived. Lily finally realizes her independence from both Mr. and Mrs. Ramsay and indeed is able to imagine the father and son landing on the rocks. Then she "looked at her canvas . . . . with a sudden intensity" and "drew a line there, in the centre. It was done; it was finished. Yes, she thought, laying down her brush in extreme fatigue, I have had my vision" (310).

Woolf has interrupted and then fractured the plotline, denying the adventure journey its authoritative coherence. And now she interrupts and decenters the actual journey by cutting back and forth to Lily Briscoe's thoughts. As Rachel Blau Du Plessis cogently argues, she also undermines the men's journey by forming a pre-Oedipal community of parent-child relationships, "geniality, sisterhood, motherhood, brotherhood" and "bisexual oscillation" (60-61). Moreover, she liberates herself from both Mr. and Mrs. Ramsay. But in the end Lily draws all the strands of the novel together in two successive images of unity: she imagines the father and son landing and completes her picture of the patriarchal family. The position of this scene in the plotline and the succession of her images—or the fact that she must complete the journey-men's story before she can finish her own—is a mark of its power to co-opt the female artist.

There is another way to read the last section of the novel, though. Ten years earlier Lily "had been looking at the table-cloth, and it flashed upon her that she would move the tree to the middle, and need never marry anybody, and she felt an enormous exultation" (262). Now she decides not to move the tree but to draw a line down the center of the painting—not to unite but to divide the family, and in so doing to divide herself from it.

What does the dividing line say about her development? And what does it say about her vision? Does she reflect what Alex Zwerdling describes so well as the "extraordinary transformation of the ideals of marriage and family life" (145)? Does she understand the patriarchal marriage that Jane Lilienfeld illuminates? Does she come to realize that marriage was more than "a man and a woman looking at a girl throwing a ball" (110)? Does she sense why Mrs. Ramsay needed to be by herself? That by wanting to shed the "attachments" to "this self," Mrs. Ramsay was not necessarily being metaphysical or mystical but giving vent to repressed feelings about her social role (95)? Of course Mrs. Ramsay was experiencing the "moment of being," in which Woolf exulted ("Sketch of the Past"). But how much of Woolf's mysticism was a sublimation of feelings that remained potent? After all, when Mrs. Ramsay thought about "this self having shed its attachments" she shifted into the discourse that governed her husband's fantasies: she would now be "free for the strangest adventures," and the first adventure would be to "the Indian plains" (95-96).

Mrs. Ramsay, Lily might also have intimated, repressed a great deal in her enthusiasm for marriage. When she reflected too long about Minta and Paul, she felt "life rather sinister." And she had to rationalize, "because whatever she might feel about her own transaction, she had experiences that need not happen to every one (she did not name them to herself)" (92). It is important that she calls her marriage a "transaction." It is even more important that she cannot name the experiences to herself—and that by feeling these experiences need not happen to everyone she implicitly blames herself.

At the end of the day, as she talks with her husband about Minta and Paul's engagement, Mrs. Ramsay comes dangerously close to seeing in an annihilating light what she has repressed and sublimated. "Slowly it came into her head, why is it then that one wants people to marry? What was the value, the meaning of things?" And she wishes that her husband would say something, anything, "for the shadow of the thing folding them in was beginning, she felt, to close round her again. Say anything, she begged, looking at him as if for help." All he says is, "You won't finish that stocking tonight." But "that was what she wanted . . . . 'No,' she said, flattening the stocking out upon her knee, 'I shan't finish it'" (183-84).

She capitulates, but rallies her independence. He wants her to tell him that she loves him. And the day that began with a quarrel about going to the lighthouse, ends with a battle of wills. "A heartless woman he called her; she never told him that she loved him." She walks to the window, turns, looks at him, and smiles. Finally she says, "'Yes, you were right. It's going to be wet tomorrow. You won't be able to go.' And she looked at him smiling. For she had triumphed again. She had not said it: yet he knew" (183-86).

Of course this is a reconciliation that makes them both feel good, a transaction between adults that enables them not only to go on but to do so in a way that is mutually supportive. But what is the price of reconciliation and who pays? What is the nature of the transaction? And what is Mrs. Ramsay's triumph?

She is able to not say that she loves him by saying "Yes, you were right." She is able to bring about a happy ending by repressing thoughts that would threaten the family romance. And what does it mean for her to have triumphed?

To have not said she loved him? Or why, we might first ask, does the woman who can make Charles Tansley feel "an extraordinary pride" (25), who triumphs at dinner by acting like the chairman of a meeting—why should this woman who has such control over social discourse have trouble expressing her feelings? Unless she was trying not to express but repress them.

Lily might have glimpsed this image of Mrs. Ramsay, or this one of Mrs. Ramsay's multiple selves, from which she needed to gain independence. And she liberates herself from Mrs. Ramsay's tyrannical hold by affirming herself as a single woman and an artist, and by finishing her picture with a line that divides the family. Nonetheless readers who see the picture as a unifying image are not wrong. For she author-izes the journey-men's story by imagining the landing. And she unifies the family by finishing their picture at the end of the novel. That so many readers take joy in a final image of unity reflects the residual power of traditional author-ity, even though it has been undermined throughout the novel.

The Waves lacks all the conventions that have traditionally provided coherence and unity. It has no storyline, no narrator, no description of the characters or the setting, no summaries of the action, no commentary—only dialogue with minimal attribution. "'I see a ring,' said Bernard . . . . 'I see a slab of pale yellow,' said Susan . . . . 'I hear a sound,' said Rhoda" (9). Moreover, the dialogue is not really dialogue. For the six characters, we soon learn, are not talking to each other. Nor is it monologue, for they are not even talking to themselves. What we hear are thoughts, that, given the quotation marks, would seem to come directly from the children's minds. Except that all the voices sound the same.

The Waves is governed by a new kind of author-ial figure who does not separate herself from the narrative to tell the story but em-bodies it. I want to distinguish this voice as female because her story is, to use Nancy Miller's terms, an erotic rather than an ambitious text. It does not strive to achieve a goal but to em-body relationships. And it does so through what Julia Kristeva calls the "semiotic": a fluid, indeed wild, and polyvalent language that transgresses denotation, syntax, logical order, and develops in the pre-Oedipal and prelinguistic stage, when we find our source of pleasure and value in the mother's body. Garrett Stewart has illuminated the novel's semiotic rhythm with great precision and persuasiveness.

Since the female authorial voice em-bodies her story, we might rather call it the embodying source. For this indeed is what we encounter in the creation myth, the myth of Aurora—which opens the novel. *"The sun had not yet risen. The sea was indistinguishable from the sky, except that the sea was slightly creased as if a cloth had wrinkles in it."* Then, instead of a male voice declaring "Let there be light," *"the arm of a woman"* raises a *"lamp and flat bars of white, green and yellow, spread across the sky like the blades of a fan."* As she raises her arm higher, the sea slowly becomes transparent, the light strikes the trees in the garden, the birds begin to chirp, and the blind of a bedroom window begins to stir (7-8).

The creation myth and italicized interchapters—focusing on nature rather than human lives and tracing the course of the sun throughout a single day—ground the continually fragmented and shifting story of Bernard, Susan, Rhoda, Neville, Jinny, and Louis. But within that story a conflict arises between the embodying source and the author-ity of her three male characters—especially Bernard.

In the beginning of *The Waves* the six friends are playing in the fields. Susan has just seen Jinny kiss Louis. And Bernard follows her "gently . . . to be at hand with my curiosity, to comfort her when she bursts out in a rage and thinks, 'I am alone'" (14). And he tells her the story of Elvedon.

In his story, Bernard leads Susan—and the reader—past a thorny hedge that the ladies clip each noon with scissors, through a ringed wood with its rank and poisonous undergrowth, where they hear the flop of a giant toad, and up to a wall. Peering cautiously over the wall, they watch the gardeners, who sweep with giant brooms, who would shoot the children if they saw them, who would nail them like stoats to the stable door. And in the center of this menacing world, between two long windows, is the lady writing.

The lady writing rules the manor. And Bernard's menacing image of Elvedon reflects his fear of female author-ity. Indeed, we might consider Elvedon to be what Julia Kristeva calls the *chora,* from the Greek word for enclosed space, or womb, which houses the wild and threatening "semiotic" rhythm that runs beneath controlled, symbolic expression. Throughout Western history, the woman's body, especially her womb, has been represented as mysterious and incomprehensible; the language associated with her body has been threatening to male author-ity because it is "other," contradictory, uncontrollable, and cannot be fixed in language.

But the menacing walls and woods and gardeners, which Bernard creates in his story, not only threaten him. They not only keep him out. They keep the lady writing in. Bernard's story may express his fear of the lady writing, but it is also designed to impose his frame upon her, to fit her into his picture, or (to use Gilbert and Gubar's term) to sentence her, imprison her between the windows of her mansion—keep her in her place.

Bernard's story is so convincing that Susan collaborates in telling it. It is so successful that we accept him as an author-ial figure even though he is a child. Indeed, we take what he says as author-itative in passages that dominate every polyvocal section of the novel. We take him at his word when he tells us that he is androgynous. And we attend to him with great anticipation in his chapter-long monologue, which begins, "Now to sum up" (238).

What we encounter in the final section is not a stylized soliloquy, like all the other monologues. It is Bernard's actual speech to a stranger sitting across the dinner table, probably at his club: "Since we do not know each other (though I met you once I think aboard a ship going to Africa) we can talk freely" (228). But—since he does not address his companion directly again until near the end—the implied "you" in this dramatic monologue gradually becomes the reader. Bernard addresses us directly. He cannot arouse the interest of his companion, but he arouses our interest and holds our attention. For we have come to care about him. But more important, we have come to rely on him for guidance in this experience of shifting viewpoints and intricate relationships. And here he is telling us: "Now to sum up. Now to explain to you the meaning of my life" (238).[3]

But note the shift. Summing up becomes finding the meaning of *his* life. As Bernard reviews the story of each character, he fits the fragmentary incidents of the past into a pattern that gives *his* life meaning and coherence. In appropriating their stories—as he appropriated the story of the lady writing—he displaces the female author, or the em-bodying source. Indeed he literally takes on the paternalistic role of an omniscient narrator—"So now, taking upon me the mystery of things, I could go like a spy without leaving this place" (291). Moreover, he co-opts the female myth of creation. For, drawing his story to an end, he tells us, "Day rises; the girl lifts the watery fire-hearted jewels to her brow: the sun levels *his* beams straight at the sleeping house" (291; italics mine). That is, he appropriates the language of the lady writing (whose *"girl couched on her sea-green mattress tired her brows with water-globed jewels"* [148]). He transfers the girl's power to a male sun god. And he reduces the female creator to the kind of figure that adorns the men's club where he is probably dining.

In the end Bernard feels "beat and done with it all" (296). Then he becomes "aware of a new desire," and identifies with Percival—who, though silent and remote, has been loved and admired by all the characters. But Bernard does not identify with the silent Percival who united the six friends in a last supper or the Percival who fell to his death in India when his horse tripped. Bernard rides against death "with my spear couched and my hair flying back like a young man's, like Percival's when he galloped in India" (297). And this is the image that unifies the novel.

There is no question that Bernard is a complex character, continually questioning the language in which he thinks and writes, changing as we see him through the eyes of other characters, thinking of himself as multiple rather than single, believing that he is androgynous. Nonetheless, in the end he takes on the combined role of omniscient narrator and phallic hero. He is driven by the desire for unity and urge toward mastery; he is aroused by a thirst for violent adventure, military invasion, and imperialist glory.

Now these are just the drives that Virginia Woolf attacked and parodied in *Mrs. Dalloway*, when she broke through her highly controlled narrative to rail against imperialism, or the Goddess of Conversion. And this is just the dual fantasy that she satirized in *To the Lighthouse*, when Mr. Ramsay realizes that he might never reach R., but would go on with the struggle. He "would seek out some crag of rock, and there his eyes fixed on the storm, trying to pierce the darkness, he would die standing." And the searchers would find him dead at his post, the fine figure of a soldier (56). And Woolf had just written *A Room of One's Own*, where she identified the power of male sentencing.

Moreover, she had just finished *Orlando* which begins, as Jane Marcus reminds us,[4] with the paragon of a young man, "slicing at the head of a Moor which swung from the rafters," a head that his father or grandfather had struck "from the shoulders of a vast Pagan." They "had ridden in fields of asphodel, the stony fields, and fields watered by strange rivers, and they had struck many heads of many colours off many shoulders and brought them back to hang from the rafters. So too would Orlando, he vowed." But since he was too young "he would steal away from his mother and the peacocks in the garden and go to his attic room and there lunge and plunge and slice the air with his blade" (13)—before settling down to spend an hour composing his Tragedy in Five Acts. The parody links the imperialist warrior with the voice of traditional author-ity. And, while in *Orlando* she turned her young hero into a woman, in *The Waves* she would turn him into Percival.

But then why do we take Percival seriously? Why don't we laugh at what is more of a pratfall than the death of an idealized hero or martyr? Why do we see him as a unifying force? Why do we glorify his innocence? Why do we invest his silence with meaning? Why, when Jinny is so lonely and Rhoda commits suicide, do we see *him* as representing the loss of human possibility? And why do we accept Bernard's author-ity? Why, when we only have his own self-serving word for it, do we trust his sympathy? Why, when he fantasizes a biographer to tell us, do we accept his androgyny? Why, after seeing what he actually writes—the romantic sketch of a back street where "a girl stands waiting. For whom?" And the story of "a purple lady swelling, circumambient, hauled from a barouche landau by a perspiring husband" with a small crane fixed to the top of a wall (115)—why do we even believe in him as a writer? And why don't we give full weight to the waves that break on the shore—the novel's final line that silently comments on Bernard's heroic gesture against Death?

To answer these questions we must turn to Mikhail Bakhtin, who distinguishes between the monologic and polylogic novel. In the monologic novel the authorial voice dominates. In the dialogic novel the authorial voice contends with another voice or voices. The ultimate dialogic or polyphonic novel is like a carnival, where the authorial voice is only one among many voices that speak, argue, harangue, cajole, mock, imply, and take joy in their contradictoriness. Julia Kristeva adds a psychological dimension to Bakhtin by seeing the monologic voice as regulatory, linguistic, and "symbolic," acquired when the child learned to accept his or her father, and the energy of the carnival as "semiotic," connected to the pre-Oedipal stage when the mother's body is the source of multiple and contradictory desires, pleasures, and values. The novel as a genre is revolutionary because of the variety of voices that contend ideologically with the authorial voice.

Bakhtin understands the power of "the unitary language" and talks about "the politics of style." And Kristeva insists that the symbolic and the semiotic are always interconnected, that the semiotic *chora* is constrained or regulated by family and social structure. But neither Bakhtin nor Kristeva deals systematically with the fact that some voices have more power than others—or with the ways they maintain their author-ity. For their author-ity derives from tradition, or a canon and way of reading, established by the class whose authority the authorial voice reflects and perpetuates. And this power may be undermined but cannot lose its force.

In *The Waves* Woolf ignored, displaced, undermined all the conventions that have traditionally empowered the monologic voice and provided coherence and unity. Moreover, she finally succeeded in eliminating all the "appalling narrative business of the realist: getting on from lunch to dinner," all the conventions so that there is "no plot, no comedy, no tragedy, no love interest or catastrophe in the accepted style," and "not a single button sewn on as the Bond Street tailors would have it" ("Modern Fiction" 212). There is no history, nothing of what Alex Zwerdling calls the "real world." She succeeded, we might say, in eliminating all the traditional conventions of fiction and history, or fiction as a his-story. But what emerges is a historical expression of the ruling class mind—and the woman's struggle within it.

The lady writing has em-bodied the shifting interrelationships of three men and three women, who were all members of the ruling class. She undermines all the author-ial conventions, decenters the novel form, replaces the journey-men's story or ambitious text with an erotic text, brings the semiotic rhythm to the surface, and exposes the historical source of political, social, and linguistic author-ity. Still, traditional author-ity maintains its hold over the narrative and over the readers' needs. And the final images of Bernard as the phallic knight and the waves breaking on the shore gives full expression to the dialogic of power relations. The semiotic and symbolic contend, and the lady writing struggles against the author-ity of the male sentence.

Notes

1. Much material in this essay was adapted from the manuscript of my *Politics of Narration: James Joyce, William Faulkner, and Virginia Woolf* (New Brunswick: Rutgers UP, 1991).

2. See my "What Joyce After Pynchon?"

3. Jane Lilienfeld strongly objects to my use of "we," for I am not describing her reading—nor that of many readers who have learned to resist the powers of convention, view authority figures with skepticism, and attend to the voices and stories that have been neglected or suppressed. I decided to retain my use of "we," nonetheless for two reasons. First, to represent most people, including myself and many female feminist colleagues, who accepted traditional author-ity up to some point in our educations. And, second, to dramatize the power of traditional author-ity over the majority of readers, scholars, critics, and teachers—for to ignore this power is to ignore textual, cultural, and historical context.

4. 1987 MLA paper.

Works Cited

Bakhtin, M. M. *The Dialogic Imagination.* Trans. Caryl Emerson and Michael Holquist. Ed. Michael Holquist. Austin: U of Texas P, 1981.

Brantlinger, Patrick. *Rule of Darkness: British Literature and Imperialism, 1830-1914.* Ithaca: Cornell UP, 1988.

Du Plessis, Rachel Blau. *Writing Beyond the Ending: Narrative Strategies of Twentieth Century Women Writers.* Bloomington: Indiana UP, 1985.

Gilbert, Sandra and Susan Gubar. *No Man's Land: The Place of the Woman Writer in the Twentieth Century.* Vol. 1 (2 vols). New Haven: Yale UP, 1987.

Green, Martin. *Dreams of Adventure, Deeds of Empire.* New York: Basic Books, 1979.

Kristeva, Julia. *Desire in Language: A Semiotic Approach to Literature and Art.* Trans. Alice Jardine, Thomas A. Gora, and Leon S. Roudiez. Ed. Leon S. Roudiez. New York: Columbia UP, 1980.

Lilienfeld, Jane. "Where the Spear Plants Grew: the Ramsay's Marriage in *To The Lighthouse.*" *New Feminist Essays on Virginia Woolf.* Ed. Jane Marcus. Lincoln: U of Nebraska P, 1984.

Miller, Nancy K. "Emphasis Added: Plots and Plausibilities in Women's Fiction." *PMLA* 96 (1981): 36~48.

Pearce, Richard. "What Joyce After Pynchon?" *James Joyce: The Centennial Symposium.* Eds. Morris Beja, Phillip Herring, Maurice Harmon, and David Norris. Urbana: U of Illinois P, 1986.

Richter, Harvena. *Virginia Woolf: The Inward Voyage.* Princeton: Princeton UP, 1970.

Stewart, Garrett. "Catching the Stylistic D/rift: Sound Defects in Woolf's *The Waves. ELH* 54 (Summer 1987): 421-461.

Woolf, Virginia. "Modern Fiction." *The Common Reader I.* London: Hogarth P, 1962. 184-195.

————. "Mr. Bennett and Mrs. Brown." *The Captain's Deathbed and Other Essays.* New York: Harcourt, 1950. 94-119

————. *Mrs. Dalloway.* New York: Harcourt Brace Jovanovich, 1953.

————. *Orlando.* New York: Harcourt Brace Jovanovich, 1956.

————. *A Room of One's Own.* New York: Harcourt Brace Jovanovich, 1957.

————. "A Sketch of the Past." *Moments of Being.* Ed. Jeanne Schulkind. New York: Harcourt Brace Jovanovich, 1985.

————. *To the Lighthouse.* New York: Harcourt Brace Jovanovich, 1955.

————. *The Waves.* New York: Harcourt Brace Jovanovich, 1959.

————. *The Years.* New York: Harcourt Brace Jovanovich, 1965.

Zwerdling, Alex. *Virginia Woolf and the Real World.* Berkeley: U of California P, 1986.

Chapter 4

Ezra Pound and the Visual:
Notations for New Subjects in *The Cantos*

Norman Wacker

I

In this volume, Downing and Bazargan argue that Plato's work keyed a broad-based shift from oral formulaic to literate analytic Greek culture. The visual and electronic simulation and processing of experience in postindustrial societies might be treated as a similar historic shift, in this case from literate to visual culture, with far-reaching implications for ideology, politics, and social organization. Platonic allegory, the principal axis of western literary representation, reflected in the parable of the cave, describes a logic of representation in which there is a tension between visual/verbal "images" and the mental and material "contents" they both substantiate and conceal. In our Platonic rereadings of Homer after Plato, we create perhaps the primary myth of western representation: Odysseus negotiating his fascination with the beautiful and the strange to recover the steadfast and the true, thus enacting the virile narrative that defines the Platonic literary symbolic from Virgil, to Dante, to Joyce and Pound. In the hands of Virgil the same myth can enact the narrative of national domination and imposition of cultural order on the irrational forces of external barbarism and internal pluralism with its spectre of Roman civil war. In the hands of Joyce, the historically dominated recover in the epic a heteroglossy carried by the ethnic and cultural multiformity of language. Joyce thus invents a protean comedy of digressive etymology and wordplay in which a scandal of duplicity runs through the whole fabric of western language, bringing to light the fact that language is "populated—over populated—with the intentions of others" (Bakhtin 294). In contemporary culture, Baudrillard suggests simulation, and the pure transport of fascination that accompanies it, renders the Odyssean drama endless. The contemporary subject negotiates cinematic logics which are perpetual and kinetic, organized by an open-ended, serial displacement of images, which simulate basic epistemological categories, including "real" and "unreal" and "experience" and "ideology" (Baudrillard 25).

Ezra Pound, fascist, arch-modernist and proponent of the "unwobbling pivot," foundational beliefs and values on which both true images and ideologies turn, nonetheless strained to capture in a new poetic the accelerating production of visual images, recognizing as he put it in "Hugh Selwyn Mauberley," "The age demanded an image / Of its accelerated grimace." Pound's prose polemics also link the poetics of the image and socio-political practice. His prose *(ABC of Reading, The Spirit of Romance, Guide to Kulchur)* functions as both diagnostic work and "how to" primer, railing against the general cultural level and proposing programs for its reform. These typographically impetuous texts place great books catalogues, university reform proposals, and social credit economic platforms side by side in texts already a pastiche of allusion, ellipsis, and quotation. No less than his poetry, Pound's prose seems to have internalized the layout of a modern newspaper and the telegraphic rhythms of the mass media of his age.

These experiments in figural and ideological basis of images were also reflected in Pound's collaboration with painter-novelist Wyndham Lewis on the oversized art magazine and literary journal *Blast* and in Pound's treatise/catalogue memorializing the sculptor Gaudier-Brzeska. As Downing and Bazargan suggest, Plato's attack on the poets conceals a more radical ideological assault on an existing Homeric culture of mnemonic representation. Pound's fascist politics and modernist poetics may similarly conceal deliberate efforts to shift the context of poetry from the literary and literate to the representational field of industrial society, a program traced through the esthetics of *Blast*, imagism, Chinese ideograms, and *The Cantos*, a long imagist poem "including history" in which lyric poetry, historical narrative, literary translation, Chinese ideograms, bursts of polemical invective, and documentary cut-ups unpeacefully coexist.

In Romantic aesthetic theory, didacticism and convention defeat the originality and creativity of poetic images as unique imaginative creations. Pound, an avowed antiromantic, envisioned poetic images as didactic with a vengeance. Images were *both* the strong inventions of strong sensibilities and the loci of possible social construction. As in the case of "In a Station of the Metro" the immediacy of the poetic image ("The apparition of these faces in the crowd; / Petals on a wet, black bough") acts as a focal point for collective experience, both representing the crowd and representing the crowd to itself. The poem enacts a moment of invention even as it evokes in the London underground the material conditions (urban crowds, speed of transport and communication, and technical and mechanical transformation of nature) invention must both work through and resist. A new poetic image, suffused by the gestural language of Lewis's post-cubism, popular film, and Chinese written characters, informed Pound's notion of how poetry might recapture the cultural centrality of Homeric poetry in early Greek culture while delineating a new politics of representation unique to modernity.

Pound opens *The Cantos* by truncating the Circe and Neukia episodes of *The Odyssey* and translating them into narrative fragments. He juxtaposes departure from Circe's isle to descent into the underworld in the Neukia episode, a montage which enacts the tension between the fascinations of image associated with Circe and the critical interrogation of shades come to life in the underworld. By making the layers of translation visible (the Greek text of *The Odyssey*—itself a transcription of an oral formulaic composition—Divus's Latin, Virgil and Dante's appropriations of Homer), Pound constructs a poetics of incessant juxtaposition and citation in which no narrative plane dominates. The tension between Circe and Neukia is also the tension between the reflective culture of individual reception of the image and of the Dantean crowds who jostle Pound-Odysseus in both the Greek underworld and the London underground, representing the mass production and public consumption of mechanically reproduced images and the volatile forms of social organization tied to mass response.

Pound's socio-poetics then has a chronological incongruity at its center, an incongruity similar to that of a postmodern esthetics of citation, appropriation, and pastiche in which "the new" carries with it embedded references to the eclipsed and a susceptibility to further appropriation. The modernist and avant-garde gesture of overcoming tradition can be reduced to the bathos of fashion and the "supply-side" schemes of merchandising and (mis)appropriation which employ it (Solomon-Godeau 209-10). Pound ("Literature is news that STAYS news" [*ABC of Reading* 29]) was among the first to experience full force the social and aesthetic dilemma of "making it new" as an esthetic principle. As academic critics of Pound's "creative" translations of Propertius and Li Po have pointed out, his treatment of these poems was anachronistic, foregrounding intervening poetic schools and an aggressive modernist reading of them. The same systematic bias has been identified by critics of Pound's treatment of historic documents. His sense of memory, representation, and tradition was in fact projective, envisioning the forms of post-history, that is, the forms of tradition that would organize post-traditional culture. If Pound failed to discover the obscenity of fascism in his lifetime, it was because he associated the open-ended transformation of nature and society promised by fascist public works and ideologies of national modernization with an emerging ethos consistent with the violent and incessant transformation of society during modernity.

The bravura and grandiosity of Mussolini promised a future as malleable and epic in scale as the stock-in-trade representations of militarism, industrialism and heroic nature in theatrical newsreels:

> "Ma qvesto,"
> 　　said the Boss, "è divertente."
> catching the point before the aesthetes had got
> 　　there;

Having drained off the muck by Vada
From the marshes, by Circeo, where no one else wd. have
    drained it.
Waited 2000 years, ate grain from the marshes;
Water supply for ten million, another one million *"vani"*
that is rooms for people to live in.
                                    XI of our era. (Canto 41, 202)

Pound fuses the larger cultural and ideological connotations of any image, referred to as "usage," or "habits of usage" to its visual impact on the reader (phanopoeia) and its shaping by the sound qualities accompanying the image (melopoeia), so that any particular image traces both its ideological antecedents and the remaking and redirection of those antecedents by the poet:

> NEVERTHELESS you still charge words with meaning mainly in three ways, call phanopoeia, melopoeia, logopoeia. You use a word to throw a visual image on to the reader's imagination, or you charge it by sound, or you use groups of words to do this.
>
> Thirdly, you take the greater risk of using the word in some special relation to 'usage', that is, to the kind of context in which the reader expects, or is accustomed, to find it. (*ABC of Reading* 37)

This connection of the image to the ideological formation and dissemination of meaning at the microscopic level of articulation parallels Pound's global concern with larger ideological formations of the thirties and forties. In addition to Pound's infamous radio broadcasts, Noel Stock describes an equally massive network of correspondence managed by Pound during the period. Its object was the dissemination of his views on the economic and cultural programs which would support *Kulchur*, as Pound sometimes styled the new ethos to be formed by the forces of distributionist economic practice, the rapid dissemination of knowledge by the ideo-grammatic method in scholarship, and the rise of totalitarian/volitionist governments able to implement cultural and economic reforms on traditional principles (Stock 342-71). It could be argued that the Rome radio broadcasts, dubbed by the editor of the broadcast transcripts "the poor man's *Cantos*," inspite of their hair-raising anti-semitism, are, like the polemical writing, integral to the articulation of an emerging ideology of "the age" on which the images of Pound's "work-in-progress" incessantly play (*Pound Speaking* 437).

Pound's massive scholarship of agitation during the interwar period parallels a principal drama of the poem, the act of the poet working up material from the documentary archives of classical antiquity, dynastic China, and colonial America into a new composition. This new composition diagnoses and corrects the vision of polity offered in its originals. As the poet stages his poem within the events and documents of the culture, construction takes on many of the qualities identified with abstractionism in the visual arts as described by art historian Harold Osborne. The abstractionist painter seeks as it were to quote the expressive characteristics of a representation, that is, initially to isolate expressive qualities and then manipulate the qualities themselves within new and unfamiliar configurations (Osborne 112). Instead of employing representation as a means of reproducing events and objects, the artist uses "abstraction and distortion for the purpose of giving prominence to the expressive qualities he saw and felt" (Osborne 112). From Osborne's perspective, the semantic properties of abstract painting are not tied to the reproduction of—or correspondence to—objects and events. Rather, having differentiated the expressive qualities of objects and deployed them in new constructions, the abstract painter develops a supple grammar of qualities and motives in which to place acts of cognition, a grammar not tied to the logos of a sponsoring culture.

If we join this sense of abstracted qualities projected as objects in new constructions to Charles Altieri's description of Classic texts as those which survive "because they capture actions and relations between actions which endure," (*Act and Quality* 310)[1] we will have moved closer to the variety of tradition implied in Pound's texts. At the same time, we will see this reification of relations (still too close to the cultural monumentalism of T. S. Eliot's "Tradition and the Individual Talent") give way in the later *Cantos* to a mechanics of the circulation of power within schemes of reification. Finally, it is not truth, but the power of poetic figuration to constitute social objects whose specificity resists new technologies of domination that is at issue. The resulting model of value, whether described as volitionist, factive, or totalitarian in his polemics, is tied like those of abstract painting to perspectives on action organized within the compositional strategies of producing a text. The writer, "using the word in some special relation to 'usage,'" produces new effects that resist those of mechanical schemes of production.

Through esthetic and polemical distortion Pound sought to identify and express what he referred to variously as "the residue of perception," "the verbal idea of action" or "the swift perception of relations," a kind of genealogy of the force of such ideas as they circulated within their historical moment, a conjunction of "authoritative" images and the concealed ideology that motivated their socio-historical centrality. The immediate apprehension and representation of this residue of intelligence was the quality Pound attributed to Dante, Cavalcanti and in general to the high watermarks of creative intelligence in northern Mediterranean culture. The preservation and emphatic delineation of this residue is a principal source of the fecundity and disseminative force Pound located in tradition:

> We appear to have lost the radiant world where one thought cuts through another with clean edge, a world of moving energies "*mezzo oscuro rade*," "*risplended in se perpetuale effecto*," magnetisms that take form, that are seen, or that border the visible. (*Selected Prose* 154)[2]

Pound states in "Cavalcanti" that a kind of humanism existed in late medieval times in which human "attitudes" that accrued to ideas were as immediate as their signifiers and that these attitudes were themselves their "own effect unendingly," being the projection of "a residue of perception, perception of something that requires a human being to produce it" (*Literary Essays* 151), a somewhat circular assertion of the cultural relationship between "truth" and the systems of representation which produce and sustain it. Once constituted, this surplus circulates within the general mechanics of power that governs the ethos of the time. Poetic images preserve an intersubjective residue of force and perception which they recover by identifying the contexts that guided and motivated powerful expressions. Acts and qualities can be preserved and reflected upon when their "energy" has not been reduced "to unbounded undistinguished abstraction" (*Literary Essays* 153). Where "lumping" and "leveling" of differences has been avoided by vigorous expression, the mind can recover the ideological patterns which act as the actual grounds of predication and logic (*Literary Essays* 153).

The text provides the poet the means of both staging and restaging his identity by reflection upon the shifting self-representations he has assumed (Altieri, *Act and Quality* 319-20) and foregrounding the cultural and ideological ground on which his self-expressions stand. Unlike the early work in *Personae* which Pound described retrospectively as a casting off with each poem of a "provisional mask" (*Gaudier-Brzeska* 85), masks are preserved here as a genealogy in which subsequent self-representations are implicated (Bush 142-82; Bernstein 54-55).[3] The identity of the poet of *The Cantos* evolves as the text of the poem-in-progress becomes a record of these positions and as the poet's reflections upon his program suggest both the powers and the limitations of his expressive acts (Pratt 136).[4] To the extent that the timing of his poetic notation produces a different time than the time-dissolving routines of discipline and ideology, the subject escapes appropriation within the mechanics of existing schemes of representation. In addition, to the extent that they deploy visual and verbal images in a notational time which both works through and works beyond the indefinite present of visual reproduction, they engage the historical, literary, and economic conditions that have erased the figure of the human and the material conditions of community.

Prior to *The Pisans* the poet is an intermittent presence in the text, characterized by an editorial logic, periodic asides, and in one instance the meditations of Pound as a Wordsworthian poet in his "young youth." However, references to the force of the poet in composing the very tradition which he cites as his authority are common throughout Pound's prose. The performative nature of the prose digests such as the *Guide to Kulchur* and *ABC of Reading* with their "how to" recipes, their idiosyncratic reading lists, and their tables of historical data, are themselves often conspicuous examples of the poet's militant redefinition of the permissions sponsored by the past (Lindberg 91-92). As discussed below, "Dateline" (1934) describes this delineation of tradition by acts of composition as including: "Criticism by Translation," "Criticism by Exercise in the Style of a Given Period," "Criticism in Prosody or Musical Treatment of an Individual Work," and "Criticism in New Composition." These modes of Criticism by Composition offer constructions of tradition by selection of "luminous details." Deployed in new compositions, "luminous details" recover suppressed or effaced cultural energies. They act as a substrate for reflections upon and reinterpretation of tradition in terms of newly identified energies. They also anticipate a fundamentally filmic understanding of composition as cutting, editing, and resequencing existing images, not to mention narrative and thematic sequences, which can be processed in the same way as the image stream. For example, once delineated by Pound's interpretation of historical fact, the nonusurious banking practices of Siena, the unity of poetry and music in Provence, and the wisdom polity of Confucian China are each recovered and deployed as alternative instruments by which to construe the documents of received tradition. (This is why Pound can without contradiction place Chinese ideograms within his reconstructions of American history and of the Eastern Empire of Rome and see in dynastic China the precedents for the bank of Siena.) Given this understanding of composition and its relationship to the construal of tradition, the act of composition itself becomes for Pound a complex self-reflective action, whereby the poet abstracts into the articulation of his own discourse the determinations made available by his own active conception of tradition, a mode of composition Pound labels "logopoeia."

As early as his statement in the "Praefatio" to *The Spirit of Romance* that "all ages are contemporaneous," (n. pag.) Pound shared with Eliot basic agreement about the simultaneity of all the artifacts of the culture. He seemed also to see the relationship between tradition and innovation as that of the "making new" of inherited values. Eliot's famous conception of tradition as an ideal order formed among existing monuments of the culture was primarily a scheme for supporting evaluation of esthetic innovation. Yet what Eliot conceived of as a means of critical judgment, Pound conceived of in terms of critical construction; that is, he saw in the associations embedded by long usage in language the material for new acts of composition. He also saw them as the means of tracing the linguistic and practical substrates of the culture. In "How to Read" Pound described the concept of logopoeia as the most difficult type of poetic logic to obtain:

> "the dance of intellect among words", that is to say, it employs words not only
> for their direct meaning, but it takes count in a special way of habits of usage,
> of the context we *expect* to find with the word, its usual concomitants, of its
> known acceptances, and of ironical play. It holds the aesthetic content which
> is peculiarly the domain of verbal manifestation. (*Literary Essays* 25)

In microscopic terms Pound is speaking of the conscious direction and ironic redirection of connotations which have accrued to words in habitual patterns of usage. In poetic composition characterized by logopoeia, language is "charged with meaning to the greatest possible degree" as it abstracts from historically accrued associations a culturally determined ground of utterance (Altieri, "First Cantos" 39). Emphatically re-placed within this ground, an act of articulation is charged by its copresence with the greatest possible breadth of those normally submerged determinations which condition its use. Throughout *The Cantos* this is allegorized by the motif of descent into an underworld (either imaginary or textual) where Odysseus/Pound provokes the shades of the underworld into offering prophecy about the world of the living—encounters with utterances of the dead which recast the designs of the living, unlike Eliot's similar encounter with wastelands to which one responds only by impersonal adjustment.

I have suggested that in making the determinations of composition available to reflection, the poet can indefinitely renew his poem. I would also argue that increasingly poetic notation moves from imagism's details luminous with sponsoring cultural antecedents to a poetics rooted in the emergence of notation from such sponsorship, in short, from allusion to genealogy and from symbolism to inscription. Equally important, new construals of the objects of tradition produce new determinations; composition suggests composition; every object can be juxtaposed to other elements in new acts of collage. The text-in-progress appropriates the determinations of precursor texts while imparting to them determinate new forms by translation, abridgement, and juxtaposition. A brief look at the function of the sea in the opening poems of *The Cantos* can serve as an example of the doubleness of construction in action and the logic of compositional transformation Pound mastered in *A Draft of Thirty Cantos*.

In *A Draft*, tradition as an unknowable substrate conditioning all discourse is gradually abstracted into tradition as the activity of reflection upon the act of articulation. This representation of the means of representation serves in turn as the constructive ground of poetic discourse, a heightening and a shaping of "old men's voices" (Canto 2, 6). The fact that initially these voices are a querulous rejection of Helen by the very Trojans who abetted her abduction, smuggles the figure of domination into the trope of *ethos* at the outset. This seed of violence at the heart of figures of value causes Pound to adjust his conception of ethico-poetic representation, even as it caused few personal recognitions of the sexism, racism, and imperialism in his source materials. Perhaps, as Bahktin might suggest, the palimpsest of multiple textual documents which Pound pastes into his text assures frequent irruptions of an underlying heteroglossia disrupting state-sponsored representations of a unified national point of view. In Canto 1 the sea acts as such a baffling medium which frustrates desire and impedes reduction to form by its ceaseless transformation, an image, as it were, of the unrepresentable and the unrepresented which motivates discourse and figuration (Kristeva 81). Neptune's hostility toward Odysseus thwarts return to Ithaca. The sea is preconscious, illusive, the body of nature defying demarcation beneath the forms of culture as well as the veiled circulation of power within them. Odysseus sails on Circe's craft, a pun for artifice, which represents the attempt of craft generally to impose the designs of human will on the transformations of nature. This desire has its own baffling imperviousness to the forms of consciousness, its own inertia and tendency to exceed the mark and to overbear the witting designs of Odysseus and his men—even as it is carried by them.

When the sea runs momentarily backward at the spot "Aforesaid by Circe" (Canto 1, 18), an abeyance which marks a reversal of determinations is experienced, and the autism of nature and culture is suspended. Abeyance creates a site where ritual contact with the suppressed rouses subconscious and moribund determinations to speech:

> These many crowded about me; with shouting,
> Pallor upon me, cried to my men for more beasts;
> . . . .
> I sat to keep off the impetuous impotent dead,
> Till I should hear Tiresias.
> But first Elpenor came, our friend Elpenor,
> Unburied, cast on the wide earth,
> Limbs that we left in the house of Circe,
> Unwept, unwrapped in sepulchre, since toils urged other.
>
> (Canto 1, 4)

Made to live among the moribund figures of tradition, the poet provokes and appropriates the figures that still live. Tiresias, the "live spot" obscured by moribundity and bloodless reflexivity in Hades, can be discerned only through a screen of competing voices, an articulation performed from within the intersubjective plethora of speech raised by the thirsting shades.

Having set this speech in motion, the poet can only arbitrarily enforce its closure by calling attention to textual transmission and its concomitant abstractionism as the poet's means of tracing the expressive features of tradition. The belated subject of images of authority, he can only expose them as images, of use only to those who have the power to deploy them:

> And he strong with blood, said then: "Odysseus
> "Shalt return through spiteful Neptune, over dark seas,
> "Lose all companions." And then Anticlea came.
> Lie quiet Divus. I mean, that is Andreas Divus,
> In officina Wecheli, 1538, out of Homer.
>
> (Canto 1, 4-5)

These images are a kind of fate which turns the figures of the poet's discourse to its own ends. If national epics are organized by tropes of domination, they

also evoke glimpses of the dominated energies and of the cultural construc-
tions/technologies which enforce domination. By reflecting on the strata of
intervening representations Pound suggests forms of inscription which can distance his figures from the aura of cultural authority invested in them, thus
asserting the localized time of poetic construction over the monumentalizing
reductions of time to space and the figure of tradition.

Odysseus's interrogation of the dead in the underworld is the prototype of
composition by the making of breaks in the plane of representation. Jump cuts
from text to text, cropping, parataxis, and montage yield the structural means by
which Odysseus/Pound can trick an identity and a destiny for himself out of the
baffling inertia of the fate concealed within cultural representations. By foregrounding the act of construction he can also stage the time of the representation's making and the tension between the subject and the economies of meaning his texts set in motion. It is as if filmic representation could be made to
unfold in literary time and fascination made to unfold in the reflective space of
reading. They also mark the transition from Pound's early effort to write to
paint from his later use of the cinematic logic of juxtaposition, metonymy, and
montage.

In Canto 2 Homer will trick a soundscape for the sea out of the demarcations of its breakers, a soundscape which will be the aural rhyme of the mur-
muring of old men's voices in deliberation over the fate of Helen, thus
obliquely patterning a destiny for Troy. Articulating constructive breaks in the
texts which actively impinge on *A Draft of Thirty Cantos* becomes one of the
means by which the poet tricks design and new modes of thinking and being
from precursor texts and asserts a growing power over the logic of representation. If the determinations of precursor texts bully the poet, the poet bullies the
forgotten texts of tradition into determinate form, alters their aural and logical
patterns of emphasis, and truncates them, juxtaposing them to other crucial documents of the culture. If the sea surge informs the aural demarcations of the
poet's soundscape, the poet's soundscape and its "interpretive rhythm" punctu-
ates the bewildering mass of the sea into breakers which become figures of
immanent orders that can be traced within any determinate moment of passage
as navigable lines of force and exploited as a path for articulate motion. The
blows rained down on the verse lines by stressed monosyllables at the opening
of *The Cantos* are perhaps the most auspicious announcement of the pressure of
construction on the materials streaming into the text's peripheries. They mark
as well a succession of discrete metonymies ("set up mast and sail," "bore
sheep aboard," "winds from sternward," etc.) which elide narrative gaps in a
way clearly informed by the semiotics of film:

>   And then went down to the ship,
>   Set keel to breakers, forth on the godly sea, and
>   We set up mast and sail on that swart ship,

> Bore sheep aboard her, and our bodies also
> Heavy with weeping, and winds from sternward
> Bore us out onward with bellying canvas,
> Circe's this craft, the trim-coifed goddess.
>
>   (Canto 1, 3)

The poet, inserted in long-standing economies of representation the instant he makes an utterance, seeks to maximize his knowledge of his placements in them. In the opening of Canto 2, Pound interrogates Robert Browning (another Tiresias from an explicitly textual underworld) about how to proceed in a world in which multiple representational strata run through each image the poet employs and where multiple Sordellos are possible, the real, the legendary, and the fictional, suggesting a proliferation of identities in which no priority can be established, but in which the specificity of transformation that forms identity can be glimpsed:

> Hang it all, Robert Browning,
> there can be but one "Sordello."
> But Sordello, and my Sordello?
> Lo Sordels si fo di Mantovana.
> So-shu churned in the sea.
> Seal sports in the spray-whited circles of cliff-wash,
> Sleek head, daughter of Lir,
>   eyes of Picasso
> Under black fur-hood, lithe daughter of Ocean;
> And the wave runs in the beach-groove:
> "Eleanor, Helenaus, heleptolis!"
>   And poor old Homer blind, blind, as a bat,
> Ear, ear for the sea-surge,
> murmur of old men's voices:
> "Let her go back to the ships,
> Back among Grecian faces, lest evil come on our own."
>
>   (Canto 2, 6)

In Canto 1 ships' keels cutting a path through the cross determinations of aural breakers moved the poet's craft forward. In Canto 2 Pound's stand-in, Homer, extrapolates from the patterned sound of breakers the figuration of destiny in the old men's voices at Troy. The thematic rhyme between Helen's abduction across the sea and the rape of Tyro by Neptune is amplified by their insinuation with Aphrodite in the substrate of the sea surge, momentarily become diaphanous and constructive of vision, then become opaque and finally painful with reflective glare. In a visual echo of the aural movement from "Eleanor, Helenaus, Heleptolis" to "blind, blind as a bat," the poet's eye composes the structure of movement from the broadened flattening beach to the broadened wings of sea birds whose nipping at the spaces between splayed

feathers repeats again the pointed marking off of immanent pattern and the convergence of motion and order grasped in the pattern of the sea and the sea's
fauna:

> And by the beach-run, Tyro,
>   Twisted arms of the sea-god,
> Lithe sinews of water, gripping her, cross-hold,
> And the blue-gray glass of the wave tents them,
> Glare azure of water, cold-welter, close cover.
> Quiet sun-tawny sand-stretch,
> The gulls broad out their wings,
>   nipping between splay feathers;
> Snipe come for their bath,
>   bend out their wing-joints,
> Spread wet wings to the sun-film,
> And by Scios,
>   to the left of Naxos passage,
> Naviform rock overgrown,
>   algæ cling to its edge,
> There is a wine-red glow in the shallows,
>   a tin flash in the sun-dazzle.
>
> (Canto 2, 6)

As in the opening canto, a zone is formed by the pressure of the poet's
delineations of patterns which are deepened and extended by a tracing of the
counterpressures of the sea on his versions of the sea's transformings. Visual
transformations represent the cognitive and affective space of a grammar of
sound and image mobilized by the aural, thematic, and imagistic montage of the
poem. These early cantos are not in any simple sense poems about the writing
of poems. Rather, they are poems written on other poems whose absorption into
the logic of new composition leaves them open to the shapes the other makings
of nature, history, and time write on the shapings of poems. They take on, as it
were, the coloration of the banks of tradition, even as they carve and bring into
relief banks altered by the poems' articulate motion:

> Art or an art is not unlike a river, in that it is perturbed at times by the
> quality of the river bed, but is in a way independent of that bed. The color of
> the water depends upon the substance of the bed and banks immediate and
> preceding. Stationary objects are reflected, but the quality of motion is of the
> river. (*Spirit of Romance,* "Praefatio")

II

At Pisa, Pound documents the passing from one representational "regime
of truth" to a new mechanics of image and ideology which anticipates both the
modernity of the cold war and the postmodernity which has decentered it. As an

enemy of the state and its prisoner, Pound comes to symbolize in his own text the interaction between the assertions and resistances of subjects and the operation of impersonal schemes of discipline employed by the state. In a world of universal surveillance the imprisoned poet works against his status as a subject of indictment and diagnosis under the codes of state discipline by working towards a poetic notation governed by narrative discontinuity, parataxis, and citation and by dwelling as well on intractable and illusive objects. Anything outside the compound—cloudscapes, birds, local peasants—takes on an almost religious fullness partly because it is outside the grids formed by the geometry of the compound. Perhaps more importantly, anything in the compound (a gerry-rigged writing table, a book of verse found in the privy, the lilt of African-American speech, the inmate social code of noncompliance) which alters the cadences of martial music and military regulation, revives the figure of the human.

Pound's notation is a celebration of improvised objects, fortuitous insight, and disruptions of fascist ideology. If Pound's politics were fascist and racist ("the sight of a good nigger is cheering/the bad'uns wont look you straight" [Canto 79, 485]), it is also clear that he wielded fascism primarily as a language of resistance to the cultural reification of late capitalism in the west, a note struck in the opening lines of *The Pisans*, "The enormous tragedy of the dream in the peasant's bent shoulders" (Canto 74, 425) and the coda "of the slaver as seen between decks" (Canto 74, 436). It might be argued—without finding Pound blameless—that neither left nor right wing resistance to modernity has escaped totalitarianism or the most extreme forms of ethnocentricity and misogyny. This is one aspect of modernist and antimodernist ideologies of the left and the right which postmodernism has sought to both reveal and escape. In *The Cantos* Pound had entertained typically modernist dreams of universal humanism (prey of course to sterile colonialist and phallocratic attitudes). Mussolini's defeat, his own incarceration, and the devastation of Europe revealed Pound's dream to be but a brittle vision of the ego driven by unreflective acquisitiveness and domination reflected in the parable of Juan Jin, "whose mouth was removed by his father/because he made too many *things* . . . the bane of men moving" (Canto 74, 427). The resulting fracture of the poet's self-conception fragments in turn the myth which has grounded his self-expression.

Canto 75 begins discussion of this process, reproducing two manuscript pages of a musical score preceded by the coda "—not of one bird but of many" (450). Musical notation inscribes the irruption of the plural into the poet's meditations. The image of musical notation, formed by birds alighting on the barb wire enclosure at the D. T. C. perimeter, combines with the march cadences of jailbirds on the drill field, snippets of inmate conversations, and pronouncements and patriotic songs carried over the D. T. C. public address system, thus intruding upon the poet's chording of his own mental experience. The intru-

sions are finally received with a kind of improvisational delight in the shifts
they produce in his reflections and the calibration of experience they offer in
terms alien to the grids of discipline or the objectifications of the languages of
the social sciences.

Repeatedly the poet makes of the minutae of his immediate surroundings
a musical score, providing a notational space in which reflection can be situated. Events in the D. T. C. intrude on the poet even as we hear in the background his *sotto voce* adjustments of notation within the mental scheme organized by the movement of birds on the wires:

> And Pétain not to be murdered 14 to 13
>   after six hours' discussion
> Indubitably, indubitably re / Scott
>   I like a certain number of shades in my landscape
> as per / "doan' tell no one I made you that table"
> or Whiteside:
>   "ah certainly dew lak dawgs,
>   ah goin' tuh wash you"
> (no, not to the author, to the canine unwilling in question)
>   with 8 birds on a wire
> or rather on 3 wires. Mr Allingham
> The new Bechstein is electric
> and the lark squawk has passed out of season
> whereas the sight of a good nigger is cheering
>   the bad'uns wont look you straight
> Guard's cap quattrocento passes *a cavallo*
>   on horseback thru landscape Cosimo Tura
>   or, as some think, Del Cossa;
> up stream to delouse and down stream for the same purpose
> seaward
> different lice live in different waters
> some minds take pleasure in counterpoint
>   pleasure in counterpoint.
>   (Canto 79, 484-85)

In Canto 80, "the ants seem to wobble / as the morning sun catches their shadows" (513). Minute observation partitions, as if by the diacritical shadows
words throw on the page, the radiance of the sun. This phenomenon is linked to
the coda, "when the mind swings by a grass-blade / an ant's forefoot shall save
you" (Canto 83, 533). Poetic authority comes not from accepting one's subjectivity, but from the capacity to represent the subject's place in an economy of
fixation, desire, and obsession which for most subjects remains pre-conscious.

This does not mean self-criticism produces enlightenment (would that
Pound had ever unambiguously recanted his fascism). It does mean that the texture of self-expression (particularly the vernacular speech and improvised code

of the inmates) produces radically temporal forms of self-location. In addition, blindness and the diacritical shadows of blindness thrown by texts, produce irregular forms of inscription not reducible to the routines which appropriate the temporal to the conceptual. This *ad hoc* system of signs allows the poet, over-run by grief, doubt, mourning, and denial, to remove himself from identification with his own meanings and to reposition himself within his own temporal production as a subject. Within this iterative economy, clouds become mythological figures, the guard roosts become ideograms, and a white ox on the road toward Pisa walks simultaneously out of the historical present, mediterranean prehistory and a panel in a del Cossa landscape. The poet's seat in the broadcast booth at the margins of the fascist empire has been replaced by a seat embedded in the production of a material notation. There he recognizes the mastery and routinization of universalizing notations is one medium in which power is exercised and that specificity and irregularity of notation are among the means by which it may be resisted.

Pound's language once tied to dreams of a Homeric role in fascist empire, is now organized by the rhythm of resistance (although still presumably a fascist, anticapitalist, resistance). If only momentarily, and in spite of his evident racism, Pound envisions an intersubjectivity secured outside the institutional and discursive routine of discipline, an alternative scheme of self-representation and communality. As the manuscript coda "—not of one bird but many" suggests, the conception of the self as rooted in plural voices mitigates treatment of the self as a unity isolated for carcereal, psychiatric, and legal processing. As Foucault has suggested in his exposition of Bentham's panopticon, the isolation of subjects into units (and ultimately the micro-units on which information processing depends), provides both a maximization of accountability to institutions and an exhaustive regime of self-regulation which allows the technology to be deployed with greater flexibility and decentralization. Such isolation and segmentation of life into micro-processes represent a quantum leap in the power of institutional arrangements to pacify and deploy population as a quasi-material force (Foucault, *Discipline and Punish* 220-21). A notation which preserves the irruption of the plural into self-representations and ties self-conception to interaction and dialogue, expands the scene of self-examination beyond the internalization of disciplinary measurements and procedures typical of the confessional, the isolation cell, and the archivist's carrel.

The Pisan poet cannot marshal precedent constructions in anticipation of ultimate closure as in the earlier *Cantos*. Nor can he depend on the formation of canons and the institution of literature to close and preserve his text as a cultural artifact. The dream of the text pointing toward history and practice, yet preserved by canons and the library from temporality, is broken by a general upheaval of cherished institutions (Habermas 11). The poet's notation no longer demands the reader decipher within his notations the lexical, syntactic, or semantic pretexts of the poem. Instead, the reader inhabits in his or her transit through this notation the path of the notation's production and glimpses his or her own social semiotic production as subject as analogous to that of the inmates at Pisa.

The Pisan poet becomes an accomplished reader of this notation of breaks and fluctuations. Value may shift and fluctuate, but where the units of measure are sharply delineated, some purchase can be gained on the potential subject positions discriminated by fluctuation and alteration. He envisions in the breakup of the Churchill government in England dreams of pastoral restoration; he reads in the rain ditches around his tent a defiant graffiti which links up with the canals of Venice and Jeffersonian America. He recalls the agricultural and maritime totems of ax, keel, and plow which have crossed and recrossed the poet's text, sometimes as profascist emblems, but more often as signs of inscription, a momentary reorganization and setting straight of a protean representational inheritance. Taken together, signs of breakage and intermittency compose a notation in which the fracture of ideals of social and historic organization is one palpable location of poetic invention and an alternative apparatus of self-construction.

The poet's recall of shipwreck and his representation of the subject's production with and against the formation of the state are accompanied by the visitation of Athena, the sponsoring diety both of difficult knowledge and the Athenian polity. Athena's visit has to do with a performative sense of knowledge not as a concept, but as an economy of fixation and irruption. What one has attempted to do, the attachments to one's productions that spring up, as well as the obsessions that one is borne on by, are embraced as the poet's "true heritage" and as a poetic economy which defies the routine processing of subjects under schemes of discipline. This notational treatment of the subject as an infinitely malleable work-in-progress is not vindicated by its approximation of plenitude or idealized conceptions of the self, just the opposite. The poet cannot grasp the *Eidos* any more than he can grasp the motility and the surplus of his own subjectivity. But he can represent the vacillation that is there from the inception of his discourse and which crosses out in Derrida's phrase "the concept of primariness." This discourse produces a situation in the world even as it erases any reference to origin: "Here error is all in the not done, / all in the diffidence that faltered . . ." (Canto 81, 522). Speaking from the "here" ceded him by his predications, punning on the not done (the yet to be accomplished and the accomplishments that have come undone), and the knots which must slip along the chain of signification, the poem ends with a critique of a failure which emanates not so much from erroneous premises as from a flagging in the force of articulation, an articulation that is valued less for its power to implement its premises than as a trace that defines qualities of affection and dissolves the hells of fixation to the extent that it defers their representation (Derrida 139).

Pound's notation, including the documentation of black speech, prison slang, and the reconstruction of an inmate code as part of a far-reaching revision of his sociohistorical moment from the point of view of "the slaver as seen between decks" (Canto 74, 436), produces new social objects and new subject positions. Pound formulates a poetics which produces specificity and temporal location in place of the slurs of social history. This poetic genealogy of power and its articulation of competing social constructions represent the specificity of marginalized persons as historically embodied persons. Truth depends in a circular way not on the truth or falsity of its discourses, but on the representational locations (the strategies, the accomplishments, and the products such discourses have the power to sustain). The inmates of Pound's poem owe their specificity not to the apparatus of discipline, but to the permissions and emancipations of the effects they construct within the inmate code ("doun you tell no one / I made you that table" . . . and the greatest is charity / to be found among those who have not observed / regulations" [Canto 74, 434]). The fascist poet writes his epic of the carcereal apparatus at a table made by an African-American inmate and from a systematic perspective on domination supplied by visions of enslavement and incarceration, "amid the slaves learning slavery" (Canto 74, 431). Resisting the representational machinery of institutions denies labor and time to the operations of discipline and produces new social relations without appeal to forms of sovereignty or legality already colonized by the mechanics of coercion: "and those negroes by the clothes-line are extraordinarily like the / figures del Cossa / Their green does not swear at the landscape" (Canto 78, 477).

It is just this articulation of the specificity of the subject in relation to the general functioning of the apparatus of truth that places the subsequent books of *The Cantos* squarely in the tradition of Nietzsche, Foucault, and contemporary pursuit of a social-semiotics that captures the way subjects experience and produce themselves within specific technologies of representation. That this occurs in the very ruins of his dreams of domination through representation, makes Pound's text one of our most pointed fables of the necessity of taking up the thinking of social practices that will not blindly and endlessly return to the figures which gave rise to those ruins. Perhaps more importantly it places Pound's poetic strategy at the center of the contemporary politics of canon (de-)formation, where the texts of marginalized writers sustain far-reaching transformations of the institutional and disciplinary arrangements that produce marginalization.

What lies in the balance is the uniqueness of Pound's project and his attempt to "write to paint," and subsequently to write "of the slaver as seen between decks," placing our categories of representation before our eyes as the medium for the rethinking of tradition at the moment of what must have seemed its most violent historical disruption. Pound was unswerving in his belief that poetry was the adequate vehicle for reflecting upon the grounds (and the ungrounding) of culture and, by extension, the political, social, and economic life of the poet's epoch. Carefully tying the constructive and developmental nature of the polemical and poetic project for a new *ethos* to the specific determinations constructed for the text at each stage of composition allows *The Cantos* to be treated as indeed a programmatic work, but one whose positions (though complexly differential) are determined by recoverable acts of construction and specific networks of discursive practice.

If Pound's programs mean different things at different times and are by turns abusive and emancipatory, the text is the record of that difference. The programs the poem does propose are functions of poetic construction. Pound's self-assertions outside his text are perhaps more morally and politically corrosive than those of any admired literary figure, in part because they were not only private vices but an attempt to stage his self-expressions as grounds for the performances of others. The fact that his vices were so public, and due in part to pursuit of a vision of the public, is also one of Pound's principal virtues, clearer to us in an age of absolute privitization of experience than it could have been to Pound's critics before the Reagan-Bush years. Since our judgments of Pound's program and his life are not easily divisible, only a full understanding of *The Cantos* will illuminate the poem's potential destructions, while tempering its errors with our recognition of the constructions it continues to permit.

Pound's project and the attempt to use abstractionism as a means to project new value continue to have a major influence (as witnessed in the large output of recent books attempting to praise or bury Pound employing the rhetoric of postmodernism) on our conception of possible grounds of modern (and postmodern) culture. The reading of *The Cantos* proposed here sees in the opening cantos of the poem an emerging sense of new ethos and a sense of the poem's polemical positions as earned by acts of composition embedded in the larger discursive economies of its times. The Adams and China cantos are viewed as attempts to appropriate positions earned in acts of composition as generalized truth claims on which to found utopian political orders. The intrusion of the record of European violence into the curriculum formed by *The Fifth Decad* returns the poem to a more radical notion of itself as both process and vehicle of its own demonstrations. The resulting resurrection of abstractionist esthetics, in resistance of the postwar state in *The Pisan Cantos*, becomes the key to the importance *The Cantos* continues to hold for modernist conceptions of tradition as well as postmodernist attempts to refigure the possibilities of the human in our present ideological and material condition.

Notes

1. I am referring all too briefly to the way in which self and reflections upon self in Pound's text are worked out in terms of self-knowledge with reference to what Charles

Altieri calls "a cultural sense of community." Professor Altieri discusses Hegel, for example, as a philosopher of the development of the forms of self within a dramatistic grammar reflective of the forms of a given cultural moment. Professor Altieri makes explicit the applications of his dramatistic model to Pound's *Cantos* in "First Cantos."

2. Pound glosses "mezzo oscuro rade" in "Cavalcanti" as "*Amor* moves with the light in darkness, never touching it and never a hair's breadth from it" (*Literary Essays* 191). The "risplended in se perpetuale effecto" is glossed in Canto 36 as "but shineth out / himself [the soul of love] his own effect unendingly." For a discussion of Pound's problematic contraction and creative translation of Cavalcanti's actual line "in mezzo scuro luce rade," see Bacigalupo 90.

3. Bush discusses the movement from the use of localized masks to the depiction of subject who was "pervasive but nowhere visible that could absorb images into the unity of an emotional *facon de voir*" in his chapter "Toward a New Narrative Voice." See also Bernstein 54-55. Bernstein sees the issue as one of authentic self-representation, largely ignoring the thesis of ethos, which suggests that self-representations are made only within terms of the representative performances of others. Bernstein sees the textual labor to produce ethos as an evasion of authentic self-expression, leading him to valorize *The Pisan Cantos* as a rehabilitation of the empty subject of the early cantos by recourse to a personal voice.

4. Pratt discusses the way in which assertions based on the potential to "tell" events (i.e., render event as narrative) also "display" venues for making judgments in such a way that the addressee is invited to make evaluations: "His [the teller's] point is to produce in his hearers not only belief but also an evaluative stance toward events" (136).

Works Cited

Altieri, Charles. *Act and Quality: A Theory of Literary Meaning and Humanistic Understanding*. Amherst: The U of Massachusetts P, 1981.

———. "Modernist Abstraction and Pound's First Cantos: The Ethos for a New Renaissance." U of Washington: Unpublished, 1984.

Bacigalupo, Massimo. *The Forméd Trace: the Later Poetry of Ezra Pound*. New York: Columbia UP, 1980.

Bakhtin, M. M. *The Dialogic Imagination*. Trans. Caryl Emerson and Michael Holquist. Ed. Michael Holquist. Austin: U of Texas, 1981.

Baudrillard, Jean. *Simulations*. Trans. Paul Foss, Paul Patton, and Phillip Bertchman. New York: Semiotext(e), 1983.

Bernstein, Michael. *The Tale of the Tribe: Ezra Pound and the Modern Verse Epic*. Princeton: Princeton UP, 1980.

Bush, Ronald. *The Genesis of Ezra Pound's Cantos*. Princeton: Princeton UP, 1976.

Derrida, Jacques. *Writing and Difference*. Trans. Alan Bass. Chicago: U of Chicago P, 1978.

Foucault, Michel. *Discipline and Punish: The Birth of the Prison*. Trans. Alan Sheridan. New York: Vintage, 1979.

————— .*Knowledge / Power: Selected Interviews and Other Writings 1972-1977*. Trans. Colin Gordon, et al. Ed. Colin Gordon. New York: Pantheon, 1980.

Froula, Christine. *To Write Paradise: Style and Error in Pound's Cantos*. New Haven: Yale UP, 1984.

Habermas, Jürgen. "Modernity, an Incomplete Project?" *The Anti-Aesthetic: Essays on Post-Modern Culture*. Ed. Hal Foster. Port Townsend, Wash.: Bay P, 1983.

Kristeva, Julia. *Revolution in Poetic Language*. Trans. Margaret Waller. New York: Columbia UP, 1984.

Lindberg, Katherine. *Reading Pound Reading: Modernism after Nietzsche*. New York: Oxford UP, 1987.

Osborne, Harold. *Abstraction and Artifice in Twentieth Century Art*. New York: Oxford UP, 1974.

Pound, Ezra. *ABC of Reading*. New York: New Directions, 1960.

————— . *The Cantos of Ezra Pound*. New York: New Directions, 1970.

————— . *Confucius*. New York: New Directions, 1969.

————— . *Ezra Pound: Selected Prose, 1900-1965*. Ed. William Cookson. New York: New Directions, 1973.

————— . *Ezra Pound Speaking: the Radio Speeches of World War II*. Ed. Leonard W. Doob. Westport, Conn.: Greenwood P, 1978.

————— . *Gaudier-Brzeska, a Memoir*. New York: New Directions, 1970.

————— . *Guide to Kulchur*. New York: New Directions, 1970.

————— . *The Literary Essays of Ezra Pound*. Ed. T. S. Eliot. New York: New Directions, 1971.

————— . *The Spirit of Romance*. New York: New Directions, 1968.

Pratt, Mary Louise. *Toward a Speech Act Theory of Literary Discourse*. Bloomington: Indiana UP, 1976.

Stock, Noel. *The Life of Ezra Pound*. San Francisco: North Point, 1982.

Chapter 5

A Good Rose Is Hard to Find:
Southern Gothic as Signs of Social Dislocation
in Faulkner and O'Connor

Margie Burns

> Between the simple backward look
> and the simple progressive thrust
> there is room for long argument but
> none for enlightenment.
> —Raymond Williams,
> *The Country and the City*

The topic of images of the South in the literature and media of the nation as a whole is rich in possibilities for cultural studies, for analysis of the processes of production, reception, and consumption of such images as they come to be formed and through which they are put to use. As anyone might recognize, cultural stereotypes about the American South are frequently projected as representations of objective reality; indeed, there exists an unanalytic habit, on the part both of the media and of canonical writers, to characterize the South through figural reification. In novels (both popular and canonical), in plays, film, and television, in periodicals, and in advertisements, versions of the same stereotypes recur, with a persistence both of form and of effect which suggests their organization by utility if not by intent. I would argue that these stereotypes both corroborate a deep-lying perception in the general consciousness, and solace an even deeper-lying doubt; without essential validity, they nevertheless fall into place with comforting neatness, to reaffirm the inferiority of the Other into which the American South has been transformed in the national consciousness. An enhanced critical consciousness, however, would perceive the political consequences of the ideological differences constituted by the various elements of the "Southern" image.

In general, the stereotypical perception of the South is organized around, literally, two *classes* of image: antebellum/magnolia/*GWTW* mythology, and cotton row/tobacco road/*Baby Doll* grotesquerie.[1] These two stereotypes embody what have been called the two greatest bourgeois perceptions of threat, the dichotomized but connected fears of a decaying "aristocracy" on one hand, and of a rebellious, primitive, "earthy" peasantry on the other.[2] The seeming triviality of these stereotypes, rather than serving to invalidate them, disguises their genuine utility—and destructiveness—in American culture. In my view, what is most illuminating about this polarized image is not the spurious distinction between its two terms but the underlying common denominators which provide the basis for the polarized image and sustain it. In this polarized construction, which is obviously a class construction and just as obviously a projection from the "central," missing term of the self-identified "middle class," the two categories correspond to two classes—upper and lower—a version of aristocracy and a version of peasantry. Furthermore, the two classes have, in these representations, three identifying characteristics in common: both are white (ironically), static, and unproductive. The gentleman of sorts lives in privileged idleness, and the redneck inhabits a Lower Slobbovia of equal idleness (although characterized as laziness rather than privilege). Both imagistic strata—the magnolia crowd and the tobacco-juice crowd—are primarily static—*stuck*—in the boonies, in ignorance, in prejudice, etc., with degenerate histories miring them down; neither group is "going anywhere," except to proceed further downward in some melodrama of degeneracy. In the typically polarized picture of the Deep South, in short, there are virtually no figures of upward mobility, no successful or productive efforts either of individual or of collectivity—there is in this regard only a glaring void waiting to be filled by the faster-moving observer from whose perspective the picture is generated. Such a perspective fulfills the formulation of Pierre Bourdieu, that for the spectator even an observed *activity* becomes an object; the South as spectacle/object, whose people all apparently sit still, presents an intensification of the phenomenon.

Hence the chief point of the characterization is surely to assert a contrast to the non-South nation, where all the action is; the characterization of static versus mobile, stagnation versus dynamism, corroborates a self-legitimating view of the *haute bourgeois* as the ideal mean, a mediating principle between the too-high and the too-low to work, industrious as well as industrial—with the latter as evidence of the former. It is the vision of the Connecticut Yankee, Hank the Boss, without the ironic awareness of a Clemens behind it. The putative absence of productivity (symbolized by an absence of mobility), in other words, gives the image its social and economic usefulness—and a fairly complex and multivalent usefulness at that—in the historical actuality which surrounds the image. Indeed, the usefulness of the image, far more than any mimetic relation to social reality, has kept it alive; and its uses have been social and economic, beyond the scope of this essay to cover.

The typical discourse on the South as object at least partly resembles colonial production, a nativist discourse dictated by essentially colonialist interests, but it is also more broadly constitutive of ideological differences along class lines.[3] Just as the trivialized stereotypes of Southern Women intensify a polarization projected onto women in general (good/sexually innocent versus bad/sexually experienced), so the sharply polarized image of two social strata in the South intensifies—crudely—its dichotomous inversion: the wish, projected from the missing term, the middle class, to lampoon or to obliterate an awareness of genuine class difference.

In other words, the view of the South self-identified as the "national" or "American" view is basically a colonial romance, with the rest of the nation identified with the forces of light and the South with the forces of darkness. And this romance shares a salient characteristic of virtually all post-Romantic romance: in it, the polarization of social highs and lows in actuality metamorphoses into a polarization of psychological highs and lows as the source of conflict in the literary representations and other representations. Thus the haute bourgeois middle term is, of course, even more thoroughly obscured. The image of dark loci which map the terrain of the South in the popular imagination (and in the scholarly imagination) directly serves the ideology which produced it.

Nowhere is the ideology-constitutive character of this image more apparent than in the literary mode known as "southern gothic."[4] In this essay on the southern gothic—a term in widespread use, but one which almost nobody attempts to scrutinize—I consider two famous short stories by William Faulkner and Flannery O'Connor and argue that the southern gothic is a literary technique which both enacts and conceals the dehumanization of response *to* the South, by representing it as a dehumanization of response *in* the South.[5] Needless to say, imaginative literature has played only one part in the construction of the South as an ideological Other for the nation as a whole. "Serious" imaginative literature has played an even smaller part; but the staggering blatancy with which these two works pursue their part in the construction justifies their analysis in postmodern critical practice.

II

Even the most casual survey of the literary mode called "southern gothic" would turn up Faulkner's "A Rose for Emily" (1924) and O'Connor's "A Good Man Is Hard to Find" (1954) as premier examples. "A Rose for Emily" presents Emily through languorous, external flashbacks which leave her own consciousness opaque but gradually reveal that she poisoned her jilting lover and cohabited for decades with his corpse. In "A Good Man Is Hard to Find," a worthless, déclassé southern family goes on a vacation, has a car wreck, and is thrown into the hands of a homicidal maniac (also southern) who kills everyone. The narrative presents the family's slaughter, moreover, as the result chiefly of its own idiocy and venality. Both short stories achieve their full horror through intense comedy, a black humor which largely accounts for the place of "southern" relative to "gothic"; if it happened anywhere else, it wouldn't be as funny. I contend that these narratives show how the consistent techniques of southern gothic mark the sites of *social* dislocations—phenomena conventionally regarded as nonliterary. In simplest terms, the *gothic* operates as a distancing: it mystifies the matter presented, removing it into an atmosphere detached from social actuality and engineering a response alienated and unsympathetic. This mystification has had consequences both within and outside the literature.

In the narratives discussed here, the most significant movements are concealment and entrapment. "A Rose for Emily" begins,

> When Miss Emily Grierson died, our whole town went to her funeral: the men through a sort of respectful affection for a fallen monument, the women mostly out of curiosity to see the inside of her house. (489)

This single, wonderfully economical sentence immediately sets up the demarcation between a crypto-military context for men and a setting of house interiors for women, which is sustained throughout the narrative. It also establishes a progression—death, morbidity, a monument, and concealment behind a wall or facade—typical of southern gothic, in which the luridness of the terms distracts attention away from their true relationship. Here, the outside-inside demarcation becomes perversely conflated—a "monument," which both blazons and conceals what it contains.[6] Any awareness stimulated by the hint of very real violence, however, is displaced—trivialized—into typically "gothic" suspense and a (feminine) morbid curiosity.

Repeatedly the narrative describes/erects some wall or facade which simultaneously blazons and conceals. In one stunning example, the generation previous to Miss Emily's produced the "edict that no Negro woman should appear on the streets without an apron" (489); I shall discuss this below. Similarly, the women whisper about Emily's sexual activities "behind their hands; rustling of craned silk and satin behind jalousies closed upon the sun of Sunday afternoon" (495). The facades thus erected ornament both persons and places with a dissolutely baroque prose; the Grierson house itself is

> a big, squarish frame house that had once been white, decorated with cupolas and spires and scrolled balconies in the heavily lightsome style of the seventies, . . . lifting up its stubborn and coquettish decay above the cotton wagons and the gasoline pumps—an eyesore among eyesores. (489)

Obviously, the old house is identified with Miss Emily (and perhaps with femaleness in general);[7] the phrases "heavily lightsome" and "coquettish decay," among others, anthropomorphize it, turning it into an old "eyesore" like

Emily herself and suggesting a threatening, veiled sexuality in both edifices.

In a rich, curious paradox of combined limpidity and occlusion, each such verbal flourish throughout the story signals a social dislocation, an injustice. Examples abound:

> And now Miss Emily had gone to join the representatives of those august names where they lay in the cedar-bemused cemetery among the ranked and anonymous graves of Union and Confederate soldiers who fell at the battle of Jefferson. (489)

Here the nostalgic, antiquarian intrigue—"cedar-bemused" itself—obscures the deaths of nameless, ordinary soldiers. Other examples concerning Emily herself arise frequently; at an early point, Emily writes:

> a note on paper of an archaic shape, in a thin, flowing calligraphy in faded ink, to the effect that she no longer went out at all. The tax notice was also enclosed, without comment. (490)

The successful mystification of the town—a successful mystification, in more than one sense—allows Emily to escape, *seriatim*, from both death and taxes:

> So she vanquished them, horse and foot, just as she had vanquished their fathers thirty years before about the smell. (492)

But while Faulkner's submerged joke on death and taxes gives some structure to the story, it also trivializes the fundamental conflict between Emily and the men—"horse and foot"—of the town. In repetitive detail, Emily is incessantly associated with the past, with the Civil War, with the *burdens* of history devoid of any understanding of history. Always, the odor of history is mystified, through her, either decayed into a stink or misperceived as the aura of nostalgia.[8] And this diffuse mystification has a highly specific use; it transforms "history" into an intimidation serving the interests of a privileged class.

> A deputation waited upon her, knocked at the door through which no visitor had passed since she ceased giving chinapainting lessons eight or ten years earlier. They were admitted by the Old Negro into a dim hall from which a stairway mounted into still more shadow. It smelled of dust and disuse—a close, dank smell. The Negro led them into the parlor. It was furnished in heavy, leather-covered furniture. When the Negro opened the blinds of one window, they could see that the leather was cracked; and when they sat down, a faint dust rose sluggishly about their thighs, spinning with slow motes in the single sun-ray. On a tarnished gilt easel before the fireplace stood a crayon portrait of Miss Emily's father. (490)

In such an atmosphere of more than adequate oppressiveness, it is hardly surprising that the men should fail in their mission to exact money from Miss Emily, or that they should be vanquished by the single, cryptic utterance: "'See Colonel Sartoris.' (Colonel Sartoris had been dead almost ten years)" (491).

Since some vague concept of "history" is often associated with outmoded ornamentation—forgetting the spareness or angularity of any artistic styles before the "modern"—the same mystification which works on Faulkner's characters has often worked on his readers. It is easy, reading Faulkner's gothic labyrinthine prose, to get lost in the style. The tremendous artistic achievement represented by this phenomenon has invited more than its share of critical commentary in strictly literary terms; Warren and Wellek might say that the outer form of the narrative corresponds to its inner form (140, 241); metacriticism would emphasize the self-reflexivity which connects plot and style. What I wish to emphasize, however, is how the narrative both blazons and conceals its mystification of history, outside the story and in it; these are lush imaginary gardens with real structures of privilege in them.

Like an X-marks-the-spot, each high-Victorian decaying narrative curlicue instances a form (literally) of concealment, partly because the ornateness of the language distances the reader, but partly because the action presented is Byzantine:

> Colonel Sartoris invented an involved tale to the effect that Miss Emily's father had loaned money to the town, which the town, as a matter of business, preferred this way of repaying. Only a man of Colonel Sartoris' generation and thought could have invented it, and only a woman could have believed it. (490)

What might be called "gothic finance" here instances Emily's exemption from paying taxes—a privilege of her class; simultaneously, however, it also marks her inability to understand or to control her business affairs, the limitation of her sex. Emily's life includes no option of financial self-sufficiency; hence the fate worse than death when Homer Barron disappoints her and, earlier, the sense of betrayal when her father died and "it got about that the house was all that was left to her" (489). Even the rather detached narrator makes the betrayal explicit:

> We remembered all the young men her father had driven away, and we knew that with nothing left, she would have to cling to that which had robbed her, as people will. (489)

The decorative flourish, which is a neat synecdoche, signals Emily's economic limitation in that she tries to earn an income by giving lessons in chinapainting.

The preeminent flourish in the narrative, however (aside from its title), occurs at the ending, in the lavish descriptive decay of the room which contains the corpse:

> A thin, acrid pall as of the tomb seemed to lie everywhere upon this room decked and furnished as for a bridal: upon the valence curtains of faded rose color, upon the rose-shaded lights, upon the dressing table, upon the delicate array of crystal and the man's toilet things backed with tarnished silver, silver so tarnished that the monograph was obscured. (500)

Fulfilling previous images which identified the house with Emily, the rose-colored curtains and rose-shaded lights (these are the only roses in the story, unless one counts "they rose when she entered") create a stereotypically "Freudian" image of female enclosure. The dusty vulva, the "bridal" chamber—like Marvell's "fine and private place" the tomb's savage travesty of the womb (or the travesty of the latter on the former, in more misogynistic perspective)—reveals the bitter turning to dust of all the camp swampiness and swampy campness of Faulkner's other ever-prevalent allusions to feminine loci of forsythia/magnolia/genitalia. "Rose, thou art sick . . . ." The symbolically enclosed rose or *hortus conclusus* turned to desert rounds off the period of the story; as the title says, it *is* the story; and the story as an ironic rose, presented with a bow and a flourish to Emily, both advertises and dissimulates what it does to Emily Grierson and to all the other Emilys, egregiously pretending not to do exactly what it does: "'Dammit, sir,' Judge Stevens said, 'will you accuse a lady to her face of smelling bad?'" (492).

With humorous, self-disclosing hypocrisy, the fondly superficial narrator presents Emily's image: "thus she passed from generation to generation—dear, inescapable, impervious, tranquil, and perverse" (499). The word "inescapable" provides the operative hint on Emily's status; at her death—which begins the story—the narrator says, "alive, Miss Emily had been a tradition, a duty, and a care; a sort of hereditary obligation upon the town" (489).

In simplest terms, Emily resembles a curse—a war debt imposed by the Civil War on the surviving South, sphinx-like creature into whose house people go and either don't escape or barely escape, the labor pursuing original sin. A selective gyneolatry projected around her image suggests the quasi-theological:

> a window that had been dark was lighted and Miss Emily sat in it, the light behind her, and her upright torso motionless as that of an idol. (493)

> When we saw her again, her hair was cut short, making her look like a girl, with a vague resemblance to those angels in colored church windows—sort of tragic and serene. (494)

> She fitted up a studio . . . where the daughters and granddaughters of Colonel Sartoris' contemporaries were sent to her with the same regularity and in the same spirit that they were sent to church on Sundays with a twenty-five cent piece for the collection plate. (498)

> Now and then we would see her in one of the downstairs windows . . . like the carven torso of an idol in a niche, looking or not looking at us, we could never tell which. (499)

On one hand, this cluster of images suggests a quasi-deification of Emily—the projection of a stiffnecked people who have deified class privilege. From another perspective, however, it should make apparent Emily's rigid isolation, her loneliness—the punishment of her sex. Emily's strenuous repulsion of intruders forms a refrain in the story—when she repels various deputations concerning her father, her courtship, "the smell," her taxes, a mailbox, etc. But this centrifugal force, generated by a male author and a male narrator, actually conceals its dialectical opposite—the men's desire to escape the enclosure which Emily represents. Emily repels, but the men run, "vanquished": her father dies, the Baptist minister wilts, Homer Barron jilts her, deputations fade away. And when Emily herself dies,

> The Negro met the first of the ladies at the front door and let them in, . . . and then he disappeared. He walked right through the house and out the back and was not seen again. (499)

Obviously, the alternate intrusion-and-repulsion of one perspective has a sexual rhythm, culminating in a grisly climax when the town forces open Emily's room. In another perspective, a deeper pattern emerges: Emily does not get out, and the men do not get in (and survive); ultimately, the narrative prohibits any exchange between outside and inside, for a woman. Men possess the outside world and women the interior, and sex privilege separates the two in sempiternity.

Only one man partly breaks the rule and survives repeated entry into Emily's house: Emily's black manservant. And the exception, of course, proves the rule—or in this case reveals its deeper structure—because one function of race privilege, reflected with staggering honesty in Faulkner's narrative, is to triangulate class privilege and gender privilege. Only a Negro man can mediate between Emily, signifier of class privilege, and the men of the town, signifiers of gender privilege, as though he somehow combines attributes acceptable to both. A single incident recapitulates the pattern of the whole story. When Emily purchases arsenic, the druggist asks why she wants it:

> Miss Emily just stared at him, her head tilted back in order to look him eye of eye, until he looked away and went and got the arsenic and wrapped it up. The Negro delivery boy brought her the package; the druggist didn't come back. (496)

A black man provides the escape valve, allowing the white man to evade overt responsibility for the murder—and to evade an emotional confrontation with a woman. Thus race privilege allows class and gender privilege to coexist, despite all their potential conflicts, cementing them in a lasting, necrophiliac embrace.

Predictably, the object of all three operations, the person who receives their brunt, is what might be called the fourth-box case, the missing term, the character who does not appear in this story: the black woman.

> Colonel Sartoris, the mayor, . . . fathered the edict that no Negro woman should appear on the streets without an apron. (489)

The edict keeps the woman of color indoors by referring her ceaselessly to her labor: if you take your apron off, you must stay indoors (the narrative does not mention church services, holidays, etc.); if you stay indoors, you can take your apron off (cf. Pip's sister in *Great Expectations*). But any suggestion of repose indoors is spurious, because the woman's work occurs indoors anyway. Again the narrative thrusts forward a dual advertisement and obfuscation, penning the black woman behind her apron and behind walls (incidentally falsely implying, in its insistence that she *must* work, that white women do *not* have to work).

In this series of dual facades, a key signifier appears in the description of Homer Barron, whose brief characterization presents him as the embodiment of masculine vitality and the antithesis of Emily: a foreman named Homer Barron, a Yankee—a big, dark, ready man, with a big voice and eyes lighter than his face (494).

It was this detail of eyes lighter than the face, employed in both "A Rose for Emily" and "A Good Man Is Hard to Find," which first drew my attention to the connections between the two stories. The highly particularized detail (one of very few in Barron's description) of eyes lighter than his face suggests in Homer Barron an element of complexity—whether in the man himself or in his situation. Another discrepancy, it marks the intersection and thus the potential conflict of race and class privilege: Barron was not born dark; he just got that way because he works outdoors. The shadow, so to speak, rests only on the surface of this carpetbagger. Compare Emily, who looks

> bloated, like a body long submerged in motionless water, and of the pallid hue. Her eyes, lost in the fatty ridges of her face, looked like two small pieces of coal pressed into a lump of dough. (491)

Notwithstanding this reassurance—as hinted by the occasion for reassurance—the eyes-lighter-than-skin image can be sinister. It suggests a hidden energy (= power) and vision (= knowledge), a knowledge or power shadowed and unreadable, behind a facade.[9] Clearly, black skin conveys something of the same threat; so does Emily's black dress:

> They rose when she entered—a small, fat woman in black, with a thin gold chain descending to her waist and vanishing into her belt . . . . She did not ask them to sit. She just stood in the door and listened quietly until the spokesman came to a stumbling halt. Then they could hear the invisible watch ticking at the end of the gold chain. (491)

Perhaps the humor involved in this intimidation of the townsmen—conveyed in details such as the unutterably sinister "invisible watch"—comes partly from a sympathy for Emily, on the part of the narrator. But always the covering darkness itself, the shadowed vantage concealing a watchful gaze, is sinister—as with the whispering behind jalousies, or The Misfit's sighting the car wreck from off the highway, etc. It suggests a consciousness hidden, on the other side of a wall, which can know (you) but not be known; and of this darkness, the light eyes set in dark skin constitute a physical sign: if those eyes were closed, one might be safer in some sense—but one might also be fooled. The threat of eyes lighter than skin conveys reassurance, but the reassurance also conveys a threat, along lines of class and race conflict, resolvable only on the high ground of gender privilege: Barron is a "real man." However, the conflicts between gender and race privilege are not as effectually cemented over as those between class and gender privilege. Barron, who works like a black man, still has many of the privileges of the white, but the manhood of a black man would not be equal protection from the operations of privilege, nor would the race of a poor white woman.

III

Sadly enough, the successful real-life operations of privilege in Faulkner's era—successful in producing the South of thirty years later—can be read in O'Connor's writing. Arrestingly, O'Connor's "A Good Man Is Hard to Find" employs the same sign noted above in Faulkner: Sammy Red Butts's wife, hard at work in the roadside food joint, is described as "a tall burnt-brown woman with hair and eyes lighter than her skin" (762). Like a hinge, this motif of eyes lighter than the skin connects the two narratives, separated by World War II. But the terrain has changed significantly since Faulkner, and so has the image under discussion. Barron's tan shows that although he labors, he has mobility: he can go outdoors, with the privilege of his gender. In contrast, Emily's dead-white skin, accentuated by her dark eyes, shows that her class privilege of exemption from labor only partly compensates for her gender oppression, being kept indoors. O'Connor's signifier, however, exhibits two differences from Faulkner's, and both differences achieve the same effect: in O'Connor's narrative, the character described is a woman, and she has not only eyes but also hair lighter than her skin. Like Homer Barron, Sammy Red Butts's wife works—and is in consequence "burnt brown"—but unlike him, she cannot fool anyone, and she cannot get away. Where the detail of light eyes in a dark face, alone, would suggest mystery, exoticism, the hint of ancestral Crusader in the face of a Turk, the added detail of light hair just suggests a cracker.

Uneasy in conflict, the different forms of privilege wish ultimately to bond into one indistinguishable upper-class- and white- and male-oriented force. And here the two narratives display a definite progression (of sorts): where the Faulkner narrative shows the different forms of oppression still, to some extent, in conflict, the O'Connor narrative shows oppression successful and beyond conflict, lifted to the level of an omniscient narrator and an infallible taste, with conflict confined to poor whites. Black adults of either sex are absent; whites of both sexes labor; the author herself is a woman; and class privilege has been subsumed into the monolithic gaze of the invisible, impersonal narrator—and thus foisted off onto the reader.

Thus while the narrative explicitly refers to economic pressures, and the grandmother even links them explicitly to race—"Little niggers in the country don't have things like we do" (761)—they are no longer a first, conscious, concern, "the old thrill and the old despair of a penny more or less" as in Faulkner's narrative (489). In the thirty years separating the South of the two stories, amenities purchasable by poorer white families increased: the sports section, baby food in jars, *Queen for a Day* (television), cars, comic books, peanut butter, olives, Coca-Cola, tap dancing lessons, vacations, and Hawaiian sports shirts—as memorialized unlovingly by O'Connor. It is one of the paradoxes of southern gothic literature that such accurate details—accurate in reflecting social actuality, or parts of it—serve not to bring the reader closer to the characters, but to alienate the reader further from the characters. We don't even want to *see* these people, except from the safe distance of an interstate highway (compare Mayor Koch's comments about Georgia). Indeed, such details tend rather to validate and to justify what happens to these people: the minor indulgences exemplify the characters' inability to defer gratification on the road to success. Nor does the narrative explore causality sufficiently to question why such indulgences should be offered to poor families when larger benefits, such as education, have clearly not been offered.

In short, O'Connor displaces the marks of class privilege so that they are less perceivable in differences of income or of possessions and fully perceivable only in differences of *taste*.[10] Faulkner's narrator, whose taste certainly distances him from much that he describes, nevertheless manifests his taste only within the limits of his persona, a Ratliff-like observer, modestly situated in the town—though perhaps representative of a modest collective ("we"). O'Connor's narrator controls a third-person universe, subsuming the reader's perspective in an alienation beyond which the reader is powerless to envision. So the story asks the reader to acquiesce in the family's deaths—gothic rather than tragic—basically because good taste demands these killings, from the instant of learning that the mother had "a face as broad and innocent as a cabbage" (760), or that the children are named John Wesley and June Star.

Taste particularly demands alienation and a privileging of the narrator/reader above those two examples of debased gentility—most threatening to entrenched taste in their own pretensions to the same quality—the grandmother and The Misfit:

> the grandmother had on a navy blue straw sailor hat with a bunch of white violets on the brim and a navy blue dress with a small white dot in the print. Her collars and cuffs were white organdy trimmed with lace and at her neckline she had pinned a purple spray of cloth violets containing a sachet. In case of an accident, anyone seeing her dead on the highway would know at once that she was a lady. (761)

> He was an older man than the other two. His hair was just beginning to gray and he wore silver-rimmed spectacles that gave him a scholarly look. (765)

Only the grandmother and The Misfit express any pretensions to intellectual curiosity:

> "You all ought to take them somewhere else for a change so they would see different parts of the world and be broad. They never have been to East Tennessee." (760)

> "My daddy said I was a different breed of dog from my brothers and sisters. 'you know,' Daddy said, 'it's some that can live their whole life out without asking about it and it's others has to know why it is, and this boy is one of the latters. He's going to be into everything.'" (766)

But such pretensions only obviate the possibility of genuine intellection among the characters.

Situating the reader behind the gaze of supercilious taste, O'Connor's narrative places the reader in an invidious position. But in so doing, it conforms to a respectable modernist aesthetic, transferring the dynamics of the story from the characters' experiences to the reader's, and bringing the reader closer to the narrator than to the characters. While such a perspective can heighten the sense of social actuality in the literary work—Ambrose Bierce's "The Boarded Window" touches a stunning note of realism on "pioneer history"—it more often results in alienation. Only once in "A Good Man Is Hard to Find" does the narrator seem detached from the matter described:

> She pointed out interesting details of the scenery: Stone Mountain; the blue granite that in some places came up to both sides of the highway; the brilliant red clay banks slightly streaked with purple; and the various crops that made rows of green lace-work on the ground. The trees were full of silver-white sunlight and the meanest of them sparkled. (761)

Not the meanest nor even the most superior of these characters sparkles, however; even the briefly painterly description quoted here just reinforces the impression of a place where every prospect pleases and only man is vile. Predictably, therefore, the landscape itself metamorphoses, as though in a Gresham's Law of debased values: "Behind them the line of woods gaped like a dark open mouth" (765). The landscape itself turns gothic; anthropomorphized only to become monstrous, more human only to be more alien, it reverses the pathetic fallacy, neither extending nor allowing human sympathy. In short, it "tells the story" itself, synecdoche for the terrain of the narrative; like the characters and the South—both in literature and in the mass media—it neither extends nor invites human response.[11]

In a humorous bit of self-parody, O'Connor has her characters learn about The Misfit by reading a newspaper, and the naturalism and detached perspective of the narrative resemble newspaper accounts. Again, however, characteristics which might heighten the realism of the writing just distance the incidents and characters further (that's-the-way-things-happen-down-there). Familial and social pressures, emotional discorders, and violence are all engineered to prevent sympathy and to produce distaste and detachment instead.

Hence the prevalence of certain loci in southern gothic settings—all secretive enclosures: darkened rooms with drawn blinds and wisteria crawling over their windows, New Orleans-style wrought-iron grillwork sheltering yet-undescribed Creole mysteries, shadowy verandas and backyards behind massed azaleas, distant woods at the edges of fields of stubble, and so forth. These loci, darkened little inner rooms of the psyche, actually signify their dialectical reverse, turned like a chevril glove inside out: what they actually express is not something "interior," but an *exteriorization*—a pushing away, a shunning, in which the pain and horror of real events are dislocated into imaginary gardens. Like the invisibility of Emily's consciousness in her story, what looks like seclusion represents an actuality of repudiation. So the southern gothic narratives here discussed reflect an actual social phenomenon of human response boxed off from human events; the forbidding closed doors and gingerbread decades signify barriers of Other-ness, the unthinkable exile of human beings to the unprestigious hinterlands of Dixie.

What is being discussed here is the production of a mystique, and a tenet of this essay is that the mystique has uses which help explain its production (like other mystiques). At least three historical uses can be posited for the mystique behind Southern gothic: (1) as an atmosphere of bemused languor projected onto the South, it rationalizes the bustling shopping malls and "strips" of exploitation by real-estate developers and others; (2) as a canny stance for some southern authors, selling the South—in effect—it discourages poaching on home preserves by non-Southern authors; and (3) as a seemingly nonpolitical and therefore safe treatment of southern history, it perpetuates oppression and the sufferance of oppression. This paper deals with the third point.

In both Faulkner's short story and O'Connor's, the single figure of an elderly woman characterizes the whole terrain of the story. Economically dependent and superfluous and personally objectionable, each "lady" is charged with the demoralization of her society and then dispatched (although not soon enough). Underscoring the suggestion of things put away, Emily and the grandmother *should* be put away; the poor old women are closet killers—indirectly in O'Connor's story, with its subliminal references to an "old cat" and the like. Incidentally, despite the submerged references to *The Mikado*—the cat named Pitty Sing; making "the punishment fit the crime" and making both "a source of innocent merriment"—I think the allusions constitute a tribute less to Gilbert and Sullivan than to Dorothy Sayers, another woman Catholic writer, also master of submerged puns, whose work also contains frequent references to Gilbert and Sullivan.[12] In displacing a situational problem onto two destructive but personally ineffectual individuals, the narratives hint at something destructive and ineffectual in their general context, a *hidden motive force* only too pertinent to the terrain they cover. This hidden motive force must have to do with race privilege. The old flowers of decayed femininity in these two stories, characterized as an eternally "feminine" essence without any sign of fruitfulness, surely signify the authors' recognition of a draining problem we have always with us, its causes only partly examined even by the literature which exploits it as a motive force.

The very concept of examining causes, however, introduces what I feel—borrowing Balmary's luminous formulation—to be the most important distinction between Faulkner's narrative and O'Connor's: where the Faulkner short story deals at least partly with *causes*, O'Connor's deals only with *mechanisms*. Whatever one thinks of an "Electra complex" as theory,[13] Faulkner at least uses it to provide Emily with a somewhat understandable motivation—understandable by inference: Emily's compulsive possessiveness has its source in her father's.[14] What lies behind the deaths in the O'Connor narrative is chiefly a Rube Goldberg sequence: kid kicks basket, cat leaps out, car goes into ditch.

This example could be multiplied a number of times. Where Faulkner's characters "*know* the old thrill and the old despair of a penny more or less," O'Connor's characters maunder about far-distant monomyths:

> He and the grandmother discussed better times. The old lady said that in her
> opinion Europe was entirely to blame for the way things were now. She said
> the way Europe acted you would think we were made of money and Red Sam
> said it was no use talking about it, she was exactly right. (763)

Where Faulkner's narrative refers to the burden of history, O'Connor's includes history only as nostalgia: "Gone With the Wind. Ha. Ha" (761). And the nostalgia is only cliché, imperfectly implied, at that—cliché already mocked in Faulkner's earlier narrative: "the very old men—some in their brushed Confederate uniforms . . . talking of Miss Emily . . . believing that they had danced with her and courted her perhaps" (499). One wonders what the old gentlemen said about their putative closeness to Emily when the dreadful bedroom is opened up. Where the Faulkner narrative deals with the problems and ironies connected to upholding tradition, the O'Connor characters sustain only debased traditions which they cheapen even in synthesizing them, such as the treasure hunt for the nonexistent secret hiding place and its Confederate riches.

These differences between the two narratives are all homologous with the main difference: while each narrative places in the foreground a character who proves more symptom than cause—Emily and the grandmother—at least the earlier narrative goes back one generation farther. That is, "A Rose for Emily" partly scrutinizes patriarchy, where "A Good Man Is Hard to Find" does not (despite its title); and the best way to turn scrutiny away from patriarchy, as Balmary illustrates, is to turn it toward "Oedipal" conflicts. Thus the O'Connor story relies on several touches of Oedipal conflict. The father in the story is the father only of small children, less a father than the grandmother's son; helpless when confronted with The Misfit, he travesties authoritarian fatherhood, any genuine authority leached out of him by the generations of "progress" culminating in his Hawaiian shirt. The grandmother herself has no parent mentioned (nothing explains how she got that way), but The Misfit had, as mentioned four times:

> It was a head-doctor at the penitentiary said what I had done was kill my daddy but I known that for a lie. My daddy died in nineteen ought nineteen of the epidemic flu and I never had a thing to do with it. (767)

At precisely the moment when, in a travesty of human contact, the grandmother identifies The Misfit as her son and reaches out to touch him, he shoots her.

"A Rose for Emily" could almost have been written to post-Lacanian specifications or to specifications for susceptibility to postmodern analysis; in it, old sins have long shadows. Its hidden fault results in defensive gestures—in both the plot of the narrative and the stylistic flourishes of its prose—which "protect and encrypt the site of incorporation" (Balmary 174), thus ensuring an ignorance of their sources. The reader looks in vain for the ordinary names in the cemetery; the townspeople might look in vain for Emily's sources of support; Emily herself might look in vain for any explanation of her own emotional state. With regard to Emily's father, to her dead lover, to Emily herself, and to racial privilege in the South, a spectral remnant of a loved object is preserved, but "only at the price of self-division" (Balmary xix). Perhaps obviously, Emily partly embodies the South, reflecting historical processes in which the South has often been projected as an American "Other," homologous with the town's projections of Emily. "We propose the following formulation: The dominated carries out the repressed of the dominant," says Lacan, following Freud (Balmary 34); "one's desire is always the desire of the Other" (Balmary 1). Homer Barron comes carpetbagging and is devoured; Emily's dead father's possessiveness metamorphoses into a ghoulish, mystified disrelish for Emily by later generations; the history of slavery fetters the South. Throughout the narrative runs the trope of a fault, a hidden history with long shadows, which manifests itself in modern dislocations which simultaneously proclaim and conceal it in postmodern criticism.

In O'Connor, the sins are still there, but their shadows are missing; there is no way to track them to their sources. In the vein of pop horror films and sensationalist journalism, the roots of The Misfit's evil (and of the family's ignorance) remain unexplored. While the history beyond Faulkner's narrative may be partly objectified by the narrative into a personalized and consciously psychological "love-hate," the history in O'Connor's narrative is even more irrevocably objectivized—as "atmosphere," lost history, inaccessible history—by fearful loathing and gallows humor. What series of forces and influences contributed to the effects visible in the grandmother's family? We never know, because they have been subsumed in the glaring synchronicity of the omniscient narrator's gaze. Thus the difference between the two stories extends to their narrative voices. Where Faulkner uses a man for his narrative persona, O'Connor does *not* use a woman or indeed any identifiable individual; any personal circuit between reader and narrative is completed only in the invisible glare of taste. Even this limited circuit is broken by the car accident, which ambushes the reader almost as thoroughly as it does the family. The film-like limpidity of O'Connor's prose, the silent void surrounding the grandmother, the absence of names for the mother and grandmother all create a shock different in degree and kind from that shared by the narrator in Faulkner's story. The sudden shock, the reader's alienation from the characters, the strict linearity of the plot which excludes any participation in reconstruction by the reader—all contribute to reduce the reader's sense of control. The absence of fathers, sources, history, and narrators creates a disembodied power of taste, floating in a kind of papal immunity from any purposeful scrutiny.

Despite all the humor in Faulkner's narrative, I think that "A Rose for Emily" still remains more of a yarn, a story, than "A Good Man Is Hard to Find"; O'Connor's narrative more resembles a joke, and a joke whose punch line is eschatological: "'She would of been a good woman,' The Misfit said, 'if it had been somebody there to shoot her every minute of her life'" (768). In this line, the most famous in the story and one of the most famous in O'Connor's writing, the narrative calls attention with a stunning limpidity to what it does, demonstrating the short-circuiting of any potential examination of causes by a subsummation into eschatology (as in the several christological allusions scattered throughout). On more than one level, and perhaps in some ways unintentionally, "A Good Man Is Hard to Find" demonstrates short cuts that don't work out. The refusal to defer gratification which contributes to—and characterizes—the family's social status; the wrong road taken, leading to an imaginary buried treasure and the family's deaths; The Misfit's version of ethics—all these are intentional illustrations of misdirected short cuts, like the grandmother's implicit valorization of class above life: "in case of an accident, anyone seeing her dead on the highway would know at once that she was a lady" (761).

So, too, is the earlier anecdote of the watermelon, as narrated by the grandmother:

> she had been courted by a Mr. Edgar Atkins Teagarden from Jasper, Georgia. She said he was a very good-looking man and a gentleman and that he brought her a watermelon every Saturday afternoon with his initials cut in it, E. A. T. Well, one Saturday, she said, Mr. Teagarden brought the watermelon and there was nobody at home and he left it on the front porch and returned in his buggy to Jasper, but she never got the watermelon, she said, because a nigger boy ate it when he saw the initials, E. A. T.! (761-62)

The ignorance and greed which snatch at immediate gratification constitute a *joke* in O'Connor's narrative, the joke in both The Misfit's line and the child's eating the watermelon, according to the grandmother: an ignorance of any transcendental signification in what is offered them or in what they do. A larger and less-funny twist in and beyond the narrative, however, suggests that transcendence itself might be another inadequate short cut, away from genuine analysis and genuine history. The imaginary gardens provide no escape from real oppression and pain, because they offer no real change: "'Shut up, Bobby Lee,' The Misfit said. 'It's no real pleasure in life'" (768).

Notes

1. For further discussion on the plethoric stereotypes/myths surrounding the image of the South, see the *Encyclopedia of Southern Culture*, ed. Charles R. Wilson and William Ferris (U of North Carolina P, 1989), especially the section titled "Mythic South," 1097-1145, by George B. Tindall.

2. This argument—my own reduction of the stereotypes to a fundamental schema of two (upper and lower)—is part of the thesis of a book-length study in progress, tentatively titled *Insignificant Other: Representations of the American South in American Media and Literature*.

3. The perspective on colonial production in this essay has been influenced by the work of Gayatri Chakravorty Spivak and Edward Said, among others. Unusual though it might seem to apply the concept of colonial production to the American South, the mode of analysis is broadly that of, and logically proceeds from, cultural studies, as in the work of Stuart Hall.

4. I am using the term *southern gothic* in the readily recognized sense in which it is understood in the *Encyclopedia of Southern Culture*, especially 1125-1127; see also 876 (on Erskine Caldwell), 917-918 (on Tennessee Williams); cf. "hogwallow politics and abnormal neuroticism." See also *The History of Southern Literature*, ed. Louis D. Rubin, Jr. (Louisiana State UP, 1985), especially 442, 475, 484, 487, and 532; also *Columbia Literary History of the United States*, ed. Emory Elliot (Columbia UP, 1988), 1139-1140; also *Fifty Southern Writers after 1900: A Bio-Bibliographical Sourcebook*, ed. Joseph M. Flora, and Robert Bain (Greenwood P, 1987), 102.

Surprisingly, given the relatively widespread currency of the phrase (and concept) "southern gothic," the concept itself has received remarkable little direct scrutiny. There are no works of literary criticism currently in print on southern gothic fiction (despite the existence of many works on southern writers, southern writing, and the gothic novel in general); "southern gothic" is not in use as a Library of Congress subject index term; there is neither a book nor an article, so far as I know, on the "southern gothic" in its across-the-board applications in both popular fiction, film, and television, and canonical literature. This lacuna indicates that few literary critics writing today have drawn extensively on abundant materials available in recent writing about the American South by historians and sociologists; to write about the "southern gothic" as a distancing of social actuality requires, of course, some study of the social actuality.

5. The psychological process identified here is, obviously, Freud's "projection." The application of psychoanalytic terms to the activities engaged in by a society, or by the dominant mode of scrutiny within that society, is among the tools of analysis used by Michel Foucault, Jacques Lacan, and Marie Balmary.

6. This dual movement or signification of both blazoning and concealing is discussed by Balmary in a very different context, with a partly Lacanian orientation to the analysis; it becomes relevant to Faulkner's writing in many more passages than discussed here.

7. Space prevents any detailed listing of items in a continuing tradition of the "room" as symbolic of woman; this story represents in some ways a final joke, grotesquely inverted, on the room-of-one's own continuum.

8. The relationship between, or antithesis of genuine history and a commodified "nostalgia" prevalent in the mass media has been discussed by, among others, Adrienne Rich, in a lecture at Delta State University, Cleveland, Mississippi, April, 1982.

9. See John D. MacDonald's Travis McGee, whose strangely light eyes belie the apparent simplicity suggested by his beach-bum tan. Precisely this image of light eyes in a blackened face is employed by *Time*, in a cover story (with special section) called "The Curse of Violent Crime," March 23, 1981; illustrations 17, 19. The illustration features a black-face map of the continental United States looking outward through two white, eye-shaped gaps; the effect, intentionally or otherwise, is certainly racist.

10. The historical uses of "taste," barely touched on here, were suggested to me first in a seminar conducted by Gayatri Chakravorty Spivak at the Teaching Institute, University of Illinois at Urbana-Champaign, summer, 1983.

11. Fully to document the stereotypicality of the "southern" would require a book-length study, at least. Citing only relatively modern examples, however, one might include almost any mention of the South in popular novels from *Tobacco Road* (Erskine Caldwell, 1932) to *Women's Work* (Anne T. Wallach, 1982); in plays from—of course—Tennessee Williams on; and in notable films such as *Easy Rider* (1969) and *Deliverance* (1972). For testimony to the longevity of the destructive-old-southern-lady motif, see Andrew Hacker's article on the E. R. A. in the resurrection issue of *Harper's Magazine*; also the popular two-actor play, *Greater Tuna*.

12. Interestingly, Sayers also has her chief female character (Harriet Vane) speculate, on the grounds of Oxford University, about possible modes of partnership between Catholicism and Freudian psychoanalysis, a synthesis which O'Connor also toys with in this story and others.

13. The idea of a pure "Electra complex" is, of course, Freudian analysis oversimplified; Freud conjectured about the possibility but never developed or applied it as extensively as the Oedipus complex, and subsequently arrived at the belief that children of *both* sexes form an early attachment to the mother, which they must later overcome.

14. The important contrast here, as developed in the discussion, is not a contrast between an "Electra complex" and an "Oedipus complex," but a contrast between a willingness to scrutinize the position of the father and a refusal to do so, as discussed in another context by Balmary, following (in part) Lacan.

Works Cited

Balmary, Marie. *Homme aux statues.* Tr. Engl. *Psychoanalyzing Psychoanalysis: Freud and the Hidden Fault of the Father.* Tr. N. Lukacher. Baltimore: Johns Hopkins UP, 1982.

Faulkner, William. "A Rose for Emily." *The Portable Faulkner.* Ed. Malcolm Cowley. New York: Viking, 1946.

O'Connor, Flannery. "A Good Man Is Hard to Find." *Fiction 100: An Anthology of Short Stories.* Ed. James H. Pickering. New York: MacMillan, 1978.

Wellek, Rene and Warren, Austin. *Theory of Literature.* New York: Harcourt, Brace, 1956.

PART III

Postmodern Images as Ideological Discourse

Chapter 6

The Narrative Text as Historical Artifact
The Case of John Fowles

Gian Balsamo

I

Monuments and documents are two among the major sources which enable a writer to create a historical novel. A portrait, a statue, a piece of machinery, a tomb, a buried city, a declaration of independence, a medical textbook, yesterday's Dow Jones Average—these are all examples of what a writer's sources amount to: mental, verbal, pictorial, perceptual images,[1] modes of representation informed by a given ideology.

My point of departure can be formulated as follows: the narrative modes of emplotment of a historical novel may be seen as structurally homologous with the nature of the historical sources (images informed by ideologies) adopted by, or made available to, the author of the novel.[2] A number of complementary topics immediately arise, among which: (1) in his selection and exclusion of historical sources, the writer of fiction must submit to different constraints than those which characterize the work of the historian; (2) besides monuments and documents, besides images and ideologies, there is another major source of fiction, imagination, whose transgressive function (Iser 223-25) consists of the disruption of the apparent homogeneity between historical sources and fictional world; and (3) what about the nature of that irreplaceable historical source—a historical source upside down, we might call it—on which the main perspective of the novel is based, namely, the tropological perspective adopted by the author himself, and its corollary "affinity with interpretation" (de Man 151)?

For now, I will leave aside these complementary topics and begin with a preliminary qualification. Figure 6-1 shows a picture taken in 1895 of the Monmouth Beach, in front of the town of Lyme Regis, on the southwestern coast of England. On this beach the Duke of Monmouth landed in 1685, to launch his doomed attempt on the crown of his uncle, James II. This photographic image can be found in *A Short History of Lyme Regis*, published in 1982 by John Fowles, honorary curator of the Lyme Regis Museum.

Figure 6-1
Reprinted by permission of Little, Brown. *A Short History of Lyme Regis*, John Fowles.

On the Monmouth Beach is located the Cobb where Sarah and Charles, the protagonists of Fowles's *The French Lieutenant's Woman*, meet for the first time. This picture—a visual image obtained with a rudimentary camera—is an example of the historical materials available to John Fowles when he wrote his most celebrated novel. The first meeting of Sarah, the "French Loot'n'nt's Hoer" (73),[3] and Charles, the soon-to-be-disinherited *rentier*, takes place in the late March of the year 1867. Only 30 years separate Fowles's romantic plot from the day the picture shown in Figure 1 was taken.

John Fowles's, *A Maggot*, tells a story which occurs 131 years earlier than the one narrated in *The French Lieutenant's Woman*. The story of *A Maggot* takes place in southwestern England, in the very area surrounding the town of Lyme Regis, at a time when the memory of the Monmouth Rebellion is still alive in the cloth trade community of the region.

A Maggot consists of a number of depositions, all of them concerning the disappearance of a young nobleman. The depositions are given by the servants who accompanied the young nobleman, whose pseudonym is Mr. Bartholomew, in a journey toward a secret destination. The interrogator of the servants is a lawyer, Henry Ayscough, hired by the nobleman's father, a power-ful duke whose identity remains a secret throughout the narration. At the begin-ning of Mr. Ayscough's inquiry into the whereabouts of his employer's son, the identities and whereabouts of three of Mr. Bartholomew's four travelling com-panions are unknown. The fourth companion, Dick Thurlow, is dead. The lawyer's inquiry begins in the month of April and ends in the month of October of the year 1736. It provides no results, no evidence, as to the fate of Mr. Bartholomew.

As can be inferred from this initial setting, *A Maggot* is a story which deals with multiple levels of fictionality. Five characters are involved in a journey toward a secret destination. None of them but one, Dick Thurlow, travel under their real name. None of them but two, Mr. Bartholomew and Dick, know the location of their destination and the true goal of the journey. In the course of the journey some of the servants are made aware that the destination toward which they are travelling is not the one they were originally told; nevertheless, they do not leave the expedition.

The identity of Mr. Bartholomew—who travels with a trunk full of alchemic papers—is a secret, and the servants either know or suspect that his name is a pseudonym. Only Mr. Bartholomew knows that the real name of the woman travelling with him is Rebecca Hocknell. The other members of the expedition are told her name is Louise. In London she is known as Fanny, or the Quaker's Maid, a notorious whore. The older man travelling with Mr. Bartholomew, supposedly an uncle of his, called Mr. Brown by the party of travelers, is a hired actor, Mr. Lacy. The self-declared ex-soldier, Farthing, is a good-for-nothing young man living in London, hired under Mr. Lacy's recom-mendation. His real name, known to Mr. Bartholomew and to Mr. Lacy but not to Rebecca, is David Jones.

And finally there is Dick Thurlow. Dick was born on Mr. Bartholomew's birthday, and has been Mr. Bartholomew's attendant since that day. He is deaf, handsome, and athletic. His eyes are inscrutable, like "twin camera lenses"; they "are of a vacant blue, almost as if he were blind . . . they betray no sign of emotions, . . . [they] suggest their owner is somewhere else" (5). This image of nonhuman eyes reveals more, indeed, than Fowles himself is willing to say; some sort of registering device seems to be in permanent operation behind Dick's pupils, a device much less rudimentary than the camera used, 167 years later, to take the picture of Monmouth Beach shown in Figure 6-1. Dick is the only character who does not travel under a false name, the only one who, appar-ently, does not pretend to be something or somebody else. And yet, toward the end of the book, his android-like attitude and aspect will raise a disquieting doubt in the reader's mind; here is the quasi- or nonhuman image of a creature whose intellect and whose emotions elude the plan of reality to which our appraisal of human deeds usually applies.[4]

Most of what we learn from the depositions given by Mr. Bartholomew's servants leads us to expect the story to develop into a conventional plot of alchemic trickery, or else into the conventional narration of the wanderings of a European freethinker of the eighteenth century. In fact, from time to time the tone of the book may remind the reader of Marguerite Yourcenar's *L'Ouevre Au Noir*, whose protagonist, a healer-philosopher named Zeno, leaves France, his home country, for the more tolerant land of England. And the extenuating depositions obtained by the patient acumen of Henry Ayscough, the lawyer-inquirer in *A Maggot*, although the vehicles for a remarkable variety of speech types, are all analogous, when it comes to their narrative moods, to the pervasive matter-of-fact levity—a dramatic ignorance of the art of introspection[5]—which can be found in the *Memories* of Giacomo Casanova, the Venetian alchemist-adventurer of the eighteenth century. But the peculiar emplotment of the narrative of *A Maggot* will reduce this potentially intriguing theme—adventure and black magic—to a mere seductive and fraudulent outline, as we shall see, out of and in spite of which the surprising theme of the novel will eventually emerge.

Either at the beginning or at the end of several of the chapters of *A Maggot*, a reproduction from the first page of *The Historical Chronicle* is inserted in the pagination of the book. *The Historical Chronicle* was the section devoted to historical information of a British Journal called *The Gentleman's Magazine*. Figure 6-2 shows one such page from *A Maggot*. This figure, whose heading exhibits the publication date April 1736, appears at the end of the first chapter. The last chapter of the book is preceded by *The Historical Chronicle* of October 1736. As the reader will recall, the fruitless inquiry of the lawyer Henry Ayscough into Mr. Bartholomew's disappearance begins and ends on those very same dates.

Here is an example of the kind of historical information that can be found in the pages of *The Historical Chronicle*. The item is dated 28 August 1736:

> On the 28th past, a man passing the Bridge over the Savock near Preston, Lancashire, saw two large Flights of Birds meet with such Rapidity, that 180 of them fell to the Ground, were taken up by him, and sold in Preston market the same Day. (Fowles, *A Maggot* 193)

From a narratological point of view, I do not see any justification for the insertion of these documents in the novel. They do not add plausibility to the plot. They do not strengthen the extent of historical knowledge exhibited by the author. They do not enhance the mimetic verisimilitude in the representation of costumes and manners. They do not contribute to the integration of narrative order and duration with diegetic order and duration. So we may ask, why are the excerpts from *The Historical Chronicle* inserted in this

Hiſtorical Chronicle, 1736.

APRIL.

Extract of a Letter from Savannah in Georgia, dated Feb. 14, 1735-6.

E arrived here the 5th Inſt. which for ỹ Time is incredibly improved; there are about 200 Houſes regularly built, ſome of which lett at 30l. Sterling a Year: Mr Oglethorpe went next Day, tho' very wet Weather, to ſee the adjacent Settlements, in which there are ſeveral Engliſh-like regular Townſhips, viz. Benzez, Thunderbolt, Fartingile, Weſtbrook, &c. in a flouriſhing Condition, beyond any Colony ever known in ſo ſhort a Time. Tho' we had a long and very ſtormy Paſſage, yet we arrived without the Loſs of a Soul out of any of our Ships, which were ſix in Number and very large; Mr Oglethorpe, during the Paſſage, was extremely careful both of the Souls and Bodies under his Care; but what ſurprizes me beyond Expreſſion is his abſtemious and hard Living, for, tho' even Dainties are plentiful, he makes the leaſt Uſe of them, and goes thro' the Woods, wet or dry, as actively as any Indian: his Humanity ſo gains upon all here, that I have not Words to expreſs their Regard and Eſteem for him: He goes To-morrow about 80 Miles farther into the Country, where he is to ſettle a Town, near which, upon the River Altamaha, a Fort with four Baſtions is to be built, that is deſign'd for the Barrier. The Country abounds with Fiſh, excellent Fruit, and Veniſon.

Sunday, 4.

Mr *Andrew Pitt*, an Eminent Quaker, &c. waited on the Pr. of *Wales*, to ſollicit his Favour in Relation to the Quakers Tythe Bill, whom his Royal H. anſwer'd to this Effect.——' As I am a Friend to Liberty in ' General, and to Toleration in particular, I ' wiſh you may meet with all proper Favour, ' but for myſelf I never gave my Vote in ' Parliament, and to Influence my Friends, or ' Direct my Servants in theirs, does not be-' come my Station. To leave them entirely ' to their own Conſcience and Underſtanding, ' is a Rule I have hitherto preſcrib'd to myſelf, ' and purpoſ'd throughout my whole Life to ' obſerve.' Mr *Pitt* overcome with this Conduct, reply'd,——May it Pleaſe the Pr. of *Wales*!——' I am greatly Affected with your ' Excellent Notions of Liberty ; and am more

' Pleaſed with the Anſwer you have given us, ' than if you had granted our Requeſt.'

Tueſday, 6.

Bryan Benſon, Eſq; was choſen Governor, *Thomas Cooke*, Eſq; Deputy Governor of the Bank of *England*. And

Wedneſday, 7.

The following Gentlemen were choſe Directors for the Year 1736.

Robt Alſop, Eſq;	Robt Atwood, Eſq;
Sir Edw. Bellamy, Kt.	Wm Snelling, Eſq;
John Bance, Eſq;	Sir John Thompſon, Kt
Sir Gerard Conyers, Kt	Mr Robt Thornton
Delil'ersCarbonnelEſq;	Stamp Brooksbank,Eſq;
Mr Jn Eaton Dodſworth	Wm Fawkener, Eſq;
Nathaniel Gould, Eſq;	Fred. Frankland, Eſq;
Samuel Holſen, Eſq;	Mr James Gualtier
Mr Benj. Longuet	Henry Neal, Eſq;
Mr Joſeph Paice.	Charles Savage, Eſq;
John Rudge, Eſq;	James Spilman, Eſq;
Moſes Raper, Eſq;	Mr Samuel Trench.

The Directors of the *Eaſt India* Company.

Robt Adams, Eſq;	Samuel Feake, Eſq;
Abra. Addams, Eſq;	Harry Gough, Eſq;
Miles Barne, Eſq;	Mr Samuel Hyde
Dodding Braddyll,Eſq;	Michael Impey, Eſq;
Sir Wm Bilters, Kt	Edw. Lovibond, Eſq;
Stephen Biſs, Eſq;	Baltzar Lyell, Eſq;
Mr Rich. Blount	Wm Pomeroy, Eſq;
Capt. Rich. Boulton	Jones Raymond, Eſq;
Chriſt. Barrow, Eſq;	Wm Rouſe, Eſq;
Charles Colburne, Eſq;	Sir John Salter, Kt
Dr Caleb Coteſworth	St Quin.Thompſon,Eſq;
Mr John Emmerſon.	Joſ. Wordſworth Jun.

Friday, 9.

Wm Bithell and *Wm Morgan*, were Hang'd at *Worceſter* for cutting down, in Company with other Rioters, *Ledbury* Turnpikes. *Morgan* died a Papiſt. The Turnpike Levellers having been very Tumultuous at the Trial, a Party of Soldiers attended the Execution; on which it paſs'd without Diſturbance.

Tueſday, 13.

Dr. Shaw, a learned Phyſician at Scarborough, was ſent for to Court, on Account of the ſurpriſing Cure performed by him on General Sutron, and was introduced to his Royal Highneſs the Prince of Wales, the Duke and the Princeſſe, by whom he was very graciouſly received, and had the Honour of kiſſing their Hands, as he had before done of their Majeſties.

G g **Wednes**

Figure 6-2
Reprinted by permission of Little, Brown. *A Maggot*, John Fowles.

book? Of what interest can they be for the reader of *A Maggot*?

The only answer appears to be a methodological one, namely, Fowles's intention to provide his reader with an explicit documentation of the historical sources adopted in the composition of *A Maggot*. It is legitimate to think, in fact, that to the majority of the educated Englishmen in the early eighteenth century the basic understanding of historical events corresponded to a plain list of chronicles like the ones found in *The Historical Chronicle*. Therefore, the apparently gratuitous insertion of excerpts from *The Historical Chronicle* may function as a reminder of the nature of the *master trope* prevailing at the time and in the place where the events narrated in *A Maggot* occur: History regarded as a mere chronicle of facts, as an aggregate of "histories" of History (Jauss 46-47).

A peculiar quality of the chronicler's work, as compared to the comprehensive effort of the modern historian, lies in the contingent quality of the truth conveyed by his reports. A chronicler, judging from Figure 6-2, is a sort of modern reporter. He reports a version of a fact. When he is the exclusive inquirer into the circumstances of the fact he is writing about, the version he writes of it goes unchallenged, and it establishes the opinion of his contemporaries about this fact. But it is well known that two reporters will have two different truths as regard the same event, three reporters will have three different truths, and so on. History, we may say, when written by reporters, results into an assemblage of eclectic truths, into that very kind of construct that to a postmodern sensibility, coincidentally, corresponds to the only acceptable notion of historic *veritas*. And we may further say, to sum this up, that the plot structure of *A Maggot* appeals to its reader as a plausible representation of the modalities of historical apprehension experienced by the very characters depicted in the book.

The group of travellers has a destination known only to two of them, Mr. Bartholomew and Dick. Only three of them, Mr. Bartholomew, Dick, and Rebecca, reach this destination and meet the mysterious beings—women "clothed . . . in plain silver . . . [who] wore narrow trowses . . . [and travelled inside] a floating maggot . . . [made] of fresh-tinned metal"[6]—who are waiting for them in a cavern. After the meeting in the cavern, Mr. Bartholomew disappears, as if into thin air. Dick is found hanged from a tree, a sprig of violets sprouting out of his mouth.[7] Mr. Bartholomew's and Dick's understanding of the meeting in the cavern would have, if accessible to the reader and to the inquirer, Henry Ayscough, the attributes of quasi-omniscience, since they prepared themselves for this meeting with the conscientiousness of two modern scientists anticipating the passage of a comet. But all their scientific and alchemic papers are destroyed before the meeting in the cavern takes place, as if no evidence of the event is to be left behind.

So the only source of information for both the reader and the inquirer is the three witnesses—Mr. Lacy, David Jones, and Rebecca Hocknell: three witnesses who, in the first place, are not aware of the nature of the experience they have gone through. They belong to the working classes; they have never received a proper education. Rebecca was raised in the cult of Quaker bigotry, then moved to London and became a prostitute; Mr. Lacy is a trained actor, whose performance in a sacrilegious and subversive play, just before he was hired by Mr. Bartholomew, earned him a good reputation in the artistic circles of London. David Jones is an outcast, a liar, a man who lives from hand to mouth. None of them know how to separate their subjective impressions from the objective description of the facts they observed in the course of the journey to the cavern.

John Fowles's resolution to duplicate, in the course of his narration, the chronicle-like structure of historical understanding that is exemplified in the pages of *The Historical Chronicle*, translates itself into a "floating" narrative structure; the denouement of his story is left to the unaccountable reliability of a number of witnesses, each one characterized by a sort of educational or temperamental blind spot, and to their conflicting versions of the facts. In the end there is no climax, no resolution of the mystery, no coalescing of themes—in a sense, there is no story at all. Our writer has willingly reduced himself to the role of a scribe.

Does the writer's metamorphosis into the figure of a scribe reflect a purpose of self-abasement? Not quite so. We must try to consider what the image of the scribe represents vis-à-vis the image of the writer of narrative. The scribe is the rival, the "other" letters-writer; an object of both fear and contempt. The contempt springs from the assurance that the scribe's writings are inferior kinds of writings, devoid of the "aura" that surrounds the voice of the artist-writer (Mitchell 153).[8] The fear stems from the recognition that the scribe's writings may be in the process of "appropriating" the mystique halo which pertains to the voice of the writer. It's worthwhile recalling here that to an anonymous scribe is attributed the compilation of *The Thousand And One Nights*; that Giovanni Boccaccio, Pietro Aretino, Italo Calvino,[9] to cite just a few among many cases, compiled collections of tales conceived by "somebody else," where the author functioned as a mere "embedder" of stories (Genette 46); and that innumerable writers, from Giacomo Leopardi to Vladimir Nabokov, claimed to be the mere translators (Leopardi, *Inno* 5 and *Odae* 29) or "preambulators" (Nabokov 5) of their own narrative inventions. Likewise, Fowles's ostensible immolation of his image as a writer conceals, as we shall see, a desecrating, iconoclastic intent.

II

So we may say that the implied author of *The French Lieutenant's Woman*, the omniscient narrator who appears in the last chapter under the guise of a French-looking man "with a touch of the successful impresario about him" (362), turns himself into a scribe in *A Maggot*. The image of the Master of Ceremony who manipulates Time at will, who "takes out his watch [and] makes a small adjustment" in order for the reader to be plunged back in the middle of the conversation between Sarah and Charles in Mr. Rossetti's house, is turned, in *A Maggot*, into the image of a "slightly bent-shouldered clerk," a passive yet strangely "sardonic" scribe (345-46).

A deposition requires the presence of an interrogator, who obtains information from the witness, and the presence of a scribe, who transcribes such information. Of the three partners who give life to a deposition, the scribe is the passive one, the silent one, totally impotent—or almost so, as we shall see—in front of the heteroglossic[10] eloquence of his speaking sources.

A scribe's task consists of reporting facts which are dictated to him as they are related to the interrogator. The scribe is not supposed to investigate into the plausibility of the words he is writing down, or into the propriety of the syntax and the speech type(s) through which these words are structured, or into the reality of the facts to which his writings, his "chronicles," give shape and texture. Between the reality of the event which is dictated to him and the fictional facticity of its written representation there is an intermediary—the witness or observer of the event—who, with respect to the scribe, is endowed with the privilege of omniscience. As we have seen above, the vindication of the truth of a fact pertains to its reporter: he becomes a source of fiction, on whose words the historian will build up a version of (a) history, the writer will build up a version of (a) narrative, the judge a version of (a) crime. At best, a scribe is a second-rate reporter.

Besides, the scribe is impotent with respect to his public. A scribe—but the time has come to give a name to our not too metaphorical scribe: he is John Tudor, the man who records the depositions given to Henry Ayscough, the inquirer in *A Maggot*—writes for his employer. His condition is different from that of the modern writer, who writes for a literary community[11] which responds to his work with a form or another of reception. Writing for an impersonal community implies an act endowed with a greater degree of freedom, as compared to the task of writing for an employer. The freedom of the writer is even greater if one considers that the literary community of the writer's time and the literary communities of future times cannot be considered as compact, monadic entities. The writer has the power—a partial power—to select the components of the literary community to which his work is directed. The correct question, here, is not: "For *whom* is the book written?" but rather: "With what components of the literary community does the book share the *questions* which justify its existence as a work of art?"

In the sixties, John Fowles's most celebrated novel shared its crucial questions with a composite audience. The sixties, after all, were years of eclecticism. *The French Lieutenant's Woman* addresses itself to the existentialists, to the

Marxists, to the Darwinists, and, last but not least, to the lovers of the Victorian novels. To be more specific, *The French Lieutenant's Woman* creates an original image of historical narrative out of an organic aggregate of "metahistories,"[12] an aggregate which intertwines the existentialist, the Marxist, and the Darwinian explanatory perspectives with the Victorian literary modes. The final result, that is, Fowles's mode of emplotment of his literary text as historical artifact, entails a specific historical configuration dominated by the tropical image of individual freedom. "Freedom," Fowles writes in *The Aristos* (68), "is the choice of action and the power of enactment I have within the rules and situation of the game." His characters' predicaments crystallize into a variety of social and cultural practices grounded in the interplay between freedom of choice and historical causality, individual self-determination and casual chance, enactment and disruption of the dominant ideologies.

In the eighties, on the contrary, John Fowles shares the questions raised by *A Maggot* with a very selected audience—with readers who, in the age of the speaking media, can read archaic English and who are open to the acceptance and enjoyment of a plot with no climax and no conventional conclusion. Readers, above all, who are willing to accept the insertion of a conclusive epilogue where they are rudely told: "I know nothing in reality of [Rebecca Hocknell], and next to nothing of various other characters" (461).

In *A Maggot*, John Fowles writes a fantastic story about the events that precede the birth of Ann Lee, the Founder of the United Society of Believers in Christ's Second Appearing, better known as the Shakers. Here is how John Fowles justifies the ideological purpose behind the creation of his book. "[Ann Lee] had a practical vision of what was wrong with [the] world." (464). And, "dissent is a universal human phenomenon, yet that of Northern Europe and America is, I suspect, our most precious legacy to the world. We associate it especially with religion, since all new religion begins in dissent." (Fowles, 466). *A Maggot* ends on the day of Ann Lee's birth. Ann Lee, a champion of dissent, the woman whose religious credo goes so far as to attribute the feminine gender to the members of the Holy Trinity, is the daughter of a prostitute, Rebecca Hocknell.

Only the reader who knows how to make sense out of such a surprising, provocative epilogue, will not be put off by *A Maggot*. What brings a self-declared atheist like John Fowles to write an imposing novel in order to celebrate the unknown events that preceded the birth of a woman, a religious leader, in his opinion a champion of dissent? And why is it that in the eighties, a decade of order and conformism, an artist of the integrity of John Fowles feels compelled to consecrate his literary efforts to the celebration of dissent?

The dissent John Fowles talks about in *A Maggot* is not too distant, however, from the notion of individual freedom on which is based the ideology of *The French Lieutenant's Woman*. In this respect, a continuity lies hidden behind the apparent ideological fracture separating the two works. In the early eighteenth century (let's recall that the story of *A Maggot* occurs in the year 1736), historiographers were trying to emancipate their professional discipline from the metaphysical aporia into which it had been plunged by the epistemological breakage introduced, with respect to the notion of reality prevailing in the Middle Ages, by the works of Descartes, Bacon, Hume, Locke. The French Enlightenment was but a feeble effort to return History to the wholeness of a conception that had been disintegrated by the then prevailing "dispersed" histories,[13] which were based on the so-called analytical episteme,[14] on the one-to-one relation between observed phenomena and classificatory signs. Jean-Jacques Rousseau, with his *Reveries of the Solitary Walker* (1782), was the first European thinker to claim for the newborn Ego of the preromantic era the right to express itself in irrational, uncodable terms. This image of an irreducibly rebellious Ego is the basic ideological paradigm by which both *The French Lieutenant's Woman* and *A Maggot* vindicate man's right to freedom.

Where does Fowles's image of individual freedom come from? To whom among the great thinkers of the past can the paternity of his vision, that is, the paternity of the utopian image of a new mode of being, be attributed? Instead of relying upon the predictable thread of the history of philosophy and wonder if the paternity of Fowles's image of individual freedom may be ascribed to Husserl rather than to Heidegger, to Sartre rather than to Marx, one should take the hints provided in Fowles's "autobiography in ideas," *The Aristos*. This book sends us back to the figure of Heraclitus, and in particular to Heraclitus's image of mankind as divided into a moral and intellectual elite (the *aristoi*) and an unthinking, conforming mass (the *hoi polloi*, the many) (9). No wonder Fowles's work has been accused of cryptofascism (8)—a suspicion I am far from sharing.

The idea of individual freedom undergoes a radical transformation between the two works under consideration, though. This radicalization can be identified with the greater importance that the political agenda of Fowles's latter work attributes to the acts of transgression and subversion in their postmodern, parodistic acceptation. *The French Lieutenant's Woman* is a love story, after all. The two endings of this book (Chapters 60 and 61) betray Fowles's ironic duplicity with regard to the theme of individual freedom. The first ending (Chapter 60) represents the triumph of conventional love, love in the form of pregnancy, birth, and reproduction—fatherhood and motherhood.[15] "The rock of ages can never be anything else but love," is one of the last statements in Chapter 60.

This conventional image of love is sacrificed to an image of love as universal piety in the ending provided by Chapter 61. "Piety is acting what one knows"—this caption, by which Fowles reveals the nature of Sarah's vocation and fate in the world, must be our point of departure in order to outline a proper appreciation of the second ending of the book.

Fowles points out that in the above caption the word *piety* might be substituted with the word *humanity* or with the word *authenticity*; this move, he suggests, would provide the caption, taken from Matthew Arnold's *Notebooks*, with the sort of existentialist flavor required by the nature of his novel. Chapter 61 leaves us with the image of a disillusioned Charles, rejected by Sarah, hopeless as to the happiness of his future life, and yet more aware than he ever was before of what life in the "city's iron heart" amounts to. Now we can recognize, in the denouement of Charles's destiny, the crystallization of a Benjaminian image of "historical configuration."[16] First, the meeting with Sarah, who may be seen at first as the personification of the Darwinian laws of origin and evolution, imposes on Charles's life the judgment of the past—the oppressed humanity of the past, the dead, who can be redeemed only through a renewed image of human nobility. Then, Sarah's refusal to become his wife, to assume the conventional role of female partner (at this point in the novel, Sarah's role becomes that of the Heraclitean child-god, who changes destinies by the playful, whimsical throwing of a dice), imposes on Charles the judgment of the future—the utopian impulse toward a future whose *master trope*, Marxian existentialism, explodes the legitimacy of conventional love into a more comprehensive image of love as ontological authenticity, as compassionate piety for one's fellow human beings, as universal freedom. Our "historical subject," Charles, experiences the shocking suspension of happening described by Benjamin in "Theses on the Philosophy of History" (263). He is the captive of an historical "configuration pregnant with tension" (Benjamin, "Theses" 262); by taking cognizance of it, he blasts his own life out of the specific era to which it belongs.

The radical transformation in the idea of individual freedom which occurs in *A Maggot* brings to completion a process that *The French Lieutenant's Woman* had left unaccomplished. In order to appreciate the extent of the contradiction hidden behind the notion of freedom as envisioned in *The French Lieutenant's Woman*, one needs only to analyze the final scene of the second ending of the book. Charles, tears in his eyes, comes to the realization that "life is to be, however inadequately, emptily, hopelessly, . . . endured" (366). This image of illumination is preceded by an epigraph at one time eloquent and elusive: "True piety is acting what one knows." Rather than formulating his personal conclusion through a final, unambiguous statement, Fowles goes back to this epigraph from Matthew Arnold's *Notebooks* and invites the reader to paraphrase such epigraph. The word "acting," Fowles suggests, should be substituted with Marx's definition of life as "the actions of men in pursuit of their ends."

Is there an ultimate, unequivocal solution to the enigmatic puzzle proposed by Fowles to the reader? Or are we facing an open-ended, unsolvable enigma? The literary critic cannot draw away from any such textual challenge. I will therefore suggest a solution to Fowles's puzzle, but not before reminding the reader that (1) to a puzzle corresponds an almost infinite number of possible solutions—each solution entailing a different permutation of the pieces of the puzzle, each discarded solution being, *in potentia*, the one the creator of the puzzle might opt for—and (2) no final verification is possible when the solution to the puzzle—and this is our case—amounts to an ontological verdict on human existence. This being said, it seems legitimate to phrase the ultimate ideological commitment of *The French Lieutenant's Woman* as follows: the imperative of piety guides man's actions in the making of his own life.

And so Charles, turned into the desolate, heroic carrier of the first germs of man's existentialist vocation, pregnant with the fetus of an original, still shapeless moral and social awareness, fades away along the deserted embankment of the Thames. The figure of this old-fashioned *rentier* is changed into an image of the imperative of piety—an image of the existentialist paradigm of individual freedom, by which man secures his own emancipation through universal emancipation. Charles's metamorphosis takes place, presumably, in the peculiar regime of freedom dictated by "the rules and the situation of the game." However, aren't we facing, at last, the intimate ideological contradiction mentioned above, the contradiction hidden behind the notion of human freedom as envisioned in *The French Lieutenant's Woman*? The beauty of Fowles's masterly text induces a sort of anesthesia in the rational response of the reader, a blindness to the trickery of his ultimate gimmickry: the freedom Fowles is talking about in this episode is the outcome of a game played by the gods with an enlightened member of the ruling class!

In *A Maggot*, on the other hand, the quest for freedom and emancipation is not assigned to the *aristoi*. Quite on the contrary, Fowles seems to embrace *in toto* the cause of the *hoi polloi*. When it comes to one of his most typical narrative devices, namely the appearance on stage of the implied author, Fowles translates this persona into the humble image of a scribe, John Tudor. The implied author's position in the schemata of the book may remind us, in a sense, of the position of the painter in Velasquez's *Las Meniñas*. From time to time John Tudor seems to stare at the reader from his writing desk; he even manages a few blinks of the eye (348). But when it comes to the narrative content of the book, John Tudor, the personification of the implied author, limits himself to the passive recording of the depositions given to Henry Ayscough by the witnesses. Here and there, between the end of a deposition and the beginning of the next, Fowles presents us with a few conventionally narrative passages, yet we are told in the prologue to the book that these passages have been *dictated* to the implied author by his own imagination, and that they are built up on a single image—"a small group of travellers, faceless" (Prologue)—which for years kept obstinately rising from Fowles's unconscious. "This book," Fowles claims, "is a maggot" (461).

In *A Maggot*, the reader is placed in the position of the *aristoi*; the king who stares at the image of Velasquez's *Las Meniñas* from the outside; the spectator who, in the movie theater described by Benjamin in "The Work of Art in the Age of Mechanical Reproduction," tests the actor's performance on the screen. As readers, we are expected to evaluate and to judge the text in front of us. We can examine the text word by word, sentence by sentence. We can anatomize the skill, the performance, the hidden and revealed intentions of the author. And yet, what we see is, most of all, "reflection." We cannot look without seeing ourselves mirrored in the picture. However, in order for us to evaluate and to judge, it is a sine qua non that we extricate the projections of our own value judgments from the cluster of images we are trying to decipher.

Whose point of view is preeminent in *A Maggot*? All in all, the point of view of *common and humble people*. Even if the events related in the novel occur because of the decision of Mr. Bartholomew, the son of a duke, to travel toward a secret destination, where he has a rendezvous with some mysterious women "in silver," most of what the reader gets to know about the nature of this journey derives from the depositions of the servants who are hired to accompany the nobleman. Mr. Bartholomew and his attendant, Dick, share a secret to which the reader will never be initiated. Mr. Bartholomew disappears after the meeting in the cavern, and Dick is found dead. So, because of a sort of abdication (no, it's not a destitution) of the *aristoi* (among whom must be counted also the persona of the implied author), the representatives of the low social strata earn the right to speak out their own versions of the facts.

Mr. Bartholomew's encounter with the women in silver is first related to Henry Ayscough, the lawyer in search of Mr. Bartholomew, by David Jones, who did not participate in the meeting but was told about it by Rebecca Hocknell, the third eyewitness of the event. Jones's version consists of a congeries of hysterical, fanatically religious images. According to him, in the cavern there was a great gallery from whose walls hung paintings in which "the figures and nature stood not fixed, as in your true pictured hangings, yet moving as in life, tho' silent" (261); among these hangings, representing "all kind of monstrous horror and cruelty of man against man" (261), was the terrifying icon of the maggot, the beast which awaits all sinners in the flames of hell (265).

The second version of the encounter, given by Rebecca, tells an altogether different story. The maggot is a flying machine, although neither Rebecca nor Henry Ayscough have a name for such a thing. As Mr. Bartholomew, Dick, and Rebecca enter inside the maggot, Rebecca is taken aside by one of the women in silver, and is shown a long sequence of moving pictures—again, for lack of a suitable term, she calls them a "gliding window"—from which she learns the terrible fate which impends over mankind. In front of this image-making marvel—a screen on which an invisible piece of equipment assembles, under a law unknown to the observer, "multiple fragments" of reality—Rebecca experiences one of the "changes in sense perception" which, according to Benjamin, will accompany the changes in "humanity's mode of existence" almost two centuries later ("The Work of Art in the Age of Mechanical Reproduction" 222). Rebecca is shown a sequence of apocalyptic images whose verisimilitude, in her eyes, grows in proportion to the illusion of spatial and human closeness conveyed by the cinematic medium. The receptive attitude of Rebecca coalesces with the religious principles she was taught as a child by her Quaker parents: images of an uncompassionate universal judgment, images of mass murder, punishment, destruction, move before her eyes, reawakening her old religious beliefs.

Nine months after Rebecca's experience in the cavern, her daughter, Ann Lee, sees the light. Rebecca will take it upon herself to instruct Ann about the apocalyptic images she was shown by the women in silver. During her interrogation, Rebecca describes these images, together with her mystical interpretations of them, to Henry Ayscough. But her matter-of-fact beliefs sound like blasphemous heresies to the ears of the religiously reverent, if not devout, lawyer; her images of universal doom do not share the hallucinatory quality of Jones's deposition. They consist of the systematical views of a profound, dogmatic religious thinker.

The emplotment of A Maggot allows the reader to see the story through the eyes of some very unconventional narrators—the kind of characters whose voice in the world of letters takes on, in most cases, a vicarious nature, and is related through the words of some or other porte-parole. It is as if, in The French Lieutenant's Woman, we could have access to Ernestina's version of her fiancé's aborted elopement with Sarah. True piety and real compassion pertain to ordinary people, rather than to extraordinary characters and titanic figures; this seems the major lesson to be learned from Fowles's novel. Twenty years after the publication of The French Lieutenant's Woman, everybody must have come to the realization that Sarah and Charles belonged to stardom long before Meryl Streep and Jeremy Irons acted them out for the screen.

There is another provisional conclusion to be drawn from this chapter. How does Fowles's implied author, in A Maggot, overcome the twofold limitation inherent in the role of the scribe, namely, the arbitrariness of its speaking sources and the compositeness of its reading audience? A scribe cannot influence the order and the duration of the chronicle, nor the syntax and the speech type(s) which structure the chronicle, nor the audience to which the chronicle is addressed. And yet it is through the orchestration of a variety of heteroglot voices and speech types, through the unfolding and systematic dispersion of the plot line into multiple levels of fictionality,[17] through an imposing array, in other words, of modern and postmodern narrative devices, that the copyist of A Maggot orients dialogically its chronicle toward those components of the literary community with which A Maggot shares the *questions* which justify its existence as a work of art. The perplexing dissonances of the polyphonic choir which tells innumerable conflicting and/or fraudulent stories about Mr. Bartholomew's journey to the cavern—innumerable half-truths, quasi-truths, and lies—are mere modulations in human relationships[18] to this selected audience, occasions to share rather than to observe the uncodable tropes of the *hoi polloi*.

III

In the second ending of *The French Lieutenant's Woman* one can detect the embryonic presence of two conflicting existential stances.

On the one hand, Sarah's inability to compromise with the conventions of a patriarchal culture turns her into a mystery impenetrable to Charles's understanding and empathy, into an opaque, almost condescending figure—the prefigurement of one of those "modern women" whom the implied author of *The French Lieutenant's Woman* "never understood" (80). Her basic fiction—that she has given herself to the French lieutenant—dupes "the Victorian age in an escape that is also a mockery of the age's imprisoning forces" (Eddins 51). She manipulates Charles in order to free herself from the manipulation of the age's artifice (Eddins 51). "I believe I was right to destroy what had begun between us," Sarah tells Charles when they meet in Mr. Rossetti's house in London. "There was a falsehood in it" (351).

On the other hand, Charles's last meeting with Sarah turns him into an image of virile endurance. When he leaves Mr. Rossetti's house in London, where Sarah lives as a permanent guest, Charles perceives the image of his beloved under a surprisingly different light. She is not a sphinx any more. His future life will not need the presence of a sphinx any more; it will not be "a riddle and one's failure to guess it" (366). His destiny will not depend on the winning or losing throw of a die. He steps out of the comfort of two ordered Victorian images of sex-gender—Sarah and Ernestina, the *femme fatale* and the orthodox companion, the riddle and its reassuring solution, the disquieting sphinx and the unquestioning, "trained-to-grace" (122) wife—into "the unadorned chaos of reality" (Eddins 52). The conflict between Charles and Sarah epitomizes the conflict between the sexes; a necessary, never-ending one. Nobody wins and nobody loses, in the end; but the awareness of this ineradicable wall constitutes a painful and perennial reminder of our fractured condition as human beings.

It is often argued that Fowles's fiction is characterized by the myth of male supremacy (Woodcock ch. 1 and ch. 6). The second ending of *The French Lieutenant's Woman* seems to confirm this hypothesis, and works like *Mantissa, The Ebony Tower, The Magus*, could be referred to in order to suggest the presence of a phallocentric world view in Fowles's fiction. Even if there may be a grain of truth in such a viewpoint, putting a special emphasis on the theme of male supremacy is likely to be detrimental to a proper interpretation of Fowles's gender-related images. After all, as we have seen, *A Maggot* was written to honor the birth of Ann Lee, the founder of a religious sect which attributed the feminine gender to the members of the Christian Trinity.

If it is undeniable that one of the masculine images most recurrent in Fowles's narrative is that of the Priapus,[19] we must also keep in mind how crucial the image of female virginity is to the economy of Fowles's works.[20] Two opposite images—the perennial erection and the inviolate hymen—find simultaneous representation in Fowles's fiction.[21] These obviously gender-related images are also related to temporal genre (Mitchell 103). Their common denominator is a state of frozen, suspended temporality, which reflects, on the one hand, "the absolute dissociation" (Fawkner 90) of man entering the timeless universe of myth and, on the other hand, "the frustrated longing and sexual irresolution stemming out of courtly love" (Woodcock 19). Two archetypes of the "eternal feminine," the classical one derived from the Greek myths and the medieval one derived from the Celtic folklore, crystallize in the image of the forever postponed sexual encounter, the "presentness beyond all time" (Fowles, *Daniel Martin* 46) which turns all of Fowles's male characters into perennial travelers toward "woman as fertile mother and mystic virgin" (Fowles, "The Trouble with Starlets" 18), toward woman as the unreachable repository of myth. The figures of Tristam and Lancelot, as well as those of Odysseus and Theseus, are the obvious literary references in this context.

Mitchell's iconological approach to the politics of genres (ch.4) illustrates how so many of Fowles's male characters participate in this reduction of feminine archetypes to frozen images of timeless magic, mystery, enchantment, myth. Fowles's female characters, on their part, acquiesce to the appropriation of their image as the projection of their male companions' archetypes only in order to radically disrupt the implications of such appropriation. This is why Fowles's female characters, in general, belong both to time and to timelessness (Fawkner 90). Sarah, in *The French Lieutenant's Woman*, and Lily-Julie, in *The Magus*, amplify the image of the unreachable, impenetrable woman, this personified duality in time, by subverting its mythical connotations. They confront Charles's and Nicholas's self-images by forcing the two men to experience the "living effect of the myth" (Jung 270-71). This amounts to arguing that in the space of Fowles's dominant tropes we witness the creative interplay between man's anxiety to imagine a terminal, unalterable state of things, and the spontaneous impulses that drive History on.

But can genres of images and images of gender convey the entirety of a writer's sexual politics? Perhaps, but in Fowles's case they should not. They can because their figurative basis, once properly understood, discloses the ideology which underlies the sexual conflict in the writer's work. But we should not fall prey to their misleading simplifications because we know that Fowles, of all people, cannot possibly be unaware that his most recurrent verbal images of gender—the perennial erection and the inviolate hymen—are images of exclusion and appropriation, or, in other words, fetishistic aberrations. Their untimeliness, their suspension of happening, can be properly understood only when seen *in toto*, like a condensed icon, or like what Mitchell calls (67) a "super-dense" symbol—a syntactically and semantically "continuous" text, in other words, in which every tiny element achieves its significance in the specific system of narratological relations to which it belongs.

IV

We may now try to articulate the relationship between the politics of genre which lies behind Fowles's gender-related images and its literary references. We will see at work, in this relationship, a realignment between gender-related images as represented in past literary traditions and the forms of their representation in the present. Such realignment overcomes the limitations inherent in the images derived from our literary past by proceeding to aggregate such images in a congeries of disconcerting arrangements—a patently fraudulent disrupture of the homogeneity between sources and modes of emplotment. It is not accidental that Fowles's self-imposed selection of literary sources reminds us of the limitations experienced by the copyist who transcribes the depositions given by Rebecca, David, and Mr. Lacy in *A Maggot*. Nor is it accidental that the constraints imposed on Fowles by his sources and those imposed on the scribe in *A Maggot* by his profession are both neutralized by the dialogical orientation of the narrative toward the components of the literary community which share with Fowles's fictions the questions which justify their existence as works of art.

The (self-) immolation of the conventional image of the writer in *A Maggot* parallels the (self-) immolation of most of the male protagonists in Fowles's novels and stories—from Clegg in *The Collector* to Nicholas in *The Magus*, from Charles in *The French Lieutenant's Woman* to David in "The Ebony Tower"—upon the altar of the *Camelot syndrome*, "this whole Celtic thing" of courtly love, mystic quest, and search for identity which Fowles sees as "seminal in the history of fiction" (Fowles, "A Personal Note" 110). The whole body of Fowles's narrative may be seen as a sequence of variations on the medieval *contes d'aventure et d'amour*. *Eliduc*, the piece Marie de France wrote between about 1165 and 1185 and Fowles translated and included in his first collection of short stories, *The Ebony Tower*, narrates of the conflict experienced by Eliduc, a Breton knight, between and within "gallantry" and "loyalty" (Loveday 83, 87). "The Ebony Tower," the story from which Fowles's collection takes its title, tells of a modern knight errant, David, torn between an elusive "damsel," Diana the Mouse, whom he meets in an isolated house surrounded by the magic landscape of Brittany, and his bourgeois wife, Beth. Through a revisitation of the enduring type personified by the knight errant, Fowles imagines the ultimate solution to the dilemma experienced by most of his male characters. The image of Tristan and Yseult lying side by side, a sword or a thorny bush positioned between their bodies, is the central icon to the interpretation of his story; the ancillary icon is that of the knight killing the dragon to save the princess. But in "The Ebony Tower" it is David's wife, Beth, who has the face of the "sacrificial and to-be-saved-princess," while the figure of the beloved damsel, Diana the Mouse, is "cast as dragon" (92).

This variation on the theme of courtly love disrupts the apparent homogeneity between the original source and the tropological perspective of the writer. On the one hand, we encounter the knight errant, who cannot endure the proximity of his beloved damsel unless a cutting blade or a bunch of thorns guarantees at one and the same time the chastity of such tempting closeness and his faithfulness to the agency of his superior duties. On the other hand, we encounter Fowles's postmodern male hero, who finds in the very woman who is permanently beside him, be it wife, companion or lover, both the sacred, untouchable "mystic virgin" and the Panic, sensuous "fertile mother"—a factual, historically concrete woman, in other words, who personifies both the riddle and the agency that informs its open-ended, disconcerting solution in terms of (self-) immolation.

V

How does this reading of Fowles's politics of genre differ from the interpretation of the critics who accuse Fowles of a phallocentric world view? What contribution does this reading bring to our analysis of the narrative text as historical artifact? Let's recall our point of departure. The sources adopted by or made available to the author of the historical novel are mental, verbal, pictorial, perceptual images, modes of representation informed by a given ideology. The first thing that should follow from such assumption—from such grouping of historical sources under the unifying heading of "imagery"—is the abolition of the reified fragmentation and thus separation of sexual, political, philosophical, and ontological rhetorics of images. Another consequence, directly linked to the first, is that our reading of the historical novel should operate as "a kind of relay" (Mitchell 2), grafting the constellation of mental, verbal, pictorial, perceptual images which set in motion the narration into the overarching tropological (re)construction of History which is found in the narration itself. The coalescing-and-diverging of genres of images and of images of gender we find in Fowles's narrative prefigures, therefore, a coalescing and diverging of dominant and counterdominant images, an original effort of engagement of those very rhetorics of images which the history of ideology has recurrently conflated and turned apart.

Seen as such unitary whole, Fowles's fiction evokes the image of a long, tentative journey among the perilous straits of a variety of existential dichotomies. Male versus female, of course, but also freedom versus oppression, submission versus emancipation, knowledge versus ignorance, authenticity versus falsity, compassion versus inclemency; Fowles's fiction ought to be grasped as the precipitate from the solution of *all* these rhetorics of images. Fowles conceives wo/man as a solitary walker whose path bifurcates endlessly. A choice between two opposite directions has to be made each time, and yet no choice can ever be the final, optimal one. While the destinies of Fowles's characters are meant to depict paradigmatic images of our fractured condition as human beings, they suggest at the same time that our possibility of individual emancipation lies in the very struggle against the un-wholeness, against the one-sidedness of such fractured condition.

So much for fictional characters, so much for human beings. But what about the existential stance of the author himself? As we have seen above, the implied author is personified by two quite opposite figures in the pages of *The French Lieutenant's Woman* and of *A Maggot*. In the first novel we meet a pretentious-looking, overdressed man, with a touch of the successful impresario about him ("the kind of man who travels first class or not at all" [364]); an all-powerful Master of Ceremonies who manipulates the time sequence of his narrative at will. In *A Maggot* we meet a silent, humble scribe. Between these two extreme images there is room, of course, for an infinite number of variations on the figure of the implied author as an intruder within the universe of his own narration. As a generic rule, we may assume that the closer the implied author's persona is to the all-powerful and omniscient condition of a god, the narrower is the range of existential choices which is left open to his characters; in narratological terms, the closer to omniscience is the narrative mode, the closer are its fictional characters to puppet-like creatures.

In *The French Lieutenant's Woman*, the implied author abuses the free will of his characters in order to subjugate them to a pre-given structural typology of historical interpretation, an original and richly articulated metahistorical approach to the actualization of their individual destinies. In *A Maggot*, the implied author is metamorphosed into the persona of a scribe, who passively transcribes the depositions given to the inquirer by a few servants.

In their radical difference, both positions—the first corresponding to the image of an omniscient narrator, the second corresponding to the image of a humble copyist, an amanuensis—are emblematic of one of the major ideological dilemmas experienced by any writer of fiction. Fowles shows himself to be acutely aware of this issue when he declares: "[writers] wish to create worlds as real as, but other than the world that is" (*French Lieutenant* 81). When Fowles's critics argue that the image of male supremacy conveys the innermost substance of the author's existential preoccupations, they mistake a symptom for a cause. Male supremacy is just a surface manifestation, a thematic imaging of the dilemma hidden behind most of Fowles's works, namely, the unresolved and possibly irresolvable enigma of the artist's dominion over his/her own materials.

As I mentioned in the first part of this essay, two opposite causal forces coexist within the plot of *The French Lieutenant's Woman*: casual chance and existential self-determination. Self-determination leads to the ultimate order-making force in the economy of Charles's and Sarah's lives, and casual chance to the chaos-making motive. However, it may be argued that in the fiction-making process, from which originates the narrative of this novel, the very structuring of the chaotic background against which Charles and Sarah will enact their "free" choices is the main vehicle of actualization for Fowles's own artistic freedom.

An analogy with the work of the professional historian may be appropriate here. The enterprise of "making sense" out of the fragmented, dispersed, virtually infinite constellations of historical monuments and documents available to the historian imposes, as a necessary first step, a process of selection and exclusion. Out of an overwhelmingly chaotic universe of unconnected, randomly distributed information, the historian structures, as a point of departure for his future work of interpretation, a specific, workable "chaotic" background. This initial background is chaotic insofar as it constitutes nothing more than the supportive skeleton of the historian's subsequent work, the canvas upon which a foreground of historical images will take on shape and substance. But this initial background is never the result of a capricious or erratic selection of historical materials. It may be argued, in fact, that its narrative patterns embody already the master tropes which will eventually encode the facts contained in the subsequent effort of historical interpretation. In a work of History, for instance, the understanding of a political revolution will be qualified by the very nature of the chaotic social and political and cultural universe adopted by the historian as the historical background the revolution under consideration struggles against and emerges from.

The same seems to be true for the writer of historical novels, once the proper differences are taken into account. The creation of a specific, workable background, the delimitation of the boundaries within which the assemblage of a great number of dominant and counter-dominant images constitutes a suitable texture for the still unwritten narrative, is equivalent to a declaration of creative independence and originality on the part of the author. By structuring a specific kind of historical background, the writer commits herself to a specific kind of fiction: the foreground of possible strategies of self-determination for her characters will be circumscribed from the very start by the specific nature of the historical paradigms with which she envelopes their actions and deeds.

We may now consider from a slightly different angle the issues related to the occurrence of multiple levels of fictionality within a historical novel.

In *A Maggot*, as we have repeatedly mentioned and commented upon, a number of conflicting versions of the same facts are related by Mr. Bartholomew's servants, and a final version of the facts can never be established by Henry Ayscough, or by the reader, with reasonable certainty.

A similar modality is found in *The French Lieutenant's Woman*. First of all, the novel provides the reader with three different endings: the two well-known and often referred-to endings (Chapters 60 and 61), plus a conventionally Victorian one (Chapter 45). Secondly, a number of conflicting versions of the origin of Sarah's nickname (the French Lieutenant's Woman, or, in the diction of the vulgus, the French Lieutenant's Whore) are presented to the reader. The first version, which consists of a virginal version of Sarah's elopement with Varguennes, the French lieutenant, is related to Mrs. Poulteney, Sarah's bigoted employer, by the vicar of Lyme Regis. The conclusion of the vicar's story conveys a crypto-Romantic judgment on Sarah's experience: "[Sarah] is not insane. Far from it. She is perfectly able to perform any duties that can be given to her. But she suffers from grave attacks of melancholia. They are doubtless partly attributable to remorse. But also, I fear, to her fixed delusion that the lieutenant is an honorable man and will one day return to her. For that reason she may be frequently seen haunting the sea approaches to our town" (33). The second version of Sarah's elopement is offered by Sarah herself to Charles, during one of their secret meetings on Ware Commons. This version of her elopement is concluded with an admission of guilt ("I gave myself to him") and a strong-willed self-justification ("I did it so that I should never be the same again" [142]). The third version of the elopement, again, is given to Charles by Sarah, after he has made love to her. A few minutes earlier she was still a virgin. She had not sinned with Varguennes. ("I saw [Varguennes] come out [of the inn]. With a woman. The kind of woman one cannot mistake. I drew into a doorway." [278]). Yet, this striking revelation is immediately followed by another surprise, by one more lie. The limp, the strained ankle that made Sarah appear so subdued and defenseless in Charles's eyes, right before they fell into each other's arms, was but a new, unforgivable deception. She cold-mindedly seduced him! "Yes," she admits. "I have deceived you. But I shall not trouble you again" (278).

The French Lieutenant's Woman is characterized by this never-ending, ceaseless flow of conflicting levels of un-truth, quasi-truth, semi-truth. The reader, for instance, will never know for certain what values or aspirations does the symbolic image of the French lieutenant, Varguennes, evoke in Sarah's mind. The one positive piece of information the reader is given about Sarah—that is, her virginal condition after the affair with Varguennes is over—comes as a revelation, out of a situation in which she is, once more, the liar, the deceiver, the hysteric. When Charles enters her room in the Exeter hotel, where she has been staying since leaving Lyme Regis, Sarah is sitting by the fire, "so pinioned, so invalid" (271). She is simulating, in fact, a limp; the same handicap, by the way, suffered by Varguennes after he recovered from his injury at sea. Sarah gives herself to Charles, a man who, like Varguennes, in her very words, "would never violate a woman against her will" (142). The slow metamorphosis of herself into the lover of the "young god" (178) which Varguennes could not possibly be but that Charles might plausibly be changed into, and the simultaneous metamorphosis of Charles into the man she "knelt before" and who "raised" her to her feet (178), are, after all, two of the most intriguing and fascinating threads within Fowles's narrative. The Exeter hotel where Charles and Sarah consummate their clandestine love is not too dissimilar from the inn in Weymouth where Sarah, according to the second version of her elopement (the first version given to Charles by herself), slept with Varguennes. "It was not . . . a respectable place," she had confessed to Charles. "I was told where his room was and expected to go up to it. I insisted he be sent for." An analogous experience to Sarah's in Weymouth occurs to Charles in the shabby hall of the Exeter hotel. "You must go up, Sir," the landlady says to Charles. And he answers, "Would you please send to ask if my visit were not better put off till she is recovered?" After saying these words, Charles "remembered Varguennes; sin was to meet in privacy" (270).

In *A Maggot*, too, the reader never manages to know for sure what happened in the mysterious cavern where Mr. Bartholomew, Dick, and Rebecca met the "women in silver." Did Mr. Bartholomew leave the planet aboard a spaceship? Was he killed by Rebecca, whom David Jones saw entering the cavern holding a knife in her hand? Were the "women in silver" local witches or visitors from outer space? Was Dick a moron, Mr. Bartholomew's mentor, a nonhuman creature, a resurrected medieval knight?

The heteroglossic voices of the servants, their divergent versions of the events which occurred during the journey toward the cavern, keep the plot of *A Maggot* in a permanent state of quasi-truthfulness which borders occasionally—particularly in the case of David Jones's deposition—on the realm of mere falsehood. By abdicating the all-powerful omniscience of the pretentious "impresario" who narrates the story of *The French Lieutenant's Woman*, the implied author's impersonation of a humble and passive scribe, in *A Maggot*, achieves that very blend of truth and un-truth, of reality and unreality, that I perceive as one of the canonic elements of postmodern fiction.

The Muses from Hesiod's *Theogony* come to mind. The heteroglot voices which disperse the plot line of *A Maggot* into multiple levels of fictionality, into innumerable conflicting and/or fraudulent stories, may almost be heard singing the Muses' words in an undertone: "We know how to tell numerous lies which seem to be truthful, but whenever we wish we know how to utter the full truth" (Hesiod 24). The authentic *porte-parole* of this seducing, polyphonic chant is the silent scribe, John Tudor, who "ventriloquates" (Bakhtin 299) the depositions of the servants. In a brief conversation with Rebecca, John Tudor's words echo quite explicitly the credo of Hesiod's Muses. "[Writing in] the short hand . . . . 'Tis a child's play, once learnt," he declares. "And where I cannot read when I copy in the long hand, why, I make it up. So I may hang a man, or pardon him, and none the wiser" (349). In typical postmodern fashion, Fowles's voice cannot "sound" (Bakhtin 278) outside of the "social dialogue" which constitutes the Tower of Babel mixing of heteroglossia surrounding his object of narration.

It is in the forever postponed occurrence of an ultimate and undisputable truth, in the closure of the narration before the longed-for final revelation takes place, in the ceaseless dialogical modulation between the implied author's discourse and the diversity of alien discourses revolving around the same object, that lie the most original contributions made by John Fowles to the canons of postmodern fiction. In his works truth and falsehood coalesce while diverging. Dominant and counterdominant images intertwine in a carrousel of infinitesimal approximations to the actualization of individual fates. Identity and piety are the inward- and outward-oriented motions toward self-determination, the *primum mobile* of human existence, which eludes History while making histories.

Notes

1. I am echoing here W. J. T. Mitchell's Introduction to *Iconology.*

2. The origins of this hypothesis can be found in the second and third chapter of H. White's *Tropics of Discourse.*

3. This version of Sarah's nickname (it means "the French Lieutenant's Whore") is used by the lower strata of the town population.

4. See the deposition—involuntarily allusive—of David Jones, in Fowles, *A Maggot* 198:
> "Q. [Was Dick] a melancholy fellow?"
> "A. Simple, Sir, as if he had dropped from the moon."

5. See Fowles, *A Maggot* 50: "[this] time has little power of seeing people other than they are in outward; which applies even to how they see themselves, labelled and categorized by circumstance and fate."

6. These words are found in the deposition given by Rebecca Hocknell (Fowles, *A Maggot* 356, 362).

7. The image of a sprig of violets in the mouth of Dick's corpse is a symbol of resurrection derived from the Celtic tradition of the courtly romance. (See for instance Guilliadun's resurrection in *Eliduc,* Fowles's translation of the medieval tale written by Marie de France.) This image adds the character of Dick, this "fellow dropped from the

moon," to the long list of Fowlesian male characters dominated by what Fowles calls the *Camelot syndrome* (Fowles, "A Personal Note" 110).

8. See also, for the definition of the aura of the work of art, Benjamin, "Mechanical Reproduction" 223.

9. I am referring to Giovanni Boccaccio's *Decameron*, Pietro Aretino's *Ragionamenti*, Italo Calvino's *Favole Italiane*.

10. I am borrowing this term from the definition of speech types, or *heteroglossia (raznorecie)*, which can be found in M. M. Bakhtin, 263.

11. The notion of "literary community" can be found in H. R. Jauss's *Toward an Aesthetic of Reception* (74).

12. I am using the term *metahistory* according to the definition given in White ch. 2.

13. My notion of "dispersed" histories is an elaboration on Jauss's concept of "plural histories" (46-47).

14. I am referring in particular to Michel Foucault, *Les mots et les choses*, ch. III *(Représenter)*.

15. The ontological radicalism of this ending, which maybe transcends Fowles's intentions, can be fully appreciated if one keeps in mind the role assigned to the experience of fatherhood by Emmanuel Levinas in *Le temps et l'autre*.

16. I am referring in particular to the images of "historical subject" and of "messianic suspension of happening" expressed by Benjamin in "Theses on the Philosophy of History" XVII 262-63.

17. This rhetoric of images, which assimilates the discourse in the novel to the symphonic orchestration of a musical theme, is derived from Bakhtin, "Discourse in the Novel." See in particular Bakhtin 263-64, 279-80.

18. Fowles, *The French Lieutenant's Woman*: "Moments like modulations come in human relationships: when what . . . is sufficient merely to classify under some general heading . . . becomes, by empathy, instantaneously shared rather than observed" (115).

19. See for instance the seduction scene between Rebecca and Dick in *A Maggot*: "both [Dick's] hands clutch, as a drowning man a branch, . . . a large, naked and erect penis, . . .[a] monstrous bloodfilled glans" (28). Or see the oppressive presence of the statue of the priapic god in the garden of Conchis, in *The Magus*: "['a] bronze manikin with a grotesquely enormous erect phallus" (84). Or see, last but not least, the quote from *Carmina Priapea* in Chapter 39 of *The French Lieutenant's Woman*: "You'd like to know why the girl kisses this spear of mine, even though I'm made of wood? . . . . 'Let's hope,' she's thinking, 'that men will use this spear on me—and brutally'" (239).

20. In *The French Lieutenant's Woman*, both Sarah and Ernestina are virgins. In *The Magus*, the character of Lily-Julie manages to preserve her virginal attributes in

defiance of all evidence to the contrary; those virginal attributes are the source of bewitching seductiveness that both her sister June and Alison, Nicholas's girlfriend, lack.

21. The most extreme personification of such state of sexual irresolution is found in *The Collector*, Fowles first published novel. Miranda Grey tells her apparently harmless kidnapper, Frederick Clegg, that he is "like Tantalus" (96). And later on she decides that in order to be freed by him she must "let him do . . . what they call Scotch love. Get me into bed if he wants. Play with me if he wants. But not the final thing" (217).

Works Cited

Bakhtin, M. M. "Discourse in the Novel." *The Dialogic Imagination*. Austin: U of Texas P, 1986.

Benjamin, Walter. "The Work of Art in the Age of Mechanical Reproduction." "Theses on the Philosophy of History." *Illumination*. New York: Schocken Books, New York, 1969.

Binns, Ronald. "John Fowles: Radical Romancer." *Critical Essays on John Fowles*. Ed. Ellen Pifer. Boston: G. K. Hall, 1986.

de Man, Paul. *Blindness and Insight*. Minneapolis: U of Minnesota P, Minneapolis, 1983.

Eddins, Dwight. "John Fowles: Existence as Authorship." *Critical Essays on John Fowles*. Ed. Ellen Pifer. Boston: G. K. Hall, 1986.

Fawkner, H. W. *The Timescapes of John Fowles*. London: Fairleigh Dickinson UP, 1984.

Foucault, Michel. *Les mots et les choses*. Paris: Gillimard, 1966.

Fowles, John. *The Aristos*. Boston: Little, Brown, 1970.

———. *The Collector*. New York: Dell, 1974.

———. *Daniel Martin*. Boston: Little, Brown, 1977.

———. "The Ebony Tower." *The Ebony Tower*. New York: Signet, 1975.

———. *The French Lieutenant's Woman*. New York: Signet, 1969.

———. *A Maggot*. New York: Signet, 1986.

———. *The Magus*. A Revised Version, Suffolk: Triad/Granada, 1983.

———. "A Personal Note." *The Ebony Tower*. New York: Signet, 1975.

———. *A Short History of Lyme Regis*. Boston: Little, Brown, 1982.

———. "The Trouble With Starlets." *Holiday* 39 (June 1966).

Genette, Gérard. *Narrative Discourse*. Ithaca: Cornell UP, 1985.

Hesiod. *Theogony. The Poems of Hesiod.* Trans. R. M. Frazer. Norman: U of Oklahoma P, 1986.

Iser, Wolfgang. "Feigning in Fiction." *The Identity of the Text.* Chicago: U of Chicago P, 1985.

Jauss, Hans Robert. "History of Art and Pragmatic History." *Toward an Aesthetic of Reception.* Minneapolis: U of Minnesota P, 1982.

Jung, C. G. *The Archetypes and the Collective Unconscious.* Vol. 9 of *Collected Works of C. G. Jung.* Trans. R. F. C. Hull. London: Routledge and Kegan Paul, 1959. 18 vols.

Leopardi, Giacomo. *Inno a Nettuno and Odae Adespotae. Versi and Paralipomeni della Batracomiomachia.* Bari: Laterza, 1921.

Levinas, Emmanuel. *Le temps et l'autre.* Paris: Quadridge, P Universitaires de France, 1979.

Loveday, Simon. *The Romances of John Fowles.* New York: St. Martin's, 1985.

Mitchell, W. J. T. *Iconology.* Chicago: U of Chicago P, 1986.

Nabokov, Vladimir. *Lolita.* New York: Berkley, 1985.

White, Hayden. *Tropics of Discourse.* Baltimore: Johns Hopkins UP, 1986.

Woodcock, Bruce. *Male Mythologies: John Fowles and Masculinity.* Brighton, Sussex: Harvester, 1984.

Chapter 7

Faces, Photos, Mirrors:
Image and Ideology in the Novels of John le Carré

James M. Buzard

I

George Smiley's colleagues in the beleaguered British Secret Service cannot understand why the taciturn Smiley hangs a photograph of Karla, his mysterious Moscow Centre opposite number, on the wall of his office at the Cambridge Circus headquarters. In *The Honourable Schoolboy*, having taken the helm of a thoroughly "blown" Service after leading the investigation to expose Karla's mole, Bill Haydon, Smiley begins with his decimated staff to take "back bearings" through the labyrinth of departmental files and memos in order to learn which operations, if any, remain secure and which have been either directed or shut down by Haydon on orders from Karla himself. In the "dingy throne room" of the former Circus chief, Control, Smiley installs his picture of Karla—"a passport photograph by the look of it, but blown up far beyond its natural size, so that it had a grainy and, some said, spectral look" (*Schoolboy* 44). This unusual decoration quickly evokes interdepartmental comment and speculation. Ironically, a Treasury official visiting Smiley's office mistakes the photo for one of Control—he assumes Smiley to be paying an ordinary tribute to the Circus tradition from which he has emerged. Those in the know, however, arrive at different conclusions. The insufferable Roddy Martindale insinuates that the photo betrays Smiley's unprofessional private obsession with the Soviet master spy who has bedeviled him for years: "It seems we've got a real vendetta on our hands. How puerile can you get, I wonder?" (*Schoolboy* 44). Oliver Lacon, Smiley's liaison with the Foreign Office, questions Smiley about the wisdom of placing such a curious icon at the center of all Circus activity:

> "Now, seriously, why do you hang him there, George?" he demanded, in his bold, head prefect's voice. . . . "What does he mean to you, I wonder? Have you thought about that one? It isn't a little macabre, you don't think? The victorious enemy? I'd have thought he would get you down, gloating over you all up there?"

"Well, Bill's *dead*," said Smiley, who had a habit sometimes of giving a clue to an argument, rather than the argument itself.

"And Karla's alive, you mean?" Lacon prompted. "And you'd rather have a live enemy than a dead one? Is that what you mean?" (*Schoolboy* 44-45)

In this 1977 work, John le Carré depicts Smiley's rededication to the Service after the repeated disillusionments the aging spy has suffered, and the many painful compromises he has endured, through five previous novels.[1] In his personal no less than in his professional affairs, Smiley is "cleaning house": he expunges every trace of Haydon from the Circus offices; he has the walls and furniture broken in order to search for hidden microphones (many are found); he calls in all operatives put in jeopardy by Haydon's fall; and he forsakes "his beautiful, if occasionally errant wife," Lady Ann (the most notorious of whose many lovers, acting on Karla's instigation, was none other than Bill Haydon himself). Smiley's "spectral" photo of Karla presides over this new beginning. Fixing the image of the elusive opponent before Smiley's gaze, the photograph inspires a new clearness and narrowness of focus, a concentration of energies for the work that lies ahead. It seems to say *here is the real being behind all the tangled deceptions I have traced; here is the one object of my labors.* Never losing sight of that ultimate end, Smiley will make his way through the tortuous complexities of two major cases—the subjects of *The Honourable Schoolboy* and *Smiley's People*—to arrive, at last, face to face with the human Karla.

Why, finally, does Smiley hang the Karla photo? What drives him to return, yet again, to his thankless career? In a manner characteristic of le Carré's novels, *The Honourable Schoolboy* offers at this point a number of possible motives for the spy's enigmatic behavior. Yet equally characteristic is the way in which the foregrounded question of motive remains unresolved, remains present in le Carré's narrative as a daunting challenge to interpreters both inside and outside the text. Each of the three explanations put forth by Smiley's colleagues is correct in its own limited sense; and each addresses a recurrent motif of le Carré's fiction. Roddy Martindale is right: there is unquestionably a personal vendetta in Smiley's renewed pursuit of Karla. But from the first Smiley novel to the last—from *Call for the Dead* (1961) to *Smiley's People* (1980)—all of Smiley's antagonists have had uncomfortably close personal ties to the British spymaster, causing Smiley's personal, professional, and political loyalties to coalesce into an amalgam of thought and feeling that must be taken as a whole rather than dissolved into its artificially isolated constituents.[2] Any rigorous personal/professional or personal/political dichotomy is also disallowed by the subtle yet consistent subtext of le Carré's Smiley novels: the subtext that casts Smiley as the Saint George of modern England, an unlikely hero for a weakened nation in an uncertain age. On this level, the constant questions raised, but never fully answered, about Smiley's personal motives become questions about the condition of a postimperial England whose degraded marginality in the international alignment grows ever more apparent to its secret servants. "What was there left," Martindale demands, "*anywhere* in beastly Whitehall—or, Lord help us, in beastly *England,* that could command [Smiley's seemingly single-minded devotion]?" (*Schoolboy* 43).[3] This rhetorical question—implying that there is, transparently, *nothing* left in England to explain Smiley's dedication—justifies for Martindale the partial "vendetta" conclusion.

Oliver Lacon, too, is right: Smiley does want a "live" enemy; though once again the explanation is qualified and complicated by considerations beyond the merely personal. Smiley employs the photo of Karla to spur his own activities, to give them purpose. "Two halves of the same apple," as the old Sovietologist Connie Sachs puts it in *Smiley's People,* Smiley and Karla are locked in a dialectical struggle, Smiley seeking to define himself in contrast to the menacing Other (*People* 211). Karla's photo becomes, in effect, a mirror for Smiley: the looming presence of Karla's image reminds the British spy of the threatening object against which his own function and identity are measured. *If that is the enemy,* the photograph invites Smiley to conclude, *then I know what I am.* The dialectic in which the photographic image participates also yields implications for the political allegory that underwrites Smiley and Karla's individual interactions: *if that image represents the international opponent,* it seems to say, *then we know what we must be to combat it.* Whatever corruption befalls the England for which Smiley strives, a sense of its collective identity may be shored up by focusing on the image of the potent opponent, who works uncompromisingly in the service of an ideology that subordinates the individual to the collective idea.

Even the mistaken Treasury official is right, in one important sense, about the meaning of the photograph hanging on Smiley's office wall: Smiley uses the photo of Karla, as he might have used a photo of Control, to locate himself in a tradition of service, to see himself in a continuous, intelligible "story" of his life and work. As it happens, the story is that of Smiley's own continuing struggle with Karla (and allegorically, that of West's struggle with East); but functionally it matters little whether it is this story or the story of pious consciousness of Circus tradition (the story that would be implied by Smiley's hanging a picture of Control in his office) that drives the British spymaster onward in his work. What matters, finally, is that the photograph is *useful* for a particular effect, and that it is so by providing a narrative of purpose for Smiley's endeavors: for whatever reasons, in the face of whatever disillusionments, Smiley continues, the West continues, and the work at hand is carried through.

Critics have long identified the relentless concern with motivation as a feature that sets le Carré's fiction apart from the standard espionage "plot thriller." As early as 1965 Umberto Eco distinguished the antipsychological "objective

structural strategy" in Ian Fleming's James Bond novels from the intense interest in human motivation evinced by le Carré's characters (Eco 146). Le Carré
has been both attacked and defended for his foregrounding of the private psychological processes of his protagonists. The Marxist critic Roger Bromley has
objected to what he calls le Carré's "evacuation . . . of the political (or, more
precisely, what is offered as the political) by a constant personal/political
antithesis which is resolved in terms of the 'personal'" (39-40). Yet the issue of
motive quickly becomes as great a morass for le Carre's readers as for his characters. With regard to Smiley's use of Karla's photograph, and indeed with
regard to all of the emotionally and politically charged actions of le Carre's
many spies, we need to distinguish between two readings of the recurrent question "Why does he/she do it?" One way of asking this question aims at the
human subject behind a given action: how can we explain this action as arising
from the intention (conscious or unconscious) of an integral psychological self?
Time and again in le Carré's novels this way of addressing the problem of
motive runs aground. From the earliest novels on, readers have watched le
Carré characters ruminate, as Smiley does in *A Murder of Quality* (1962), on
the unknowability of motive so conceived: "I don't believe," Smiley avers,
"that we can ever entirely know what makes anyone do anything" (130).
Already in this early novel we watch Smiley reflecting

> for the hundredth time on the obscurity of motive in human action: there is no
> true thing on earth. There is no constant, no dependable point, not even the
> purest logic or the most obscure mysticism; least of all in the motives of men
> when they are moved to act violently. (113)

To accept the constant invitation to consider this unanswerable question of
motive is to place oneself in the uncomfortable position of le Carré's protagonists themselves. Readers who take up the question of motive in this way commit themselves to the search for confirmation of a coherent volitional subject,
of a "constant" or "dependable point" from which to understand the complex
chains of events and the extraordinarily tangled narrative arrangements of le
Carré's novels. The spy's career is a series of deceptions, assumed identities,
fabricated stories; how can one hope to retrieve the underlying self, the true
story?

Another way of posing the question "why" seeks instead to understand for
what function, for what practical effect, the subject acts: that is, *in what way
does the action make the actor an effective agent for some specific end?* While
the first, subject-seeking, way of formulating the question is so regularly
offered to le Carré's readers and characters alike, no resolutions are finally
reached on this score of psychological investigation; meanwhile, effective
agency goes on, making use of le Carré's psychologically uncertain subjects as
agents. This is the manner in which we should consider Smiley's use of the

image of his Soviet opponent, and it is the manner in which we should consider the functioning of the many conflicted, "unhappy consciousnesses" who perform the espionage work of the West throughout le Carré's novels. The image of Karla is *used* by Smiley for numerous (ultimately unfathomable) reasons; the image is *of use* to Smiley, to England, to the West, because of the way it ideologically transforms Smiley into an effective agent. *Ideologically*, because the image encourages Smiley and his colleagues to formulate "stories," connections, traditions, narratives, that situate the agent as a vital, coherent, explicable subject; the photographic image and the various stories to which it gives rise all serve to name, to "hail" Smiley, to tell him who he is. To approach the function of the Other's image in this way is to invoke Louis Althusser's radical reconception of the Marxist concept of ideology: *"ideology hails or interpellates concrete individuals as subjects"* (173). Althusser's examination of the central ambiguity of "subject" might be taken as a description of what happens to the agents inhabiting the espionage world of John le Carré's fiction:

> In the ordinary use of the term, subject in fact means: (1) a free subjectivity, a centre of initiatives, author of and responsible for its actions: (2) a subjected being, who submits to a higher authority, and is therefore stripped of all freedom except that of freely accepting his submission. [Through ideology,] the individual *is interpellated as a (free) subject . . . in order that he shall (freely) accept his subjection*, i.e. in order that he shall make the gestures and actions of his subjection "all by himself." (182)

Ideology makes subjects by encouraging individuals to recognize themselves as psychologically, legally, and morally discrete entities. At the same time it makes of its illusory "subjects" effective agents for the continuation of the social order. Doggedly seeking that constant, "dependable point" that lies behind their and others' actions, le Carré's characters hold fast to the category of subjectivity even as their relentless duplicities and vacillations call it into question. And we need to keep in mind the two levels on which their persuasions operate. They rely on token images and tell themselves, and each other, stories to keep alive the the the illusion that constitutes Althusser's first meaning of "subject": the humanistic "center of initiatives, author of and responsible for its actions." On the level of political allegory, they sustain the notion of collective society that derives from this ideal free subjectivity: the Western ideology which proposes that the West has no ideology, that it has only its cherished

> way of life (national, democratic, humanist, individualist, natural) [that] contends with "communism" as an unnatural "ideology" superimposed by idealists, intellectuals, and/or power seekers on peoples to whom it is both foreign and frightening. (Barley 15)

By reconceiving the question of character motivation in this way, by considering the dialectical function of Karla's image—and the function of other photographic and mirror images throughout le Carré's work—one can gain a valuable perspective on the central ideological problem dramatized by le Carré's fiction: that of maintaining the illusion of a coherent Western (liberal humanist) subject in the face of considerable evidence of that subject's dispersal, corruption, or loss. In the following pages I will chart through three novels—*The Looking Glass War, Smiley's People*, and *A Perfect Spy*—the way in which le Carré's characters make use of photographs, mirrors, and faces ostensibly to confirm the integrity of the Western subject—the integrity, that is, of both individual subjects and of a positive, believable English or Western collective identity.[4] At the same time, I will argue that the novels can be read as undercutting that eagerly sought integrity by exposing the deceptions, illusions, and futile desires that give meaning to the photos, mirrors, and stories with which those characters continually bolster themselves. Such an argument will also necessarily impinge upon the debates concerning the status of the postmodern, for as I am characterizing them here, John le Carré's novels lend themselves well to Jean-François Lyotard's description of the postmodern's "incredulity toward metanarratives" (xxiv), evincing an incredulity toward those motivating stories le Carré's spies are always seeking, the predominant metanarrative of which is that tired old tale of Britain's and the West's leading role in the progressive destiny of humankind. But in the end it will be necessary to push beyond both Althusser and Lyotard in order to account for the deeply ambivalent messages le Carré's novels send their (Western) readers about the fates of the West's restless, relentlessly produced, quintessential subjects: its secret agents, fitfully laboring on the frontier between domestic (both private and national) and geopolitical exigencies.

II

An attempt to understand the role of photographic and mirror images in le Carré's work can best begin with an examination of his fourth novel, *The Looking Glass War* (1965), which evokes the illusory world of Lewis Carroll in mounting a strong criticism of the way nostalgia and self-perpetuating bureaucracy impel the unnecessary, misconceived, and disastrous efforts of a vestigial branch of the World War II War Intelligence Department. "Staffed by a handful of remnant veterans" and the young agent John Avery, the Department lost its *raison d'être* at the end of hostilities in 1945; in the twenty years since then, almost all its functions have been usurped by the offices in Cambridge Circus run by Control and Smiley and administered by the Foreign Office. Its charter now severely limited, the meagerly funded Department "seeks to perpetuate the spirit of some long-departed camaraderie" among its members, to instill in them some illusory purpose for continuing their operations (Barley 48-49). The novel details the final failure of the Department, the profoundly mishandled Operation Mayfly, in which the organization garners its few resources to send an agent into East Germany on a mission that proves, in the end, chimerical. The novel's title suggests that out of their own need to sustain the illusion of their necessity, the Department's members have projected a reflection of an enemy operation that may not even exist. *The Looking Glass War*, as le Carré has described it, is concerned with

> the phenomenon of committed men who are committed to nothing but one another and the dreams they collectively evoke. . . . The source of their energy lies not in the war of ideas [between East and West] but in their own desolate mentalities. ("To Russia" 5)

Photographs, a central element in all espionage activity, here play a crucial role both in the perpetuation of the Department's illusions and in the fatal decision to run the East German operation. Operation Mayfly has its origins in some undeveloped film, shot from an airplane, of what Leclerc and his colleagues are eager to believe is a large new military installation near Rostock. Taylor, the clumsy agent sent into Finland to retrieve the film, drinks too much while waiting for his contact in the airport bar, attracts too much attention, and, after receiving the film, is run down on the road to his hotel. The undeveloped film is lost. Was Taylor murdered by enemy agents seeking to recover the film? This is the conclusion that suits the Department's own interests, but le Carré hints that Taylor's death was an accident caused by his own drunkenness—he is stumbling in darkness on the wrong side of the road when the car strikes him.

Department head Leclerc summons the youthful Avery to his office for briefing on a "run" into Finland to recover Taylor's body and, if possible, the film. It is Avery's first campaign, and it begins with his taking note of the photographs with which Leclerc has decorated his office walls—images in their way as "spectral" and inspiring as Smiley's snapshot of Karla. Avery is "suddenly aware of the pictures round the room, of the boys who had fought in the war. They hung in rows of six, either side of the model of a Wellington bomber, rather a dusty one" (27). Leclerc's keepsake images of the men he had commanded in the war connect the Department to the bygone glories of purposeful wartime Britain; Leclerc can situate himself in the tradition of dedicated service represented by the photos, and Avery is to carry on that tradition. But of course the tradition, like the Wellington bomber, is, to say the least, "rather a dusty one." Le Carré describes the pictures and the signatures of the young men beneath them with a mixture of pathos and irony:

> There were no surnames, but sobriquets from children's magazines: Jacko, Shorty, Pip and Lucky Joe. . . . [The men] seemed to like having their photograph taken, as if being together were an occasion for laughter which might not be repeated. The men in front were crouching comfortably, like men used to crouching in gun turrets, and those behind had put their arms carelessly

over one another's shoulders. There was no affectation but a spontaneous goodwill which does not seem to survive war or photographs. (28)

Leclerc and his whole Department are an unnatural survival of the war; the empty forms and protocol of the wartime forces persist, but not the unaffected, confident purpose to be seen in Leclerc's photo display. As he gives Avery his commission, Leclerc is also preparing the larger mission that will send an agent into East Germany to survey the suspected new Communist military base. He shows Avery a photo of the man chosen for the job—Fred Leiser, a British-naturalized Pole who has not worked for the Department since 1945—and asks,

> "What do you make of a face like that?"
> "I don't know. It's hard to tell from photographs."
> It was the head of a boy, round and blank, with long, fair hair swept back.
> "Leiser. He *looks* all right, doesn't he? That was twenty years ago, of course," Leclerc said. "We gave him a very high rating." (26)

This early scene makes clear that Leclerc has dwelt for some time amid the comforting images of a past era. But the key pieces of evidence adduced in support of the new ambitious Operation Mayfly have come to hand only a month before. At the organizational meeting for the operation, Leclerc produces a set of snapshots passed on by the Department's old Hamburg agent, Jimmy Gorton; Gorton has purportedly received the pictures from an East German refugee named Fritsche who had worked as a railwayman near Rostock. The pictures are said to show a rocket launching pad under construction. Taking the enlarged photographs from the drawer of his desk to show them to his team, Leclerc is "smiling a little, like a man looking at his own reflection," and the group crowds around to examine the evidence. "Something was there":

> You could see it if you looked quickly; something hidden in the disintegrating shadows; but keep looking and the dark closed in and the shape was gone. Yet something was there—the muffled form of a gun barrel, but pointed and too long for its carriage, the suspicion of a transporter, a vague glint of what might have been a platform.
> "They would put protective covers over them, of course," Leclerc commented, studying their faces hopefully, waiting for their optimism. (52)

Less important for what they purport to represent than for their capacity to reflect the desires of their user, to substantiate the user's mythic sense of purpose and identity, the photographs featured in *The Looking Glass War* become, like Smiley's photo of Karla, mirrors. The pictures from the halcyon days of the Department consecrate Leclerc's desire for a story of unbroken, noble tradition in which to place himself and his Department. But the old photos of Jacko, Shorty, Pip, and Leiser remain images fixed in their remoteness, hinting provocatively of values that "[do] not seem to survive war or photographs"; the original meaning and context of the pictures are no more retrievable than the Fred Leiser of twenty years ago. The photographic image emerges from a history but cannot supply that history; instead its present users appropriate it and overlay it with a new meaning arising from their own "desolate mentalities," from their own needs and exigencies. In itself equivocal, forever susceptible to new uses and new stories, the image participates in the production and maintenance of the subject by illustrating the subject's self-confirming story of free and vital subjectivity. By extension, the story giving meaning to the Rostock photographs is, for Leclerc, a dialectical guarantee of the Department's continuing importance: the photos must be seen to show the efforts of a "live enemy" in order to support this Western collective subject.

But these reconnaissance images are equivocal in even a more direct sense. Not everyone in the Department is as quick to accept them on face value: Adrian Haldane, Leclerc's reluctant second-in-command, questions not only the poor quality of the exposures but the curious story Gorton has provided about how the Department obtained them. Fritsche is supposed to have escaped to the West by swimming across a river: but if so, "how did he preserve the film?" Given the photographer's story of shooting the film through the ventilator of a boxcar in siding near the suspected site, Haldane asks, "Why isn't there any trace of camera shake? He'd been drinking, he was balancing on tiptoe." And most important of all, since the Department knows that the defector attempted unsuccessfully to sell his pictures to the British Consulate, "Why did he give Gorton for nothing what he'd offered elsewhere for money?" (69). Later in the novel, after Leiser has already been trained for his mission, Haldane unearths some information that justifies this scepticism about Leclerc's cherished evidence. Searching through a file of "the depressing miscellany of rogues, double agents and lunatics who in every conceivable corner of the earth, under every conceivable pretext, had attempted . . . to delude the Western intelligence agencies," Haldane finds the old report that damns Fritsche's photos.

> It was marked: Should not use. Fabrication. There followed a long justification citing passages in the report which had been abstracted almost verbatim from a 1949 Soviet military manual. . . . Attached were six photographs, very blurred, purporting to have been taken from a train with a telephoto lens. (192)

By the time Haldane makes this discovery, the wheels of Leclerc's plan are already in motion, and Haldane will not exert himself to halt the operation. "Before Leiser sets out, it is a foregone conclusion, except to the self-deceivers of the Department, that he will find nothing to support Fritsche's bogus intelligence" (Lewis 84). In fact, the Circus of Control and Smiley, in a position to profit from the demise of its moribund rival in the War Office, has already seen and rejected the Fritsche report, but Smiley does not apprise any of the Department officials of this salient fact. In the end, Smiley appears at the West German base of Operation Mayfly with orders to roll up the whole campaign and cut losses. Leiser, who has made a muddle of his radio transmissions and has called attention to himself by killing a sentry during his border crossing, is abandoned to the East Germans.

At the end of *The Looking Glass War*, Leiser is holed up awaiting his inevitable capture in the apartment of a young woman who has agreed to harbor him; he drops his cover and shows her the faked pieces of identification the Department has provided him. Rummaging through his wallet, the woman comes across the commemorative snapshots that are part of the agents's usual equipment:

> She held up a photograph of a woman; a blond, round head.
> "Who is she? What is her name?"
> "She doesn't exist," he said. . . .
> She found a picture of a child, a girl in spectacles, eight or nine years old
> perhaps, and again she asked, "Who is it? Is it your child? Does *she* exist?"
> "Nobody. Nobody's kid. Just a photograph." (254-55)

Once the sustaining fiction of Leiser's cover has lost its purpose, the photos in his wallet are reduced to disturbingly meaningless fragments, caught moments of an irretrievable distant history. The spy denies the very *existence* of the photographs' subjects, but of course the woman in the photo does (or did) exist, the child is (or was) *somebody's* kid; they simply do not exist any longer for Leiser or the Department. But then, neither does Leiser or the Department exist any longer. As the end of them both, Operation Mayfly exemplifies the dependence of agent and cause on ideology's fusion of image and story: with photo and tale bound to each other, the operation "may fly" only cast doubt on the relevance or consistency of the parts or the bond, and the fragility of operators and operation—named for an ephemeral vernal insect—is revealed. Leiser's "She doesn't exist" and "Nobody. . . . Just a photograph" express a central truth about the ideological functioning of photographic images in the le Carré world: the images have meaning only insofar as they impel actions that look convincingly *as if* they are based on a firm belief in the story linking those images to the agent. An agent's "belief" in the objective truth of the images is as chimerical as the "dependable point" giving meaning to character motivation—Leclerc, Avery, and Leiser all have their fundamental doubts; what matters is that the subject act his part[5] for a given end. The agent's *desire* to believe himself a valid subject—and to believe in the validity of his cause—is what effectively drives the story-making and story-sustaining consensus that keeps le Carre's spies in motion.

III

In *The Looking Glass War,* the characters participating in this consensus are clearly distinguished from others (like Smiley and Control) who know the truth

about the Fritsche report and Operation Mayfly: the latter stand outside the
doomed mission and allow it to run its course. The functions of knowing and
acting are divided in similar ways throughout le Carré's novels: in *The Spy Who
Came in from the Cold*, for example, the operative Alec Leamas is deliberately
sent on a mission into Germany with an incorrect understanding of his true
objective: Control and Smiley make Leamas their effective agent by giving him
only that information which will drive him to achieve the ends *they* have fully
in view.[6] The agent himself receives partial explanations, stories to boost his
confidence, token images on which to focus his attention. Full knowledge of a
case is available—if it ever is—only to those who have no functional role to
play in it.

In those novels in which Smiley does play a major active role, he forfeits
this omniscience and enters the uneasy round of questioning and self-persua-
sion that is the agent's usual lot. Thus Smiley hangs his "spectral" photo of
Karla and seeks to discover himself, his motive, his goal—and the larger collective identity, motive, and goal for which he works—through the contemplation
of that image. He refers to his own past to find the wellspring of his continuous
espionage activities: at the end of *The Honourable Schoolboy,* Smiley recalls
the beginning of his career as a time when the undeniable presence of a threatening opponent—Nazi Germany—gave his dedication a self-evident meaning.
"So far as I can ever remember of my youth," he writes, "I chose the secret road
because it seemed to lead straightest and furthest toward my country's goal. The
enemy in those days was someone we could point at and read about in the
papers" (532). As for the officers of Leclerc's dusty Department in *The Looking
Glass War*, the paradigm of Second World War clarity and purpose has never
ceased to function for Smiley—has never ceased to make *him* function, in spite
of innumerable misgivings. In the postwar, even the post-Cold War world of the
Quest for Karla trilogy (*Tinker, Tailor, Soldier, Spy, The Honourable Schoolboy*,
and *Smiley's People*), Smiley still holds true to the "we/they" model of The
Good Fight, which drives him most effectively against Karla, but which recon-
ciles him (and us?) all too easily to the way the agents of "we" are produced,
impelled, and squandered, whenever the image of "they" is displayed before us
like the terrible aegis of the Homeric epics.[7]

Smiley's progress in the trilogy leads him by a route that is anything but
straight to a confrontation with Karla as "someone [he can] point at"; and the
spectral photograph installed on his office wall in the middle novel guides him
on this circuitous course. Indeed, in the three novels Smiley moves through
three different types of encounter with the face of the Other. In *Tinker, Tailor,
Soldier, Spy*, and again in *Smiley's People*, Smiley remembers that he has once
encountered Karla face to face without realizing it. In the 1950s, Smiley had
been sent to Delhi to interview one Gerstmann, "identified by London as a
Moscow Centre agent, and now awaiting deportation to Russia" (*People* 157).

Only after failing in his bid to persuade Gerstmann to defect does Smiley learn that he has been dealing with "none other than Karla himself, Bill Haydon's recruiter, case officer, mentor" (*People* 159). It is this subsequent identification that enables Smiley to attach a face to his nemesis; and so the spectral photograph appears in *The Honourable Schoolboy*. From these two initial steps—from the face-to-face meeting with the unrecognized Karla, followed by the concentration on Karla's known face in the photograph—le Carré's trilogy proceeds ultimately to the final confrontation of Smiley and the real Karla in full recognition of each other—a confrontation with the Other that at last dialectically yields self-knowledge. When they meet at the end of *Smiley's People,* their faces act as mirrors for each other.

> Smiley saw [Karla's] face, aged and weary and travelled. . . . They faced each other; they were perhaps a yard apart, much as they had been in Delhi jail. . . . They exchanged one more glance and perhaps each for that second did see in the other something of himself. (386-87)

In le Carré's murky, uncertain world, this scene, with its qualifications of "perhaps," "for that second," and "something of himself," is our closest approach to resounding novelistic closure.

The face-to-face encounter between rivals that concludes the *Quest for Karla* triptych—each man a representative for the entire system he supports—is one of the most firmly established features of espionage and mystery fiction and one which le Carré has manipulated in a variety of ways throughout his career. In *Call for the Dead,* his first novel, le Carré brought Smiley to a similar culminating confrontation with his opponent—in this case, Smiley's old friend from the anti-Nazi days in Germany, Dieter Frey, who has since become an agent of the East German government. In a dramatic struggle, Smiley kills Frey and is left to mourn the necessity of his action. The struggle has affinities with the battle between Holmes and Moriarty at the Reichenbach Falls, and with the many concluding episodes in which James Bond faces off against the criminal mastermind at the headquarters of his evil empire. As these examples might suggest, the conventional face-to-face encounter involves a strong element of closure; readerly gratification is guaranteed when, after gathering clues and surviving perils on the periphery, the spy/detective gains the inner sanctum of crime and looks in the face of its prime mover.

But here we need to consider the further complications of the face-to-face meeting as le Carré presents it in the *Quest for Karla*. The convention interacts with the metaphorical system of photo and mirror images to become a symbolic, as well as a structural, element in the novels. What is the symbolic value of the human face in the logic of these metaphors? First we should note that Frey, Haydon, and Karla are all seen as working on behalf of a social arrangement that is conventionally regarded by their Western counterparts as *faceless*—that is, as implying the subjection of the individual "with a human face" to the merciless collective idea. In *Call for the Dead*, Smiley realizes that

> everything he admired or loved had been the product of intense individualism. That was why he hated Dieter now, hated what he stood for more strongly than ever before: it was the fabulous impertinence of rejecting the individual in favour of the mass. . . . Dieter cared nothing for human life: dreamed only of armies of faceless men bound by their lowest common denominators. (130)

Yet the very facelessness, the imagined inhumanity of the Eastern bloc opponent is what gives that opponent a daunting appearance of superior dedication, of surer commitment to his political work than the Western agents can ever attain. Anxiety before the Enemy's apparent self-sufficiency has been a regular element of the le Carré formula from the beginning. Dieter Frey "was a man who thought and acted in absolute terms, without patience or compromise" (124).[8] And, as Smiley recalls, Karla (as Gerstmann) had remained completely impassive before his attempts to lure the Russian spy into defection; promising Gerstmann a free life in the West and threatening him with the probable death or internal exile that awaited him in Moscow, Smiley had

> waited, on and on, vainly, for the slightest response to his increasingly desperate entreaty. . . . Yet the more Smiley implored him, the more dogmatic Gerstmann's silence became. . . . Gradually Gerstmann's completeness was awesome. He was a man who had prepared himself for the gallows; who would rather die at the hands of his friends than live at the hands of his enemies. (*People* 158-59)

And here we should also connect the daunting *completeness* of the Other to his status—until to the very end, at least—as sheer *image* on the walls or in the memories and imaginations of le Carré's Western spies. Aloof, silent, impassively staring, betraying nothing of need or confusion or desire, the Enemy invites comparison with the iconic art image in romantic and modernist aesthetics; Stephen Dedalus's description of the beautiful art work's *integritas, consonantia,* and *claritas*—wholeness, harmony, and radiance—is oddly opposite to Karla as Smiley encounters and commemorates him (Joyce 212-15).[9] During his peripatetic lecture on beauty in Joyce's *A Portrait of the Artist as a Young Man,* Stephen's attention is drawn to the girl he desires, as if to remind him of the difference between himself and the contemplator of that ideal "self-bounded" art work he describes; his mind "emptied of theory and courage," he gazes bitterly at the girl, and the bitterness seems to taint that theoretical confidence he had exuded just moments earlier. The same awareness of difference, the same *ressentiment* of the human viewer toward the work, can be attributed to Smiley, who has in great measure created the Karla who looms over him in the dingy Cambridge Circus throne room. And a face that does not speak, merely smoking and waiting on the other side of the table, is a totemic mask, an art object that covers or substitutes for an expressive, responsive human face. Looking at it, imploring it, Smiley resembles another troubled theorist, the self-professedly "sentimental" Friedrich von Schiller in his initial confrontations with "naive" geniuses like Shakespeare and Homer, those "strangers at whom one stares," who merge so fully, so *facelessly*, with their works that they "incense" the sentimental searcher with their "coldness" and "insensitivity." Schiller and Smiley could sigh together of their respective naive Others that "it was intolerable to me that here there was no way to lay hold of the poet, and nowhere to confront him," since "*he* is the work, and the work is *he*" (Schiller 106-10).[10]

Smiley's special project in *Smiley's People*, in the symbolic terms of *face* and *facelessness*, is to find the human face beneath Karla's implacable mask, just as he had found the human face of Dieter Frey in *Call for the Dead*. In both instances, "finding the human face" means revealing the enemy as a conscientious subject not fully "subjected" to that collective idea he represents: as neither an iconic artwork nor a naive genius of ideology, in other words. Smiley is able to kill Frey in their life-or-death battle because Frey cannot finally overcome his own personal affection for Smiley: "Dieter had let him do it, had not fired [his] gun, had remembered their friendship when Smiley had not" (*Dead* 137). By the end of *Smiley's People*, Carré's protagonist has discovered a similar unsuspected human weakness in his adversary: Karla's protective love for a mentally ill daughter (whose very existence he has kept secret) has led him to make unauthorized use of Moscow Centre funds and personnel in order to spirit her out of the Soviet Union and into a Swiss asylum for safe keeping. Smiley uses this knowledge to force Karla to defect.

The revelation of Karla as an "unsubjected" individual with personal priorities is foreshadowed at the beginning of *Smiley's People* by a similar reversal of the expected political equation of *face* and *faceless*. The novel opens as Smiley is called out of retirement to investigate the suspicious death of the old Estonian emigré Vladimir, who had worked with the Circus in bygone days but who has since, in the era of détente, been pensioned off as a potential embarrassment to the new international arrangements. Smiley receives his commission with strict orders to minimize the impact of the incident. On Hampstead Heath to view the body, Smiley asks first to be shown Vladimir's face, but the Police Superintendent in charge is reluctant to satisfy this request:

> "Ah, now you are sure about that, sir? . . . There'll be better ways of identifying him than *that*, you know."
> "Yes. Yes, I am sure," said Smiley earnestly, as if he really had given the matter great thought. (35)

What Smiley discovers is that Vladimir's corpse is *literally* without a face—it has been demolished, the old spy concludes, by the soft-nosed bullet used routinely by KGB assassins. This clue impels him to pursue his inquiries beyond the limits of his charter, ultimately to the final showdown with Karla. In this reversal of the expected symbolic values of the opposed terms, the murdered Estonian patriot—defender of the free individual "with the human face" against faceless Communism—is left faceless: a significant absence that leads Smiley on his course towards the human face of the supreme agent of facelessness.

Broadening our perspective once again to the *Quest for Karla* trilogy as a whole, we may say more specifically that Smiley's ultimate defeat of Karla involves the replacement of the "spectral" image of Karla's face with the *merely human face*, worn and haggard and fully visible before the triumphant British spy. And yet the culminating "facing" of Karla is accompanied by—is the dialectically necessary cause and effect of—a simultaneous "defacing" of Smiley in two important ways. First, Smiley becomes an effective agent in the victory over Karla only by violating that respect for the individual, that devotion to the human face, which has been his guiding principle and which constitutes the supposedly nonideological conviction of the individualistic West. Once he locates that vital center in his opposite number, Smiley *subjects himself* entirely to effective agency in order to exploit it. The recognition that comes with this betrayal of self is the same as that which Smiley had felt after triumphing over Dieter Frey in *Call for the Dead*: Dieter had remembered the human bond when Smiley had not. The Enemy proves to be less complete than expected—less a self-created and self-bounded work of art, as Stephen Dedalus would have it—and it is the Western agent who in the end exhibits the "coldness" and "insensitivity" he formerly saw in the "naive" Other.

The second manner in which Smiley is "defaced" at the conclusion of the *Quest for Karla* takes us back to the point that began this section: knowing and acting remain strictly distinct functions in the le Carré world. Once the British agent knows his enemy fully, face to face for the first time, he achieves a consequent fullness of self-knowledge, a consequent profundity of disillusionment about the personal subject and political ideals he has labored to support, that seem to disqualify him for further action. This is a practical truth about the literary productions of John le Carré, a truth about which the novelist has been forthright: the resolution of a lifetime of struggle and confusion at the end of *Smiley's People* seems to preclude the possibility of future Smiley novels. "There can be little doubt," most readers would agree, "that *Smiley's People* brings to an end the cycle of George Smiley novels. [Having defeated Karla,] Smiley . . . has his thoughts fixed on death rather than future secret enterprises" (Monaghan 123).[11] Full knowledge of Self and Other obviates further action and terminates the illusory subject so long sustained by "spectral" images and the ideological stories that gave them action-promoting meaning. After he has defeated Karla, Smiley is complete.

IV

Though George Smiley has not returned, John le Carré has continued his complex investigations of the constitution and maintenance of illusory subjects in
four post-Smiley novels: *The Little Drummer Girl* (1983), *A Perfect Spy* (1986),
The Russia House (1989), and *The Secret Pilgrim* (1991). In each work the
dialectic of Western agent and Enemy has been extended and complicated. It is
in *A Perfect Spy*, however, that le Carré's questioning of the ideology of free
and integral subjects has reached its most radical conclusions: for this novel,
while making use of many of the conventions of the earlier fiction, submits that
ideology and its supporting stories and images to a set of profoundly ironic
reversals. At the same time, *A Perfect Spy* requires us to go beyond the
Althusserian framework I have been deploying, calling into question ideology's
efficacy in interpellating individuals as subject/agents.

Once more, the functions of knowing and acting are set firmly in opposition. Le Carré's story is really two separate stories: one tells of a British intelligence officer (Jack Brotherhood) and his attempt to uncover a mole inside the
Western secret service networks: the other is told by that mole himself (Magnus
Pym), who has spent twenty-five years diligently burrowing in the service of
the Czechs. In the manner of the Smiley novels, Brotherhood acts in a conventional story of self-perpetuating agency: we watch him drive himself toward the
capture of Pym, his friend and protégé, by means of the familiar ideological use
of story and image. He stares, as so many of le Carré's agents have done, at a
haunting photograph of his Other—in this case, not Pym but Pym's Eastern
bloc controller, Axel. Jack sees in Axel's worn features that image of the potent
opponent which is necessary to dialectically reinforce his own mission.

> [Jack] stared yet again at the eaten-out features of Herr Petz-Hampel-
> Zaworski [Axel's several aliases], Pym's presumed controller. . . . The down-
> turned eyelids. The down-turned moustache. The hidden Slav smile. Who the
> devil are you? Why do I recognize you when I have never set eyes on you?
> (362)

Like most of le Carré's agents, Jack is an ambivalent and disillusioned man: his
hard-bitten "realism" is fueled by years working at a trade which, as the novels
never let us forget, soon puts paid to callow idealism and patriotism.[12] Rather
than impeding his pursuit of Magnus, however, Jack's disenchantment is transformed into a remorseless energy pushing him toward the apprehension of Pym,
his erstwhile "brother." As he sets the official wheels in motion against Pym, he
tells himself a typical fragmentary, hardly credited story to stoke his determina-
tion:

> Reluctantly Brotherhood phoned Head Office and asked to speak to Nigel of
> Secretariat. Belatedly, in the teeth of more larcenous instincts, he knew he

must conform. . . . Just as in the end he had always conformed, not out of slav-
ishness but because he believed in the fight and, despite everything, the team.
(280-81)

Resigned to fighting the Good Fight, Jack dismisses as "larcenous" those very
instincts of his own that answer to Magnus's experience: we listen to him rally
himself with the oldest of saws, the sporting ethic of "not letting down the
side." It is a lesson Jack Brotherhoods have been intoning, in India, at Ypres, in
the Ardennes, to the rhythms of Sir Henry Newbolt's "Vitaï Lampada" since
that "classic equation between war and sport" appeared in 1868—the lesson of
lines like:

> The river of death has brimmed its banks,
> And England's far, and Honour a name;
> But the voice of a schoolboy rallies the ranks:
> "Play up! play up! and play the game!"
> (qtd. in Fussell, *Great War* 25-26)

Here the disillusioned Brotherhood exemplifies the condition of the entire espionage "fraternity" as le Carré depicts it. Having long since arrived at an
"incredulity toward [the particular] metanarrative" which legitimated his youthful efforts as a spy (the metanarrative of British imperial destiny), Brotherhood
has not broken through to some perspective of incredulity toward metanarratives *as such*. His cynical recital of the sportsman's creed suggests that Brotherhood has made his very cynicism and disillusionment into a new metanarrative inspiring "perseverance in the face of disillusionment."[13]

Yet while Brotherhood's mission fits into the well-worn groove of previous
le Carré novels and of the established ruling-class ideology behind both le Carré
and Newbolt, the second story of *A Perfect Spy* represents a new departure.
When we first see Magnus Pym, he is striding manfully into a stiff wind and
enacting what we only gradually realize is a parody of Newboltian imperialist
perseverance:

> His stride was agile, his body forward-sloping in the best tradition of the
> Anglo-Saxon administrative class. In the same attitude, whether static or in
> motion, Englishmen have hoisted flags over distant colonies, discovered the
> sources of great rivers, stood on the decks of sinking ships. (1)

Reading on, we learn that the treasonous Magnus has actually abandoned his
post (he is Head of Station in Vienna) and run to ground—under an alias, as
usual—in a simple boarding house in a Devonshire coastal town, where he aims
to straighten out once and for all the tangle of his years of double agency. After
a career spent deceiving father, wife, son, colleagues, and friends, Magnus plans
to write the true story of his life, aiming to fully possess his own subjectivity for
the first time. With *Wilhelm Meister* as his model, Pym tries at last to complete

his own *Bildungsroman*, the "great autobiographical novel" he has planned and fitfully labored at for years (223).

But his full confessions can be written only when there is no going back to the subject-producing, illusion-sustaining world of action: Pym's autobiography is in fact an extended suicide note which the quondam agent writes for his son, Tom; it is the story a *finished subject* tells about his own formation *as* subject. "You do it once," Magnus reminds himself about his truthful tale; "once in your life and that's it. No rewrites, no polishing, no evasions. No would-it-be-better-this-ways. You're the male bee. You do it once, and die" (22). What Jack Brotherhood must learn through the course of his pursuit of Magnus, and what readers learn through the story Pym writes, is that Pym's whole career has been spent in the attempt to atone for an early sin: as a young spy newly recruited by Brotherhood, Magnus had informed against Axel, his close friend and housemate in Bern; deported from Switzerland, Axel had subsequently joined the Czech Secret Service and had exploited Magnus's guilty conscience to "turn" Pym. Pym's final reckoning makes up a large portion of le Carré's 517-page novel, and it aims toward a final answer to that so-often deferred question: Who is Pym? Magnus's problem is that of all of le Carré's spies: where is the "dependable point" behind a lifetime of manipulated images and stories? "Magnus is a great imitator," Axel once puts it, "even when he doesn't know it. Really I sometimes think he is entirely put together from bits of other people, poor fellow" (427). Magnus's goal of complete disclosure is expressed through his "male bee" analogy: the desire to determine and communicate the truth about the subject outweighs the desire to bolster and perpetuate it.

But the immediate cause spurring Magnus to write an autobiography that will set forth a continuous narrative of the spy's formation is the death of his father, Rick, an incorrigible big-time confidence man. In a fragment of the "great autobiographical novel," Magnus had wavered between third- and first-person narration in attempting to come to terms with the father's decline:

> The systems of [Pym's protagonist's] life are all collapsing. . . . All his life he's been inventing versions of himself that are untrue. Now the truth is coming to get him and he's on the run. . . . Rick invented me, Rick is dying. What will happen when Rick drops his end of the string? (129)

Pym fears the loss of a sustaining connection that is threatened by Rick's "letting go of the string." Rick "invented" Magnus; so Magnus writes of his father in order to discover the terms of his inheritance, the way in which the father's identity has given shape to the son's. Con man and double agent,[14] Rick and Magnus are of a kind, each relying on his presentation of cover stories and convincing images. Yet Magnus's full examination of the connecting string, his exposure of the unbroken lineage from which he emerges, is not undertaken to provide him with a renewed inspiration to carry on that lineage or the identity it has bestowed on him. Rather, Pym's story lays bare his patrimony as essentially fraudulent.

He accomplishes this, in part, through a consideration of significant photographs which he describes and passes on to Tom as illustrations for his text. The main exhibits are views of Rick, depicting the father in an array of false guises; many come from Rick's strange, mendacious campaign for election to the Parliamentary seat of a remote Yorkshire constituency. Magnus gives an extended description of Rick's official campaign photos, each of which seems phonier than the others. On "an imposing red-and-black pamphlet" for the voters, Rick appears "flanked by somebody's adoring spaniels, . . . reading a book before an unfamiliar fireside, a thing he has never done in his life" (310). And the display cards set up at Rick's speeches depict Pym's father in the variety of phony roles he had assumed to pass himself off as "the Common Man's Candidate":

> Rick at Napoleon's desk with his law books ranged behind him. Rick on the factory floor for the first and only time of his life, sharing a cup of tea with the Salt of the Earth. Rick as Sir Francis Drake gazing towards the misted armada of Gulworth's dying herring fleet. Rick the pipe-sucking agriculturalist intelligently appraising a cow. (312)

Objectifying his father's many false poses, Magnus inverts the standard le Carréan use of photographic images: the value of these pictures lies precisely in his recognizing them as both shams *and* models on which his own subjectivity has been constructed. Pym's narrative illustrates that, contrary to the comforting promise of ideology, "complete knowledge" yields only the paralyzing recognition of an intrinsically duplicitous, fragmented subject: the perfect spy, the quintessential agent, is false to the core. His writing finished, "placing himself for the last time before the shaving mirror," Pym watches himself prepare to commit the suicide that is the only, the eagerly awaited end of the subject he has revealed: "And he noticed how he was leaning: not away from the gun, but into it, like someone a little deaf, straining for the sound" (516-17).

Just as in the writing of his autobiography Pym reverses the expectations that the earlier novels raise about photographic and mirror images, Pym's whole history entails a reversal of the many expectations that have slated him as "perfect" for the roles consonant with the position of an upwardly mobile star of the British Foreign Service. From the time that Brotherhood discovered the young Pym in postwar Switzerland and began to ease him into "semi-conscious" espionage work amidst the refugee population of Bern, Magnus had seemed a natural, a perfect spy. Having impressed his Foreign Office interviewers with his imitation of their rhetoric, Pym entered the "Firm" and entered into a seemingly perfect marriage—to the proper upper-middle-class Belinda—at the same time; he remembers thinking, "that's me taken care of, then. . . . With the Firm getting

172

JAMES M. BUZARD

one half of me and Belinda the other, I'll never want for anything again" (454).
Even the break-up of this first marriage only led Pym toward an even more perfect second one, to Mary, a former decoder with the Firm who is consequently
a helpmate more attuned to the strains of career espionage work and to the need
for a proper household cover for Magnus. Even the irrepressible Rick, who in
spite of his life of crime had always espoused a highly sentimental patriotism,
did not disqualify Magnus in the eyes of his Foreign Office sponsors. "I don't
think we can hold you responsible for the sins of your old man, can we?" one of
Pym's interviewers had said; and when Pym looks back on the scene in his
autobiography, he concludes that "Rick was an asset. A healthy streak of criminality in a young spy's background never did him any harm, they reasoned.
'Grown up in a hard school,' they told one another. 'Could be useful'"(453).

But Pym is a dangerous teammate for any "side" that tries to make him
play its game. The criminality in his nature turns out to be uncontainable for the
purposes and within the structures of authorized British espionage, and Pym's
treason takes the form of a rejection of the identities which those purposes and
that structure have provided for him. Far from being the conscious act of a self-
determining, nonideological, liberal-humanist subject, moreover, Pym's repudiation of Pym emerges from the fissures and contradictions in and among the
very "hailings"—son, husband, father, Oxford graduate, career intelligence officer—to which he has been subjected. To read his career in this way is to follow
the lead of critics who have extended Althusser's model of ideological interpellation in such a fashion as to theorize resistance to ideology without recourse to
a nonideological domain of free subjectivity. As Paul Smith argues,

> to regard resistance to ideology as anything but a by-product of the ideological
> itself must be to posit some kind of innate human capacity that could over-ride
> or transcend the very conditions . . . of social existence. Resistance does take
> place, but it takes place only within a social context which has already con-
> strued subject-positions for the human agent. The place of that resistance has,
> then, to be glimpsed somewhere in the interstices of the subject positions
> which are offered in any social formation. (25)

While Pym's complete knowledge and disclosure leaves him, at the conclusion of
his autobiography, as a finished subject—"perfect" in the grammatical sense of a
completed action—his story does not oblige readers to derive a univocal conclusion, either that of total identification with Magnus or that of indignant condem-
nation of his treason. To assume either option as the necessary result of reading *A
Perfect Spy* would be to imagine the novel as an efficiently functioning *lisible* text
that unproblematically assigns responses to passive "implied" readers.[15] Indeed,
any approach that seriously addresses both of the intertwined narratives that comprise le Carré's novel must needs avoid such univocality. Rather, Pym's story can
give readers a view both of ideological interpellation at work and of the ways ideology may *fail* to encompass the person it subjects to interpellation.[16]

In this it contrasts with its forerunner *The Little Drummer Girl*, which despite its own considerable ambiguities and different circumstances still tends to emphasize the effective restraint and rechanneling of "larcenous impulses"—in this case in the service of Israel—by means of image and story. When, in the middle of a mission that involves the exploitation of an English actress as bait to lure a notorious Palestinian terrorist, Israeli masterspy Gadi Becker glimpses himself in a mirror, his reaction repeats the theme on which so many le Carré variations have been played.

> Becker caught sight of his attractive features in the mirror, and stared at them with sharp distaste. For a moment, they were like a wrecker's light to him, and he had a morbid and overwhelming wish to extinguish them for good: Who the hell are you? . . . What do you feel? He drew closer to the mirror. I feel as if I am looking at a dead friend, hoping he will come alive. I feel as if I am searching for my old hopes in someone else, without success. I feel that I am an actor . . . surrounding myself with versions of my identity because the original somehow went missing along the road. But in truth I feel nothing, because real feeling is subversive and contrary to military discipline. Therefore I do not feel, but I fight and therefore I exist. (231-32)

The crisis averted—the man feeling larcenous impulses back in protective custody—Gadi goes on with the fight. "I fight and therefore I exist": the phrase encapsulates the strange reversal that befalls the spy who drives himself against the implacable Other-as-image: he parodies the naive Other's self-completeness, that quality Schiller attributed to poets like Homer and Shakespeare. *Gadi is the work, and the work is Gadi.* Magnus Pym, on the other hand, is finished with all that.

V

Le Carré's novels are, finally, every bit as equivocal as the myriad images, stories, and identities that recur throughout them. As is especially true of *A Perfect Spy*, with its split stories of subject and agent, the novels can support conflicting readings. On one level, they fully indulge the reader's urge to maintain the spectral illusion of a dualistic world, in which George Smiley and Jack Brotherhood persist in spite of their troubled consciences, in a ritual stoicism that appears to support a tenacious belief "in the fight and, despite everything, the team." What returns again and again, from this standpoint, is the image of the international Other, the Soviet threat, to reinstate the unhappy Western spy as an effective agent. Significantly, all of the West's espionage activities appear in le Carré's novels as specific responses to suspected Eastern bloc initiatives, as makeshift schemes hatched purely in order to safeguard Western interests. Smiley's predecessor Control assures Alec Leamas in *The Spy Who Came in from the Cold* that "the ethic of our work . . . is based on a single assumption. That is, we are never going to be aggressors. . . . Thus we do disagreeable things, but we are *defensive*" (15); this single assumption makes the international menace "determining in the last instance" for le Carré's spies, underwriting the many images and stories they use to keep themselves in the fray.[17]

Alternatively, in dramatizing the ongoing fabrication of subjects, in detailing the provisional and sometimes unsuccessful nature of that fabrication, le Carré's fiction can be read, as I have tried to read it, as problematizing both liberal-humanist and strict Althusserian interpretations of subjectivity. In their divided consciousnesses, in the divisions between their conscious knowledge and their effective agency in processes they do not control, le Carré's characters exhibit the strains of inhabiting that polarized world in which East/West geopolitics override all other considerations, reducing each act to a gesture of either support or betrayal of the status quo. This reductiveness robs political choice of its specificity, and may explain why we never fully understand why the le Carré spies do what they do: they are taking up the densely particular question of motive in a world that can conceive only that there is behavior *for* the West and behavior *against* it. In this setting, politically significant actions simply find their agents as they find their opponents, and the insistent question of human motivation gives way to attempted rationalizations, the seeming finality of which is belied by internal contradiction. Once le Carré's spies call a stop to their self-doubts in order to get on with the job, they have doomed themselves to becoming parodies of the very image they pursue: instead of the enviable self-boundedness of the Other-as-image, they attain a state of immersion in their labors that so emotionally impoverishes them that they resemble automata waiting for the next push of the button. At the moment of his capture after the Mayfly fiasco, Leiser stands "very straight [with] his small face . . . empty, held by some private discipline, a man once more intent upon appearances, conscious of tradition" (War 274). Similarly, arriving on the scene too late to prevent Pym's suicide, Jack Brotherhood faces the melee "standing to attention like a dead centurion at his post" (Spy 517).

In *The Russia House* (1989), the dialectic of subjected agent and spectral Enemy is extended into the glasnost world of contemporary geopolitics. "Goethe," a Soviet scientist who is privy to secrets not destined for official openness, attempts to reveal the great hoax of Soviet nuclear capability to the West, choosing an unlikely British publisher, Barley Blair, as the recipient for his message. After almost thirty years of his fiction, John le Carré and the international alignment have so shifted that it is possible to find the Other speaking of what both our sides do: "in life, in certain types of life"—we might almost think Goethe a biologist describing amoebae—"you can have a situation where a player has such grotesque fantasies about another one that he ends up by inventing the enemy he needs" (*House* 85). It should also be possible, after those nearly thirty years, to construe the fates of le Carré's spies and counterspies as evidence of a need for a different politics, one not yet in view in either le Carré's fictional world or in ours: a politics more attentive to the ways ideology is reproduced and resisted within Western societies than to that spectral image of the Other which looms over us and can be relied on to call our straying members to order.

Notes

1. Smiley is the protagonist of *Call for the Dead* (1961), *A Murder of Quality* (1962), and *Tinker, Tailor, Soldier, Spy* (1974); he plays small but significant roles in *The Spy Who Came in from the Cold* (1963) and *The Looking Glass War* (1965). After *The Honourable Schoolboy* (1977), Smiley makes what would seem to be his final appearance in *Smiley's People* (1980). Smiley has a cameo role in le Carré's latest novel, *The Secret Pilgrim* (1991), which appeared as this volume was going to press.

2. In *Call for the Dead*, Smiley breaks up the spy ring run by Dieter Frey, a former student of Smiley's from the 1930s, when Smiley worked under academic cover inside Nazi Germany; at the end of the novel Smiley kills Frey in a struggle and suffers intense remorse. In *A Murder of Quality*, Smiley arrests for murder Terence Fielding, the brother of one of his wartime Circus colleagues, and his investigation takes place near the ancestral home of his estranged wife's family. In *Tinker, Tailor, Soldier, Spy*, of course, Smiley uncovers the mole Bill Haydon, distant cousin and lover of the faithless Ann.

3. Martindale's answer is too limited, but he does identify the important historical problem for Smiley: England is no longer the nation to which he devoted himself so many years before. Even when he reaches one of his career's peaks in exposing Bill Haydon, Smiley cannot avoid this realization:

> Even now he did not grasp the scope of [Bill's] appalling duplicity; yet there was a part of him that rose already in Haydon's defence. Was not Bill also betrayed? Connie's lament rang in his ears: "Poor loves. Trained to Empire, trained to rule the waves . . . You're the last, George, you and Bill." He saw with painful clarity an ambitious man born to the big canvas, brought up to rule, divide, and conquer, whose visions and vanities all were fixed . . . upon the world's game: for whom the reality was a poor island with scarcely a voice that would carry across the water. Thus Smiley felt not only disgust, but, despite all that the moment meant to him, a surge of resentment against the institutions he was supposed to be protecting . . . The Minister's lolling mendacity, Lacon's tight-lipped moral complacency, the bludgeoning greed of Percy Alleline: such men invalidated any contract—why should anyone be loyal to them? (*Tinker* 345-46)

In the terms of Jean-François Lyotard's characterization of the modern as involving the legitimation of a discourse "with reference to a metadiscourse . . . making an explicit appeal to some grand narrative [*grand récit*]," this imperial destiny is the metadiscourse that first impelled Smiley and Haydon into the secret service; its "story" gave them legitimation for their earliest efforts in that service. See Lyotard, xxiii.

4. It is important to recognize what Paul Smith calls "the lure that is offered in the

very word 'individual,'" with its strong positive connotations of indivisibility: it offers "a fiction of cohesion that bears as its symptom a belief in a fully enabled and self-conscious power" (Smith xxxiv). Since it is still nearly impossible to avoid the word in any discussion of discrete *persons*, I use it advisedly here.

5. And in the le Carré world it almost always is "his" part, since except for *The Little Drummer Girl*, which differs in other important ways as well, all of the novels focus on male agents and their functional self-deceptions. In *Taking Sides: The Fiction of John le Carré*, Tony Barley argues convincingly, with special reference to *The Looking Glass War*, that women in le Carre's work regularly undercut the masculine delusions and fantasies that fuel espionage activities.

6. Specifically, Leamas is sent to deflect suspicion away from Mundt, a mole working inside the East German *Abteilung* for the Circus; but he does not know that Mundt is a mole until he has already performed this function in spite of his own intentions.

7. Paul Fussell has recently and controversially challenged the ideology of the Second World War as a completely "righteous" one for the Western allies in *Wartime: Understanding and Behavior in the Second World War* (1989).

8. Many other examples of the enemy's fixed sense of purpose could be adduced; the most well-known may be found in the interrogation of Alec Leamas by Fiedler, the dedicated East German *Abteilung* officer, in *The Spy Who Came in from the Cold* (119-26).

9. I say "oddly," since Stephen's notion of the work of art as neither attracting nor repelling viewers—as impelling no action—would seem flatly contradictory to Smiley's use of Karla's photo precisely to inspire his own action. Yet Joyce's ironic setting of the aesthetics lecture in *Portrait* should at least lead us to wonder whether any such iconic work as Stephen describes has ever existed, for him or for anyone else. What is plain is Stephen's *desire* for an art that would foster in him a contemplative, undesiring state of being, that would make *him* feel "selfbounded." The pertinent critical work on the continuity of romantic and modernist aesthetics of the image is still Frank Kermode's *Romantic Image*.

10. David Monaghan employs Schiller's "naive and sentimental" distinction in a somewhat different manner in *The Novels of John le Carré: The Art of Survival*, especially pages 2-41. Le Carré has himself alluded to Schiller's dichotomy in his one non-espionage novel, *The Naive and Sentimental Lover* (1971).

11. David Monaghan quotes a series of interviews in which le Carré has "more or less admitted that he has no intention of resurrecting his 'anchor man and familiar' of seven novels" (123).

12. This aura of disillusioned "knowingness" is a hallmark of the le Carréan spy novel; it goes hand in glove with a constant debunking of that Ian Fleming technology-, property-, and commodity-fetishism which continues to enthrall movie audiences today. If James Bond wields a gold fountain pen that is also a state-of-the-art

laser (the product of a profligately funded research department), the le Carré spy carries a clotted Bic. The le Carré style has had some august detractors: Jacques Barzun scorned *The Spy Who Came in from the Cold* for purporting to be "a really real realistic tale of modern spying" (167).

13. Brotherhood's gesture here should give us some critical perspective on the modern/postmodern distinction as offered by Lyotard: Lyotard's own notion of postmodernist "incredulity" may unintentionally rely on just such a progressivist metanarrative of "lost illusions," such as we recognize in the *Bildungsroman* form le Carré is ironically employing in *A Perfect Spy*.

14. To this pair of roles we should add also "novelist," not only because Magnus gives shape to his life in a *Bildungsroman*, but because *A Perfect Spy* is in one sense an autobiography of the novelist with the assumed identity "John le Carré" (David Cornwell). For comments on le Carré's father, the original of Rick Pym, see Noel Annan's "Underground Men," which reviews *A Perfect Spy* (3). This association of artist, spy, and con man should also help us appreciate the degree to which *A Perfect Spy* is a novel in the modernist tradition. Emphasis on the artist as "artificer" is of course a modernist *topos*: the works of Mann and Gide provide obvious examples, but Joyce's *A Portrait of the Artist as a Young Man* is perhaps most pertinent, concluding as it does with Stephen Dedalus's appeal to Icarus as "father, old artificer" who must "stand [Dedalus] in good stead" as he embarks upon his independent career. *A Portrait's* status as a *Bildungsroman* makes the comparison still more compelling. Le Carré's continuation of modernist conventions is also evident in the Conradian juxtaposition of narratives characteristic of many of his works.

15. Paul Smith has recently challenged the notion that a text can be

> empowered to *force* the reader to adhere to the discursive positions it offers—the text is not, in Althusser's terms, a repressive state apparatus. . . . It can, of course, offer *preferred* positions, but these are by no means the conditions with which a reader must comply if he/she wishes to read a text. . . . In other words there is, first, no necessary correspondence . . . between "real" readers and "inscribed" ones . . . and equally, there can be no predictable or intended meaning-for-the-subject in any given text. (34)

Smith's argument here, which applies to texts of all varieties, is particularly useful in combatting the alluring assumption that popular literary forms like the spy novel can be distinguished from "high" literary ones on the basis of the former's putatively intrinsic character as a mere dispenser of ideology to a wholly passive audience.

16. In describing how Pym's autobiography "gives a view" of its author's interpellation by ideology, I am echoing Althusser's general description of art's relation to ideology. Art "give[s] us a 'view' of the ideology to which [it] alludes and with which it is constantly fed. . . . [It makes] us 'perceive' . . . in some sense *from the inside*, by an *internal distance*, the very ideology in which [it is] held" (222-23). An implication of my argument is that le Carré's novel, as opposed to Pym's autobiography, takes readers a step further in allowing them a more critical, rather than a merely spectatorial, perspective.

17. I am alluding, of course, to the Marxist notion of the economic base as "determining in the last instance" of both the shape of history and the forms taken by super-
structural phenomena in a given society; in the "late capitalist" world of global political
polarization, the perception of the International opponent seems to have assumed a large
part of this role.

Works Cited

Althusser, Louis. *Lenin and Philosophy*. Trans. Ben Brewster. New York: Monthly
Review P, 1971.

Annan, Noel. "Underground Men." Rev. of *A Perfect Spy*, by John le Carré. *The New
York Review of Books* 29 May 1986: 3-7.

Barley, Tony. *Taking Sides: The Fiction of John le Carré*. Milton Keynes, England:
Open UP, 1986.

Barzun, Jacques. "Meditations on the Literature of Spying." *American Scholar* 34.2
(Spring 1965): 167-78.

Bromley, Roger. "Natural Boundaries: The Social Function of Popular Fiction." *Red
Letters* 7 (1978): 34-40.

Eco, Umberto. "Narrative Structures in Fleming." Rpt. in *The Role of the Reader:
Explorations in the Semiotics of Texts*. Bloomington: Indiana UP, 1984.

Fussell, Paul. *The Great War and Modern Memory*. Oxford: Oxford UP, 1975.

——— . *Wartime: Understanding and Behavior in the Second World War*. Oxford:
Oxford UP, 1989.

Joyce, James. *A Portrait of the Artist as a Young Man*. Ed. Chester G. Anderson. New
York: Viking, 1976.

Kermode, Frank. *Romantic Image*. 1957. New York: Vintage, 1964.

Le Carré, John. *Call for the Dead*. London: Victor Gollancz, 1961. New York: Bantam,
1985.

——— . *The Honourable Schoolboy*. New York: Knopf, 1977. New York: Bantam,
1978.

——— . *The Little Drummer Girl*. New York: Knopf, 1983. New York: Bantam, 1984.

——— . *The Looking Glass War*. New York: Coward, McCann, 1965. New York: Bantam, 1984.

——— . *A Murder of Quality*. London: Victor Gollancz, 1962. New York: Bantam,
1983.

——— . *The Naive and Sentimental Lover*. 1971. New York: Knopf, 1972.

——— . *A Perfect Spy*. New York: Knopf, 1986. New York: Bantam, 1987.

———. *The Russia House*. New York: Knopf. 1989.

———. *The Secret Pilgrim*. New York: Knopf, 1991.

———. *Smiley's People*. New York: Knopf, 1980. New York: Bantam, 1985.

———. *The Spy Who Came in from the Cold*. London: Victor Gollancz, 1963. New York: Bantam, 1983.

———. *Tinker, Tailor, Soldier, Spy.* New York: Knopf, 1974. New York: Bantam, 1985.

———. "To Russia, with Greetings: an open letter to the Moscow Literary Gazette." *Encounter* 26 (1966): 3-6.

Lewis, Peter. *John le Carré*. New York: Ungar, 1985.

Lyotard, Jean-François. *The Postmodern Condition: A Report on Knowledge*. Trans. Geoff Bennington and Brian Massumi. Minneapolis: U of Minnesota P, 1984.

Monaghan, David. *The Novels of John le Carré: The Art of Survival*. Oxford: Basil Blackwell, 1985.

Schiller, Friedrich von. *"Naive and Sentimental Poetry" and "On the Sublime": Two Essays*. Trans. Julius A. Elias. New York: Frederick Ungar, 1980.

Smith, Paul. *Discerning the Subject*. Minneapolis: U of Minnesota P, 1988.

Chapter 8

The Gyroscope and the Junk Heap: Ideological Consequences of Latin American Experimentalism

Harry Polkinhorn

I. Introduction

The following discussion examines several views of history as seen through the lens of Latin American experimental art. These views provide an alternative to standard arguments over the significance of postmodernism in the cultures of developed countries. More specifically, Latin American experimentalism provides a radical critique of the ideologically dominant images of static, linear history characteristic of Western modes of self-representation. Examples are drawn from the visual poems of the Uruguayan Clemente Padín (1960s), Chicano murals (1970s), and contemporary U.S. Latino performance art. With regard to the latter work, it is important not to forget that:

> U.S. Latin culture is not homogeneous. It includes a multiplicity of artistic and intellectual expressions both rural and urban, traditional and experimental, marginal and dominant. These expressions differ from one another according to class, sex, nationality or assimilation and time spent in the U.S. California Chicanos and Nuyorricans inhabit different cultural landscapes. Even within Chicano culture a poet living in a rural community in New Mexico has very little in common with an urban cholo-punk from L.A. (Gómez-Peña, "Multicultural Paradigm" 22)

Because of the recent flurry of interest in Latin American culture in the U.S. arts establishment, of which Chicano art forms a subset, a reappraisal of the role of ethnicity in critical debates over the avant-garde and the postmodern would seem especially appropriate at this time. Such a reappraisal shatters the dominant discursive separation of "autonomous" imagery and political ideologies.

The experimental art of New World Hispanics critically examines conventional notions of historical understanding. To begin with, a strictly *historical* approach to experimental art requires the theoretical construction of a position *external* to that history in order to even begin to establish a controlling, chronological sequence of events. Latin American art forms propose themselves as a critique of just such ideological control and "objectifying" distance characteristic of dominant Western modes of historical representation. Indeed, such ideological controls are smuggled into high culture under the rubric of a marginalizing theory of ethnic "genres" sustained by the material social formations manifested in the distinct but oftentimes interlocking gallery, museum, publishing, and reviewing hierarchies. The oppositional force of Latin American experimental art derives from a fundamental acknowledgement that one's means of historical understanding are completely embedded in the processes of contemporary experience. Even if historical understanding is temporarily separated from these processes, it is only to return to them in a subsequent cycling. Such a separation must not be concealed, for the dominant, monological (chronological) historical paradigm stems from that act of concealment.

This dynamic opposition has become the marking feature of Latin American experimentalism and operates according to two distinguishable moments.[1] The first extreme is based on an idea of history all but identical to what is being critiqued, that is, linear serialization through a chronological sequence in which time is arbitrarily divided into equal, theoretically exchangeable units—seconds, minutes, hours, periods, epochs, and so forth. Accordingly, the model of revolt and subversion is conceived to a large degree in terms of those patterns being opposed: the succession of historical events which has generated patterns of economic and social repression through exploitation of a Third World labor surplus. Thus the pattern itself is constituted on the basis of an act of repetition of identical parts; it is as if Hegel's master-slave dialectic kept mechanically repeating itself without progress. The conceptual theoretical model, however, conceals a controlling image of an idealized machine fetishized by the industrial revolution's obsession with progress. History, that is, works like a machine, and for our purposes a gyroscope provides a fruitful image of such controlled historical understanding. Whereas any simple machine could serve as an example, the gyroscope is particularly fitting, since it provides orientation in space through balancing physical movements. The spinning motion is controlled by a single axis that touches ground at only one stable point. Meaning itself is thereby imagined as an interacting division of signs and referents stably balanced and controlled by the single dominant axis.

The other extreme features the dissolution of such a process of creating stable structure and determinate meaning: its very disintegration under the pressures of economic oppression, disenfranchisement, and political torture regimes propped up by the U.S. government. Here oppressive social reality spawns its own cultural demolition. The serialization mentioned above and upon which the first moment is based breaks down into a raw state, becoming the very ground of art. At this level no hierarchy exists, no privileged status granted any "autonomous" image, no controlling gyroscope, merely the basic elements from which the art work will be "assembled" (that is, context-less words, pigment, random imagery for collage, and so on). Thus instead of an art of repetition, which requires order and hierarchy, we have one of turning away. Each time the stage of crystallization is reached, there is disappearance through transformation. Whenever a parallel aesthetic dimension seems about to form, ugliness and chaos recur. Here the gyroscope of history is smashed; it is thrown on the junk heap which becomes an irreverent source for the recycling of particular cultural artifacts whose experimental modes of local, ethnic solidarity provide as well for new, historically contingent and "decentered" images of global ecology.

II. Practitioners

The former view is perhaps best represented during the late 1960s and 1970s by the Marxism of Clemente Padín, whose aesthetic was based on the reincorporation of poetry in life. Padín's *Poesía Inobjetal* (Objectless Poetry) took the act as sign, thus implicating all human activities and directly impacting upon ideology. As publisher of *Ovum 10*, a widely distributed journal dedicated to investigating new poetry, Padín received international exposure for his art and criticism and brought such currents to the attention of the Uruguayan public through sponsoring exhibitions such as *Liberarse: Exposición Internacional de la Nueva Poesía* (12-22 August 1969) and *Exposición Exhaustiva de la Nueva Poesía* (7 February-5 March 1972). An ironic measure of the success of these activities, and proof of their politically subversive nature, is that he and Jorge Caraballo, another Uruguayan experimental artist active in visual writing, were incarcerated for them by the ruling military tribunal. Implicit in Padín's aesthetic is the collapse of the socially maintained distinction between art and life, *in favor of life*.

> Man is responsible for what happens; he is a historical being, works on reality in spite of himself, and pretends to forget it by taking the easy road of symbol making. The new poetry induced the act, and by analogy this attitude is carried over into the rest of man's activities. Poetry is act, not thought. The old aspiration of the traffickers in illusions was to disappear under the weight of its own impossibility; identification now must be incorporated, or these objects called visual poems must be rejected, but in all cases by movement and not by the intermediation of elements foreign to the actualization of poetry. Words used to fulfill this heavenly function, bearers of concepts; now, their foreignness, that of objects, has been overturned. ("La nueva poesía" 30-32; my translation)[2]

Padín sums up this position as one of a strategically politicized search for new artistic idioms which find their place within a context of historical change:

> Characteristics can be discerned in their own development of the Latin American artistic avant-garde that will define art in the near future: artistic experi-

ence and the search for new languages and forms inserted into cultural production as one more social practice, unprivileged and at the service of the progressive sectors of society; creative participation that favors consumer's
choice, inducing him to discover on his own, without ideological impositions
or pre-established value judgements, the information transmitted by the work
and the artist, and finally the compromise of the unrestricted liberty of the
individual and the group to decide their own destinies (which merge), and of
justice, without which all artistic action becomes meaningless. ("El arte latinoamericano"; my translation)[3]

As Gómez-Peña puts it, "Metier is being redefined. In Latin America, the artist
has multiple roles. He/she is not just an image-maker or a marginal genius, but
a social thinker/educator/counter-journalist/civilian diplomat and human rights
observer. His/her activities take place in the center of society and not in special-
ized corners" (Gómez-Peña, "Multicultural Paradigm" 22). Examples of
Padín's aesthetic can be seen in the visual poems he produced during this early
period in his career.

The second view of history operates according to a different set of forces.
Here art takes relative predominance over life, but through expanding its repertoire of strategies. A performance aesthetic is implicit in work like Padín's early
visual writing. However, the experimentalist, visual-writing dimension gives
precedence to its complement in live performance in the work which establishes
this second view; additionally, contemporary Chicano performance uses multimedia, bilinguality, code-switching, and so-called site-specific installation as
ways of ignoring serial chronology through appropriation of disparate materials,
motifs, themes, and imagery from a variety of contexts, all modes of visual
writing itself.

Performance art as practiced by Chicano groups has roots first in spontaneous street events in the barrio as well as in the cities of Latin America,[4] then
in the Teatro Campesino, formed in 1965 with the purpose of organizing Chicano farm workers in California (Valdez and Steiner 360-61). In all cases, however, "art and political activism were either equivalent or complementary, and
their objectives were mostly outside the parameters of art"(26). Subsequent performance groups have striven for street actions of pieces designed to further
awareness of Chicano concerns. Example groups are Asco of Los Angeles and
the Border Arts Workshop of San Diego. The artists of Asco (Spanish for dis-
gust, nausea), with roots in Berlin Dada and 1960s conceptualism, distinguished
themselves among other things for performances that alienated a wide variety
of audiences. In one of these, done in 1971,

> Gronk got dressed up like Pontius Pilate, a clown throwing popcorn. Willie
> Herron got dressed up as a Christ figure with a skull and a big, horribly
> designed, cardboard cross that he was dragging. I [Harry Gamboa] was
> dressed like an altar boy with a large animal skull strapped on to the top of my

Figure 8-1
Border Art Workshop/Taller de Arte Fronterizo. "Oh George, Oh Carolos, Oh Panama." Intervention/Performance at Canyon Zapata, Soccer Field, Colonia Libertad, Tijuana, BLN, Mexico. Jan. 1990. Photo credit: Bertha Jottar. Permission to reprint from the Border Arts Workshop.

> gown. We walked down Whittier Blvd. and delivered it to the Marine Recruit-
> ing Station and blessed it with all this popcorn, made an enormous mess.
> (Burnham, Durland, and MacAdams 51)

The group, whose members also included Diane Gamboa, Patssi Valdez, and Daniel J. Martinez, produced plays, videos, graphics, fashions, murals, and manifestos whose effect is "both hilarious and frightening" (51).

In San Diego, the Border Arts Workshop/Taller de Artes Fronterizos (Guillermo Gómez-Peña, Emily Hicks, Victor Ochoa, Berta Jottar, Rocio Weiss, Robert Sanchez, Michael Schnorr) has likewise produced a number of pieces which focus on the violence inflicted on segments of the population by a racist legislation as passed through media images (i.e., sensationalistic news-paper accounts). Their work has taken as its main concern the multiple impacts of the U.S.-Mexican border, and often adopts an overt, politically subversive stance. In a 1986 performance,

> The performance set . . . consisted of a chain-link fence and an altar that filled
> the stage. The effect was of an altar placed at the border crossing. To the left
> of the altar was a screen for the projected slides; the bilingual piece included
> a taped musical soundtrack. One memorable scene showed Berman (a former
> member) as a border patrol figure with a gun, evoking sadomasochistic
> imagery through a juxtaposition of sex and violence, but the centerpiece of the
> performance was Gómez-Peña's drunken monolog, the entire text of which is
> included in the exhibition. . . . In the concluding vignette, Gómez-Peña wore
> a shaman mask and removed some green goop from a bottle, saying "caca-
> lata" (a generic term for commodities invented by capitalism and sold to Latin
> America)—literally, canned excrement. (Hicks, Border De(con)struction, n.
> pag.)

Other performances have been organized at the westernmost end of the U.S.-Mexican border itself.

As a nonobject, intergenre, variable form, street and site-specific perfor-mance launches an attack on the commodification of art in the bourgeois sys-tem of goods production and consumption which structures non-Chicano art. The abrasions of power between classes (Chicano and Anglo-American) cat-alyze these diverse materials into an art of mockery, attack, subversion, critique. Division and confrontation not only undo historical evolution through uses of pornography, violence, obscurity, but also willfully retrograde attachment to popular forms, *indigenismo* or embracing alternative cultural traditions, appro-priate mass-media processes, and politicize the new technology-generated inter-media genres.[5] At the multiple and shifting juncture points between cultures, classes, linguistic codes, art genres, and nations, Chicano performance art launches its erosion of the dominant historical paradigm based on a carefully controlled chronology of political and military "events."

III. Avant-Garde vs. Postmodern

At the heart of Chicano art lies a complex process best characterized as avant-garde, a term with strong historical antecedents in the European avant-garde of the 1920s and 1930s. In general, the avant-garde advocates an irreverent critique of all forms of a-historical, elitist, and universalizing artistic activity in the name of an experimentalism aimed at local and popularizing sociopolitical contexts. However, its application to Chicano art will involve modulating it in the direction of a significant and much-needed broadening of its parameters. Such broadening will be particularly necessary given the debates over the utility of the avant-garde, in traditional Eurocentric or North American cultural politics, whereby the linear chronology of modernism, avant-garde, and postmodernism involves a serial usurping of each epoch by the ensuing one. Implicit within these formulations lies the gyroscope paradigm of history and the capitalist values which such a paradigm rationalizes. Thus "avant-garde" as end point to the chronological succession of style movements (baroque, neoclassical, romantic, modern) simply reinforces conventional historical succession and the economic patterns which such a view of history attempts to pass off as universal (i.e., from feudalism through monarchy to the bourgeoisie with its wage-class divisions). Postmodernism then becomes the final overcoming of the avant-garde style. In contrast, what I am arguing for in this essay is a non-gyroscopic view of the postmodern which does not surpass the avant-garde but engages in its critical politics, much as William Spanos and the *boundary 2* writers have argued that a politically aware postmodernism must.

Taking the Latin American avant-gardes in general and Chicano art as the case in point simultaneously undercuts value-blind discourse on the function of avant-garde art, as indicated above, and opens that discourse up to its own modulation, to the possibility of a change in the function of the category. This is clearly grasped by Eduardo Subirats, whose analysis underscores the missing dimension to this discourse:

> In preindustrial areas like Spanish culture or Latin American countries, there weren't exactly the conditions of cultural crisis caused by industrialization and technological development; neither were there known the morally devastating effects of the World War and subsequent revolutionary crises. . . . Revolutionary, eschatological, and critical elements were lacking in the epigonic manifestations of the international expansion of the avant-garde. (36)[6]

Subirats's insight historicizes the category of the avant-garde, relating it unequivocally to the social conditions which engendered it. His discussion highlights the importance to this notion of the spirit of utopia: "The social and cultural utopia of the avant-gardes, of a revolutionary, emancipating character, carried implicitly the moments of its integration into a regressive process of the technological colonization of life, and a coactive rationalization of society and the cultural" (19; my translation).[7] Such critical utopianism does not imply a move to restore the past, for "This has nothing to do in any way with preserving the spirit of the historical avant-gardes. Nevertheless, going beyond them is conceivable only through reinstating their critical goals and their principle of utopia" (22; my translation).[8] Thus, if not all avant-gardes are as politically oppositional as the European, this idea of utopia has a social utility which goes beyond the conditions of its immediate engendering. Chicano art, of course, inflects notions of confrontation, revolution, and utopia according to its own dynamic, one of whose marking images is the border.

IV. The Border Equation

To understand the model of history which informs Chicano art, one must understand the notion of borders—what they are, how they function socially and psychologically, their role in the decentering of signification and imagery. Geopolitical boundary, sociocultural membrane, no-man's land where contraband flows in both directions, borders perform a wide range of functions in the structuring of consciousness through separation or division. Perhaps what all these functions share is their role as concentration points of power. At borders the raw power relations which constitute societies are revealed. Crossing the border, one must identify oneself, show documentation stating country of citizenship or birth, place oneself in the hierarchy of traditional socialization patterns. For a citizen in the heart of his or her own country, this is not necessary, but on leaving or reentering it, a statement must be made. That is, a public, comprehensible definition of affiliations is required at gunpoint. Unmonitored travel between countries is not permitted. At the border, the torque of differential power is applied to all but political dignitaries, whose crossings are smoothed by special gates and privilege. Citizenship for the masses of course is not vague but means quite concretely the obligation to do military service and to pay taxes to support the government; both imply continued centralization of power by means of which a society exists. Borders thus are political signs and images through and through; crossing one will make all this immediately evident, especially one such as that between the U.S. and Mexico, that is, between one of the most powerful of the developed nations and a country in development. The failure of discussions of the avant-garde to consider the multiple impacts of borders through adopting a transcultural perspective reflects the blindness of power exercising its necessary function: imposition upon subjects which it reconstitutes as objects (the subject-citizen, that is, responds to the reality definitions that emanate from the center of power).

V. Language and Experimentalism

If a politically aware theory of language is needed to comprehend how borders function, it is equally necessary to an understanding of the notion of history which Chicano art manifests. That is, some of the features of a specifically *linguistic* analogue are embedded in the conceptualization of borders and of Chicano art. The language of exposition mediates power; the transparency of this language as a purged system of point-for-point referentiality exactly mirrors and transmits the mythological *donnée* of power as an absolute category. This is the language of the law, of pronouncement, of the analytical philosophy of the British and American varieties. Meaning passes through, as it were, undisturbed on its frictionless way to passive consumers of truth, who receive and are remolded. There is no room for ambiguity or differential interpretation, since the metaphorical dimension of language is ignored, seen as superfluous to the discourse of "truth," and thus tropes and images have been sublimated or stripped away altogether.

Threatening the totalizations of this hegemonic linguistic model, however, is a radical poetic potential, that is, language's poeticity, the core of the unanalyzable that inheres in verbal images and figures of speech. This transgressive power to cross borders, both literary and political, has understandably enough been that dimension which has been cordoned off as "literature," the realm of autonomous images as inscribed by New Critical textual and pedagogical practices which tend to neuter the political dimension of literature as a constituent of the humanities. For some, the key trope is metaphor, a figure which has exercised rhetoricians and philosophers since the Greeks. Even the definition of metaphor proposed in the traditionally oriented *Princeton Encyclopedia of Poetry and Poetics* opens the doors to a nontraditional reading of metaphor. Metaphor is "neutrally" defined as a relation of "comparison, contrast, analogy, similarity, juxtaposition, identity, tension, collision, fusion"(Preminger 490). Metaphor thus addresses those high-energy points where language resists abstraction, where it insists on its materiality and its ideological consequences. Metaphor is further defined as "the radical process in which the internal relationships peculiar to poetry are achieved"(490) and "a condensed verbal relation in which an idea, image, or symbol may, by the presence of one or more other ideas, images, or symbols, be enhanced in vividness, complexity, or breadth of implication"(490). Its importance to imagistic and alogical expression has thus been long recognized, but the traditional definition then distinguishes it from the more valuable "literal" dimension: metaphor "marks off the poetic mode of vision and utterance from the logical or discursive mode"(490). This definition and "marking off" of its terrain derive from Aristotle for whom "metaphor consists in giving the thing a name that belongs to something else; the transference being either from genus to species, or from species to genus, or from species to species, or on grounds of analogy" (*Poetics* 1475b; qtd. in Preminger 490). It is this transference between classificatory levels which makes metaphor the wild card, but even though Aristotle felt that metaphor made possible a revitalization of language (from it "we can best get hold of something

fresh" [*Rhetoric* 1410b; qtd. in Preminger 491]), his formalistic classificatory
system broke its effect off from infiltrating the literal. Avant-garde and postmodern linguistic theories open up to just such infiltration.

The fear that meaning would not pass unaltered from level to level has led
some rhetoricians to argue that "metaphor not only transfers and alters meaning
but may also pervert it" (Preminger 490), the thrust of such a statement turning
upon the term *pervert* (from Latin *pervertere*, to turn the wrong way, turn
around). In this turning, even Wittgenstein in his early work, prior to formulating his more situational notion of language games, saw a form of dishonesty;
metaphor, he felt, is "an 'improper' connection of terms . . . decorative but inex-
act alternative to what honest and forthright consideration would disclose in a
literal form" (Preminger 490). Wittgenstein himself represents a turning point,
as he later repudiated such a narrow investment in the a-contextual exposition
of the literal. In Derrida's subsequent assessment, metaphor is recognized as the
trope undoing Aristotelian metaphysics; as Derrida mentions, metaphor
involved "a homonymy in which Aristotle recognized . . . the very figure of that
which doubles and endangers philosophy" (271). According to the affirmative
side of such a view, metaphor involves "two (occasionally four) operative
terms . . . used for adornment, liveliness, elucidation, or agreeable mystification," and is "a trope of transference in which an unknown or imperfectly
known is clarified, defined, described in terms of a known" (Preminger 490). It
is precisely through the relational characteristic of the trope or verbal image that
the necessary conceptual slippage between the terms is traded off for a gain in
clarity. This "gain," however, is accompanied by a tremendous loss, namely,
that of philosophy itself: "Metaphor, therefore, is determined by philosophy as
a provisional loss of meaning, an economy of the proper without irreparable
damage, a certainly inevitable detour, but also a history with its sights set on,
and within the horizon of, the circular reappropriation of literal, proper meaning. This is why the philosophical evaluation of metaphor always has been
ambiguous: metaphor is dangerous and foreign as concerns *intuition* (vision or
contact), *concept* (the grasping or proper presence of the signified), and *consciousness* (proximity of self-presence)" (Derrida 270). The danger to Western
philosophical discourse with its valorizing of the literal and the transhistorical
follows: "Metaphor, then, always carries its death within itself. And this death,
surely, is also the death *of* Philosophy" (Derrida 271). Put otherwise in the
terms of Paul Ricoeur, rather than recuperating a disappearing sense of presence
and an ontologically stable meaning, the "perception of incompatibility (which)
is essential to the interpretation of the message in the case of metaphor" (186)
involves a suppression of the undifferentiated chaos which gives rise to such a
perception.

While it is beyond the scope of this paper to fully develop the application
of the linguistic models to the visual and performative arts, it should be clear

that the metaphoric rupturing of the dominant modes of literary realism and philosophical foundationalism is equally a rupturing of the institutional and disciplinary borders between art, literature, and politics. The advantage of the linguistic model is, first, that it recognizes the system of signs and codes sustaining all forms of cultural life, and second, that it provides more exact ways of discussing material that on the surface may seem non-linguistic. My basic assumption is that the social and cognitive processes involved in decoding visual images may be comparable to those involved in decoding verbal art. It is an often neglected fact, for instance, that these considerations preoccupied Roman Jakobson in his early formulations of structural linguistics: "When asked what inspired the new conception of language and linguistics in the Moscow and Prague Circles, Jakobson regularly cites as most important the avant-garde trends in painting, poetry, and music immediately preceding the First World War" (Steiner 195).[9] There is no suggestion here of a naive or happy blending of the arts, but rather of an interactive and often conflictual relationship that clearly ruptures any fixed borders. Wendy Steiner thus concludes her study by remarking: "For what is most characteristic of modern literature may very well be what exceeds that discipline, integrating verbal art in a system that includes the visual arts, criticism, and philosophy" (218). Central to this "system" will be a theory of the operations of metaphor in art.

Even from such a brief overview, we can see that as a point of rhetorical orientation, the trope of metaphor will allow us to see the interconnections between borders and Chicano art's advances over the historical avant-gardes, for metaphor "is not simply a problem of language. Though metaphor is seen in a highly developed form in poetry . . . it may also prove to be the radical mode in which we correlate all our knowledge and experience . . . juxtaposition and interaction," since it manifests "a desire to communicate, to enter into communion—without either the emerging or unification of elements or the destruction of integral individuality" (Preminger 490, 494). This surely summarizes the position of Chicano art, which correlates knowledge and experience through juxtaposition and dialectical tensions among its indigenous pre-Columbian, *mestizo*, and Native American elements (much the same way that visual image writing itself depends on juxtaposition, layering, collage, or collage-like effects), relying on the mechanism of communal production.

Such a politically self-conscious view of the interrelations of language, image, and ideology can better account for changes through time crosscut by a vertical dimension in which static comparisons of artistic styles and periods operate. This view, which shares much with the traditional diachronic model inherited from gyroscopic history, has built into it some way of explaining change based on antagonism, mutation, evolution, and discontinuity. In other words, it leads not only to an acknowledgement of the mediating, subjectivizing, socially embedded conditions of the critical activity, but also to a view of the avant-garde and the postmodern as both historically differentiated while politically interactive in their populist activism and their concern for altering the institutional status of art. It also avoids a reductive sense of the postmodern in terms of a mere stylistic innovation, a new artistic "period" which supercedes and eliminates the previous phases of the modernist and the avant-garde movements in the continuing serial of gyroscopic history.

VI. Aztlán: The Triumph of the Imaginary

In 1969 at a Chicano conference in Denver, *El Plan Espiritual de Aztlán* was formally adopted, calling for reappropriation of lands stolen from Mexico during the U.S. westward expansion. The point was to provide the basis for a social reconstruction of historical identity of oppressed peoples. Aztlán, the legendary home of the Aztecs in the Southwest, quickly became an ideological marker, inherent in which is division or separation from middle-class materialism, technological/imperialist military arrogance, and the reductionism of the profit motive. The utopian impulse, fired by the unleashed rage of groups long discriminated against in housing, education, employment, and so on, focused these forces and drove them forward. The art form which perhaps best captures these concerns is posters and murals of the period. As Goldman and Ybarra-Frausto observe, "A high sense of idealism was intrinsic to the 1968-1975 period. It explains the emphasis on community-oriented and public art forms like poster-making and muralism and on the development of artistic collectives, as well as an insistence on political and ethnic themes. Art was part of a whole movement to recapture a people's history and culture, albeit at times romantically, as part of the struggle for self-determination" (32). These public forms may be seen as complementing the intimacy of much experimental art (such as visual poetry, mail art, and artists' books), at times necessarily inward, difficult, refractory.

The inherently politically subversive nature of mural art in the modern period is traceable not to the role it played in post-Revolution Mexico, as is so often argued, but to its formal qualities as they operate in a context of contemporary urban decay. If avant-garde art is driven by a doubled code (subjectivity of artistic expression versus avant-garde difficulty), then the mural form clearly exemplifies this process. Working with representational imagery in a mode of melodramatic juxtaposition, metahistorical narratives, and monumentality, Chicano murals are an art *of* the Chicano community, produced by teams of artists and assistants; as such, they share with the historical avant-gardes a move to eliminate the imposed division between art and life which the industrialization of aesthetics in a European social context required (Goldman 139-54). Russian cubo-futurism and constructivism, Italian futurism, Berlin dadaism, French surrealism, and the Bauhaus all in one way or another consciously sought to merge art and life. In addition, all of these movements placed importance on the notion of group production, especially the most politically sophisticated, namely, Russian constructivism,[10] which excelled among other things in poster production.

Chicano mural and poster work has spawned an alternative art-socialization process; unconditional linear descent from the European schools is rejected, replaced with a popular upsurge, as the value hierarchies and their commercialization are structurally critiqued. Chicano muralists learn their trade in community workshops in the streets, not in art school. The context of lateral influences on the muralists has been oriented rather toward the Latin American avant-gardes. This problematizes a misperception noted by Goldman and Ybarra-Frausto in the following: "The young 'avant-garde' of Mexico has assumed a critical stance vis-à-vis the failed promises of the Mexican Revolution, and its members were astonished in the late 1970s to realize that the Chicano avant-garde was nostalgically glorifying aspects of Mexican culture which the Mexicans themselves had long since brought under questioning scrutiny" (8). One must realize that while the use of images of Villa, Zapata, Quetzalcoatl, or *mestizo* uprisings in a Chicano mural may seem to the Mexican viewpoint as nostalgic glorification, from that of the artists themselves as well as the art's audience, a complex strategy of cultural socialization is being pursued; that is, a mural in the social context of Chicano art, with its built-in antagonistic stance and hostile reception by the surrounding culture of oppression, is very different from a mural in the Mexican context, whose orientation towards European-conditioned experience (the chronological, historical paradigm mentioned above) has in many ways been much more telling. In general, the Latin American movements of Noigandres concretism, intersign poetry, poem/process, and others have developed, like Chicano art, in circumstances of deprivation and political oppression; these currents while understood by the Mexican avant-garde are only recently penetrating U.S. consciousness.[11]

VII. Conclusion

As I hope the above discussion has made clear, in order to avoid deriving Chicano art from that of purely Eurocentric and Anglo-American practices, while at the same time not quarantining it as autonomous and therefore nostalgic for mythological origins, one needs to revise critical practices so as to place this art in a more sophisticated intellectual/cultural context than has heretofore been the case. This context is Latin American experimentalism and the international avant-garde, with which it shares certain characteristics, yet from which it differs in its negativizing stance in relation to the cultural politics of non-Chicano, North American art. Whereas the historical avant-gardes oriented their political stances towards critiquing the bankrupt liberalism of their time, for Chicano art the target has been considerably less visible. For the Chicano avant-garde artists the stance of a rejection of a monolithic, gyroscopic history still has a strategic function in allowing for admission of mediation and the utopian reorientations which such an acknowledgement permits; these reorientations are necessary for a statistically significant, socially and economically oppressed group inhabiting a superpower nation. For the non-Chicano Latin American avant-gardists, caught up in the crossfire of the superpowers in a state of passive warfare, the ideological array of images, institutions, and representations that drive forward gyroscopic history are taken up as much more direct ammunition.

At the heart of such a revision lies the adoption of a poststructuralist conception of language, signs, and images which grants a complex, gendered, historically conditioned subjectivity. In spite of certain problems raised by the recent publication of Paul de Man's early wartime writings, the following formulation provides a useful guidepost: "One is interested in the subject-matter primarily because it confirms that the unseen can be represented: representation is the condition that confirms the possibility of imitation as universal proof of presence. The need for the reassurance of such a proof stands behind many characteristic statements of the period (modernism) and confirms its orthodoxy in terms of a metaphysics of presence" (134-35). De Man goes on to give a characterization of modernity which is not based on the flat rejection or acceptance of an unproblematized notion of history: "modernity, which is fundamentally a falling away from literature and a rejection of history, also acts as the principle that gives literature duration and historical existence" (162). This permits further efforts in the direction of theorizing the avant-garde, as does Büchloh's notion that "it seems more viable to define avant-garde practices as a continually renewed struggle over the definition of cultural meaning" (21). Büchloh's emphasis on a fully mediated struggle of a strategically constructed subjectivity denies any reified, romantic, or bourgeois notion of individuality. According to Bürger, "The avant-garde not only negates the category of individual production but also that of individual reception" (53). The divided art of resistance, conditioned throughout by the social oppression of a large national minority with intimate ties to Latin America, continues this struggle for the definition of cultural meaning, thereby demonstrating a significant advance over the mission of the historical avant-gardes.

The two views of history outlined above between them set up a spectrum of possibilities for undermining the hegemony of contemporary aesthetic theory whose bases in cultural power are all too often left unexamined. An example is the bid of certain critics to install a "protopolitical" version of postmodernism as a category in order to extend the serial unfolding of genetic movements.[12] If the postmodernist debates are to locate a politically self-conscious critical practice, then it is into this contemporary conflict that the Latin American context comes with a real sense of liberation. Thus we see that not only have the fundamental issues in the great movements of romantic, symbolist, modernist, and contemporary art been thoroughly worked through in Latin America but that also the key constellation summed up by the term avant-garde has been *extended*, not superseded or hypostatized, by a wing of Latin American practice, namely, Chicano art. Performance art and visual poetry both pry apart image/power systems, establishing the spread of options open to those artists today whose work grows out of a fuller awareness of the play of power on the high seas of culture.

Notes

1. For a different formulation of this doubleness in the context of postmodernism in general see Linda Hutcheon. For example: "The postmodern, then, effects two simultaneous moves. It reinstalls historical contexts as significant and even determining, but in so doing, it problematizes the entire notion of historical knowledge" (89).

2. "El hombre es responsable de lo que sucede; es un ser histórico, obra sobre la realidad mal que le pese y pretende olvidarlo por el camino fácil de la simbolización. La nueva poesía induce al acto y, por analogía, esa actitud se traslada al resto de sus actividades. La poesía es acto, no pensamiento. La vieja aspiración de los traficantes de ilusiones, la identificación, desaparece por su propia imposibilidad; ahora habrá que incorporarse o rechazar esos objetos llamados poemas visuales, pero en todo caso por movimiento y no por intermediación de elementos ajenos a la actualización de la poesía. Las palabras cumplían esa función celestinesca, de acarreadoras de conceptos; ahora su ajenidad, propia de los objetos, se vuelca" (Padín n. pag.).

3. "Del propio desarrollo de la vanguardia artística latinoamericana se desprenden las características que definirán el arte en su futuro próximo: la experiencia artística y la búsqueda de nuevos lenguajes y formas insertos en la producción cultural como una práctica social más, no privilegiada, al servicio de los sectores progresistas de la sociedad; la participación creativa que favorece la opción del consumidor y le induce a descubrir por sí mismo la información que la obra y el artista le trasmiten, sin imposiciones ideológicas ni juicios de valor pre-establecidos y, finalmente, el compromiso con la libertad irrestricta del hombre y los pueblos a decidir sus propios destinos (que confluyen) y con la justicia, sin la cual, cualquier acción artística, pierde sentido" ("El arte latinoamericano" n. pag.).

4. Guillermo Gómez-Peña, "The Multicultural Paradigm" 25; see also Emily Hicks, "The Artist as Citizen" 32-38.

5. For related examples, see the works reproduced in issue no. 3 of *La Linea Quebrada/The Broken Line*. "There are, in fact, many Latino artists working in computer arts, media art, video, audio and sophisticated multimedia languages, but they utilize technology in a socially responsible manner to reveal the contradictions of living and working between a preindustrial past of mythical dimensions and a postindustrial present in permanent states of crises" (Gómez-Peña, "The Multicultural Paradigm" 23).

6. "En zonas preindustriales como la cultura espanõla o los países de Latinoamérica no se daban precisamente las condiciones de una crisis cultural provocada por la industrialización y el desarrollo tecnológico; tampoco allí se concocían los efectos moralmente devastadores de la Guerra Mundial y las subsiguientes crisis revolucionar-

ias. . . . Los elementos revolucionarios, escatológicos y críticos faltaron en las manifestaciones epigónicas de la expansion internacional de la vanguardia" (Subirats 36).

7. "La utopía social y cultural de las vanguardias, de signo revolucionaria y emancipador, llevaba implícitos los momentos de su integración a un proceso regresivo de colonización tecnológica de la vida, y racionalización coactiva de la sociedad y la cultural" (Subirats19).

8. "No se trata, pues, de conservar en modo alguno el espíritu de las vanguardias históricas. Sin embargo, su superación solo es pensable a través de la restitución de sus objectivos críticos y de su principio de utopía," (Subirats 22).

9. Note also Jakobson's persistent identification of the sources of his conceptualizations with the Russian avant-garde: "what must have primarily influenced my approach to poetics and linguistics was my proximity to the poets and painters of the avant-garde" ("My Favorite Topics" 7). Elsewhere he says: "Young unorthodox linguists heeded the rallying slogans of the avant-garde poets, and we were at one with the brave and moving call jointly launched by Xlebnikov, Krucenyk, Burljuk, and Majakovskij: 'To stand on the boulder of the word WE amid a high sea of catcalls and hatred'" (*Selected Writings* vii). Jakobson's own treatment of metaphor is well known and can be found in *Fundamentals of Language*.

10. For a full discussion of Russian constructivism, see: Stephen Bann, ed., *The Tradition of Constuctivism* (New York: Viking, 1974); Charlotte Douglas, *Swans of Other Worlds: Kazimir Malevich and the Origins of Abstraction in Russia*, (Ann Arbor: UMI Research P, 1980); John Elderfield, "On the Dada-Constructivist Axis," *Dada/Surrealism*, 13 (1984): 5-16; Camilla Gray, *The Russian Experiment in Art 1863-1922* (New York: Harry N. Abrams, 1962); and George Rickey, *Constructivism: Origins and Evolution* (New York: George Braziller, 1967).

11. See N. N. Argañaraz, "La poesía experimental en Latinoamérica y Uruguay," *II Bienal Internacional de Poesía Visual y Alternativa en México*, ed. Núcleo Post-Arte (Mexico: Direción General de Difusión y Relaciones Públicas del Departamento del Distrito Federal, 1987) 36; and by the same author *Poesía Visual Uruguaya* (Montevideo: Mario Zanocchi, 1986); Clemente Padín, "Las vertientes del concretismo," *Revista del Sur* 11 (1986): 20-25; César Espinosa, "Poesía alternativa: una poetica polidimensional," *Crítica: Revista de la Universiada Autónoma de Puebla*, 28 (July-September 1986): 141-48; Louis Camnitzer, "Access to the Mainstream," *New Art Examiner* (June 1987): 20-23; also essays collected in *Signos Corrosivos*.

12. See, for instance, Fredric Jameson's articulation of this problem in his "Foreward" to Jean-François Lyotard's *The Postmodern Condition*.

Works Cited

Büchloh, Benjamin. "Theorizing the Avant-Garde." *Art in America* 72.10 (November 1984): 21.

Bürger, Peter. *Theory of the Avant-Garde*. Minneapolis: U of Minnesota P, 1984.

Burnham, Linda, Steven Durland, and Lewis MacAdams. "Art with a Chicano Accent." *High Performance*. 9.3 (1986): 51.

de Man, Paul. *Blindness and Insight: Essays in the Rhetoric of Contemporary Criticism.* New York: Oxford UP, 1971.

Derrida, Jacques. "White Mythology." *Margins of Philosophy.*Trans. Alan Bass. Chicago: U of Chicago P, 1982.

Goldman, Shifra. "Elite Artist and Popular Audiences: Can They Mix? The Mexican Front of Cultural Workers." *Studies in Latin American Popular Culture.* 4 (1985): 139-54.

Goldman, Shifra M., and Tomas Ybarra-Frausto. *Arte Chicano: A Comprehensive Annotated Bibliography of Chicano Art, 1965—1981.* Berkeley: Chicano Studies Library Publication Unit, 1985.

Gómez-Peña, Guillermo. "The Multicultural Paradigm: An Open Letter to the National Arts Community." *High Performance* 47 (Fall 1989): 18-27.

———. "A New Artistic Continent," *High Performance* 35 (1986): 24-31.

Hicks, Emily. "The Artist as Citizen," *High Performance* 35 (1986): 32-38.

———. "Border De(con)struction." *Artweek* 17.13 (5 April 1986): n. pag.

Hutcheon, Linda. *A Poetics of Postmodernism.* New York: Routledge, 1988.

Jakobson, Roman. "My Favorite Topics." *Verbal Art, Verbal Sign, Verbal Time.* Minneapolis: U of Minnesota P, 1985.

———. *Fundamentals of Language.* The Hague: Mouton, 1975.

———. *Selected Writings.* Vol. 2. The Hague: Mouton, 1975. 6 vols. 1971-85.

Jameson, Fredric. Foreword. *The Postmodern Condition.* By Jean-François Lyotard. Minneapolis: U of Minnesota P, 1984.

Padín, Clemente. "La nueva poesía," *Ovum 10* 1 (December 1969) n. pag. (Rpt. in *Signos coorosivos: selección de textos sobre poesía visual concreta-experimental- alternativa.* Ed. César Espinosa. Mexico: Ediciones Literarias de factor, 1987. 30-32.)

———. "El arte latinoamericano de nuestro tiempo." Unpublished paper, 1988.

Preminger, Alex, ed. *Princeton Encyclopedia of Poetry and Poetics.* Princeton: Princeton UP, 1974.

Ricoeur, Paul. *The Rule of Metaphor: Multi-Disciplinary Studies of the Creating of Meaning in Language.* Toronto: U of Toronto P, 1977.

Steiner, Wendy. *The Colors of Rhetoric: Problems in the Relations between Modern Literature and Painting.* Chicago: U of Chicago P, 1982.

Subirats, Eduardo. *La crisis de las vanguardias y la cultura moderna.* Madrid: Ediciones Libertarias, 1985.

Valdez, Luis and Stan Steiner, eds. *Aztlan: An Anthology of Mexican American Literature.* New York: Vintage Books, 1972. Rpt. in *Signos corrosivos: seleccion de textos sobre poesia visual concreta-experimental-alternativa.* Ed. Cesar Espinosa. Mexico: Ediciones Literarias de factor, 1987.

Chapter 9

Apostle to the Techno/Peasants:
Word and Image in the Work of John Berger

Michael W. Messmer

Gushing from the end of a rusting pipe, a stream of water signifies refreshment. This is water to be drunk from a ladle with a long handle on a sweltering summer day, or splashed on a sweating face with cupped hands. Such associations spring easily to mind if one focuses solely on the single photograph of the water. Then imagine that positioned directly to its left on the facing page is another, a reproduction of a folk artist's depiction of a kerchiefed woman baring her breast to nurse a swaddled child. Immediately the associations to the first photograph shift to those of sustenance, of water as the fountain of life. And they shift again when one discovers, by moving several pages back in the book, that the picture of the pipe end and its rivulet of water is a close-up sectioned from a larger photograph of the whole of the pipe itself, dispensing water into a small cistern against a background of a grove of trees. A worn scrub brush lies on the edge of the cistern, intimating repeated scrubbings of dirt from laborers' hands, a suggestion immediately confirmed by the picture on the facing page of three brushes, at different stages of use, the diminishing length of whose respective bristles confirm the frequency and vigor with which they are used to cleanse the hands that wield them.

Trains of such associations emerge as soon as one inserts oneself into the sequence of images titled "If each time . . . " in John Berger and Jean Mohr's *Another Way of Telling*. But the associations are not confined to the innumerable possible permutations of this sequence of 153 images in which Berger and Mohr seek to trace the course of an old peasant woman's reflections on her life. The images of water which I have isolated resonate directly into one of Berger's stories of peasant life in *Pig Earth*, "An Independent Woman," in which an elderly woman, her brother, and a neighbor (all over seventy years old) dig in almost frozen turf to uncover a pipe buried a meter beneath the surface. Tracing the pipe will lead them to the spring whose basin has become clogged, thus cutting off the flow of water to the woman's house. After three days labor, the basin is uncovered, the clogging sediment cleared away, and water flows again:

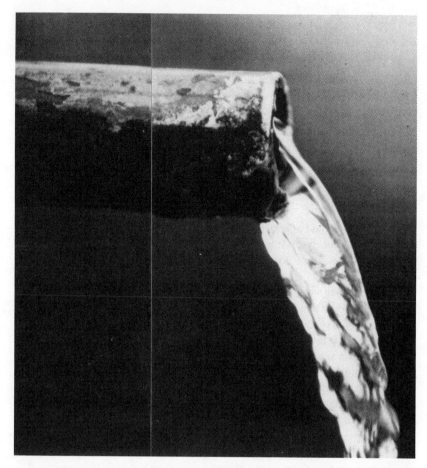

Figure 9-1
Reprinted by permission of Random House. *Another Way of Telling*, John Berger and
Jean Mohr.

"Close against the wall, in the shelter of the eaves, water gushed out of the
mouth of the pipe. As it fell, it became tangled and silver [as does the water in
the photograph described above]" (*Pig Earth* 39-40). Readers of Berger will
recall easily other examples of the weaving back and forth from image to story
which occurs in his works of recent years focusing on the peasant experience.

But the juxtaposition of associations need not end here either; they can proceed beyond as well as among Berger's texts. A recent French film, *Jean de
Florette*, centers precisely around some of the themes which now preoccupy
Berger's writing. In the film an urban family assumes ownership of and begins
to cultivate some rural property which the husband has inherited. Distrustful of

the newcomers and skeptical of the scientific agronomy which the city man attempts (initially with great success) to employ on his land, two of the local peasants scheme to ruin him. They secretly block a buried spring on the new family's land, so that when summer's heat and drought wither the crops, they will be unaware that the solution to the water problem lies on their own property. The cunning peasant, the intrusive presence of urban ways in the countryside, the vagaries of agricultural lives still subject to the whims of the forces of nature—these aspects of the film embody themes which have become crucial to Berger's peasant writing.

The primary focus of Berger's recent writing has thus been on the representation of peasant experience. This essay will unpack the complexities involved in that task by analyzing the theoretical base and the textual practice of Berger's various texts focused on the peasantry. I will argue that Berger's examination of peasant experience is founded on a theory of how photographic images and verbal narratives can be used to construct ways of depicting the experiences of human collectivities other than those dominant in contemporary late capitalist culture.

I

"Of all the changes that have come to European and world society in the wake of the industrial revolution, this transformation of agricultural life seems likely to prove the most important . . . . By breaking down peasant patterns of life across the whole of Europe within a mere two centuries, the industrial revolution clearly severed the mass of European mankind from age-old ancestral ways of life" (McNeill 160-61). Thus writes the historian William McNeill, and in doing so he articulates well a central focus of Berger's recent work. Echoing McNeill, a major section of the sociologist Peter Worsley's *The Three Worlds: Culture and World Development* centers on what he calls "The Undoing of the Peasantry." Berger is hardly unique in his concern with the massive transformations world peasantries have undergone in the past two centuries—a minor academic industry examines these changes. But he does bring a distinctive combination of talents—novelist, poet, art and culture critic, film maker—to his efforts to represent this threatened peasant world. He himself has lived in a peasant village in the Giffre River Valley in French Haute-Savoie for the past fourteen years. This blend of immersion in peasant life with the imagination of an artist has enabled Berger to produce what Worsley calls "the finest summary of the nature of peasant society and its values and its institutions—its culture" that we possess (Worsley 119). Close examination of several of Berger's recent works will reveal both the moral force of his vision of peasant experience and the methods by which he constructs the hybrid texts which are the vehicles for his expression of that vision.

I want to argue that it is only by examining several of Berger's texts together that we obtain a full sense of his re-creation of the peasant ethos. It is not just the two published volumes of the "Into Their Labors" trilogy (*Pig Earth* and *Once in Europa*), but the collaborative books with the photographer Jean Mohr (*A Seventh Man*, on European migrant workers, and *Another Way of Telling*, which they note is "a book of photographs about the lives of mountain peasants") that compel attention. My suggestion is that the four books complement one another, each producing threads of stories and/or skeins of images which weave together in intricate ways to produce the dense fabric of Berger's evocation of peasant ways.

There is little of the nostalgic or the elegiac in Berger's descriptions of the lives of peasants. If anything, the impact of his work is to suggest that McNeill's judgement may err by underestimation of the durability of peasant modes of life even after two centuries of industrialization. When McNeill writes that it "may well require another two centuries or longer before any comparably stable adjustment to the altered realities of human interdependence emerges—if it ever does," Berger might well emphasize "or longer" (McNeill 161). What fundamentally energizes Berger's work is not just the attempt to show what the determinants of the changes in the lives of peasants have been and will continue to be, although this is certainly part of his project, but the effort to depict "the way peasants look at themselves" (*Another Way* 84).

It will be useful at this point to examine briefly Berger's ideas concerning the relationship between image production in capitalist society and contemporary visual practice first advanced in his influential book *Ways of Seeing*. There he argued for a special relationship between oil painting and property relationships in emergent capitalist society, from the late fifteenth century until the end of the nineteenth. For example, he demonstrated that the genre of the nude in Western oil painting was one in which women were typically depicted as the passive visual property of a male viewer. Similarly he argued that the very properties of oil paint itself and the techniques for applying it to canvas were especially successful in the accurate depiction of the variety of material things of all kinds which were the increasing obsession of the bourgeoisie. This historical relationship between a specific art form and the sociohistorical formation in which it was embedded was then obscured in the twentieth century by the extraordinary proliferation of photographically reproduced images. In the twentieth century, advertising appropriated the visual language of oil painting, drawing much of its stock repertoire of images from that earlier visual language, and thereby preserving the core values of the tradition of oil painting in a moribund form.

Berger later modified some of his claims in *Ways of Seeing*, but it is important here to note his abiding concern with the intimacy of the relationship between art forms and their social locus, with the ideological uses to which images are put in capitalist society, and with the ways such uses act to erase historical consciousness.[1] Finally, it is crucial to keep in mind that three of the seven essays in *Ways of Seeing* had no words, but were composed solely of series of photographic images. An argument can be made without words, these essays asserted, and the process of identifying such an argument demands a participatory role for the viewer different than that of reading a text.

A concrete application of Berger's ideas in *Ways of Seeing* directly germane to this essay occurs in a short piece on the work of the French painter Millet which he wrote in 1976. In that essay Berger argued that, despite the fact that Millet more than any other single artist is identified as the painter of the European peasantry, nevertheless his works failed to embody his intention of capturing peasant experience. Berger suggested that the language of traditional oil painting could not accommodate Millet's intended subject. Since landscape painting traditionally addressed a spectator who was (most of the time) from the city, therefore: "The peasant's interest in the *land* expressed through his actions, is incommensurate with scenic landscape" (*About Looking* 76). There was no formula within the traditions of landscape for depicting "a peasant's labor *on*, instead of *in front of*, the land" and to invent one would destroy the traditional language for depicting landscape (emphasis Berger's, *About Looking* 77). Anticipating his future concerns in the texts upon which this essay will focus, Berger further suggested that the inadmissibility of the peasant into the traditions of European oil painting prefigures exactly the conflict between the First and Third Worlds in the twentieth century.

As far as Berger's own recent practice is concerned, he clearly considers it possible to do with other art forms, notably photography and writing, what oil painting could not accomplish, namely the representation of peasant experience. In a 1978 essay on the "Uses of Photography," he began to speculate about an alternative photographic practice, one which would be based upon the incorporation of photographs into what he called "social and political memory." The way to accomplish this would be "to construct a context for a photograph, to construct it with words, to construct it with other photographs, to construct it by its place in an ongoing text of photographs and images" (*About Looking* 60). This context-construction would develop in a radial, as opposed to a linear way. The context into which a photograph was to be embedded "must mark and leave open diverse appearances," thus allowing the photograph to be seen in terms "which are simultaneously personal, political, economic, dramatic, everyday and historic" (*About Looking* 63). In suggesting such an alternative use for photographic practice Berger was outlining the concerns which have continued to preoccupy him. To these we can now direct our attention.

A statement from the "Historical Afterword" to *Pig Earth* provides a convenient beginning point. Berger writes: "Recently the insulation of the citizen has become so total that it has become suffocating. He lives alone in a serviced limbo—hence his newly-awakened, but necessarily naive, interest in the countryside" (206). One can read a certain autobiographical content into these words, finding there one of the reasons for Berger's relocation to a French peasant village. But the naivete of the newly-awakened interest of the city dweller breeds nostalgia or elegy, precisely what Berger seeks to avoid, and the seeming permanence of his remove to the French peasantry ensured against it. He has followed the reverse course from that which his writings trace: from the advanced urban industrial world to the peasantry. Of course, and this is one of his points, the line of demarcation has never been so clearly cut: the boundaries between urban and rural have been increasingly permeable from the beginnings of the industrial era, with the primary vector of change initiating in the industrialized metropolises. Berger seeks a partial reversal of that vector.

It is thus a living peasant world Berger wants to re-create and his means of doing so are noteworthy. His most significant work oriented toward the depiction of peasant life constitutes a series of experiments which, taken together, comprise a (still-emerging) whole whose various parts interweave in striking ways. Several examples will illustrate this. The longest and most fully developed story in *Pig Earth* is "The Three Lives of Lucie Cabrol," a tale of the grim survival and fundamental humanity of a peasant woman. The cover photograph of Berger and Mohr's *Another Way of Telling* shows a wizened peasant woman whose hands grasp the end of the handle of what is likely a spade (although the photograph does not show the full length of the tool) and whose kerchief recalls that of the madonna in the folk picture from this same book. Is this woman Lucie Cabrol? In one obvious sense she is not, for the list of photographs at the book's end identifies the woman as a Swiss peasant and Lucie Cabrol is a product of Berger's imagination, albeit based upon his own experience of peasant life. But in another sense, that which Berger implies in the prefatory note to *Once in Europa* when he writes that: "Certain details apart, this [fictional] village could exist in a number of countries across the continents of the world" (prefatory "Note"), this *is* a photograph of Lucie Cabrol, her lined face, small stature, and strong hands. This image of a Swiss peasant is a quotation, as Berger writes that all photographs are quotations, from the infinite series of appearances of peasant women in global history. Reading Berger's story and looking at Mohr's photograph are mutually supporting and reinforcing; they complement one another.

Repeatedly in *Pig Earth* the magnetic pull of urban metropolises on peasant ways is captured, often in just one or several short sentences within a larger fragment of a story, as when we find out that Lucie's brother Emile "had left in the autumn to work in Paris as a stoker for the central heating of the new department store of Samaritaine" (*Pig Earth* 108) or that the old woman Catherine in the story about the blocked spring "had worked once as a waitress in a cafe near the Gare de Lyon in Paris" (31) or that the peasant man in the story "Addressed to Survivors" (in *Pig Earth*) had once been an army conscript.

The pull of power—the power of the state to conscript, of the labor market to offer better wages, of international capital to disrupt traditional ways of life and displace millions—is another central concern of Berger's, perhaps most straightforwardly in *A Seventh Man*, his and Mohr's book on the experience of contemporary migrant workers in Europe. This latter text's theme is "the new phenomenon of millions of peasants migrating to countries with which they had no previous connection" (*Seventh Man* 8). Here (and in *Another Way of Telling*) the connection between images and words is more straightforward than it could be in *Pig Earth* or *Once in Europa*, but in these latter works the connections are nevertheless there with those of Berger's books which do include photographic images. The photo essay in *Another Way of Telling* is interspersed with images from the metropolitan world: a railroad poster, scenes from Istanbul contrasting with ones from rural Turkey, a reproduction of a postcard of the Eiffel Tower. Some of these immediately trigger associations with Berger's written work. For example, in the story "Boris Is Buying Horses" in *Once in Europa*, one of the characters remarks: "Once you brought me a packet of cigarettes whilst I was grazing the sheep above the factory" (*Europa* 42). Juxtaposed here into one scene are two archetypal images of urban industrial and rural life—grazing sheep and a factory. Readers familiar with *Another Way of Telling* will then recall the photograph of a Geneva suburb in which two shepherds move their flock down a street running alongside a factory with a contemporary high-rise building in the background (*Another Way of Telling* 180-81). (See Figure 9-2.) This insistent mutual reinforcement of image and text, both within individual works and between and among them, is a key methodological tool in Berger's project of depicting peasant experience.

The combination of stories told with images alone and of writing powerfully shaped by ways of seeing enables Berger to evoke the lived quality of peasant life. The specificity of these evocations he combines with an overarching explanation of why the transformation of peasant life has proceeded along the paths it has assumed over the past two centuries. Not surprisingly for those acquainted with Berger's work over four decades, that explanation is a broadly Marxist one.[2] The only extensive sustained attempt to frame such an argument occurs in the afterword to *Pig Earth*, but its essence is contained in one sentence from *A Seventh Man*: "Only if we understand that imperialism brings to its widest possible application the universal law of uneven and combined development, can we understand world history in the twentieth century" (*Seventh Man* 35).

For the most part, the theoretical apparatus Berger brings to his peasant writing is unobtrusive, allowing foregrounding of his primary concern with the cultural specificity of peasant life. But there is a "fit" between the formal means Berger employs in his peasant texts and the historical changes he seeks to comprehend. An interesting example occurs in "The Three Lives of Lucie Cabrol."

Figure 9-2
Reprinted by permission of Random House. *Another Way of Telling*, John Berger and Jean Mohr.

The last part of this story contains a (literally) fantastic scene in which the now-dead Lucie conducts the narrator, Jean (her former lover), to a community house building, where he works with a group of deceased men of his village in building a new house. It is a scene strongly reminiscent of those in the magic realist novels of contemporary Latin American authors such as Gabriel García Márquez. One commentator on Berger's work specifically uses the description "magic realist" to characterize this story.[3] What interests me here is the relevance to Berger's writing in *Pig Earth* of some comments on magic realism by Fredric Jameson. Jameson notes that two tendencies seem to achieve synthesis in the work of García Márquez: his work contains "a transfigured object world in which fantastic events are *also* narrated" and such a conception of magic realism is "anthropological." Magic realism would then be understood as a kind of "narrative raw material derived essentially from peasant society, drawing in sophisticated ways on the world of village or even tribal myth." This captures a key aspect of Berger's story. Later in the same article Jameson advances a provisional hypothesis that "the possibility of magic realism as a formal mode is constitutively dependent on a type of historical raw material in which disjunction is structurally present; or, to generalize the hypothesis more starkly, magic realism depends on a content which betrays the overlap or the coexistence of precapitalist with nascent capitalist or technological features" (Jameson 301-2). The organizing category of magic realism is therefore the struggle of different modes of production, and I would suggest that, if Jameson's hypothesis is correct, then Berger's most successful peasant story should *necessarily* have been cast in the mode of magic realism.

It is also appropriate to link Berger's work with a current project within anthropology, one identified most clearly by George E. Marcus in his contribution to the important collection of essays *Writing Culture: The Poetics and Politics of Ethnography*. Marcus is concerned in his essay "Contemporary Problems of Ethnography in the Modern World System" with how "contemporary experimentation with the ethnographic genre" can contribute "to the understanding of the operation of the capitalist political economy." He points out that "ethnographers who write within the Marxist theoretical tradition . . . have the powerful advantage of placing the larger order in the background while focusing intensely upon a closely observed locale as ethnographic subject." This advantage is characteristic of Berger's peasant works as well and is at least one of the reasons for their power. Berger too writes within a broadly Marxist framework. The lineaments of that framework—still, in Marcus's words, "the most sophisticated and coherent framework for conceptualizing modern societies to survive the nineteenth century"—can be taken to be familiar to Berger's readers and hence, as with Marxist-oriented ethnography, "much of the work of inventing a representation of the larger order is accomplished by orienting or referring the situated ethnography to issues of Marxist theory," as Berger does in the afterword to *Pig Earth*. It is also noteworthy that Marcus turns to some programmatic paragraphs from the work of the British literary and cultural critic Raymond Williams, approving his call for the production of experimental texts as the most appropriate vehicle for attempts to integrate "the macro into the micro, combining accounts of impersonal systems into representations of local life as cultural forms both autonomous and constituted by the larger order" (Marcus 169-73). Again, this precisely captures the importance of Berger's works on the peasantry in contemporary France: they are experimental texts, combining images and words, or fiction, poetry, and historical analysis, in a series of attempts to capture the lived reality of peasant experience as it is subject to the constantly disruptive pull of the capitalist world economy.

Berger, however, is not a professional ethnographer, nor is he, even after a decade and a half of life among them, a peasant. This forces upon us a question Berger himself raises: "What is the writer's relationship with the place and the people he writes about?" (*Pig Earth* 5). It is a question very similar to the one which Marcus suggests that any ethnography sensitive to political economy must answer: "Why precisely are you in this locale rather than another?" Berger has written sensitively about these questions at the beginning of *Pig Earth*, where he makes it clear that he himself is not a peasant and that his writing is "both a link and a barrier" in his relationship to the peasants among whom he lives. His description of himself as both novice and independent witness is reminiscent of ones in anthropological writing, where the ethnographer finds herself or himself in the position of a child within the new culture which he or she seeks to study, a person who must learn the ways of life of the people whose lives he or she will share, but one whose expertise places the ethnographer (or Berger) in a special position, an independent witness with access to a body of knowledge beyond that of local cultural knowledge. When Berger notes that this double role of novice and independent witness establishes a "certain reciprocity" between himself and the peasants with whom he lives he is touching upon an area in contemporary anthropological writing which is receiving sustained self-reflective attention. As Berger has it, "the stranger who is a witness [to local culture] may also, under certain circumstances, be able to contribute" (*Pig Earth* 11). As the novice is taught by those with whom he lives, they recognize that he may include them in one of his stories, or in an ethnographic monograph, and this places a heavy burden upon the writer, one which is at the same time an opportunity: how to attain and maintain respect *as equals* for those with whom one has come to live, despite the often vast difference in the bodies of knowledge to which each has access from within their respective cultures.

Several comments are necessary at this juncture. Berger became interested in attempting to comprehend the peasant way of life during the course of working on *A Seventh Man* with Jean Mohr. He came to understand that the migrant workers whose lives he was documenting were, by and large, the sons of peasants, from Turkey, Portugal, North Africa, and the other areas peripheral to the European heartland from which the overwhelming majority of migrants are drawn. The more he sought to imagine the peasant world, the more he realized that in order to write about it, about what mattered to its inhabitants, he would have to live among them. As he noted in a recent interview: "I wanted to tell the peasants' story before they were gone from the earth." So Berger opted to relocate among the French peasantry of the Vallée du Giffre. Unlike the ethnographer, whose residence with another people is periodic, Berger's with the peasantry appears permanent. Over the years of residence with them two bases of mutual respect emerged between him and his neighbors. He shares their work—making hay, tending cows, other agricultural tasks—and in doing so has found a basis from which to understand peasant life. As he notes: "The best way to know peasants is not by talking but by doing things, working together" (Marzorati 46, 50). But Berger is a writer, not a peasant, just as the anthropologist is not a native. Here, too, however, a basis for respect developed, founded on the local peasants' understanding that, like their own labors, that of the writer is arduous and difficult as well. Respect for effort and skill provided a basis for common appreciation across the gulf that separated the urbane Berger from his rural compatriots.

An equally potent foundation for equality is the mutual recognition between Berger and the peasants of the importance of storytelling in their respective lives. As he intimates in *Pig Earth*, this, more than shared labor or mutual recognition of labor's difficulty, constitutes the basis for the perception of equality between himself and his peasant friends. He writes of trying to puzzle out precisely what was the source of the look of complicity he caught in the eyes of one of his friends as they drank coffee after working together during a morning. It wasn't the work itself, he thought. After some time he knew: "It was his recognition of our equality: we were both storytellers. As storytellers we both see how events fit together" (*Pig Earth* 12). Thus it is that Berger has been able to establish a reciprocity with the French peasantry among whom he has chosen to live, and it is from that foundation in common lived experience that he writes.

II

Another aspect of Berger's enterprise takes the discussion onto a more theoretical level. Here I will address the ways in which he grapples with the problem limned by Marcus, that of precisely how to represent the experience of lives lived under the global pull of the world economy but to do so in such a way as to ensure that local forms of life can be represented in their autonomy as well as in their character as constituted by the larger order—the problem of the micro and the macro. In addressing this question, a passage from *A Seventh Man* is helpful. Berger is discussing the importance of giving proper value to any attempt to depict the actual experience of migrant workers within the context of the world economic system. He notes that economic theory can explain how the conditions which lead to emigration emerge and it can show why the global economic system needs the labor power peculiar to migrant workers. But then he notes that: "Yet necessarily the language of economic theory is abstract. And so, if the forces which determine the migrant's life [and the peasant's] are to be grasped and realized as part of his personal destiny, a less abstract formulation is needed. Metaphor is needed. Metaphor is temporary. It does not replace theory" (*Seventh Man* 41).

Several oppositions—macro/micro, theory/metaphor—have now emerged and together they point toward a fuller consideration of Berger's ideas concerning the relationship between images and social memory, which is another key element in his peasant works. The most extensive development of these ideas is in a 1980 essay titled "Another Way of Telling," and I want to examine it in some detail.[4] Berger there interrogates the nature of the mediation which a photograph makes between reality and the viewer. He reminds us that, unlike a painting which begins with an empty surface, a photograph begins with an event to be photographed, with appearances in the world. From its nineteenth-century origins the power of photography was always related to its ability accurately to capture and record appearances. A photograph is a tiny fragment of past time, resulting from a single choice, that of the photographer opting to record *this* particular instant. Thus, in comparison with a painting or a story, a photograph for Berger is weak in intentionality. Marvelous recording instrument that it is, the camera nevertheless does not itself deploy a language, as does painting. It *quotes* from what Berger calls the language of appearances, as opposed to a painting, which *translates* from that language.

It is precisely because photographs themselves are weak in meaning for Berger (Roland Barthes's view, similar to Berger's, was that a photographic image is "a message without a code"[5]) that they are so readily subject to manipulation and simplification and can be used to hide rather than reveal the truth. This is why Berger can argue that there is a "congruity" between the current uses of photography and capitalism. As mere traces of experience rather than re-creations or re-presentations of them, photographs (especially photographs in their myriad public uses—advertising, news, etc.) are curiously mute with regard to their subjects. Further, photographs are records of the past and Berger argues that in the ways photographs are used in the modern world, the photographed past never rejoins the present. Finally, the weak intentionality of photographs makes then easily manipulable by the kind of slogans or captions that are so frequently attached to them. This means for Berger that photography in its public uses conforms to the needs of capitalism to deny sensitivity, to negate the past, and to provide means to enhance capitalist credibility. It is against this predominant use of photography that Berger works.

His primary question is this: given that the language of appearances is the "working material" of photography, "Is there a way of using photography so that it becomes a means of *making sense* of experience through the language of appearances?" ("Another Way" 71; Berger's emphasis). How can photography, which is conducive to a fragmented view of the world, be used against the grain of this fragmentation? How can photographs be made to tell a story? That single photographs *do* frequently tell stories is part of virtually everyone's experience of them. A personal photograph instantaneously establishes a complex web of connections between past and present because personal memory identifies the subject and immediately triggers a concatenation of associations. Berger thinks that public pictures can be made to do what private photographs typically do. How?

If, he argues, photographs are treated as a "vast inchoate memory of collective experience" then it should be possible to mobilize parts of this memory by centering them "around the recounting of a specific experience" (74). The result would be the construction of a universal public memory analogous to the private memories that are always already there for the individual and for small groups of people sharing common experiences. Since photographs offer "a kind of historical evidence" they can be used to present images as belonging to "a *living* memory" rather than being treated as they typically are in capitalist society, as relics of the past, the "perfect nostalgic objects" which act to eliminate the past as a reality (72; Berger's emphasis), The appropriate means for accomplishing this alternative use of photographs is montage, the construction of sequences of still photographs, as in *Another Way of Telling*. Such sequences "can be read forwards and backwards many times," hence putting the viewer in a position where he or she "makes his [or her] own way," independently (72). The eye of the viewer can wander, searching for connections, following a "way of seeking understanding in a language other than words" (78).

Accomplishment of this objective (and it is part of the argument of this essay that Berger has accomplished it in *Another Way of Telling*) would then challenge what he sees as the two "alibis" which current uses of photography offer for contemporary capitalism. As he notes, "late capitalism rejects the social function of any human subjectivity and, consequently, all subjectivity is treated as private," and in current uses of photography "the experience of the other, while open to observation, has little or nothing to do with the experience of the viewer" (73). Berger's peasant work, then, is meant to confront these alibis and to show how it is possible to use photographs "on behalf of the photographed" (75).

This dual aim of the recovery of subjectivity and the erasure of the separation between viewer and other is at the basis of Berger's demand for both metaphor and theory, although I think it is helpful to rewrite this demand in other terms. The separation of metaphor and theory in the lines from *A Seventh Man* quoted earlier obscures the irreducible metaphorical component of all theories. If we use a very general definition of metaphor, that "the essence of metaphor is understanding and experiencing one kind of thing in terms of another," then I think it is arguable that all theories are metaphors and hence that Berger's separation of metaphor and theory is misconstrued (Lakoff and Johnson, 5). A more helpful contrast, and one closer to Berger's meaning, would be between "abstraction" and "concrete studies."[6] The abstractions of theory must not only be tied down with the specificity of concrete studies, but the latter are in fact more important, as Berger himself accepts when he writes in "Another Way of Telling" that "work done is more useful than theory, not only because it encourages rather than discourages (the critical spirit of theory is always negative), but also because practice never respects the limits of theory.

The area staked out by theory is invariably too small and too pure. Practice complicates and enlarges it" (75).

This valorizing of practice over theory is embodied in the structure of *Pig Earth*, where the brief theoretical afterword comes at the book's end. Berger likens this afterword to what he calls a nineteenth-century "tradition" in which novelists and storytellers gave their readers an explanation of their work, typically in the form of a preface. The reason for this was that "it is not usually possible in a poem or a story to make the relation between particular and universal fully explicit" (*Pig Earth* 195). The necessity for such prefaces was the revolutionary changes in the nineteenth century which increasingly made "the relation between the individual and history . . . a conscious one." The twentieth century has experienced even greater changes, yet, Berger thinks, it is now rare for a writer to attempt an explanation for his or her book because the work of imagination is seen as self-sufficient and "literature has elevated itself into a pure art." (Perhaps it would be more accurate for Berger to have written "the work of the *modernist* imagination.") Berger himself challenges that modernist assumption by asserting that most literature, even that intended for an "elite" readership, has "degenerated into pure entertainment." He opposes both developments, especially because they are "an insult to the dignity of the reader, the experience communicated, and the writer" (*Pig Earth* 196). Hence, as in nineteenth-century practice, his concluding essay is meant to offer his reader an explanation of how the stories of *Pig Earth* establish a relation between the particular and the universal, the micro and the macro. Berger is making sure his own literary work will not be interpreted in modernist terms.[7]

Another methodological comment, this one from *Another Way of Telling*, implicitly acknowledges this emphasis on the concrete as prior to the abstractions of theory. Berger writes: "All photographs are ambiguous. All photographs have been taken out of continuity. . . . Discontinuity always produces ambiguity. Yet often this ambiguity is not obvious, for as soon as photographs are used with words, they produce an effect of certainty, even of dogmatic assertion" (*Another Way* 91). Like the linking of photograph and text, so too with theory: since the risk is that of dogmatic assertion, Berger's preferred mode will be that of ambiguity, of the concrete, what he calls "metaphor." It is from such a position that he can emphasize as strongly as he does that the photographs which comprise a substantial part of books like *A Seventh Man* and *Another Way of Telling* must be read independently of the texts themselves; they are not meant simply to illustrate points which the written text makes. Complementarity and mutual reinforcement is the relationship that must exist between them. As he notes at the beginning of *A Seventh Man*: "The book consists of images and words. Both should be read in their own terms. Only occasionally is an image used to illustrate the text" (*Seventh Man* 7). Or, in the prefatory comment to the sequence of photos which occupies 140 consecutive pages of

Another Way of Telling: "We are far from wanting to mystify. Yet it is impossible for us to give a verbal key or storyline to this sequence of photographs. To do so would be to impose a single verbal meaning upon appearances and thus to inhibit or deny their own language. In themselves appearances are ambiguous, with multiple meanings. This is why the visual is astonishing and why memory, based upon the visual, is freer than reason" (*Another Way* 133). It is also why Berger's current project on the peasantry consists of photographs, fiction, and poetry: here the power of memory, anchored in lived experience, couples with Berger's intensely visual imagination to establish the conditions for his own access to the French peasant world and for his representation of it.

I would argue further that Berger's peasant works belong within the emergent genre of experimental texts which Marcus and Williams suggest as appropriate vehicles for enabling an ethnographer to grapple with the problem of situating lives lived at the local level within the broader framework of the global economy. James Clifford writes of good ethnographies as "ethnographic fictions," emphasizing the strong sense of that apparently oxymoronic phrase: "Ethnographic writings can properly be called fictions in the sense of 'something made or fashioned,' the principal burden of the word's Latin root, *fingere*. But it is important to preserve the meaning not merely of making, but also of making up, of inventing things not actually real."[8] Whereas some of the more creative contemporary anthropological work approaches the notion of ethnographic fiction from the ethnography side, Berger approaches it from the side of fiction, as the paperback edition of *Pig Earth* unwittingly documents when the back cover indicates that the book should be classified as "Fiction/Anthropology." That Berger's work belongs within this interpretive category of ethnographic fictions can be grasped by comparing it with several recent works, two of which take their inspiration from his own writings.

The distinguished cultural critic Edward Said has collaborated with Jean Mohr on the book *After the Last Sky: Palestinian Lives*. Said himself has praised Berger's work, suggesting that in his most recent writing "there is the basis of a major critique of modern representation" (Said, "Opponents" 24). His own book is clearly patterned after the collaborative work of Berger and Mohr, and he is eloquent in describing its purpose and the methodology for accomplishing it. He writes that he wants to engage "the problem of writing about and representing the Palestinians generally," and hence "to deny the habitually simple, even harmful representations of Palestinians, and to replace them with something more capable of capturing the complex reality of their experience" (Said and Mohr 6). Substituting "peasant" for "Palestinians" would precisely capture Berger's intentions. Said then goes on to argue that "essentially unconventional, hybrid, and fragmentary forms of expression" should be used to represent the Palestinian experience, because of its main contemporary features of "dispossession, dispersion, and yet also a kind of power incommensurate with our stateless exile." The text he and Mohr produce attempts precisely this, by mixing genres, modes, and styles, by the interplay of texts and images, by eschewing any attempts to tell a consecutive story or formulating a political essay. What I would argue is that, unlike Berger and Mohr's coauthored books, Said's does not manifest that mutual reinforcement between image and text which I have earlier argued is a crucial aspect of *A Seventh Man* and *Another Way of Telling*. In *After the Last Sky* the powerful written texts always threaten to overwhelm the photographs, reducing them to the role of supplements to the written words. This is partly the result of the inclusion of captions which anchor each photograph specifically to passages in the text. It is far harder, indeed virtually impossible (because of the captions and the texts) to read the photographs on their own terms, as Berger and Mohr had stated that those in *A Seventh Man* should be read. This is not to diminish either the power or the significance of *After the Last Sky*, only to note that it is less successful in maintaining the equivalence of image and word which Berger seeks.

A similar point can be made about an important recent essay by Susan Buck-Morss: "Semiotic Boundaries and the Politics of Meaning: Modernity on Tour—A Village in Transition." Buck-Morss explicitly acknowledges her theoretical indebtedness to Berger. Her incisive essay examines the struggles for power over the production of meanings which occur in a Cretan village which has recently become a popular tourist attraction for northern Europeans and hence the locus for a complex interweave of cultural, sex, and class systems within the broader framework of tourism and its impact on political and economic relationships in an international context. (Among other things, her study parallels Berger's *A Seventh Man*, but from the opposite direction: she studies the relationship of northern European tourist migrants with their southern European host communities; he studies southern European worker migrants' relationships with their northern European hosts.) What is relevant to our discussion at this point is Buck-Morss's statement that: "Specifically for reasons that are both philosophical and political, I rely heavily on images which, as concrete representations of material reality, have the power to challenge conventional theory, not merely to illustrate it" (200). 1 would argue that where the challenge in fact is issued is with the text's appropriation of the photographic images, which can be elucidated only through a reading of the text itself. As in Said's book so too here: the photographic images are supplements of the argumentative structure of the written text; they cannot be read on their own with the expectation that conclusions at all congruent with those drawn in the text would be forthcoming from such an independent reading.[9]

I would like to suggest that a striking recent book by the anthropologist Richard Price, one valorized by Clifford as a successful example of experimental ethnography, is closer in methodological approach and impact on the reader to Berger's work than that of authors like Said and Buck-Morss who have explicitly sought to follow Berger's example. In *First-Time: The Historical Vision of an Afro-American People*, Price presents a complex text composed of oral testimonies about the lives of eighteenth-century Saramaka maroons who escaped from slavery and settled in the tropical rain forests of Suriname where their contemporary descendants provided the sources from which Price obtained the recollections which comprise part of his book. These oral texts are arranged to run across the top half of the page in *First-Time*, while Price's commentaries occupy the bottom half. This produced a book divided into what he calls two "channels," and they together involve the reader in a complex interweave from commentary to text and back. This opening up of two separate channels of communication into the past and present of the Saramakas is closely akin to Berger's methods, in which image and text are intended to open up two different, but mutually reinforcing channels of communication. Similarly, in *Pig Earth*, the channels opened are those of poetry, fiction, and authorial commentary, although not presented in the innovative manner of Price's text.

Price's suggestion about how best a reader can use his book might apply to Berger's texts as well. He counsels a process of "double reading," hoping that "most readers will be sufficiently patient to try out the following procedure, for which the presentation was designed. First, read a text (or bundle of texts) indicated by a single title. . . . Then turn back and read the commentary indicated by the same title. And finally, reread the text with the commentary in mind before going on to the next text and continuing the process" (Price 40). The specifics of these reading guidelines cannot apply to Berger's texts, which are organized along their own lines, but they capture well the impact Berger's texts can have. In effect, both Berger and Price ask that the typical linear direction of the reading process be fractured into a series of back and forth movements, from oral text to commentary or from image to written text, or from one image to another, and that two or more co-present channels of communication thus be allowed to filter into each other in an oscillating reading maneuver over which the reader herself has a significant amount of control. Although Berger uses both written and pictorial "channels" while Price employs two different written ones, the impact is quite similar in that the texts of both authors invite the reader's eye (and consciousness) to wander, to search for connections, to make her or his own way and thus render the reader/viewer more independent in confronting texts than would have been the case if only one channel had been open. Thus the organization of the texts themselves helps to pull the reader into the text and hence into the lives of the peoples represented therein.

At the conclusion of Said's essay in which he argued that Berger's recent work constitutes a basis for a critique of modern representation, he briefly outlined a "program of interference" in cultural politics for which he suggested two concrete tasks, both of which he thinks are adumbrated by Berger. These are "opening the culture to experiences of the other which have remained 'outside' (and have been repressed or framed in a context of confrontational hostility) the norms manufactured by 'insiders'" and using "the visual faculty . . . to restore the nonsequential energy of lived historical memory and subjectivity as fundamental components of meaning in representation" (Said, "Opponents" 25). In Berger's work (and in that of Price) the oscillation between channels and the requisite double reading directly taps this nonsequential energy through the reading process itself.

<h1 style="text-align:center">III</h1>

Focus on these crucial aspects of Berger's work—representation of peasant experience, location of that experience within a global historical trajectory, and interrogation of the relationship between photography and writing—compels a further question: how to situate Berger's writing within that complex of discourses which in the past decade has placed the concept of postmodernism at the center of contemporary critical thought. Berger's work, I will argue, is an ambiguous signpost standing at the junction of modernism and postmodernism, pointing in both directions.

I suggested earlier Berger's effort to distance his work from one fundamental modernist impulse, that of art for art's sake. But in an illuminating discussion of the photographic essay, W. J. T. Mitchell emphasizes how such texts as Said and Mohr's *After the Last Sky* or Agee and Evans's *Let Us Now Praise Famous Men* insist on "the distinctive character of each medium" (writing and photography) which constitutes them, pursuing thereby a "search for a 'purity' of approach that is both artistic and ethical" (Mitchell 13). From within the now-classic formalist version of modernism associated with the criticism of Clement Greenberg, this is a modernist emphasis, one Berger's work clearly shares. And yet, Mitchell also notes that the origins of the photographic essay lie "in documentary journalism, newspapers, magazines, and the whole ensemble of visual-verbal intersections in mass media [which] connect it to popular forms of communication that seem quite antithetical to modernism in their freedom of exchange between image and text." This erosion of the separation of high and mass culture is emphasized consistently in current attempts to map the terrain of postmodernism.

In his provocative book *Hiding in the Light: On Images and Things* Dick Hebdige constructs an illuminating contrast between what he describes as two very different "Worlds" which he calls "Planet One" and "Planet Two." On Planet One "relations of power and knowledge are so ordered that priority and precedence are given to written and spoken language over 'mere (idolatrous) imagery'"; it is a World which unfolds along a single line of historical time (Hebdige 158). Recently a progressive group within the intellectual priesthood on Planet One has arisen which has attempted to adjust the subordinate relation of images to words and to provide the former with expanded autonomy, still however within the same historical vision. By contrast, there is a Second World, that of Planet Two, which is strikingly different: here the supremacy of word over image has been upended, language serves as supplement to the now dominant image, historical sense has been flattened out into a synchronic horizontality, and truth (still approachable if only asymptotically on Planet One) dissolved into language games and rhetorical strategies. This Second World is the world of what Hebdige calls the "People of the Post": postmodernism and poststructuralism.

One of the examples he gives of the difficulty in traversing the gap between Planet One and Planet Two is that of photography and of writing on photography, and he cites Berger's work as an instance of a First World attempt "to place the photograph within a web of narratives which are designed to authenticate its substance (i.e., that which is depicted) in order to make the image 'tell' its true story" (163). By contrast the People of the Post on Planet Two seek the opposite, "to liberate the signifier from the constraints imposed upon it by the rationalist theology of 'representation.'" There is a truth somewhere beyond or beneath appearances for a First Worlder like Berger, but for denizens of the Second World such an assumption is nothing but a theological illusion.

The position Hebdige finally takes in his staged confrontation between the Worlds of Planets One and Two would be Berger's as well. Hebdige writes of the necessity to remind himself constantly that "there will never be an end to judgement," that there is a line separating truth from lies, justice from injustice, and that the order of both his two Worlds is built on the chaos of all the "avoidable disasters" of contemporary history such as Chile and Biafra (176). Berger's position is perfectly congruent with this, for he clearly believes that a series of photographs, for example, can be used to speak truth to a world based on injustice and domination, even though readers should be able to make their own way through such image sequences. By contrast, in Hebdige's Planet Two such a series of photographs as that in *Another Way of Telling* would be "cruised" by a reader picking up whatever he or she found useful. Such a reading of Berger and Mohr's text would be at odds with their own First World intentions.

If it is Berger's historical vision coupled with his belief that photographs record reality that makes him a Planet One critic, it is precisely those notions which are the basis for a critique of his work by John Tagg, who in his *The Burden of Representation: Essays on Photographies and Histories* takes Berger to task for his effort to develop a world historical consciousness and for his confidence that photographs do record appearances automatically, as it were, quoting directly from the language of appearances. Working from within a perspective strongly influenced by the work of Michel Foucault, Tagg argues that "the pretentious role of critical overseer and commentator" must be abandoned and that "real historical research" will accomplish that abandonment most effectively (Tagg 204). Such historical analysis will uncover, as several of Tagg's essays demonstrate, the complexly interwoven codes of knowledge and power which produced the web of discourse ("the regime of truth," to use the Foucauldian term) from within which "photography's privileged status as a guaranteed witness of the actuality of the objects or events it represents" is displaced from "the alleged intrinsic nature of the photographic process . . . to the level of the operation of certain privileged apparatuses within the given social formation, such as . . . scientific establishments, government departments, the police and law courts" (189). Tagg's historical microscopy cannot therefore reveal any general plan (as he says Berger tries to do), but rather seeks to identify micropolitical sites for struggle in the present. Equipped as he is with the tools of semiotics, Althusserian ideological critique, and Foucauldian dissection of regimes of truth (tools frequently described as postmodernist or poststructuralist), Tagg might be described as an inhabitant of Planet Two who has replaced the cruising of images with their genealogical decipherment a la Foucault. Again, as in Hebdige's example, Berger appears as a critic opposed to the People of the Post, although Tagg's negative appraisal contrasts with that of Hebdige.

Tagg's suspicion of what he takes to be Berger's future-oriented search for a world-historical consciousness is reminiscent of Jean-François Lyotard's now-familiar suspicion of modern master-narratives in his *The Postmodern Condition*. Within Lyotard's perspective Berger's work would still be captive within the moribund project of the Enlightenment. Taking the opposite tack, Said has argued that Lyotard's version of postmodernism is an "amnesiac vision," one which "*separates* Western postmodernism from the non-European world, and from the consequences of European modernism—and modernization—in the colonized world" (Said, "Representing" 224, 222; Said's emphasis). For Said, experiences such as exile, immigration, and the crossing of boundaries demand "new narrative forms" or, and here he cites Berger, "*other* ways of telling" (225; Said's emphasis). In his moving obituary assessment of Foucault, Said characterized his histories as "self-aware, mixed-genre performances" whose "deliberate extraterritoriality" mark them as postmodern (Said, "Foucault" 3). He gives a number of other examples of such mixed-genre texts and again points to Berger's work. Thus for Said, as for Mitchell, it is the hybrid character of Berger's texts which defines them as postmodern. Further, Berger's work is one example, Said argues, of an appropriate move toward the construction of new narrative forms which would counter the Eurocentric postmodernism of a Lyotard. Berger's work might then be seen as an instance of that postmodernism of resistance which Andreas Huyssen has invoked as a means of opposing what he calls an affirmative postmodernism of the "anything goes" variety (roughly analogous with Hebdige's Planet Two).[10]

Said's joining of Foucault and Berger, in contrast to Tagg's opposing of them, is echoed by the geographer Edward Soja in his book *Postmodern Geographies: The Reassertion of Space in Critical Social Theory.* Soja calls for a "spatialization" of critical thought as an antidote to the historicization he argues dominated the paradigmatic social theories developed in the late nineteenth and early twentieth centuries. He locates the origins of this (still to be accomplished) postmodern geography in the work of Foucault, Henri Lefebvre, Fredric Jameson, Berger, Marshall Berman, and others, but his pinpointing of Berger's work as prefigurative of his own project is what is of interest here. Soja quotes a long passage from Berger's 1974 book of essays *The Look of Things* in which Berger called for new modes of narration in the modern novel, modes which would come to grips with the fact that "it is scarcely any longer possible to tell a straight story sequentially unfolding in time. And this is because we are too aware of what is continually traversing the storyline laterally." Berger went on to emphasize the globality of exploitation and inequality in the contemporary world and hence that "it is space not time that hides consequences [of exploitation] from us" (Soja 22). Soja extracts from Berger's work a declaration of the death of historicism and guidelines toward the project of spatializing critical thought in order to strike "an appropriate interpretive balance between space, time, and social being" (23).

Berger's image for the changed narrative modes which could come to grips with the "simultaneity and extension of events and possibilities" in the contemporary world is that of lines radiating from a fixed point, rather than of a point as part of a series composing a straight line (22). It is the same image he later used for the construction of the appropriate context for photographs if they would become the basis for an alternative social and political memory. These narrational experiments which Soja pinpoints as indicative of Berger's postmodernism led him to works like *G.* and *Pig Earth*, texts characterized by Linda Hutcheon as historiographic metafictions, which are for her perhaps *the* paradigmatic postmodernist works. It is worth emphasizing once again the increasing importance in Berger's recent writing of groups who are ex-centric (to borrow another of the terms Hutcheon uses to characterize postmodernist concerns): postcolonial migrant workers, peasants, women. Like Said, Hutcheon and Soja would see Berger as a representative example of the postmodern search for new narrative forms which can more appropriately come to grips with the ex-centricity of people marginalized by class, race, gender, or ethnicity. Similarly, they would join with Said (against Tagg) in seeing in his work attempts to develop a coherent challenge to what Soja calls the "hegemonic historicism" of most twentieth-century critical social theory (16).[11]

Ultimately the point here is not to decide whether or not Berger's work is definitively modernist or postmodernist but rather to emphasize the ways in which many of the key issues in the debates surrounding the concept of postmodernism are mediated in his writing. His texts are symptomatic of many of the issues crucial to that debate, and his commentators further reflect that symptomaticity in the various ways in which they place Berger's work across that disputed terrain where the crossroads between modernism and postmodernism lies.

IV

The position within contemporary cultural struggles which writers like Said and Berger occupy has been interestingly mapped by the anthropologist Paul Rabinow. He locates four different groups of thinkers involved in various ways with a series of crucial concerns: "questions of truth and its social location; imagination and formal problems of representation; domination and resistance; the ethical subject and techniques for becoming one." His "interpretive federation" involved with these problems includes interpretive anthropologists, critics, political subjects, and critical, cosmopolitan intellectuals. His description of the last of these captures Berger's stance very well. For Rabinow, a critical cosmopolitanism is an oppositional position, one which takes the ethical as its guiding value. Its second value is understanding, "but an understanding suspicious of its own imperial tendencies." Thinkers within this frame recognize that "specificity of historical experience and place" and "world-wide macro-interdependency encompassing any local particularity" characterize the condition of all of us at present. He can then define critical cosmopolitanism as "an ethos of macro-interdependencies, with an acute consciousness (often forced upon people) of the inescapabilities and particularities of places, characters, historical trajectories, and fates" (Rabinow 256-58). It is from within that ethos that Berger writes, and it is to that ethos that his works compel his readers.

Why, then, have peasants become so important for Berger? Why should their stories bear relevance for the readers of his books, the overwhelming majority of whom are likely to be from the industrialized metropolitan center of the world rather than from the peasant world itself? One motive is surely that of preserving a way of life which is disappearing. But Berger's project is not just an example of what Clifford has tellingly called "salvage ethnography": the anthropological concern to document "primitive" cultures before their demise, which was a prominent motive in the ethnographic monographs of earlier generations of anthropologists over the past century. Rather, Berger finds in the peasant way of life a commitment to survival which he feels may be more relevant in the foreseeable future of humankind than the remnants of what he calls the "culture of progress" in either its Western or Eastern forms. Within the peasant culture of survival as Berger depicts it there has emerged an ideal of equality based upon the necessity of work in a world of scarcity, an idea whose promise "is for mutual fraternal aid in struggling against this scarcity and a just sharing of what the work produces." If there is a move toward the future in the peasant's thoughts and feelings it is "directed toward the survival of his children" (*Pig Earth* 202). Berger sees in this sober, skeptical attitude not only the basis for the typical peasant distrust of "progress," but as well a moral position better adapted to the future of humankind than any other. He writes: "if one looks at the likely future course of world history, envisaging either the further extension and consolidation of corporate capitalism in all its brutalism, or a prolonged, uneven struggle waged against it, a struggle whose victory is not certain, the peasant experience of survival may well be better adapted to this long and harsh perspective than the continually reformed, disappointed, impatient progressive hope of an ultimate victory" (*Pig Earth* 212-13).

The crux of Berger's work, and the basis of its importance, is of course *how* this peasant experience is re-presented, depicted, shown. Summarizing the argument of this essay, I would suggest that Berger's textual practices (photographs carefully arranged in montages, written texts, a series of books which provide a complex interweave of associations) are meant both to secure access to the peasant experience and at the same time to challenge those techniques of cultural production in late capitalist society, which he criticized in *Ways of Seeing*, and which have as their ideological precipitate the erasure of others' experience and the negation of historical continuity. Berger thus attacks the "culture of progress" in its late capitalist phase with formal means (magic realism, montage) which themselves are a necessary component of his critique.

Berger is not optimistic that peasant suspicion could be the basis of an alternative political development. As he is quick to point out, such a possibility would imply that peasants could achieve power as a class, and this would, if achieved, transform the basis upon which the peasant vision itself has for centuries been formed: lack of achieved political power. Nevertheless, that there is a modest hope to be derived from the culture of the pig earth, and a lesson to be drawn from it for the denizens of the advanced industrial societies is captured in the title of a book published several years ago called *The Techno/Peasant Survival Manual*. Its purpose was to present essential information in an accessible form on what its authors thought would be the "tools for accessing the 80's": microcomputing, fiber optics, lasers, genetic engineering, and so on. It was an interesting effort in the popularization of knowledge. What is noteworthy here is the book's definition of a techno/peasant as a person the nature and quality of whose life is increasingly determined by others, technocrats, who monopolize knowledges which overwhelm most of us. Consequently, we remain "too uninformed to have any say in [our] own future" (Print Project 1). This condition of having the quality of life determined by others is one to which the world's peasantries have long been exposed, under a variety of political regimes and within different social frameworks, but at no time more conspicuously and pervasively than in the past two centuries. As the title of the book makes clear, "survival" is what the techno/peasant needs to have tools to accomplish. My suggestion would be that the books of John Berger can be even more useful tools to approach that task than cookbook knowledge of new technologies. The epigraph for the "Into Their Labours" trilogy of which *Pig Earth* and *Once in Europa* are the first two parts comes from the Gospel of John: "Others have laboured and ye are entered into their labours." The context is Jesus's encounter with the Samaritan woman and the words Berger quotes are immediately preceded by Jesus's own quotation of the saying that one man reaps what another has planted. It expresses well the kernel of Berger's view of peasant life and its meaning and, if the original Greek sense of *apostle*—messenger—is kept in mind, it is perhaps not wholly inaccurate to describe Berger himself as an apostle to the techno/peasants.

In the final analysis, then, Berger's work is not only about the peasantry, it is equally about all those who inhabit what he calls "the North Atlantic world system." Raymond Williams has written that contemporary peasant experience is primarily a form of what he calls "residual" experience, still living remnants of older ways of life encysted within new forms of experience now become dominant. Williams also suggests that such residual forms of experience may in limited ways have alternative or oppositional aspects, and he specifically instances the idea of rural community as an example.[12] Certainly this is one aspect of the lives of the French peasantry Berger too finds compelling and it is why he believes that the peasant experience has lessons to be learned by those in the hegemonic culture of late capitalism. But it is also crucial to note that Berger conceives it to be a "radical task for intellectuals" within the dominant North Atlantic system to "struggle to undo, to unwrite, the false axioms on which the culture around them has often been based." He thinks it likely that only those, like himself, whose enculturation has been tied into those axioms, will be able to succeed in untying them. Thus, it is not just the meaning of peasant experience, but the means for untying some of the axioms of "our" experience which is at the core of Berger's message and which determines that its audience be the techno/peasants of the late twentieth century.[13]

Notes

1. His doubts about some of the arguments in *Ways of Seeing* are expressed in a 1978 essay "The Work of Art" (Spencer, 197-204).

2. Fred Inglis situates Berger among his fellow British Marxists of the post-1945 period, thinkers such as E. P. Thompson, Raymond Williams, and Peter Worsley. See especially pages 186-192 on Berger.

3. See Ryan 184. For other helpful commentaries on Berger's fictional work see George Szanto and Raymond A. Mazurek.

4. A different version of this piece appears in *Another Way of Telling* as the theoretical introduction to the long montage of photographs.

5. See Barthes's justly influential essays "The Photographic Message" (1961) and "Rhetoric of the Image" (1964) in Roland Barthes, *Image-Music-Text*. Berger's writing on photography and image reproduction can be seen as part of a four-way conversation whose participants are Berger, Barthes, Susan Sontag (to whom the essay "Uses of Photography" was dedicated), and Walter Benjamin, whose famous 1936 essay "The Work of Art in the Era of Mechanical Reproduction" Berger has acknowledged as a formative influence on *Ways of Seeing*.

6. Richard Johnson proposed this substitution of "abstraction" for "theory" in opposition to "concrete studies."

7. Linda Hutcheon writes that: "Unacknowledged modernist assumptions about closure, distance, artistic autonomy, and the apolitical nature of representation are what postmodernism sets out to uncover and deconstruct" (*Politics* 99). This certainly captures one of Berger's intentions, most fully realized perhaps in his 1972 novel *G.* Hutcheon instances *G.* as an exemplar of what she calls "historiographic metafiction," a genre which she explicitly characterizes as postmodern. (*Poetics* 105-23; *Politics* 47-92). My point here is that in works like *G.* and *Pig Earth* Berger is engaged in what critics like Hutcheon would characterize as a postmodernist critique of modernism. When Berger as author intervenes directly in his texts it is not with the intention to return to a nineteenth-century practice, but rather to force a re-thinking of the relationship between the individual and history from within the dramatically changed historical space of the late twentieth century. The critique of modernist assumptions is a necessary first step.

8. James Clifford, "Introduction: Partial Truths," *Writing Culture* (complete citation is in Works Cited). In a provocative essay "On Ethnographic Surrealism" Clifford has made some comments which illuminate aspects of Berger's work. He is addressing what he calls "the paradoxical nature of ethnographic knowledge" which seeks both to render the different familiar (the moment of what he calls anthropological humanism) and the familiar different (the moment of what he calls ethnographic surrealism). Both moments he sees as part of a broader process—"a permanent ironic play of similarity and difference, the familiar and the strange, the here and the elsewhere"—which he says is "characteristic of global modernity." He writes that in most ethnographies and in every beginning anthropology course there are points "in which distinct cultural realities are cut from their contexts and forced into jarring proximity," hopefully to produce a "defamiliarizing effect" on the reader or listener. He associates this juxtaposing strategy with the mechanism of collage, but goes on to suggest that "it is essential to distinguish this movement of metonymic juxtaposition from its normal sequel, a movement of metaphorical comparison in which consistent grounds for similarity and difference are elaborated." The principle of montage which Berger uses in constructing the photo essays in *Ways of Seeing* and *Another Way of Telling* is also an instance of the metonymic juxtaposition of images, many "cut from their contexts and forced into jarring proximity." What then must occur is the moment of metaphorical (theoretical) comparison, either in the consciousness of the viewer or, thinking of Berger himself, in a separate, but related theoretical reprise. See James Clifford, *Predicament*, especially 145-46 from which I have quoted. An earlier version of Clifford's essay appeared in *Comparative Studies in Society and History*, 23 (1981), 539-64.

9. In *The Politics of Postmodernism*, addressing herself to the work of contemporary artists such as Barbara Kruger and Victor Burgin, Hutcheon suggests that their postmodern photography seeks "to de-naturalize the relation between the visual and the verbal and also any evaluative privileging of one over the other." She goes on to argue that such work presents two different discourses, verbal and visual, which produce meaning through their interaction and therefore force the viewer toward an awareness of "the theoretical implications of the differences between . . . meaning producing within the two separate and differing discourses and . . . any meaning created through their interaction" (125, 138). I think that this pinpoints one of the effects which books such as *Another Way of Telling* and *Ways of Seeing* produce in their reader/viewers; in contrast, while Said and Buck-Morss may have intended their works under discussion here to have such an effect, my argument is that they do not.

10. The distinction between an affirmative postmodernism and an alternative postmodernism of resistance is elaborated in Huyssen's essay "Mapping the Postmodern," included in his important book *After the Great Divide*. Huyssen's essay and Hebdige's "Staking out the Post" (plus the four Post-scripts which follow it, all included in *Hiding in the Light*) are to my mind two of the very best efforts to encompass the complexities which the postmodernism debate has assumed in the past decade. (Huyssen's essay originally appeared in *New German Critique*, 33 (1984): 5-52. A third encompassing effort to assess postmodernism is Hutcheon's. She attempts to overcome such dichotomies as Huyssen's between an affirmative and a resistant postmodernism by stressing the ways in which "postmodernism is a contradictory cultural enterprise, one that is heavily implicated in that which it seeks to contest." For Hutcheon a "poetics of postmodernism" would strive "to enact the metalinguistic contradiction of being inside and outside, complicitous and distanced, inscribing and contesting its own provisional formulations" (*Poetics* 106, 21).

11. Hutcheon has written interestingly of the parallels between the historigraphic theory of contemporary thinkers like Hayden White and Dominick LaCapra and much postmodern fiction, citing their common "self-consciousness (both theoretical and textual) about the act of narrating in the present the events of the past, about the conjunction of present action and the past absent object of that agency." (*Politics* 71; see 69-92; *Poetics* 87-101, 124-40). These have been concerns of Berger as well.

12. See the chapter "Dominant, Residual, and Emergent" in Raymond Williams, *Marxism and Literature*. Williams writes interestingly in a way that I think illuminates Berger's project: "Thus certain experiences, meanings, and values which cannot be expressed or substantially verified in terms of the dominant culture, are nevertheless lived and practiced on the basis of the residue—cultural as well as social—of some previous social and cultural institution or formation. . . . Again, the idea of such community is predominantly residual, but is in some limited respects alternative or oppositional to urban industrial capitalism" (122).

13. An interrogation of the notion of experience in Berger's work can be found in the important article of Bruce Robbins.

Works Cited

Barthes, Roland. "The Photographic Message." *Image-Music-Text*. Trans. Stephen Heath. New York: Hill and Wang, 1977. 15-31.

———. "Rhetoric of the Image." *Image-Music-Text*. Trans. Stephen Heath. New York: Hill and Wang, 1977. 32-51.

Berger, John. *About Looking*. New York: Pantheon, 1980.

———. "Another Way of Telling." *Journal of Social Reconstruction* 1 (1980): 57-75.

———. *Once in Europa*. New York: Pantheon, 1987.

———. *Pig Earth*. New York: Pantheon, 1979.

Berger, John, et al. *Ways of Seeing*. New York: Penguin Books, 1977.

Berger, John, and Jean Mohr. *Another Way of Telling*. New York: Pantheon, 1982.

———. *A Seventh Man*. London: Writers and Readers Publishing Cooperative, 1982.

Buck-Morss, Susan. "Semiotic Boundaries and the Politics of Meaning: Modernity on Tour—A Village in Transition." *New Ways of Knowing: The Sciences, Society, and Reconstructive Knowledge*. Eds. Marcus G. Raskin, Herbert Bernstein, et al. Totowa, New Jersey: Rowman and Littlefield, 1987.

Clifford, James. "Introduction: Partial Truths." *Writing Culture: The Poetics and Politics of Ethnography*. Eds. James Clifford and George Marcus. Berkeley: U of California P, 1986.

———. *The Predicament of Culture: Twentieth-Century Ethnography, Literature, and Art*. Cambridge: Harvard UP, 1988.

Hebdige, Dick. *Hiding In the Light: On Images and Things*. London: Routledge, 1988.

Hutcheon, Linda. *A Poetics of Postmodernism: History, Theory, Fiction*. New York: Routledge, 1988.

———. *The Politics of Postmodernism*. New York: Routledge, 1989.

Huyssen, Andreas. *After the Great Divide: Modernism, Mass Culture, Postmodernism*. Bloomington: Indiana UP, 1986.

Inglis, Fred. *Radical Earnestness: English Social Theory 1880-1980*. Oxford: Martin Robertson, 1982.

Jameson, Fredric. "On Magic Realism in Film." *Critical Inquiry* 12 (1986): 301-25.

Johnson, Richard. "What Is Cultural Studies Anyway?" *Social Text* 16 (Winter, 1986-87): 38-80.

Lakoff, George, and Mark Johnson. *Metaphors We Live By*. Chicago: U of Chicago P, 1980.

Marcus, George E. "Contemporary Problems of Ethnography in the Modern World System." *Writing Culture: The Poetics and Politics of Ethnography*. Eds. James Clifford and George E. Marcus. Berkeley: U of California P, 1986.

Marzorati, Gerald. "Living and Writing the Peasant Life." *The New York Times Magazine* 29 (1987): 38-39, 46, 50, 54.

Mazurek, Raymond A. "Totalization and Contemporary Realism: John Berger's Recent Fiction." *Critique* 25 (1984): 136-46.

McNeill, William. *The Shape of European History*. New York: Oxford UP, 1974.

Mitchell, W. J. T. "The Ethics of Form in the Photographic Essay." *Afterimage* 16 (1989): 8-13.

Price, Richard. *First-Time: The Historical Vision of an Afro-American People*. Baltimore: Johns Hopkins UP, 1983.

The Print Project, *The Techno-Peasant Survival Manual*. New York: Bantam, 1980.

Rabinow, Paul. "Representations are Social Facts: Modernity and Post-Modernity in Anthropology." *Writing Culture: The Poetics and Politics of Ethnography*. Eds. James Clifford and George E. Marcus. Berkeley: U of California P, 1986.

Robbins, Bruce. "Feeling Global: Experience and John Berger." *Boundary 2* 11 (1982-83): 291-308.

Ryan, Kiernan. "Socialist fiction and the education of desire: Mervyn Jones, Raymond Williams, John Berger." *The Socialist Novel in Britain: Towards the Recovery of a Tradition*. Ed. H. Gustav Klaus. Brighton, Sussex: Harvester P, 1982.

Said, Edward W. "Opponents, Audiences, Constituencies, and Community." *Critical Inquiry* 9 (1982): 1-26.

———. "Michel Foucault, 1927-1984." *Raritan* 24 (1984): 1-11.

———. "Representing the Colonized: Anthropology's Interlocutors." *Critical Inquiry* 15 (1989): 205-25.

Said, Edward W. and Jean Mohr. *After the Last Sky: Palestinian Lives*. New York: Pantheon, 1986.

Soja, Edward W. *Postmodern Geographies: The Reassertion of Space in Critical Social Theory*. London: Verso, 1989.

Spencer, Lloyd. *The Sense of Sight: Writings by John Berger*. New York: Pantheon, 1985.

Szanto, George. "Oppositional Way-Signs: Some Passages Within John Berger's History-Making, History-Unravelling Experiment." *College English* 40 (1978): 364-78.

Tagg, John. *The Burden of Representation: Essays on Photographies and Histories.* Amherst, Mass: U of Massachusetts P, 1988.

Williams, Raymond. *Marxism and Literature.* New York: Oxford UP, 1977.

Worsley, Peter. *The Three Worlds: Culture and World Development.* London: Weidenfeld and Nicholson, 1984.

PART IV

Theoretical Issues:
Images of Ideology/Ideologies of Images

Chapter 10

Allegories of History:
The Politics of Representation in Walter Benjamin

Azade Seyhan

> It is characteristic of philosophical
> writing that it must continually
> confront the question of represen-
> tation.
> —Walter Benjamin,
> *The Origin of German Tragic Drama*

Although attempts to define the fine line of distinction/opposition/continuation between modern and postmodern discourse are legion, I will start with the simple premise that these two modes of discourse are, by and large, a concern with representation in the first instance and a confrontation with it in the second. In "Die Zeit des Weltbildes" ("The Age of the World Picture"), a lecture delivered in 1938 but not published until 1952, Martin Heidegger provides an incisive analysis of social and cultural configurations that characterize modernity. He maintains that the mission of modern scientific research is fulfilled only when "truth has been transformed into the certainty of representation" (127). Heidegger's investigation into the nature of modern science aims at understanding its "metaphysical ground":

> Metaphysics grounds an age, in that through a specific interpretation of what is and through a specific comprehension of truth it gives to that age the basis upon which it is essentially formed. This basis holds complete dominion over all the phenomena that distinguish the age. Conversely, in order that there may be an adequate reflection upon these phenomena themselves, the metaphysical basis for them must let itself be apprehended in them. Reflection is the courage to make the truth of presuppositions and the realm of our own goals into the things that most deserve to be called in question. (115-16)

An understanding of the metaphysical ground of modern science provides an accurate assessment of the essence of the modern age. The essence of an age, in turn, is reflected in its "world picture." And just what is the world picture of the modern age? Heidegger suggests that posing this very question may in itself constitute the essence of modern consciousness. The transition to modernity, he argues, was marked not merely by the replacement of the medieval world picture by a modern one but rather by the transformation of the world itself into a picture: "The fundamental event of the modern age is the conquest of the world as picture." This picture, however, is no longer a copy or an imitation of the world: "The word *picture (Bild)* now means structured image *(Gebild)* that is the product of the subject's representational capacity *(des vorstellenden Herstellens)*" (134). The modern subject creates reality in representation. He produces *(herstellen)* the world by reproducing it in representation *(Vorstellen)*. This radical shift from the perception of an "objective" world to a perception of its subjective construction brings in its wake a heightened realization of the problem of representation.

In what follows, I would like to investigate how Walter Benjamin's examination of representation and his radical restoration and diversification of allegory map the critical path from the modern to the postmodern. This early map of the postmodern condition is decidedly historical and polemical and often antidirectional. The apparent paradoxes of Benjamin's theoretical apparatus are characteristic of the contradictions of postmodernism itself which, as Linda Hutcheon observes, "may well be those of late capitalist society, but whatever the cause, these contradictions are certainly manifest in the important postmodern concept of the 'presence of the past'" (4).[1] In "Theses on the Philosophy of History," a series of aphoristic reflections on the concept of historical materialism, Benjamin subjects the ideological implications of the imagistic presence of the past in the *Jetztzeit* to critical scrutiny. *Jetztzeit*, which literally means "the time of the now," is one of the many words in Benjamin's vocabulary that refer to a constellation of visual and historical ideas. It designates the impulse to disrupt the complacent continuum of history. It "presupposes that the present cannot be seen as restorative, collective, and seclusive (as in Hegel, at least in the later years) but as the focus of historical tendencies, as the turning point of handed down contents, as the origin of new values" (Holz 103). Benjamin thematizes the notion of *Jetztzeit* to demonstrate the relation of the truth of history to language and representation and thereby affirms our more recent critical awareness that "every representation of the past has specifiable ideological implications" (White 69). Benjamin's free appropriation and accumulation of the images of the baroque, quotations, and excerptations subvert the notions of authenticity and originality and underline the role of intending subjectivities in the creation of reality. In a similar vein, Lionel Gossman has argued that both modern history and modern literature have "rejected the ideal of representation that dominated them for so long. Both now conceive of their work as exploration, testing, creation of new meanings, rather than as disclosure or revelation of meanings already in some sense 'there,' but not immediately perceptible" (38-39).

The problem of representation is inherent to the never fully answered question of how philosophical or poetic language can mediate and account for "reality." The question pursues the ideal correspondence of object to subject, word to meaning, image to concept. Michel Foucault has observed that the definite transition to modernity was marked "when words ceased to interact with representations and provide the spontaneous grid for the knowledge of things" (304). The modern awareness that any intimation of "truth," of presence or being is possible only through representation "imposes upon language, if not a privileged position, at least a destiny that seems singular when compared with that of labour or of life" (Foucault 304). Since representation can never ideally coincide with its object, it always involves the presentation of the latter by means of something that it is not. It presents the object or the concept in word, symbol, or image, that is, in subjectively constructed form. This form is always historical and points to an extremely complicated interweaving of social and cultural practices. Our perceptions of the universe are not governed by a u-topic or atemporal logic of nature but by our own sphere of understanding which is conditioned by a particular scientific, moral, or aesthetic heritage and is, thus, subject to change. Therefore, any form of representation constitutes a text which needs to be broken down in order to make visible the multiplicity and contingency of meaning hidden in words (Foucault 304).

The anxiety over the adequate way of representing "truth" attacks periods on the threshold of major social and cultural changes, when the validity of accepted norms of understanding is subjected to critical scrutiny. In the postmodern condition, this anxiety takes the form of an unsettling confrontation with the pervasiveness of representation and leads to a challenge and contestation of this pervasiveness. In an essay on the politics of the postmodern in art and architecture, Hal Foster differentiates between "neoconservative postmodernism" and "poststructuralist postmodernism." The first attempts to restore representation by guaranteeing the referential status of its images. Poststructuralist modernism, on the other hand, is a critique of representation. It "questions the truth content of visual representation, whether realist, symbolic or abstract, and explores the regimes of meaning and order these different codes support" (129). In this sense, representation is understood as the seat of both formal and ideological interests. The heightened self-consciousness of postmodern fiction about its form, for example, prevents, in Hutcheon's words, "any suppression of the literary and the linguistic, but its problematizing of historical knowledge and ideology work to foreground the implication of the narrative and the representational in our strategies of making meaning in our culture" (183). The often interlinked destinies of fiction and historiography in postmodern novels further highlight the "issues surrounding the nature of identity and subjectivity; the question of reference and representation; the intertextual nature of the past; and the ideological implications of writing about history" (Hutcheon 117). In short, the not always clearly demarcated passage from the modern to the postmodern involves a move away from the referential claims of representation to a questioning of the ideologies and histories housed in representational images.

Benjamin's sustained interest in the question of representation and its fateful role in material history marks an important contribution to modern critical discourse. Representations of the present time may promote, entrench, or mask dominant ideologies embedded in certain rhetorical practices. However, representational form simultaneously contains a prehistory or forgotten memory that harbors seeds of difference and discontent. In Benjamin's "tame historical materialism," as Habermas has called it, this prehistory functions as a liberating image. In "Theses on the Philosophy of History," Benjamin states that this image "unexpectedly appears to man singled out by history at a moment of danger. The danger affects both the content of the tradition and its receivers. The same threat hangs over both: that of becoming a tool of ruling classes. In every era the attempt must be made anew to wrest tradition from a conformism that is about to overpower it" ("Theses" VI, 255). The dynamic content of tradition, which presents itself in a recovered constellation of images, needs to be pried loose from the oppressive continuity of history. For example, "to Robespierre, ancient Rome was a past charged with the time of the now *[Jetztzeit]* which he blasted out of the continuum of history" ("Theses" XIV, 261). In other words, our ability to engage with the context, condition, and mode of representational production determines whether our confrontation with history is paralyzed by a conservative historicism or enriched by an effective reading of historical materialism.

Historicism "musters a mass of data to fill the homogeneous, empty time." "Materialistic historiography," on the other hand, studies not only the flow but also the arrest of ideas or images in time. In other words, it reads time as iconized history. "Where thinking suddenly stops in a configuration pregnant with tensions, it gives that configuration a shock, by which it crystallizes into a monad. A historical materialist approaches a historical subject only where he encounters it as a monad" and exploits the tension in this structure "to blast a specific era out of the homogeneous course of history" ("Theses" XVII, 262-63). This shock, the stripping away of a historical structure from its fossilized background, paves the way to revolutionary and liberating change. Benjamin's concept of historical materialism operates by recalling and arresting moments of history that are then re-configured in new narratives in such a way as to release their liberating potential. This re-configuration distorts official or institutional histories that preserve and protect ruling class interests. The praxis of materialistic historiography prevents the making present of the past or the re-presentation of history from being a reduction of periods to ruling class ideologies. In dismantling the claims of representations sanctioned by ruling classes and replacing monolithic images of official histories by multilayered discourses, Benjamin's writing recalls and enacts Mikhail Bakhtin's notions of polyphony, dialogism, and heteroglossia which characterize the modern novel. Bakhtin's *Rabelais and his World* (1940), written in the same year as Benjamin's "Theses," "blasts" Rabelais's aesthetic from the "homogeneous" course of literary history. As Eagleton observes "Rabelais is the memory that Bakhtin seizes hold of as it flashes up at a moment of danger" (144). Bakhtin reclaims the explosive configuration of the politics of the erotic, the semiotic, the arabesque, and the grotesque in Rabelais and pits it against the authoritative voice of the unnamed Stalinism. The resynthesized voices of history constitute the polyphonic field which drowns out the monologue of authority. Likewise, "Benjamin pries images loose from the authority of the past so that they may plurally interbreed; and this liberation of the image into polyvalence has for Bakhtin the name of carnival" (Eagleton 145). The analytics of representation or the examination of the constitution, decomposition, and resynthesis of images is a recurrent concern of Benjamin's political aesthetic.

Benjamin presents a lengthy and somewhat paradoxical definition of representation in the "Epistemo-Critical Prologue" to the *Origin of German Tragic Drama*. In German philosophical thought, representation is designated by three related words, *Vorstellung, Darstellung,* and *Repräsentation*.[2] Of these three, only *Darstellung* attains to a materiality of figural form. In other words, *Darstellung* refers to the material form of poetic or aesthetic representation. Therefore, we need to bear in mind that when Benjamin valorizes *Darstellung* as the site of "the transcendent force of the sacred image and the truth itself" (*Origin* 28-29), he is referring to a formal and ultimately poetic (and, more specifically, allegorical) principle. Benjamin starts his discussion by distinguishing between knowledge *(Erkenntnis)* and truth *(Wahrheit)*. The distinction takes aim at the positivistic position that a mere accumulation of knowledge about phenomena can provide access to truth. Knowledge, argues Benjamin, is a possession *(ein Haben)* and can be presented. "Its very object is determined by the fact that it must be taken possession of—even if in a transcendental sense—in the consciousness" (*Origin* 29). Knowledge is fully informed by the idea of possession or ownership *(Besitztum)*. Possession makes self-representation impossible. But truth, which cannot be possessed, exists as self-representation *(ein Sich-Darstellendes)*. It is "bodied forth in the dance of represented ideas" (29). The method of knowledge is the acquisition of mastery, that of truth is representation. Representation presupposes a form which is immanent to truth. In a way, representation constitutes a "response to the human condition of being exiled from the truth that it would embrace. The existence-in-absence of truth is a condition that has been explained in various origin-myths of fall, rupture, or exile; it can be understood, however, only by examining the way in which it exists in representation" (Cowan 114).

Thus, truth or intimations thereof are visible only in the representational form. From the critical discourse of early German romanticism Benjamin inherits the idea that the absolute is accessible to consciousness only in poetic form. Benjamin's dissertation *Der Begriff der Kunstkritik in der deutschen Romantik (The Concept of Art Criticism in German Romanticism)* demonstrates that in the critical project of Friedrich Schlegel and Novalis, two major theorists of romanticism, the representational form of the work of art and the idea of form replace the idea of the absolute. For Schlegel and Novalis, representation designates not an imitation but an intimation of the real. Novalis arrests the problem of representation in this formulation: "all representation rests on making present what is not present" (3: 421). In other words, representation is the process of embodying or giving form to absence, of re-presenting what is no longer present. Novalis also states that only the poetic process can "represent the unrepresentable" (3: 685). And in Benjamin, "philosophical representation" *(die philosophische Darstellung)* itself is an act of locating truth (Holz 64). As Cowan observes, "truth exists as a goal, though not beyond signification" (113). The dialectic of representation "knows no fixed cognition" (Holz 65). Therefore, philosophical truth as opposed to scientific knowledge is "unpossessable and impossible to present. . . . This impossibility of *presentation* leads in Benjamin's thought to the designation of truth's proper mode as *representation (Darstellung)*" (Cowan 113-14).

Thus, the form of representation itself embodies what we call "truth." In other words, truth is the form of neither an originary presence nor an absolute but of self-representation. In the epilogue to *The Origin of German Tragic Drama*, Benjamin maintains that the history of philosophy is the history of a struggle for the representation of ideas. Ideas represent the "virtual arrangement" and "objective interpretation" (34) of phenomena, and they do this through the intermediary of concepts *(Begriffe)*. Unlike concepts, ideas constitute a realm of sensible representation. Thus, Benjamin equates ideas with language and image. The image is that of the "monad" in which "the pre-stabilized representation of phenomena resides" *(Origin* 47). When Benjamin calls ideas "monads," he means that "every idea contains the image of the world. The purpose of representation of the idea is nothing less than an abbreviated outline of this image of the world" *(Origin* 48). Like monads, ideas are informed by an "irreducible multiplicity" *(Origin* 43) and "are displayed, without intention, in the act of naming, and they have to be renewed in philosophical contemplation. In this renewal the primordial mode of apprehending words is restored" *(Origin* 37). Thus, ideas do not mimic an absolute truth, but rather represent the multiplicity of truth. In this context, Benjamin remarks, "it is not surprising that the philosopher of the *Monadology* was also the founder of infinitesimal calculus" *(Origin* 48). Scattered phenomena are available to consciousness only when "salvaged" by ideas and represented in them *(Origin* 35). By locating the essence of truth in representation, Benjamin valorizes representational form as the actual realm of ideas. Thus, it is the form and not the content of philosophy that participates in the search for truth. "The conclusion of Benjamin's prologue in brief is that the form of philosophical writing is an allegory of truth" (Cowan 114).

Thus, representation or form emerges as an elusive index of truth, subject to the interstice between the representable and the unrepresentable. Whereas knowledge creates a regulative form of reasoning, truth resists the order of possession, observation, and mastery of the object and inconspicuously resides in moments of discontinuity. Like monads or stars in a constellation, ideas form a discontinuous whole and are characterized by continuous change of form and renewal. Thus, truth demands a form that holds out against the totalizing conceit of dominant histories and the transcendental plan of a self-assured metaphysics. The act of representation investigates our relation to truth. Allegory represents the necessarily inconstant or variable condition of that relation. In Benjamin's work, allegory emerges as the *topos* and trope of interlinkage between the modern and the postmodern. In other words, Benjamin's concern with representation marks the conceptual profile of his modernity. His valorization of allegory as the emblem of iconic history, on the other hand, prefigures postmodernism's challenge to representation. Benjamin's allegory is a palimpsest of past and present codes. The modernist project in architecture and literature tended to highlight its representational originality or to showcase its "nowness" and "newness." The postmodernist encounter with tradition, on the other hand, incorporates the past and a sense of "secondhandedness" into the present. Many postmodernist novels such as Umberto Eco's *The Name of the Rose* ironically recall their own intertextual beginnings. Several times in the story mention is made of how books always refer to other books. "I had thought, each book spoke of the things, human or divine, that lie outside books," says the narrator, "now I realized that not infrequently books speak of books: it is as if they spoke among themselves" (342). Here, as in Benjamin's understanding of allegory, representations refer not to things in the world but to other representations. Similarly, postmodern architecture houses past traditions as ever present artifacts. It "cites"[3] such forms as the classical column, the pointed gable, or the Roman arch, which were "taboo" in the past several decades, as historical intertexts.

The history of the symbol/allegory opposition is not the subject of my study.[4] However, I shall briefly dwell on this dichotomy invented by the romantics in order to show how Benjamin "salvages" allegory from the "inferior" position assigned to it in romantic usage and reinvents it as the informing trope of historical change. In a brief article, entitled "Über die Gegenstände der bildenden Kunst" ("On the Objects of Plastic Arts"), Goethe states that the symbolic points to a space beyond representation where pure feeling indirectly grasps the loftiest objects. The allegorical, on the other hand, destroys our interest in representation because of its direct designation of the object. The opacity of the symbolic is valorized over the transparency of the allegorical which demystifies the romantic glorification of experience (407). "As a symbolic construct, the beautiful is supposed to merge with the divine in an unbroken whole," writes Benjamin, "the idea of the immanence of the moral world in the world of beauty is derived from theosophical aesthetics of romantics" (*Origin* 160). The concept of allegory simply served as "the dark background against which the bright world of the symbol might stand out" (*Origin* 161).

Benjamin, furthermore, maintains that the concept of the symbol as a unity of form and content, appearance and essence, lacks dialectical rigor and represents a misplaced nostalgia for myths of origin. It is typical of a mentality that cannot tolerate the tension and ambiguity that characterize life and history. As a counter strategy to this mentality, Benjamin establishes allegory as the trope of temporality (or history). Reviewing the work of German romantic critics Görres and Creuzer on allegory, Benjamin notes that their introduction of the category of time into the semiotic comparison of allegory and symbol made possible a formal definition of the relationship between the two tropes: "Whereas in the symbol destruction is idealized and the transfigured face of nature is fleetingly revealed in the light of redemption, in allegory the observer is confronted with the *facies hippocratica* of history as a petrified, primordial landscape" (*Origin* 166). In other words, both tropes involve a violation of linear time and a transfiguration of that violated moment. However, symbol glosses over the rupture in the transcendent image. Allegory freezes the shocked face of history in memorable form. As Richard Wolin observes, "whereas for the symbol the ideal of time is found in the fulfilled mystical instant *(Nu)*, for allegory it is represented by the idea of an unfulfilled infinite progression. For the one the relation to redemption is immediate; for the other it is infinitely removed" (66). In the baroque drama, redemption is beyond nature. That is, it is realized only in the attrition and decay of nature. Redemption moves into history at the expense of nature. Therefore, images of death are the recurrent emblems of the baroque:

> Everything about history that, from the very beginning, has been untimely, sorrowful, unsuccessful, is expressed in a face—or rather in a death's head. And although such a thing lacks all "symbolic" freedom of expression, all classical proportion, all humanity—nevertheless, this is the form in which man's subjection to nature is most obvious and it significantly gives rise not only to the enigmatic question of the nature of human existence as such, but also of the biographical historicity of the individual. This is the heart of the allegorical way of seeing, of the baroque, secular explanation of history as the Passion of the world; its importance resides solely in the stations of its

decline. . . . But if nature has always been subject to the power of death, it is also true that it has always been allegorical. Signification and death both come to fruition in historical development. (*Origin* 166)

Another prominent baroque image, the ruin as the emblem of lost cultural riches, is the object of the melancholy gaze of allegory. This gaze sees history as a heap of fragments. The image of the ruin subverts the imaginary unproblematic continuum of the past and the present. Not only history but also nature is subject to the ravages of time. The allegorical understanding rejects the notion of a timeless harmony both in nature and in human life. "By its very essence classicism was not permitted to behold the lack of freedom, the imperfection, the collapse of the beautiful, physical nature," writes Benjamin, "but beneath its extravagant pomp this is what baroque allegory proclaims with unprecedented emphasis" (*Origin* 176). The allegorical form captures the shattered images of time in its re-collections.

The question that is of interest at this point is how the baroque allegory assumes its modern face in Benjamin's critique of contemporary social and political discourse. How does it emerge as a strategy of dislocation that wrests its hitherto unacclaimed share from the victorious scribes of history? How does it graduate from its status as the sign of the absence of presence and become a regulative metaphor of historical materialism? "How is it possible that such a thoroughly 'untimely'—at least apparently—attitude characteristic of the allegoricist has the foremost place in the poetic work of the century?" (677)[5] asks Benjamin in "Zentralpark" ("Central Park"). "Central Park" is a central text on modern allegory. Ostensibly a reading of Baudelaire, more than half of its forty-five fragments are on allegory. The baroque allegory epitomized a world where objects and meanings, having made the transition from the sacred to the profane, no longer coincided. Modern allegory, in a more or less similar fashion, marks what Baudrillard would see as "the transition from signs which dissimulate something to signs which dissimulate that there is nothing." He adds that "the first implies a theology of truth and secrecy (to which the notion of ideology still belongs)." Benjamin would equate this category with the auratic space of the symbol. "The second inaugurates an age of simulacra and simulation, in which there is no longer any God to recognise his own, nor any last judgment to separate true from false, the real from its artificial resurrection, since everything is already dead and risen in advance" (*Simulations* 12).

Baudrillard's formulation expresses the postmodern sentiment that signs generate meaning and value only in terms of relation and difference to other signs, not as representations of things in the world. Similarly, Benjamin's allegory posits no image/reality duality. The objects on the baroque stage exist only as images or as the simulacrum of the simulacra. In the baroque drama, any form of *Darstellung*, the figural as well as the scenic, can be an allegory (Holz 85-86). Allegory "creates a world of representations where everything can take

the place of something else" (Holz 84). Thus, Benjamin opposes the allegorical
mode to the symbolic or the auratic which preserves the irreplacable status of
the original. Allegory fragments the apparent uniqueness and unity of the original. Benjamin attributes a similar function to mechanical reproduction. He
states that "the stripping away of the object from its case, the destruction of the
aura, is the signature of a perception whose sense for sameness in the world is
developed so highly that even the unique is divested of its uniqueness by means
of its reproduction" ("Photographie" 379). In a certain sense, allegory resembles a filmic image. It can be preserved, cut, edited, reproduced. However, this
reproduction is not mere repetition. It serves to "defetishize the aura of the original" (Eagleton 40). In fact, "origin and repetition are themselves locked in
imaginary collusion: the 'original' moment is bound to reduce what follows to
mere repetition; repetition itself is the empty pulsation of a process striving to
return to an origin it continually displaces" (Eagleton 40). The allegorical operation, on the other hand, creates meaning always anew by re-collecting fragments. However, this is only "posited meaning; it does not derive from the original context of the fragments" (Bürger 69). The critic as allegoricist mortifies
the text and its pretensions of totality and "salvages," in bits and pieces, its historically recyclable material.

Although allegory subverts the false unity of the real by fragmenting it, the
moment of recovery at a higher level follows its destructive impulse. "That
which is affected by the allegorical intention," writes Benjamin, "will be separated from the context of life: it is simultaneously destroyed and conserved.
Allegory holds on to the ruins. It offers the picture of arrested unrest *(erstarrte
Unruhe)*" ("Zentralpark" 666). Allegorical writing paralyzes itself in scenes; it
interrupts nature and linear time to draw the portrait of the historical moment.
Modern allegory lays claim neither to origin nor to transcendental meaning.
The emblematization of temporal consciousness fulfills itself in allegory. "Writing history," states Benjamin, "is giving years their physiognomy" ("Zentralpark" 661). History presents itself in these scenes in all its conflicts and ruptures. Thus, allegorical expression reaches maturity in texts of crisis, for
example, in the 17th century baroque, turn-of-the-century Vienna, Baudelaire.
The tormented physiognomy of history in the moment of its arrest negates the
Hegelian concept of a linear, progressive history. Benjamin rejects the notion of
modern that produces progress and is informed by it: "The concept of the historical progress of mankind cannot be sundered from the concept of its progression through a homogeneous, empty time. A critique of the concept of such a
progression must be the basis of any criticism of the concept of progress itself"
("Theses" XIII, 261).

History is not predicated on a natural master plan that unfolds in cumulative time. Benjamin valorizes another impulse of modernity characteristic of
Nietzsche, Baudelaire, and Kafka. "Arrested unrest" is, according to Benjamin,

"the formula for Baudelaire's life picture that knows of no progress" ("Zentral-park" 668). And "Kafka did not consider the age in which he lived as an advance over the beginnings of time" ("Franz Kafka" 139). The allegorical moment of modernity does not sanction a peaceful synthesis. It is radically secular without transcendence and telos. Secular salvation lies in the destructive forces of social history that reflect the dual operative principle of modern allegory—disfiguration and rehabilitation. The concept of progress is embedded in catastrophe. That things go on as they should is what Benjamin sees as catastrophe. Benjamin likens the picture of this catastrophe to the images of the kaleidoscope which go from chaos to order. The hand that shakes the kaleidoscope belongs to the dominant powers that create the illusion of restoring order to disorder. The order simulated is merely a pastiche of the history of ruling-class styles. Dictated by a masked authority and masquerading as a representation of universal "truth," this image of order holds out against the chaos of history. "The kaleidoscope must be smashed," declares Benjamin ("Zentralpark," 660). "Salvation *(Rettung)* hangs on to the small leap in the continual catastrophe" ("Zentralpark" 683). The leap originates in allegory where progressive history is replaced by disjunctive memory.

"Memory" is the "key figure of modern allegory" ("Zentralpark" 683). However, this is no longer the reconstructed memory of Hegelian phenomenology that ensures the ontological status of representation. In other words, it is no longer the representation of the absolute spirit that fulfills itself in history. History is not the representation of the absolute. Rather it is the self-representation of the present. "To articulate the past historically does not mean to recognize it 'the way it really was' (Ranke)" ("Theses" VI, 255). Rather it means to capture memory and investigate its use in the present. If memory cannot be revitalized for the present, if history cannot be textualized in such a way as to render it a critically effective praxis, then the cumulative effect of knowledge and experience is invalidated. The modern allegoricist strives to reinscribe the redemptive moments of tradition threatened by oblivion. What is transmitted through tradition are for Benjamin not sacred artifacts of past knowledge but, as Eagleton sees it, "strategies that construct and mobilize them. It is not that we constantly revaluate a tradition; tradition *is* the practice of ceaselessly excavating, safeguarding, violating, discarding and reinscribing the past. There is no tradition other than this, no set of ideal setmarks that then suffer modification. Artifacts are inherently available for such reinscription" (59).

The modern allegoricist is also embodied in the figure of the *flâneur*, "for both dip randomly into the ruck of objects to single out for consecration certain ones that they know to be in themselves arbitrary and ephemeral" (Eagleton 26). Benjamin's most memorable *flâneur* is Baudelaire. He is the quintessential modern, alienated, displaced, and saturnine who collects images left in the jungle of the cities in the wake of modernity. Baudelaire's poetry records the experience of the big city, the crowds, as a series of shocks. Shocks are registered at the site of the *Jetztzeit* and jolt the modern experience out of the monotonous flow of history. "Shock is among those experiences that have assumed decisive importance for Baudelaire's personality," writes Benjamin, "Gide has dealt with the interstices between image and idea, word and thing, which are the real site of Baudelaire's poetic excitation" ("On Some Motifs" 164). This site marks, in Benjamin's reading, a historical shift to the modern that fulfills itself not in large-scale societal changes but in changes in sociocultural artifacts and in the way they are experienced and reevaluated. Baudelaire is the *flâneur*, strolling through the mercantile arcades, collecting representational artifacts lining urban pathways. The mission of the collector is informed by the allegoricist spirit of salvaging the past. However, in its initial stage, the act of collection requires a process of destruction. "For to redeem objects," observes Eagleton, "means to dig them loose from the historical strata in which they are embedded, purging them of the accreted cultural meanings with which they are encrusted. The collector releases things from the traditional hierarchies into the free space of sheer contiguity"6 (61). The passion of the collector "fastens on the contingent and unregarded. Collecting is in this sense a kind of creative digression from the classical narrative, a 'textualizing' of history that reclaims repressed and unmapped areas" (Eagleton 61). The artifacts the collector finds are no longer recoverable in their totality or as a coherent narrative but only as fragments of lived accounts. Experiential fragments necessitate a new mapping of history, generate new meanings and tensions, as they reposition themselves in configurations of other cultural artifacts.

In Benjamin, memory remains fragmented. However, these fragments enter into configurations of altered significance during their passage through the *Jetztzeit*. Thus, in the course of its history, truth *(das Wahre)*—as representation or allegory—becomes commodity *(die Ware)*: "the emblems return as commodity" ("Zentralpark," 681). The representation of the "Wahre" turns into the reproduction of the "Ware." In *For a Critique of a Political Economy of the Sign*, Baudrillard argues that in the postmodern consumer society, commodity is produced as sign and sign value, just as signs are produced as commodity (147-48). The form of commodity constitutes an allegory of modern truth in Benjamin's later work. Benjamin fills the space of history with the distinct materiality of the *Jetztzeit* ("Theses" *XIV, 261). He illustrates the physical re*-membering of the past in the regulative metaphor of fashion, a metaphor grounded in a distinctly material context: "Fashion has a flair for the topical, no matter where it stirs in the thickets of long ago" ("Theses" XIV, 261). In coming to terms with the material and emblematic nature of the recurrent, Benjamin deploys, though inconclusively, a dialectic of salvation: "Fashion is the eternal recurrence of the new. Nevertheless, aren't there motives of salvation precisely in fashion?" ("Zentralpark" 677). Allegory salvages the "truth" content of history and recycles it as material signs that regulate fashions in art, culture, and commodity consumption.

Historical materialism invests the fragmented material signs of history with new significance. For his part, Benjamin locates a revolutionary potential in the ruins of nineteenth-century bourgeois life. The re-presentation of these fragmented signs in time, which remain forgotten in official histories, constitutes the foundation of modern critical praxis. Allegory as the "armor of modernity" ("Zentralpark"681) shields its emblems (collections) from the losses of time. Collection tries to salvage things from nonrepeatable time, but recollection refers them back to their contingent fate. Benjamin's conception of the dual nature of allegory illustrates the entangled orders of simulacra. On the one hand, the Benjaminian allegory is the collection of time's emblems. However, it also dismantles and disseminates this collection across time. In Baudelaire, for example, the allegorical impulse constitutes "the tearing away of things from their usual context—which is normal in the process of exhibiting commodities" ("Zentralpark" 670). This act of violence destroys the stability of the image embedded in social time and deconstructs the ideology—a form of negative theology that serves as the unequivocal referent of the image—maintained by dominant systems of representation.

The allegorical imagination fragments the cultural object, reduces it to discontinuous images that subvert traditional history's pretentions of totality. In this process, moments of revolutionary promise can be saved from stagnation and death in history. The reduction of objects to fragment destroys the representational conceit of an uncritical aesthetic vision: "In the field of allegorical intuition the image is a fragment, a rune. Its beauty as a symbol evaporates when the light of divine learning falls upon it. The false appearance of totality is extinguished" (*Origin* 176). The redemption of these fragments involves, however, more than a subversion of falsity. The allegorical attack challenges masses to reflect on their own sense of alienation, on the oppressive character of history. In *The Genealogy of Morals*, Nietzsche states how in every age dominant powers have reinterpreted existing structures to invest them with their own intentions. Thus, power has resided in the activity of outstripping, reinterpreting, and, thus, overcoming. In the rewritten documents of declarations of power, which take on the form of palimpsests, preexisting meanings and intentions are necessarily obscured, erased, or lost. Nietzsche's antihistoricist stance that acknowledges the legitimacy of conflict, rupture, and radical revision in the course of history is not lost on Benjamin. However, Nietzsche's attack on the metaphysics of history also subverts what Benjamin designates as tradition. For Benjamin tradition houses suppressed, forgotten, or marginalized texts and contexts of general history. The allegorical operation releases these by shattering and fragmenting the fossilized layers of that history hitherto inscribed by ruling ideologies.

The emancipation and re-cognition of the marginal and the oppositional is a recurrent item on the postmodern agenda. When the allegory strips the sign "from its mimetic intimacy with the thing, it has nevertheless been released into a new freedom with which fresh 'iconic' correspondences may be constructed" (Eagleton 41). Indeed, postmodern art and theory are repeatedly reminded of and moved to reflect on their centrality by the "previously silenced ex-centrics, both outside (post-colonial) and within (women, gays) our supposedly mono-lithic western culture" (Hutcheon 179). In "Catastrophic Utopia: The Feminine as Allegory of the Modern," Christine Buci-Glucksmann observes how Walter Benjamin's critical writings acknowledge the marginalized image of woman as a structure of "interpretive radicality" (220). Fictions of the feminine and visions of the female body in Baudelaire—prostitute, lesbian, androgyne—con-stitute shocking allegories of the modern. Allegory's destructive gaze rests on the violated, fragmented figure of the prostitute. The forgotten casualty of modernity, the commercialized, marketed body of woman is retrieved in Ben-jamin's criticism through the images in Baudelaire. The marginal always sub-verts the dominant discourse, disrupts it in time, links it with other pasts and forgotten practices. "Indeed, the prostitute is one of those monads that open the way for the archeological work of reconstructing history," writes Buci-Glucks-mann, "Benjamin's interest in the 'nameless' *(Namenlosen)* and the depths of history as well as literature, his constant desire to '*fix the image* of history in the humblest of crystallizations,' will produce a constellation of thoughts and images, a chaos of metaphors around this form of the feminine, the tragic form of modernity" (223).

The cutting edge of allegory paves the way to a corrosive job of criticism. The work of criticism looks for the sources of this knowledge in diverse places, even in traditional forms that may harbor allegorical beliefs. "The outer form [of the German tragic drama] has died away because of its extreme crudity. What has survived is the extraordinary detail of the allegorical references: an object of knowledge which has settled in the consciously constructed ruins" (*Origin* 181). One separates out the eternal "from the events of the story of sal-vation, and what is left is a living image open to all kinds of revision by the interpreting artist" (*Origin* 183). An understanding of allegory provides the alert reader with access to the complex social operations that construct image and ideology. In the hands of the allegoricist "the object becomes something differ-ent; through it he [the allegoricist] speaks of something different and for him it becomes a key to the realm of modern knowledge; and he reveres it as the emblem of this" (*Origin* 184). The historian as allegoricist "must highlight the seemingly inconsequential details of any given larger structure because they have been ignored in the larger process whereby the dominant class ascribes truth value to its ideologically inspired version of history " (Jennings 26).

Benjamin re-reads "the theory of eternal recurrence," which represented for him the always modern re-configuration of relics salvaged from history, "as a dream of the imminent colossal inventions in the field of reproduction technology" ("Zentralpark" 680). In Baudrillard's chronology of the postmodern, this moment marks the shift from representation to simulation. Simulation technology radically opposes the basic axiom of representation based on the equivalence (albeit u-topically) of the sign and the real. It sublates the difference between the real, original presence and the imaginary. Baudrillard argues that "whereas representation tries to absorb simulation by interpreting it as false representation, simulation envelops the whole edifice of representation itself as a simulacrum" (*Simulations* 11). Simulation is constituted in a "procession of simulacra" (*Simulations* 2). Similarly, Benjamin had observed that with each passing day, the need to take possession of objects in "reproduction" or "copy" *(Abbild)* rather than "picture" *(Bild)* became more prevalent. *Abbild*, which is characterized by transience and replicability, is the staple of illustrated dailies and weeklies. *Bild*, on the other hand, is informed by uniqueness and duration ("Photographie" 379). Furthermore, the "precession of simulacra" resembles the operations of allegory and technical reproduction in Benjamin's terms. The technique of the film camera, like that of allegory, penetrates deeply into the physiognomy of a temporal procession, "deranging the 'natural' viewpoint by its ability to probe and isolate, freezing, magnifying or disarticulating the fragments of an action in order to reassemble them in multiple forms" (Eagleton 39).

Benjamin's conception of allegory stands at this crossroad of modernity and postmodernity, because its operations unsettle representation and acknowledge simulation where there is no coextensivity between the map and the territory it represents or between the signifier and the signified. We no longer see the territory but read the map which endlessly refers to other maps. Today, "the real is produced from miniaturised units, from matrices, memory banks and command models—and with these it can be reproduced an indefinite number of times" (Baudrillard, *Simulations* 3). An extreme example of such a prison house of models and images is, according to Roland Barthes, "the United States, where everything is transformed into images: only images exist and are produced and consumed" (118). In *America*, Baudrillard reaffirms Barthes's assertion. Here "everything is destined to appear as simulation. Landscapes as photography, women as the sexual scenario, thoughts as writing, terrorism as fashion and the media, events as television. Things seem only to exist by virtue of this strange destiny. You wonder whether the world itself isn't just here to serve as advertising copy in some other world" (32).

This extreme generalization of images "completely de-realizes the human world of conflicts and desires, under cover of illustrating it" (Barthes 118). In this sense, image and ideology are joined in an unholy alliance, for "postmodern" ideology in Baudrillard's words "only corresponds to a betrayal of reality by signs" (*Simulations* 48). In Benjamin, allegory is the consciousness of the pervasiveness of images, but it does not yield to this inevitability of the sign without a fight. The work of allegory is to write sign systems out of the causal order of the historical maps commissioned by dominant classes. The allegorical operation separates signs from their assumed mimetic correspondence to things and rechannels them into the *Jetztzeit* as re-membered icons. Benjamin's allegorical gaze disrupts even the representational truth of the photographic image. What fascinates the beholder is not the stillness of the captured "reality" but the telltale signs that signify contingency and link the photographic reality to the present. ("Photographie" 371). The beholder confronts in the image a breaking down or fragmentation of the codes of perfect illusion whereby the time of the picture and that of the gaze become dialectically linked.[7] Likewise, the fragmented memory of history has to be captured in dialectical images, re-grounded in contemporary contexts and understood as a periodizing of culture in terms of socioeconomic concerns. In these dialectical images or confrontations, "a present moment may re-read itself in the past and allow the past to interpret itself anew in the present" (Eagleton 41).

Notes

I have used English translations of cited works when readily available and with minor changes. If an English translation of a work is not given in *Works Cited*, then the translations are mine.

1. Hutcheon adds that "presence of the past" was the title of the 1980 Venice Biennale "which marked the institutional recognition of postmodernism in architecture" (4).

2. Without attempting an etymological detour, I shall briefly point to the contextual use of *Vorstellung* and *Repräsentation* in romantic idealism. *Vorstellung* is an "inside" metaphor and designates an imaginary picture in the subject's mind. Friedrich Schlegel emphasizes the conceptual nuance between *Darstellung* and *Vorstellung* in an analogy to the inside/outside dichotomy: "The inner *Vorstellung* can become more understandable to itself and most lively only through *Darstellung* toward the outside" (2: 306; translation mine). Although *Repräsentation* also means making present, it often designates philosophical representation, whereas *Darstellung* almost exclusively refers to poetic or aesthetic representation. For a close examination of the use of these terms in eighteenth-century philosophical and aesthetic writings, see Fritz Heuer, *Darstellung der Freiheit: Schillers transzendentale Frage nach der Kunst* (Köln: Böhlau, 1970) 19-36.

3. In fact, postmodern architecture is often called the "citation style," for certain historical styles it incorporates are seen as quotations. I am thankful to Professor Ingeborg Hoesterey of Indiana University for this information.

4. For a very comprehensive treatment of the symbol/allegory opposition in German romanticism, see Tzvetan Todorov, *Theories of the Symbol*, trans. Catherine Porter (Ithaca: Cornell UP, 1982) 198-221.

5. All translations from "Zentralpark" are mine. An English translation by Lloyd Spencer is in *New German Critique* 34 (Winter 1985) 32-58.

6. It is interesting to recall that Jacques Derrida originally used the term *déconstruction* as a mode of "being alert to the implications, *to the historical sedimentation of the language which we use*" *(emphasis mine)*. Thus, the deconstructionist critic, like the allegoricist-collector frees words and images embedded in them through a long history and subjects them to critical scrutiny. See Derrida 271.

7. Similarly, in *Camera Lucida*, Roland Barthes speaks of the "two ways of the Photograph." The one is "tame" photography where spectacle is subjected "to the civilized code of perfect illusions." The other is "mad" photography or "photographic *ecstasy*" where the beholder confronts "the wakening of intractable reality" in the spectacle (119).

Works Cited

Barthes, Roland. *Camera Lucida; Reflections on Photography*. Trans. Richard Howard. New York: Farrar, Strauss and Giroux, 1981.

Baudrillard, Jean. *America*. Trans. Chris Turner. London: Verso, 1988.

————. *For a Critique of the Political Economy of the Sign*. Trans. Charles Levin. St. Louis: Telos, 1981.

————. *Simulations*. Trans. Paul Foss and Paul Patton. New York: Semiotexte, 1983.

Benjamin, Walter. *Der Begriff der Kunstkritik in der deutschen Romantik. Gesammelte Schriften*. Eds. Rolf Tiedemann and Hermann Schweppenhäuser. I. I. Frankfurt: Suhrkamp, 1972. 6 vols. 11-122.

————. "Franz Kafka: On the Tenth Anniversary of His Death." *Illuminations*. Trans. Harry Zohn. New York: Schocken, 1969. 111-40.

————. "Kleine Geschichte der Photographie." *Gesammelte Schriften*. 2.1. 368-85.

————. "On Some Motifs in Baudelaire." *Illuminations*. 155-200.

————. *The Origin of German Tragic Drama*. Trans. John Osborne. London: NLB, 1977.

————. "Theses on the Philosophy of History." *Illuminations*. 253-64.

————. "Zentralpark." *Gesammelte Schriften*. 1.2: 657-90.

Buci-Glucksmann, Christine. "Catastrophic Utopia: The Feminine as Allegory of the Modern." *The Making of the Modern Body: Sexuality and Society in the Nineteenth Century*. Eds. Catherine Gallagher and Thomas Laqueur. Berkeley: U of California P, 1987. 220-29.

Bürger, Peter. *Theory of the Avant-Garde*. Trans. Michael Shaw. Minneapolis: U of Minnesota P, 1984.

Cowan, Bainard. "Walter Benjamin's Theory of Allegory." *New German Critique* 22-25 (1981-82). 109-22.

Derrida, Jacques. "Discussion" to "Structure, Sign, and Play in the Discourse of the Human Sciences." *The Structuralist Controversy*. Eds. Richard Macksey and Eugenio Donato. Baltimore: Johns Hopkins UP, 1972.

Eco, Umberto. *The Name of the Rose*. Trans. William Weaver. New York: Warner, 1984.

Eagleton, Terry. *Walter Benjamin or Towards a Revolutionary Criticism*. London: Verso, 1981.

Foster, Hal. "(Post)Modern Polemics." *Recodings: Art, Spectacle, Cultural Politics*. Seattle: Bay Press, 1985. 121-37.

Foucault, Michel. *The Order of Things: An Archaeology of the Human Sciences*. Translation of *Les Mots et les choses*. New York: Random, 1970.

Goethe, Johann Wolfgang von. *Sämtliche Werke*. Vol. II. Berlin: Propylän, 1891. 45 vols. 405-08.

Gossman, Lionel. "History and Literature: Reproduction or Signification." *The Writing of History: Literary Form and Historical Understanding*. Eds. Robert H. Canary and Henry Kozicki. Madison: U of Wisconsin P, 1978. 3-39.

Heidegger, Martin. "The Age of the World Picture." *The Question Concerning Technology and Other Essays*. Trans. William Lovitt. New York: Garland Publishing, 1977. 115-54.

Holz, Hans Heinz. "Prismatisches Denken." *Über Walter Benjamin*. Frankfurt: Suhrkamp, 1968. 62-110.

Hutcheon, Linda. *A Poetics of Postmodernism: History, Theory, Fiction*. New York: Routledge, 1988.

Jennings, Michael W. *Dialectical Images: Walter Benjamin's Theory of Literary Criticism*. Ithaca: Cornell UP, 1987.

Nietzsche, Friedrich. *Zur Genealogie der Moral. Werke*. Ed. Karl Schlecta. Vol. 2. Munich: Hanser, 1956. 3 vols. 763-900.

Novalis (Friedrich von Hardenberg). *Schriften*. Eds. Paul Kluckhohn and Richard Samuel. Vol. 3. Stuttgart: W. Kohlhammer, 1960. 4 vols.

Schlegel, Friedrich. *Kritische Ausgabe*. Eds. Ernst Behler. Vol. 2. Paderborn: Schöningh, 1967. 35 vols.

White, Hayden. *Tropics of Discourse: Essays in Cultural Criticism*. Baltimore: Johns Hopkins UP, 1978.

Wolin, Richard. *Walter Benjamin: An Aesthetic of Redemption*. New York: Columbia UP, 1982.

Chapter 11

Figuring Rupture:
Iconology, Politics, and the Image

Brian Macaskill

I

A primary concern of iconology, by which I mean the *theory* of imagery rather than an iconographic investigation of this or that particular image, is to trace "the ways that images in the strict or literal sense (pictures, statues, works of art) are related to notions such as mental imagery, verbal or literary imagery, and the concept of man as an image and maker of images."[1] The palimpsests of such tracing reveal the image as participating within a zone of control and the ever-attendant potential for conflict that accompanies control; within a zone, that is, shaped by the ideological pressures of hegemonic enforcement and counter-hegemonic resistance. In this respect, the image is crucially a site of power, a dominant figure in the representation, governance, and manipulation of cultural constructs. The image figures prominently, for instance, in the controlling mechanisms of political mythology, where it serves to illuminate the nationalistic stories that cultures tell themselves about who they are: to illustrate plastically, graphically, and semiotically a sense of communal identity in flag, emblem, monument, statue, and in the narrative seduction of histories (his-stories) which lay claim to the assimilation and regulation of individual mysteries (my-stories).

The deployment of images in the hegemonics and counter-hegemonics of political regulation, the crafting of image as idol or fetish by iconophiles and iconoclasts, is sufficiently obvious to indicate the significance of the image as a volatile element within the politics of making, shaping, controlling, and resisting. Images are literally subject to the power of policing, as recent events make clear: the South African government's response to emblems of the African National Congress printed on T-shirts, say, or congressional debate over the legal and constitutional issues surrounding the act of burning the Stars and Stripes of the United States. Likewise, though not always as obviously so, the aesthetic image has been implicated within paradigms of ideological conflict from Plato to the present, in the course of which it has as frequently occasioned suspicion as it has attracted staunch defense. In either instance, whether ostensibly negated by or affiliated to some validating axiology, the aesthetic image has historically been conjugated in a register that repudiates or affirms other registers of power—philosophy, say, or theology, history, science, psychology, mathematics, and, more recently, photography also. Hence Plato's distrust of the artist as dealer in aesthetic images thrice removed from the real and the true (to which political legislators, philosophers, and even artisans have more immediate access) is ostensibly repudiated by a romantic valorization of "the Image as a radiant truth out of space and time" (Kermode 2). In its turn, this romantic concept of the image is a valorization generated against (but also in nervous acknowledgement of, in complicity with) a notion of some "superior" scientific power which is assumed to have dominion over the physics of space and time. In brief, the image has long been a locus of value for those who insist on the power of art, and both artists and theorists have often defined that value defensively, so as to affirm it in the face of epistemological competition from other orders of discourse.

But the competition has come not only from orders of discourse other than those of the arts, for a rivalry exists also within the arts: a conflict between the respective potencies of pictorial and literary images. In particular, the literary image has had to confront the pictorial image, or image proper, in the skirmishes of what Leonardo da Vinci refers to as the *paragone* or war of signs between painting and poetry, between image and word, which has become—for later semioticians—a war also between photograph and text. Once again, some measure of resolution to this conflict has been achieved by means of an uneasy complicity between word and image whereby the image is commonly and typically defined as "a picture made out of words."[2] And so opposing claims for the literary image have struggled their way into the twentieth century. The imagist poets, for instance, have granted a special privilege to the "masculinity" of antiromantic images, a "hardness" that Ezra Pound, for one, believed crucial to the new "science" of twentieth-century poetry. In an attempt to distance art from the proliferation of images in commercial advertising, much Anglo-American criticism of the twentieth century (loosely, the "New Criticism"), has granted ever-increasing powers and complexities of value to the image: "a poem may itself be an image composed from a multiplicity of images," writes Day Lewis (18). In yet another development surrounding the foment of ideas about images in the twentieth century, the Russian formalists promoted the concept of formal "devices" over that of discrete images in literature and launched a programmatic attack on the notion that "Art is thinking in Images."[3]

The image exists in the context of conflict, then, and critical theory has sought to police the domain of the aesthetic image and its specifically literary manifestation. With this conflict as background, I propose to pursue the political potential available to a particular deployment of the image: a *rupturing* deployment, whose operation I shall exemplify in pictorial as well as in narrative forms by first metamorphically transposing da Vinci's concern with the *paragone* into Derrida's fascination with the *parergon*, a supplemental boundary or frame to the work of art.[4] The transformation of *paragone* into *parergon* is in fact more than a rhetorically compelling metamorphosis, given that the paralinguistic investigation practiced by the likes of Derrida and Roland Barthes retains a healthy skepticism about the power of linguistic "science," and thereby directs attention precisely to limits—not only the limits of linguistics as scientific discipline, but also to the boundaries, intersections, and complicities between linguistic arts and their extralinguistic supplements. Poststructural linguistics in this sense operates across the domain of "debate, quotation, partisanship, betrayal [and] reconciliation" that Rosalind Krauss calls the space of "paraliterary work" (37); more pointedly, such linguistic procedure operates fully aware that the image is after all not *linguistic* in nature, and thus poststructuralism adds its own (cultural) doubts to da Vinci's *paragone*. As Roland Barthes explains it, linguistics doubts that the image is linguistic in any crucial sense, and is not alone in this suspicion: "public opinion as well vaguely regards the image as a site of resistance to meaning, in the name of a certain mythical notion of Life: the image is re-presentation, i.e., ultimately resurrection, and we know that the intelligible is reputed antipathetic to the experiential" (*Responsibility* 21). If the image is thus widely held somehow to touch upon the *limits* of meaning, it is surely pertinent to investigate the possibilities of its intelligibility at the parergonal margins which bring the image into being: its "denotative" outline and the ideologically connotative procedures of its framing—in sum, at the interstices of its modality as re-presentation of the experiential by a particular culture at a particular time.

As Linda Hutcheon has recently stressed—and as my brief overview of the image's entry into modern/postmodern theory and praxis is intended to imply—the activity of ex-centric literary practice and "paraliterary" cultural work cogently contributes to the definition of that particular time and place, that space, in which postmodern culture operates. Quoting one of the Merry Pranksters from Tom Wolfe's *The Electric Kool-Aid Acid Test*, Hutcheon reiterates a common perception of postmodern praxis as *borderline* activity, suggesting that "perhaps the postmodern motto should be . . . 'Hail to the Edges!'" (73). This should not be taken to imply that a celebration of or concern with "the Edges" adequately defines the postmodern, nor indeed that a preoccupation with borderlines contributes only, exclusively, to a definition of postmodernism. In theoretical and historical periodization of the arts, as in drawing or in other art works—and in political maps—the border is the place where continuity and discontinuity meet: a space nicely suggested by the barrier that emerges when "postmodern" is written as "post-modern." Furthermore, the hyphen can operate similarly—as graphic sign of discontinuity *and* continuity—between the modern and its predecessors. Modernism, after all, is also post-Victorian, post-romantic, and so on; rather than dividing only into binary distinctions, such "post-" formulations suggest the complicities and continuities that division negotiates. So although attention to the border is crucial in postmodern practice, where borderlines explicitly display themselves as ironic, my concern with edges is not confined to the postmodern, but extends to include that upon which the irony operates: earlier borderlines, the contiguities with and rupture from pre-modern ideology and artifice which the post- comes to interrogate. Hence I proceed with a rhetoric of rupture that is particularly appropriate to postmodern inquiry, but that simultaneously recognizes relationships of (dis)continuity, taking as my starting point the continuity that iconic, narrative, and cinematographic images can evoke among themselves and the referents they denote.

The illusion of continuity effected by images in the service of representation is achieved by concealing a gap between art and life, a gap which can be reopened for examination whenever attention is focused on the parergonal margins of representation: the frame or outline, indispensable to the image's denotative function, but also important loci of cultural connotation. Alluding to this gap, Socrates points out to Hermogenes in the *Cratylus* that "the image must not by any means reproduce all the qualities of that which it imitates, if it is to be an image [rather than a duplicate]" (432b, 163). It is precisely the loss occasioned by the image's inability to reproduce "all the qualities of that which it imitates" that suggests the political dimension of aesthetic imagery. Recognition of this loss as a boundary between the mimetic and political extends from Plato to Barthes, who has noted that "where politics begins is where imitation ceases" (*Barthes by Barthes* 154). The cognition of mimetic loss as a boundary does not mean, however, that the political cannot be represented, but rather that the boundary itself is a political one, that representation is *already* politicized. The image, moreover, is able to realize its political potential when representation imagines the boundary or gap; that is, when the image figures the rupture between depicted world and that other world on which it is modelled.

The gap takes place—situates itself—between the cultural sign-system exterior to the frame (which we know and inhabit as the world) and the stylistically framed interior of the various artistic media used to represent or to address that world. Narrative, the pictorial arts, and cinema draw their images across this gap: redraw their images inside the frame, seek to supplement cognitively, incrementally, the images they ultimately give back to the world.[5] The gap is thus figured most obviously by—and can be exploited most obviously by—the outer boundaries and margins of the modelling system: the picture frame, say, or the conventions of pictorial perspective and cinematographic transitions; or the epilogues, prologues, and frame tales of medieval and Renaissance story collections; or the "fictional" footnotes to texts like *Tristram Shandy* and *Finnegan's Wake*.[6]

This marginalia of outer borders and paginal supplements that offset and make use of the gap between representation and represented quickly becomes conventionalized—as already noted—and is frequently pressed into generating the illusion of continuity. As we shall see, however, fascinating emblems of the gap between representation and the represented occur also internally to the work, where they operate as *images* (rather than as framing edges), and where their rupturing effects are less likely to be neutralized than at the outer margins of the frame. It is to three instances of such internal disruption or frame-breaking—in icon, film, and narrative—that I now turn my attention. Aligning itself with the border, the margin, the *débordement* of the work in which it figures, the rupturing image always involves a play of intra-referentiality (to the extent that the frame-break points inwards to that which is marked as being internal to the frame) and simultaneously involves also a semiosis of extra-referentiality (to the extent that the rupture indicates the represented "inside" as something other than, though beholden to, the "outside" which it serves to model, from which it draws its intelligibility, and upon which it in turn incrementally acts as supplement).

II

That this *débordement* or "overflow" from work to world involves what might be called a politics of the gap is quite clearly evident in medieval representation, which tends to conceive itself as a necessarily incomplete and insufficient key to a richer, invisible, and divine reality. Although "Man" was created "in the image and likeness" of God, he was not created as a material "copy" of God, as annotated Bibles frequently explain:

> Now as the Divine Being is infinite, he is neither limited by parts, nor defin-
> able by passions; therefore he can have no *corporeal image* after which he
> made the body of man. The image and likeness must necessarily be intellec-
> tual. (*The Holy Bible . . . with a Commentary and Critical Notes by Adam
> Clarke*; qtd. in Mitchell 31n)

In this order of things, "the image of the Word is the true man, that is, the mind of man, who on this account is said to have been created 'in the image' of God and 'in His likeness,' because through his understanding heart he is made like the divine Word or Reason, and so reasonable" (Clement of Alexandria).[7] Furthermore, the images that man makes of himself and his world are but transitory things: the books he writes are imperfect glosses on God's Book of Scripture or God's Book of Nature, the statues he fashions "in human form, being an earthen image of visible, earthborn man, and far away from the truth, plainly show themselves to be but a temporary impression upon matter" (Clement). The true image, that is, is encoded in the spiritual, not the material, and as Mitchell notes, "the distinction between the spiritual and material, inner and outer image, was never simply a matter of theological doctrine, but was always a question of politics, from the power of priestly castes, to the struggle between conservative and reform movements (the iconophiles and iconoclasts), to the preservation of national identity (the Israelites' struggle to purge themselves of idolatry)" (35).

From the ideology that sustains such an environment, I draw my first example: the miniature of Otto II on the frontispiece of the Aachen Gospels.[8] (See Fig. 11-1.) Executed towards the end of the tenth century, this celebrated miniature depicts the emperor seated on his throne, which is supported from below by a female figure, presumably Earth herself; from above, the Hand of God reaches down to Otto's crowned head in a gesture of benediction. The emperor and God's hand are each framed by a conventional sign of sacred space: the emperor is surrounded by a mandorla, a common configuration in the representation of Christ, and the Hand by a cruciform nimbus, unequivocal signifier of divinity. Furthermore, the mandorla and nimbus intersect on either side of the emperor's head, thus creating there an unusually dynamic pictorial centre.[9] The framing hierarchy evoked by imperial mandorla and divine nimbus is replicated by the symmetrically hieratic arrangement of the other figures within the outer framing arch of the miniature: around the emperor's upper torso are depicted the four beasts of the apocalypse, who also function as symbols for the four evangelists (Matthew is the winged man, John the eagle, Mark the lion, and Luke the ox);[10] two high-ranking princes flank the emperor's feet, and the bottom third of the miniature is occupied by two archbishops and two warriors, whom Kantorowicz notes as "representing the princes spiritual and secular" (62).

The most interesting feature of this miniature is the veil held by the four beasts of the apocalypse: a figure for the veil of the tabernacle, a curtain of sky which not only marks the boundary between heaven and earth, but thereby also divides Otto's body into supra- and sub-celestial segments. The interpretative space this figure makes available within the image projects an ideological vision of the dual nature—body natural and body politic—of the emperor as *christomimetes*, literally the "actor" or "impersonator" of Christ. As Kantorowicz points out, the veil is positioned

> in such a fashion that the fall of the fold leaves head, breast, and shoulders as well as the brachial joints of the emperor "above," that is in heaven, whereas the body, including the hands, remains "below." We have to remember that head, breast, shoulders, and brachial joints were the places where the emperor was anointed with holy oil. Those parts of his body therefore refer, so to speak, to the *christus domini*, whereas the trunk and limbs are those of an ordinary man. (74)

The veil which here divides Otto's body seeks to transform the mere "temporary impression upon matter"—all a portrait of "visible earthborn man" could hope to achieve—into a more potent signifier: the body politic as made "in the

Figure 11-1
Reprinted by permission of the Cathedral Treasury, Aachen. Frontispiece to the *Aachen Gospel Book*, c.a. A.D. 975.

image" of Christ, in the likeness not only of his spiritual presence, but of his political power as well. The emperor as Christ-ruler is human by nature, but divine by grace and consecration, a notion whose political ramifications provided the grounds of dispute in the eleventh-century Investiture Conflict, a struggle for power and authority between secular and ecclesiastical interests launched by Gregorian attacks on, and royalist defenses of, the privileges of royal theocracy.[11] The artist of the miniature portrays in this work the paradox of Otto as simultaneously man and *christomimetes*, and presumably intends the representation to hold the conflict between the two bodies in transcendent tension. But the principal means whereby transcendence is to be achieved, the image of the veil, surely deconstructs this harmonious intent. The veil does more than divide and hold together Otto's body in paradox. The veil functions as an image that sutures the rupture between heaven and earth, Christ and Emperor; and yet, it is only able to achieve this suture to the extent that it also enacts an ideological rupture between royalist and papist, between "internal" representation and "external" politics. It is able to achieve the suturing of rupture only to the extent that it becomes a rupturing image. The artifice of the veil effects the transcendent paradox of imaging in one unified body a two-bodied ruler, but in the process it demonstrates itself as deconstructively *para*-doxical in ideological terms. The image reveals itself, in other words, as one that *runs against* the *doxa* of divine law, as one that reinterprets divine law polemically, for its own political ends.

The aesthetic paradox captured by means of the image in this miniature cannot but overflow the lines of its artistic delineation, its denotation as spiritual transcendence devoid of politics. In the act of overruning its denotative outline (the signification of an existence beyond and independent of material experience), the image cannot avoid connoting also—by virtue of its own materiality—the ideological terms of a conflict that will culminate in the pamphlets circulated during the Investiture Conflict, "the first medieval crisis to call forth a considerable propagandist literature" (Tellenbach 115).

Much of this "propagandist" literature follows the tone of tracts written by the Norman Anonymous of York, a cleric of passionately royalist and determinedly anti-Gregorian sentiments, who, by way of example, has this to say of the anointed kings of Israel:

> We thus have to recognize [in the king] a *twin person*, one descending from nature, the other from grace. . . . One through which, by the condition of nature, he conformed with other men: another through which, by the eminence of [his] deification and by the power of the sacrament [of consecration], he excelled all others. Concerning one personality, he was, by nature, an individual man: concerning his other personality, he was, by grace, a *Christus*, that is, a God-man. (Qtd. in Kantorowicz 46)

Such a notion of the two-natured king persisted in the political domain long after the liturgical concept of kingship championed by the Norman Anonymous became superceded by a more secular concept of jurisprudence. As Kantorowicz further points out, for instance, the affiliation and distinction between king as mortal body natural and King as immortal body politic made it possible for

Parliament to summon, "in the name and by the authority of Charles I, King body politic, the armies which were to fight the same Charles I, king body natural" (21).

Despite the ideological and politicized conflict in which the miniature of Otto II becomes involved, the project undertaken by (the inside of) the miniature remains clearly directed towards incorporation rather than separation, towards suture rather than rupture. The controlling principle at work within the miniature is a systematic gesture towards universal *historia*, a view which emphasizes the coherence of world and scripture, politics and theology, Emperor and Christ, ideology and image.[12] The world the miniature frames and secures is coherently hieratic and historiated. The veil that polemically ruptures the frame operates as a "hidden polemic" (to use Bakhtin's term), and is motivated by incorporation, not anarchy; hence it serves as an internal trace of the frame, and does not call attention to itself as a rupturing challenge. What the example conveniently demonstrates, however, is the interruptive valence of the image. Whatever specific conjectures we may formulate with regard to intentionality in the production of this miniature, the rupturing image of the veil—no doubt despite itself—performs work that allows the informed viewer to perceive in the overrun between image and ideology a disruption of precisely the (neutral, natural, inevitable) transcendence the image seems designed to achieve. Thus the design of the miniature—its attempt to portray the dual-bodied Emperor as spiritual fact, its curtailment of tension and achievement of transcendence through the aesthetic reification of spiritual paradox—reveals the conflicting ideologies which make its politics intelligible and reveals also the hegemonic interests of a royalist project it indubitably serves. And it does all of this despite its clearly harmonic intentions. This example reveals, finally, a disruptive potential that more recent artisans of the image have consciously sought to foreground through the creation of their artifice within the politics of contemporary culture.

Given the political nature of this disruptive potential, here accidentally revealed by the Imperial miniature, it is no longer possible in this discussion to ignore the distinction between politics proper (in the sense of political action, taking sides in the investiture conflict, say) and the metamorphic transformation of political impulses into indices of stylistic choice which seemingly distance and separate the aesthetic object from the power relations whereby social life is organized. Addressing such issues, and principally in an attempt to qualify high modernism's social influence, Frederic Jameson has made a distinction between "political" and "protopolitical" impulses, referring to the latter as "[modernism's] 'Utopian' substitution of cultural politics for politics proper, the vocation to transform the world by transforming its forms, space or language" (109). Jameson's project grapples with at least a two-tiered problem: at one level, aesthetic artifacts can be "about" politics (Picasso's *Guernica*, say, or Orwell's

Animal Farm) or appear not directly to concern political issues (modernist "intransitivity," the legacy of Flaubert and Mallarmé); at another level, however, any cultural artifact is in some crucial sense a product of its time and hence also a response to the relations of power that constitute the politics of that time (the position that "avoids" or "transcends" politics is itself a political position, as the preceding discussion of the Imperial miniature has indicated). One has thus to contend with the political program explicitly announced by some works of art (though not by others), *and also* with the at least protopolitical force of certain stylistic and generic devices signaling a relationship between artifact and the social structure which has enabled the work to take place.

Once again attention to acts of framing suggests ways of bringing into view the significance of protopolitical style as an activity related to but not identical with political action. Consider the eighteenth-century novel, for example: here the function of framing as an aesthetic device to supply a reifying and defining outline for the work of art exactly reveals the frame's importance in a narrative literature seeking to come to terms with, perhaps even to create the terms of, its emerging status as object of secular culture *entitled* to claim cultural privilege. It is in this sense that the title pages and prefatory mechanisms of the eighteenth-century novel may be seen to constitute a narrative frame, one of whose crucial functions is protopolitically to assert for the generic neonate an identity as valuable commodity (*Literature*), despite the early novel's self-conscious aura of insecurity about matters of parentage and pedigree.[13] Hence too the frame (in narrative as well as pictorial terms) becomes crucial in yet another moment of commodified art's genealogy—a moment equally fraught with insecurities of self-definition—when the Art-film seeks to distance itself from the Hollywood hegemonics of commercial cinema. This latter protopolitical development is predicated in part on the significance of cinematic framing as a revisionary instrument, in which the cinematic frame is acknowledged as a "reconstitution of the scene of the signifier, of the symbolic, into that of the signified, the passage through the image from other scene to seen" (Heath 260).

The denotative thrust of the Imperial miniature, as we have seen, seeks to signify a spiritual "non-fiction": the dual-natured Otto as transcendent ruler. In the wake of the self-conscious experimentation that has accompanied narrative and cinematographic representation—an index of insecurities about the status and power to which the representational endeavors of these artforms may lay claim—the novel and film too have often relied on the denotative power of "non-fictional" reference, now in secular rather than religious terms. As in the miniature, this maneuver has in turn come to constitute a double articulation, in which the non-fictional reference comes to connote a second order of meaning, roughly translatable as "this fiction is true." In such a semantics, the image thus becomes involved in a process of splitting, whose primary function is to validate aesthetic "authenticity" and to legitimize the artificial act of representation. By way of example, we thus encounter, along with intimate "biographical" details substantiating the authorship of *Gulliver's Travels* as that of "LEMUEL Gulliver, first a Surgeon and then a CAPTAIN of several SHIPS," a portrait of Captain Gulliver in an etched image on the frontispiece of some 1726 printings. And in the opening shot of Karel Reisz's *The French Lieutenant's Woman* a tripling effect is announced by the clapperboard which introduces the viewer to a film about the filming of a film in which Meryl Streep is to be recognized as Sarah (the French Lieutenant's Woman) and Anna (the actress playing Sarah) and therefore also (in a quasi-documentary sense) as a well-known actress playing two (in fact, three) parts in Reisz's film. As this last example might suggest, the practice of frame-breaking is especially foregrounded in postmodern production, a claim even the most casual acquaintance with the literary and cinematographic work of, say, Calvino, Borges, Robbe-Grillet, and Buñuel will confirm.[14]

Hence it is to the political and protopolitical use of "non-fictional" frame-breaking in postmodernism that I now turn, first by briefly considering the rupturing potential of images in a French new wave film, and finally by examining the politics of a verbally constructed image from a Nadine Gordimer novel.

III

Hiroshima mon amour, filmed by Alain Resnais from a screenplay by Marguerite Duras, manipulates the boundary between fiction and non-fiction by straddling different representational spaces and times—notably those of documentary and desire. It overflows from one domain into the other and back again, and creates for criticism the fascinating problem of accounting for the nature of reference in which the cinematographic images here participate. In her "synopsis" to the published screenplay, Duras explicitly designates *Hiroshima* as a "false documentary" ("une espèce de faux documentaire" [12]). The protopolitical dimension of the film's display of images thus becomes in part a question of determining the validity of "false documentary" in the context of a commonplace banality, a romantic "histoire banale . . . qui arrive chaque jour" (11), and in the context of the outrageous *fact* of Hiroshima, a fact commemorated within the film by newsreels and photographs of the event itself. Conscious of precisely this problem (several months before beginning the film, Resnais had found it impossible to fulfill his initial commission to shoot a short documentary on Hiroshima and the bomb [Monaco 34]), Resnais and Duras thematicize it in the work as the impossibility of talking about (or making a film about) Hiroshima. As Duras says of the initial exchange between the lovers,

> Their first remarks will thus be allegorical. *In brief, these remarks will constitute an operatic exchange.* Impossible to talk about HIROSHIMA. All one can do is to talk about the impossibility of talking about HIROSHIMA. The *knowledge of Hiroshima* being granted a priori as an exemplary decoy for the mind (un leurre exemplaire de l'esprit). (My translation 10)

Confronting the paradox of communicating a subject about which it is impossible to speak, Resnais of course responds by way of visual communication, creating cinematographic images that function in the film as complex, primary signifiers—images that often rely, in addition, on the *para*-doxical impulses of rupture.

The film proper, for instance, opens with an image of two pairs of naked shoulders. (See Fig. 11.2.) In accordance with Duras's screenplay, "All one sees are these shoulders, cut off from the body at the height of the head and the hips.

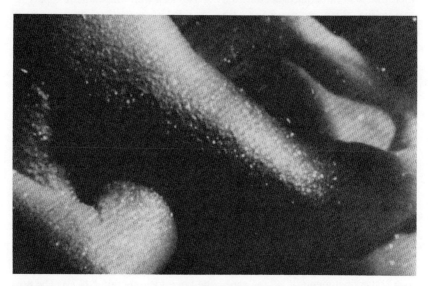

Figure 11-2
Reprinted by permission of New Yorker Films. A still picture from the opening sequence of *Hiroshima mon amour*.

Locked in an embrace, the shoulders seem to be drenched with ashes, rain, dew, or sweat, whichever the viewer prefers (*comme on veut*)" (21). The carefully cropped image creates a defamiliarizing effect. By forcing the bodies' extremities outside the picture frame, and by capturing what remains, equivocally, in the grip of rain, dew, radioactive ash, or the sweat of lovemaking (*comme on veut*) Resnais's directing here creates the impression that we are looking at unfamiliar, unidentifiable parts of the human body. This opening image foreshadows, precisely, precociously, the film's exploration of what one critic describes as "how psychological recuperation and moral awareness emerge out of new ways of perceiving relationships" (Dittmar 196). The cropped framing of this particular image is more, however, than a psychological signifier. It is also at least a protopolitical act attempting to reflect in some sense the political event that preceded it, an act which plays the gap between individual identity and abstract form, between banal love story and the horror of Hiroshima, between the cinematic "inside" and the historical "outside" of the celluloid frame. Metonymically, the image suggests the dependency of preclusive histories and partial memories on other historical acts and mental fabrications, personal as well as public. A sense of this dependency in effect generates the framing of the film as a whole: documentary framed by desire; or is it perhaps the other way around—desire framed by documentary?

Uncertainty about what frames what in this work is fundamental to the structure of the film itself, and the equivocation stresses the extent to which frame-breaking, here manifest as an oscillation, a periodic forcing of images into and out of the "containing" cinematic frame, undermines the notion of a supposedly prediscursive experience of life "exterior" to representational codes and the signifying practices that make the "interior" of representational artifice. As Michael Ryan notes of transcoding between film and social discourses, "the notion of a material circuit [linking film discourse to social discourse] implies that there is no exteriority of the referent, no objective ground to the film signifier. Rather, the two are part of one system, or a multiplicity of interconnected systems that relay social ideas and feeling from the extracinematic culture to film and back into culture, where they circulate further" (480). It is precisely in this sense that a rupturing *débordement* or overrun of narrative and pictorial boundaries in *Hiroshima*, and even in the miniature of Otto II, simultaneously disrupts and yet also contributes towards the fiction of unbroken and containing boundaries. The *débordement* of image is always a supplemental and incomplete act whose protopolitical program perhaps threatens to overrun its "proto-" technics, becoming political to the extent that it seeks to change the viewers' perception and to encourage their participation in contributing something back to the overrunning image: to neutralize the incompleteness of an insufficient human order from the perspective of a royalist, say, or to confront the lack of certainty generated by multivalent or equivocal representation in *Hiroshima mon amour*.

Resnais's film is more challengingly disruptive in its effects than those achieved by the Imperial miniature, but like the miniature, and despite its oscillation between history and "love story," *Hiroshima mon amour* is finally incapable of extricating itself from the ideological dilemma it portrays: the (im)possibility of living the (im)possibility of a banal love affair under the mushroom cloud of Hiroshima. Indeed, the marker of variance available to an ideological "reading" of *Hiroshima mon amour*, a variance indicated by the parenthetical prefix of the preceding sentence, undoes itself when it negates the *im*possibility of living the banal possibility by projecting exactly the possibility of that "impossibility." In a crucial sense, then, the rupture made available by this film's protopolitically sophisticated recording fails (or refuses) to rupture: *Hiroshima mon amour* seeks to demonstrate the film industry's power to engage in cultural critique, but domesticates its criticism by showing only how it remains possible (banally) to cope—by itself coping with, rather than dismantling, the assumptions of a power system that made its own recording possible.

IV

As the foregoing account of *Hiroshima* has indicated, it is not only the pictorial properties of the image which claim access to the subversion between inside and outside; nor is the semiotic doubling of pictorial elements even privileged in terms of political potential. Despite commonly held suspicions that significained cannot exhaust the ineffable wealth of the image proper, that is, of the visual image (Barthes, *Responsibility* 22), and that only visual images can thus be genuinely disconcerting, the double articulation of language surely points to the possibility of radical disruption in the constitution of the verbal image. My final example, which will also prove to be the most germanely *political* instance of a rupturing image at work, is indeed a verbal construct brought into being by Nadine Gordimer's 1974 novel, *The Conservationist*. This final example will serve as a culmination to the trajectory of political potential thus far traced through imagery in icon and film, for the effect of the verbal image in this case clearly goes beyond that of protopolitical gesture and cannot easily be said to achieve its political resonance *despite itself*, or by accident.

The dominant image in *The Conservationist* is that of a dead black man carelessly buried by indifferent policemen in a shallow grave on a farm belonging to Mehring, the protagonist and principal focaliser of the novel. The police, as Mehring later muses, "shovelled [the black man] in as you might fling a handful of earth on the corpse of a rat" (248). The unidentified black corpse is, however, inadequately buried in more ways than those suggested by the indifference of a police force reluctant to take seriously anything outside the periphery of white, hegemonic interest: the black labourers on the farm also refuse to accept any responsibility for the dead man ("Nobody can know for this man. Nothing for this man" [15], "Is not our trouble" [32]), and the corpse remains only half-buried in the consciousness of Mehring, who becomes obsessed with the dead presence in a process wrought of both identification and revulsion.

Quite aside from the effect the dead man exerts on the characters within the novel, Gordimer exploits the image of the corpse as a narrative vehicle of interruption, for the image motivates and engenders an entirely alternate underplot to the principle narrative. This subnarrative eventually comes to dominate the text's final pages, where it narratively displaces the privilege previously granted by *style indirect libre* to the white protagonist's consciousness. Speaking for the dispossessed, this crucial strand of the narrative originates in the ligature between the image of the dead man as unknown ancestor and the irruption into the text of quotations from the Reverend Henry Callaway's mid-nineteenth-century text, *The Religious System of the Amazulu*. The image of the corpse serves Gordimer as a complex political device to intimate a tradition of sociopolitical organization quite different from that familiar to the lineage of white colonizers from whom Mehring is descended; Callaway's text is an account, amongst other things, of the Amatongo or spirits of the dead—*"they who are beneath"* (163). Furthermore, the image of the corpse contributes towards an interruptive discourse specifically opposed to the realist register in which that colonial lineage represented by Mehring has traditionally told its tales on and about South African soil. The alignment between conservationist, conservative, and conversationalist that comes to characterize Mehring (and that has historically characterized the aesthetics of realism) is here challenged by Gordimer's text itself, which thereby ceases to produce meaning from within the aesthetic hegemony of liberal realism, but which instead opposes that hegemony from some other and genuinely radical position—from under the ground.[15]

The underground challenge is effected by the image of the black corpse, who motivates a narrative politics within *The Conservationist*. Following suggestions by Genette and Benjamin, I have elsewhere described this politics as a politics based on the strategy of "hypertextual" quotation.[16] Expanding upon the concept of "intertextuality," Genette elaborates a taxonomy of "transtextual" relationships, one of which he labels "hypertextuality." Hypertextuality is the fundamentally *critical* relation of a "hypertext" to its anterior "hypotext." As hypertext, *The Conservationist* modifies, elaborates, or extends its hypotext, Callaway's *Religious System of the Amazulu*.[17]

For his part, Benjamin locates the "basis of quotation" in the strategy of interruption, and notes that his own critical writings are permeated with such interruptions, adding that "Quotations in my works are like robbers by the roadside who make an armed attack and relieve the idler of his convictions" (38).[18] Benjamin, that is, draws attention to the paradoxical sense in which quotation preserves the past, but only through the destructive operation of tearing the past out of its own context and submitting it to another, a present reading of the past: quotation "contains the hope that something from this period will survive—for no other reason than that it was torn out of it" (39). Gordimer's use of quotation from the "non-fictional" Callaway source complexly duplicates the operation alluded to by Benjamin, and is far more compelling in the effects it achieves than is *Hiroshima's* related interplay between nonfictional documentary and fictional romance.

In the first instance, Callaway's transcriptions from Zulu informants itself represents a destructive preservation of ancient Zulu religious myths. The preservation is imperfect and destructive for the simple reason that the transliterated Zulu myths are recorded under the aegis of colonizing Christian myths. Secondly, Gordimer then draws on this already corrupted but nevertheless "documentary" source of transliterated quotation, and selectively presents extracts

from it to serve a hypertextual function in her own developing narrative mythology of preservation and destruction. In their hypertextual capacity, the extracts
from Callaway in *The Conservationist* thus repeat and critically modify the process of preserving and alienating simultaneously. These extracts cumulatively
"preserve" a system of belief which runs roughly parallel to the narrative depiction of the life of the black community on the farm. In this sense the quotations
emphasize for the reader an alternative to Mehring's "conservationist" practices, practices which the reader comes to know as particular instances of more
general capitalist, sexist, and colonialist patterns of exploitation (Mehring is a
businessman and not a farmer; he thinks of the farm as an opportunity to
manipulate income tax obligations and as "a good place to bring a woman"
over weekends).

The amalgam of fictional narrative and quotation from Callaway in *The
Conservationist* not only critically comments on Mehring's "conservation,"
however, but in addition modifies also the Callaway hypotext by implicitly calling the latter's neutral and non-fictional status into question. Furthermore, the
entire montage of fiction, anthropology, and myth ultimately and deliberately
reveals inadequacies as well in black "conservation," insofar as the extracts represent an already debased mythos submissively accommodating itself to a new
political order:

> *So we came out possessed of what sufficed us, we thinking that we possessed
> all things, that we were wise, that there was nothing we did not know. . . . We
> saw that, in fact, we black men came out without a single thing; we came out
> naked; we left everything behind, because we came out first. But as for white
> men . . . we saw that we came out in a hurry; but they waited for all things,
> that they might not leave any behind.* (213)

Or, as a previous quotation notes, "*since the white men came and the mission-
aries, we have heard it said that there is God*" (193).

The image of the corpse in *The Conservationist* is thus the pristine locus
from which a complex and sophisticated political critique of South African consciousness may be developed. Such a critique brings to the surface, in the relationship between interruptive subnarrative and the "principal" narrative, questions of incommensurability, political blindness, and moral responsibility.
Gordimer does not simply replace "white" with "black" mythology; indeed, she
emphasizes the extent to which white consciousness has already permeated that
black mythos, just as the presence of the corpse has infiltrated the consciousness of the protagonist. The corpse contradicts Mehring's initial conviction that
this black body is completely other and unrelated to him, and Gordimer's
description of the dead man emphasizes the interrelationship between both parties: the corpse wears a secondhand pinstripe jacket ("that must once have been
part of some white businessman's suit"), a fake snakeskin belt over "smart tight

pants," outdated "stylish" shoes, and is overweight (15). Washed out of his shallow grave by torrential rains towards the end of the novel, the dead man emblazons Gordimer's narrative project: the corpse is the site of rupture between the living and the dead, between different cultural and political aspirations, between narrative fiction and non-fictional narrative.

Crucially, however, the body's operation in this text no longer follows only a protopolitical paradigm which forces the reader to revise his or her reading of the novel in the light of a developing counter-hegemonics within the text. The image of the body encourages more than revision and comes finally to constitute a political call for action. As a dead man, the body signifies its linkage to the ancestors and to the buried aspirations of black political action, thereby inaugurating a counter-hegemonic attack; as a *corpse* for whom the blacks on the farm will initially not accept responsibility, however, the body as image also implicitly points towards inadequacies in current black resistance. The full political force of the image is revealed only when the corpse is brought to the surface (by the torrential rains, by the narrative strategy of the novel). Only when the corpse *comes back*, is he finally put to rest by the black labourous who had previously disowned him: "They had put him away to rest, at last; he had come back. He took possession of this earth, theirs; one of them" (267). And only at this point does the body finally reveal the full extent to which it functions as a political exhortation uttered by the text itself in the vocabulary of bodily image; for at this point it at last becomes perfectly clear that this image of the body, placed here by fiction, metonymically stands also in the place of another (non-fictional) political body, the African National Congress, whose slogan, "Afrika—Mayibuye," is here realized: "Africa—May it come back."[19]

Images may thus be seen to operate within the larger domain of politicized conflict whereby hegemonic and counter-hegemonic power relations shape the organization of our social lives. Operating at the limits of intelligibility, in plastic as well as in verbal forms, the aesthetic image affords some compelling instances of the interconnections between aesthetic objects and the sociohistorical networks which not only made possible the production of those objects as works of culture, but upon which the aesthetic objects subsequently also offer a more or less direct commentary. In particular, the aesthetic image identified above as a rupturing image, an image whose valence resides in its attempt to imagine the gap between representation and the represented, has at its disposal a quite considerable political force which overruns, in both directions, the gap between aesthetic work and social world. Quite aside from the rupturing image's propensity to foreground the inevitably politicized aspect of images as cultural constructs, the rupture employed by such images may further serve politically or protopolitically to support or to undermine the power relations actually in effect at the time and place in which the work is produced.

Thus, as we have seen, the suturing/rupturing veil in the miniature of Otto

II functions as an inscription in one particular version of totalizing politics, a version opposed to another and equally totalizing theology; its function is ultimately conservative, and it attempts to disguise its connotative project ("royalism is good") by representing it as a denotative fact (Otto is simultaneously man and *christomimetes*). The slippage between denotation and connotation is here at the same time concealed and revealed by the seemingly innocent emblem of the rupturing veil, whose function of achieving harmony in the portraiture of paradox nevertheless reveals the conflict between royalist and papist sentiments it is designed to transcend. Indubitably more interested in actively manipulating the disruptive potential of double articulation, postmodern practice has sought ways to exploit the rupturing image and to foreground the conflicts it makes available. The disjunction created by *Hiroshima*, in the opening image and in the larger series that enfolds this image, protopolitically generates a critique of habituated perception; but the disruptive effects it thereby achieves are ultimately recontained by the recuperative ideology on which the film's intelligibility is based. A documented historical past (Hiroshima, the German occupation of France) is situated in the context of two presents: the present of the narrative as experienced by the characters and the present of the spectacle as viewed by the audience. The latter experience is shaped by the conjunction of the two former times, whose cumulative effect is one of mutual marginalization: documentary suppresses narrative time and is in turn suppressed by and subsumed within the visual narrative of Resnais's film. Rupture here is ultimately reconstructive and even forms a kind of pattern that can be anticipated—all of which further serves to contain the political potential of rupture safely within the "proto-" technics of its delivery.

The corpse in *The Conservationist*, in conjunction with other devices, plays ironically with the semantic alignment between "conservative" and "conservationist" and without question goes politically further in its effects than either of the pictorial images previously discussed. Textual disruption in this work invites the reader to examine closely and critically various instances of superficial conservation undertaken in the different cultural milieux of the novel (white, black, Indian). These instances are ultimately "conserved" in the language of Gordimer's text, a language which itself serves as a disruptive vehicle of political and social vision. Through language, then, the reader is incorporated into the process of determining what it means to read the past in terms of the present and in hopes of the future. Through linguistic rather than pictorial means, the aesthetic image ruptures most strikingly in this text. Turning in upon itself—self-critically—tearing itself open, the text reveals in the locus of a corpse and in various loci of belief—in black and white—a pregnant absence—no pictures—waiting to come back: "Afrika—Mayibuye."

Gordimer's praxis thus comments ironically upon—supports and undermines—the theoretical observations with which this essay began. I have appropriated Gordimer's manipulation of the image into that borderline space of the paraliterary, from which it now suggests that although the image may not be linguistic in nature, and although the literary image may mark that point where imitation ceases, the linguistic image may equally mark the point at which politics begins. It does so, I have argued, by figuring a gap which it fills with political potential: by making of loss a link. The interrelationship between postmodern praxis and theory is every bit as intimate as the ideological complicity we have here observed between icon and politics—and postmodern practice can use this link, typically allows a place for it in its borders, whose activity can then come back to surprise theory: not least by turning reflexivity into political involvement.

Notes

1. The quotation is from W. J. T. Mitchell (2); as will become evident, I am indebted to Mitchell for much of the present discussion. For an earlier distinction between iconology and iconography, see Panofsky.

2. This particular quotation from C. Day Lewis (18) is recent (1947). The tendency to define the verbal image in such terms, however, has a long history. In the first-century discourse attributed to Longinus, the author notes that "at the present day the word [image] is predominantly used in cases where, carried away by enthusiasm and passion, you think you see what you describe, and you place it before the eyes of your hearers" (86). In the same segment of the discourse, Longinus also emphasizes affiliations between image and power. Not only do images "contribute greatly, my young friend, to dignity, elevation, and power as a pleader," but "oratorical imagery . . . actually makes [the hearer] its slave" (86-87).

3. For the Russian formalist program, see especially Victor Shklovsky.

4. See Derrida's "Parergon" and, for an unabridged version, *The Truth in Painting*. For the notion of *débordement* (overflow or overrun), upon which I later rely, see also "Living On: *Border Lines*."

5. I borrow the notion of such a "cognitive increment" from Darko Suvin; see especially 666ff.

6. In Boccaccio's *Decameron*, for instance, the complex outer frame of prologue, epilogue, and plague cornice stresses the distance between world and the "garden of literature," and thereby protects the stories it encloses from charges of moral subversion and blasphemy: the *Decameron* stories are delivered from within the marginal space of conventional courtly tradition, and are explicitly, exclusively, addressed to "ladies in love." However, and in addition to the protective screen it thus sets up, the outer frame also exploits the marginality of literature as a means of attacking contemporary clerical and social abuses. For a more detailed account of framed collections of stories in general, see Robert Clements and Joseph Gibaldi. On the picture frame, see Richard Brettell and Steven Starling; on perspective, see Miriam Schild Bunim, and Ernst Gombrich; on

epilogues and prologues, see Gérard Genette; on fictional footnotes, see Shari Benstock.

7. This and the following quotation from Clement of Alexandria are cited by Mitchell 34n45.

8. A frontispiece may, of course, also serve a framing function to the text it prefaces. More than mere ornament, the frontispiece may serve as an emblem or visual epitome of aspects crucial to the text it introduces. For an account of such emblematic title pages in Renaissance England, see Margery Corbett and R. W. Lightbown. For an account of the significance of frontispiece and preface in early Byzantine Gospel Books, see Robert Nelson. My discussion of "Otto II in Majesty" is much indebted to Ernst Kantorowicz.

9. On the nimbus and on pictorial convention during the Middle Ages, see Emile Mâle ch. 1. For a study of the pictorial centre, see Rudolf Arnheim.

10. Mâle 6-7 and 35-37; the conventional positions occupied by Mark and Luke are inverted in this miniature. Nelson devotes considerable attention to depictions of the apostles in the Byzantine Gospel Book.

11. For a history of the Investiture Struggle, see Gerd Tellenbach.

12. On the relationship between *historia* and theosis, see Stephen Nichols, especially ch. 2.

13. Terry Lovell discusses in some detail the fascinating ideological context of desire and respectability which so shaped the early novel.

14. To cite only two concrete examples of such frame-breaking in postmodern production: Calvino's *If On a Winter's Night a Traveler* "begins in a railway station [where] a locomotive huffs, steam from a piston covers the opening of the chapter, a cloud of smoke hides part of the first paragraph" (10); and Buñuel's *Cet obscur objet du désir* (1977) employs *two* actresses (who do not at all resemble one another) to play the female lead in this film, thereby deliberately disrupting the viewer's habits of vicarious identification and in fact challenging the very notion of consistent representational identity.

15. My reading of *The Conservationist* is thus diametrically opposed to some recent pronouncements of Donald Morton and Mas'ud Zavarzadeh, in which Gordimer's oeuvre is assumed to be self-evidently realistic in presentation, and in which her "discourses of realism" are dismissed as "collaborationist discourses" that "help to forestall a radical reorganization of social arrangements in South Africa" (171). While it is indisputable that Gordimer cannot escape the influence of the South African political hegemony, and that her works are thereby affected by that dominant, this by no means invalidates the genuinely counter-hegemonic critique conducted by *The Conservationist* (an argument I conduct at greater length in "Interrupting the Hegemonic"—see note 16 below). Morton and Zavarzadeh do not specifically refer to *The Conservationist*, do not in fact name any Gordimer text in their blanket dismissal of her work.

16. I pursue the question of narrative rupture at greater length in "Interrupting the

Hegemonic: Textual Critique and Mythological Recuperation from the White Margins of South African Writing." This and the following two paragraphs paraphrase in brief one of the lines of argument from the more detailed study.

17. I am here in fact conflating Genette's third (metatextual) and fifth (hypertextual) types of transtextuality.

18. Qtd. by Hannah Arendt, the editor of Benjamin's *Illuminations*, as is the following quotation. Page numbers refer to Arendt's edition of the *Illuminations*. Since Benjamin, it has become increasingly common to identify the ironic use of quotation as one of the most striking characteristics of the postmodern, especially in architecture. For example, see Paolo Portoghesi.

19. In an interview with Stephen Gray, Gordimer says of this clause, "It's the only beautiful, poetically valid slogan I've ever heard. That I put in, really, for myself, hoping perhaps that somebody would take note of my affirmation" (268).

Works Cited

Arnheim, Rudolf. *The Power of the Center: A Study of Composition in the Visual Arts.* Rev. ed. Berkeley: U of California P, 1983.

Barthes, Roland. *The Responsibility of Forms: Critical Essays on Music, Art, and Representation.* Trans. Richard Howard. New York: Hill and Wang, 1985.

———. *Roland Barthes by Roland Barthes.* Trans. Richard Howard. New York: Hill and Wang, 1977 .

Benjamin, Walter. *Illuminations.* Trans. Harry Zohn. Ed. Hannah Arendt. New York: Schocken, 1969.

Benstock, Shari. "At the Margin of Discourse: Footnotes in the Fictional Text." *PMLA* 98 (1983): 204-25.

Brettell, Richard R. and Steven Starling. *The Art of the Edge: European Frames 1300-1900 .* Chicago: The Art Institute of Chicago, 1986.

Bunim, Miriam Schild. *Space in Medieval Painting and the Forerunners of Perspective.* New York: Columbia UP, 1940.

Callaway, Henry. *The Religious System of the Amazulu.* 1870. Facsimile rpt. Cape Town: Struik, 1970.

Calvino, Italo. *If On a Winter's Night a Traveler.* 1979. Trans. William Weaver. San Diego: Harcourt, 1981.

Clements, Robert J. and Joseph Gibaldi. *Anatomy of the Novella: The European Tale Collection from Boccaccio to Cervantes.* New York: New York UP, 1977.

Corbett, Margery and R. W. Lightbown. *The Comely Frontispiece: The Emblematic Title-page in England 1550-1660.* London: Routledge, 1979.

Da Vinci, Leonardo. "Paragone: Of Poetry and Painting." *Treatise on Painting*. Ed. A. Philip McMahon. Princeton: Princeton UP, 1956.

Day Lewis, C. *The Poetic Image*. New York: Oxford UP, 1947.

Derrida, Jacques. "Living On: *Border Lines*." *Deconstruction and Criticism*. Ed. Geoffrey Hartman. New York: Seabury, 1979.

———. "The Parergon." Trans. Craig Owens. *October* 9 (1979): 3-41.

———. *The Truth in Painting*. Trans. Geoff Bennington and Ian McLeod. Chicago: U of Chicago P, 1987.

Dittmar, Linda. "Fashioning and Re-fashioning: Framing Narratives in the Novel and Film." *Mosaic* 16 (1982): 189-203.

Duras, Marguerite. *Hiroshima mon amour*. Paris: Gallimard, 1960.

Genette, Gérard. *Palimpsestes: la littérature au second degré*. Paris: Seuil, 1982.

Gombrich, Ernst. *Art and Illusion*. Princeton: Princeton UP, 1956.

Gordimer, Nadine. *The Conservationist*. 1974. Harmondsworth, Middlesex: Penguin, 1978.

Gray, Stephen. "An Interview with Nadine Gordimer." *Contemporary Literature* 22 (1981): 263-71.

Heath, Stephen. "On Screen, in Frame: Film and Ideology." *Quarterly Review of Film Studies* 1 (1976): 251-65.

Hutcheon, Linda. *A Poetics of Postmodernism: History, Theory, Fiction*. London: Routledge, 1988.

Jameson, Frederic. "The Politics of Theory: Ideological Positions in the Postmodern Debate." *New German Critique* 33 (1984): 53-65. Rpt. in *The Ideologies of Theory: Essays, 1971-1986*. Vol. 2. Minneapolis: U of Minnesota P, 1988. 2 vols. 2: 103-13.

Kantorowicz, Ernst H. *The King's Two Bodies: A Study in Medieval Political Theology*. Princeton: Princeton UP, 1957.

Kermode, Frank. *Romantic Image*. London: Routledge, 1957.

Krauss, Rosalind. "Poststructuralism and the 'Paraliterary.'" *October* 13 (1980): 36-40.

Longinus. *On the Sublime*. *Critical Theory Since Plato*. Ed. Hazard Adams. New York: Harcourt, 1971: 77-102.

Lovell, Terry. *Consuming Fiction*. London: Verso, 1987.

Macaskill, Brian. "Interrupting the Hegemonic: Textual Critique and Mythological Recuperation from the White Margins of South African Writing." *Novel: A Forum on Fiction* (Winter 1990): 156-81.

Mâle, Emile. *The Gothic Image: Religious Art in France of the Thirteenth Century.* Trans. Dora Nussey. 1913. New York: Harper, 1958.

Mitchell, W. J. T. *Iconology: Image, Text, Ideology.* Chicago: U of Chicago P, 1986.

Monaco, James. *Alain Resnais.* New York: Oxford UP, 1979.

Morton, Donald and Mas'ud Zavarzadeh. "The Cultural Politics of the Fiction Workshop." *Cultural Critique* (Winter 1988-89): 155-73.

Nelson, Cary and Lawrence Grossberg, eds. *Marxism and the Interpretation of Culture.* Chicago: U of Illinois P, 1988.

Nelson, Robert S. *The Iconography of Preface and Miniature in the Byzantine Gospel Book.* New York: New York UP, 1980.

Nichols, Stephen G., Jr. *Romanesque Signs: Early Medieval Narrative and Iconography.* New Haven: Yale UP, 1983.

Panofsky, Erwin. "Iconography and Iconology: An Introduction to the Study of Renaissance Art." *Meaning in the Visual Arts.* Garden City: Doubleday, 1955.

Plato. *Cratylus.* Trans. H. N. Fowler. Cambridge: Harvard UP, 1926.

Portoghesi, Paolo. *Postmodern: The Architecture of the Postindustrial Society.* New York: Rizzoli, 1983.

Ryan, Michael. "The Politics of Film: Discourse, Psychoanalysis, Ideology." Nelson and Grossberg: 477-86.

Shklovsky, Victor. "Art as Technique." *Russian Formalist Criticism: Four Essays.* Eds. Lee T. Lemon and Marion J. Reis. Lincoln: U of Nebraska P, 1965: 3-24.

Suvin, Darko. "Can People Be (Re)Presented in Fiction?: Toward a Theory of Narrative Agents and a Materialist Critique beyond Technocracy or Reductionism." Nelson and Grossberg 663-96.

Tellenbach, Gerd. *Church, State and Christian Society At the Time of the Investiture Contest.* Trans. R. F. Bennett. Oxford: Blackwell, 1959.

Wolfe, Tom. *The Electric Kool-Aid Acid Test.* New York: Farrar, Strauss and Giroux, 1968.

Chapter 12

Feminist Politics and Postmodernist Style

Kristina Straub

Feminist criticism seems to be in a particularly fortuitous position in American culture to act as an agent of social change and, concurrently, to bring the academy into a more vital relation with the American left. Academic feminism has corollary voices in mass culture as the "high" theories of Lacanian psychoanalysis and Derridian deconstruction, for example, do not; academic feminists tend to be conscious of their connections with nonacademic feminist discourse and to incorporate popular feminism into both their classroom discussion and their criticism. The connections between academic feminism and popular feminism are particularly striking in the project of articulating feminine subjectivity. Part of both academic and popular feminisms' work, from the period of seventies consciousness-raising to the present, has been to articulate feminine subject positions that at the very least require some shifting in dominant ideology if they are to be accommodated into American capitalist culture. Feminist re-readings and revisions of popular and "literary" images of femininity are central to giving women place and voice in the representations of ideologies both inside and outside the American academy. Feminist English teachers and activists in the anti-rape movement alike find themselves teaching their students and clients how to re-read the imagery of gender and sexuality and, concurrently, to re-image themselves as women both oppressed and articulated by that imagery.

As a feminist who has worked both inside and outside the academy, I am now speaking from the position of an academic who wants to see the theoretical possibilities of my trade retain their pragmatic connections with nonacademic feminism. With this broad-based project of re-reading and re-imaging in mind as academic feminism's most valuable political connection with life outside the academy, I want to examine a significant drift in feminist theory that might seem to be at odds with the populist potential of feminist criticism—the drift towards postmodern, especially deconstructionist, theory. This drift would often seem to widen the linguistic gap between academic and popular feminism; on the other hand, it offers strategies for re-articulating relations between image and ideology that would, along with feminist-materialist projects, provide a healthy corrective to the essentialism that can limit some radical and cultural feminist projects.

Feminists in the academy are, with good cause, warily circling deconstructive theory rather than rushing to embrace this possibly enabling addition to feminist thought. Barbara Creed, Tania Modleski, Alice Jardine, Domna Stanton, and Mary Poovey, along with Janice Doane and Devon Hodges, have examined the relation between American feminist and postmodernist theories of subjectivity, in both male-written and female-written manifestations, with thoroughness, erudition, and varying degrees of uneasiness about the mutual effect of the juncture. Jardine, on one end of the discussion's spectrum, says that feminists have no choice—or at least no good ones. It would be reactionary and suicidal for feminism to ignore what she calls "modernity," a term she uses to describe the French phenomenon most closely correspondent to what is called postmodernism in the States (*Poetics* 98, 101). Creed agrees that feminism cannot seal itself off against postmodernism, but, with Modleski, sees a loss of feminist political clarity in the encounter. Stanton regretfully and carefully argues that the maternal metaphor of French postmodernist feminisms and anti-feminisms threatens American feminism with a reactionary essentialism.[1] In a far-ranging and forceful essay, Poovey agrees with Stanton on the essentialism implicit in French feminism, but, with Doane and Hodges, argues that deconstruction's attack on the essentialist tendencies implicit in binary thinking may serve feminism's political commitment to social change *if* feminism can, in turn, deconstruct deconstruction: "deconstruction itself must be historicized and subjected to the same kind of scrutiny with which it has dismantled Western metaphysics and women's experience" (15). The very proliferation of academic writing on this juncture suggests that there is no going back—or forward—without a feminist "us" continuing to consider and re-consider what feminism in the American academy is becoming and has become in the context of this juncture. I also think, with Modleski, Creed, and Stanton, that a feminist "we" has reason to be wary of accepting that "becoming" too readily. This essay will proceed, warily, I hope, to consider the problematic juncture between American feminism and postmodernist theory through a reading of *The Poetics of Gender*, the published papers delivered at a conference of the same name at Columbia University's Maison Française (sponsored by Michael Riffaterre and Nancy K. Miller, the latter of whom also edited the anthology). This reading will approach the problematic juncture between postmodernism and feminism in what may seem a frivolous way: as a question of style.

What I mean by "style" here is not so much a question of diction and syntax or what my composition students defensively refer to when I correct grammatical errors in their essays, although these are certainly related ideas. I mean "style" in the sense of "I like your style": as a manner of presentation, a mode of action and self-imaging that may be deployed by a group or individual.

Specifically, I want to examine what American feminists gain or lose by relating themselves to postmodernism *as a style* of critical discourse. What is too often lost sight of in theoretical discussions of the relations between image and ideology is that theory itself is a form of self-imaging, a linguistic construction of subject positions, and that theoretical self-imaging takes on stylistic conventions as readily as the images that form the subject of theory's analysis. I do not use the term "style" lightly, then; as Kaja Silverman says of clothing, style is "a necessary condition of subjectivity . . . in articulating the body, it simultaneously articulates the psyche" (147). Nor do I use it without precedent. This particular way into an examination of the relation between feminism and postmodernism was suggested to me by Jane Gallop's essay located approximately in the middle of *The Poetics of Gender*. Gallop's essay, "Annie Leclerc Writing a Letter, with Vermeer," implicitly formulates feminism's relation to "high" theory in terms of fashion and style, and in doing so it manifests a political awareness of the imagery by which the feminist critic represents herself as she analyzes the representation of other women. Gallop's consciousness of feminist style initiates, for me, a way of articulating a relationship to postmodernism more enabling to feminism than the self-trivializing "Annie Hall" approach detected by Elaine Showalter: the feminist critic dressed up in postmodernist clothes.

Gallop's essay begins with a contemplation of what might be called academic fashion, the imagery, the color and style by which feminism is represented: the book jacket of *Writing and Sexual Difference*, the 1982 republication of *Critical Inquiry's* 1981 feminist issue, edited by Elizabeth Abel. Gallop notes that, like the "Poetics of Gender" colloquium, *Writing and Sexual Difference* is evidence of feminism's recent entrance "on the stage of high literary theory," an entrance facilitated, in part, by another juncture, the juncture of American and French theory, of English and French departments. The re-formulation of Derrida's "Writing and Difference" into "Writing and Sexual Difference," the title's evocation of "sexy" French relation to sexual difference, and the chic, mauve—not naive, feminine pink—color of the book jacket all suggest a "high feminine culture" both in the sense of *haute couture* and in the sense of America's intellectual, theoretical elite (136-39). This commentary on fashion precedes what may *seem* to be an unrelated political caveat: Gallop's reading of the French feminist Annie Leclerc goes on to suggest how political unself-consciousness can slip into feminist discourse, particularly when spoken/written by a middle-class woman about her working-class sister. But the integral connection between fashion and politics, image and ideology is made clear when Gallop notes, at the end of her essay, another cover, the cover of *La venue a l'ecriture*, a mutilated reproduction of Vermeer's "The Letter" that gives us the painting's original image of a middle or upper-class woman writing, while it suppresses the original's figure of a female servant standing behind her mistress. Gallop admonishes us not to "forget the other woman," an implicit warning to us, in our consideration of the juncture between feminism and postmodernist theory, that the "fashionable" packaging which goes along with feminism's entrance into high theory may subvert feminism's political work (154). I would read Gallop's self-imaging in relation to both "high theory" and "the other woman" as a sort of parable for feminist critics who, like myself, are drawn to both deconstruction's heady strategies and our sense of connection with popular feminisms. While Gallop critiques feminist attentiveness (implicitly her own) to theoretical fashion, she also uses the metaphor of fashion to enable the feminist critic (implicitly herself) in relation to high theory. Gallop imagines the relation of feminism to high theory as a very sophisticated and intellectual form of dress-up; a feminine subject in relation to a fashion, a style that gains her entrance into and power within male-dominated academic realms—but that also may cause her to forget her political responsibilities to other women.

It may also, I might add, cause her to be forgotten or, at least, blotted out in her bid for academic legitimacy. In a brilliant essay on "Female Grotesques," Mary Russo points out the dangers as well as the advantages of feminists making a feminized spectacle of themselves on the high theoretical stage. The feminist critic might deploy masquerade, put on theory just as women have traditionally put on femininity—"with a vengeance." Gallop's musings on color, style, and fashion foreground the "put-on" nature of feminism's deployment of postmodernist theory as a means to gain attention and a voice in the academy. This masquerade entails the danger, however, of being misread by those who do not "get" the irony of this particular form of self-representation. Russo points out that feminine masquerade has a long history of misogynistic laughter, a history that works against women's use of masquerade for their own advantage (214-17). Representations of femininity are often close to self-parody in our culture today: witness Madonna, who embodies both a self-referential femininity "with a vengeance" and a feminine image all-too vulnerable to victimization by the male gaze, depending on how she is "read." As a growing body of feminist film criticism tells us, even the *self-conscious* assumption of image is often difficult to read as an empowering "ironic distance" when the masquerader is feminine. There is a long tradition for the recuperation of women's duplicitous self-imagings by patriarchal ideologies of the feminine: the woman who puts on theory like a new dress may merely be classified as yet another Duessa. In short, the feminist critic/masquerader who self-consciously foregrounds her "putting-on" of postmodernist theoretical "style" may find herself taken all too literally as the trivialized floozy of high theory. Gallop's strategy is, therefore, by no means a safe one. But it may help us—feminists—to look at the relationship between feminist politics and deconstructive theory in ways that give us a consciousness of our power, however qualified and delimited that power may be by the misreadings of masculinist criticism.

Gallop's implicit metaphor of dress-up is one formulation of a tension that emerges in the juncture of feminism with postmodernist theory in *The Poetics of Gender*: a tension between postmodernist, high theoretical "chic" and the ideological and material positions of women—a tension, in other words, between the style of critical discourse and feminist political commitment. The metaphor of dress-up articulates this tension as a relation between clothes and body, fashion and subject, image and ideology, a relation that, by "common-sense," traditional priorities, would *seem* to privilege the latter terms. The historically specific ideological and material positions of women are placed in a position of "body" in relation to the theories of "woman" or "feminine subjectivity" that form that "body's" image in the realm of theoretical discussion. Feminist criticism in Gallop's essay, the metaphor follows, takes on both sets of terms, but with an implicit privileging of women over "woman." At the same time, the association of theory with fashion suggests that postmodernist critical discourse is more than just a little something that feminists picked up. As Silverman tells us, fashion is an important determinant not only of what we wear but of who we are: our relations to each other, the way we think of ourselves, even the shapes of our bodies (147). Image makes ideology, as well as the other way around, and high theory remakes feminism as surely as feminism decides to put it on. The metaphor of fashion as an image for feminism's connection with postmodern critical theory does not ultimately privilege one side over the other, nor does it solve the problems that feminists feel when they take on the self-imagings implicit in high theory while trying to keep tabs on their explicitly political agendas.

It does, however, articulate the juncture in a way that seems to have a significant political advantage, an advantage that may help the feminist critic keep her political edge amidst the image makings implicit in postmodernist theory. Fashion is, by definition, particularly resistant to theory's drift towards assuming an "always/already, totalizing" position in the discussion. The formulation of high theory as fashion denies fixity to the premises of postmodernism (including the displaced subject) by suggesting postmodernism's own subjection to historical pressures. This is an important political move for feminists: the de-mystification, among other things, of a twentieth-century (masculine) subjectivity veiled in its own stories of loss, fragmentation, deconstruction. Postmodernist theories of subjectivity look, to me, very much like male hegemony in yet another guise. The postmodernist subject as a fragmented, "lost" construct existing only through repeated displacements onto mask after mask, has a tendency to fill all available interpretive space with its substancelessness, allowing no room for the feminist articulation of feminine subject positions. What Alice Jardine has named "gynesis," the postmodernist writing of Woman into male-dominated language,[2] occurs within a theoretical frame in which the "rules" for what constitutes subjectivity are determined by a mostly male and, pardon me for the name-calling, elitist few. The feminists in *The Poetics of Gender* seem to be struggling to find a relation to postmodernist theory that uses the prestige of high theory and its theoretical disruption of opposition without closing off feminism from populist channels for social change: at the heart of this struggle is the question of subjectivity.

Nancy K. Miller lays out the political stakes in this struggle. In "Arachnologies," Miller replies to Barthes's poetics of the "already read" that "only the subject who is both self-possessed and possesses access to the library of the already read has the luxury of flirting with the escape from identity . . . promised by an aesthetics of the decentered (decapitated, really) body" (274). In other words, the decentered postmodernist subject is itself a particular, historical construct, dependent for its inception on a rather elitist set of conditions and applicable, as a theoretical tool, in some, not all, class-, race-, and gender-determined circumstances. It is, in a sense, an image or pose that is tied to a particular ideological position. Miller points out that the fragmented postmodernist subject is *not* a "always/already" condition defining the limits of our artistic and critical world, as it often seems to in male postmodernist texts. While Miller does not explicitly deploy it, her strategy here is parallel to Gallop's label of fashion—a label that de-fixes this decentered subject by placing it in cultural time and space, de-mystifying the imagery by which it is created. The importance of this "de-fixing" in relation to the question of political agency is that it opens up space in the closed, hermeneutic world of postmodernism to articulate under-articulated feminine subjectivities as well as masculine subjects outside the domain of privileged, masculinist high theory.

Many of the feminist essays of *The Poetics of Gender* seem to work their way through a potentially debilitating tension between American feminist political imperatives and postmodernist theories of language and subjectivity by placing an emphasis on historical specificity, the changing material and ideological conditions of women writing and reading. In the essays by Nancy K. Miller and Naomi Schor, most explicitly, historical time intercedes in the tension or "impasse" (Schor's word) between feminism and postmodernism to open up interpretive space between the two opposed terms. Naomi Schor, in "Reading Double: Sand's Difference," acknowledges and uses "the place of history in the play of difference" (269) to open a deconstructionist reading process to the political "real" world of historical specificity.

Miller even more directly interjects the factor of time into the postmodernist formulation of a fragmented or "lost" reading and/or writing subject. Barthes's "deconstructed subject, restless with what he already knows" exists, Miller points out, in a history of readers and writers whose material and ideological conditions are partially determined by gender. Miller positions Barthes's image of the subject in relation to gender ideologies that have shaped the experiences of men and women writers, respectively. Her strategy of "over-reading" women's under-read texts for the specific conditions of "the production of the female artist" is proposed as a "counterweight" to interpretive assumptions such as Barthes's, which do not account for a subject—decentered or otherwise—outside of the ideological conditions of masculinity. It does not ignore the postmodernist, deconstructed subject, but it challenges its authority as the only reading and writing game in town. This challenge to postmodernist theories of subjectivity and language occurs implicitly or explicitly in essays by Nancy J. Vickers, Mary Ann Caws, Ann Rosalind Jones, Sandra M. Gilbert and Susan Gubar, and Elaine Showalter, suggesting that history may, after all, be the master discourse that slips in while feminism and postmodernism are duking it out for control over the imaging of women's subjectivities; I hasten to correct this suggestion by returning to Gallop's metaphor of fashion.

While this metaphor implicitly opens the constructs of postmodernist theory to time and space, it de-fixes the fixity of the postmodernist subject in another, related way: through ironic distance. This is, as I stated earlier, a risky stance, but it does allow for feminist readings of criticism and theory (like this one), readings that resist a sober acceptance of the postmodernist, deconstructed subject that erases ideologies of gender. Gallop's essay, particularly in its opening pages, playfully considers postmodernist (as well as feminist) theory as something associated with fashion, an irreverence that enables us to see theoretical positions without awe—and without the assumption that theory, as we know it, is and always will be the only way to conceive of subjectivity. The serious tone and political commitment at the end of the essay work against the ironizing of feminism, perhaps in some views (not mine) too little and too late, but Gallop's treatment of high theory gains and keeps an ironic distance on its subject. Kaja Silverman's article, "Fragments of a Fashionable Discourse," cited several times above, delightfully suggests retro-dressing as a way for women to assume the feminine with an enabling irony (150), and I see Gallop as performing a parallel act of ironic dressing-up—putting on theory, in this case, instead of femininity. Susan Rubin Suleiman less playfully, but as effectively, deploys postmodernist reading strategies and assumptions in a feminist reading of Bataille's pornography—as a more effective means to ends not gained for theoretically sophisticated audiences by readings such as Andrea Dworkin's.[3] In their very different ways, Gallop and Suleiman both gain a measure of distance from and control over the postmodernist reading strategies they deploy. The intercession of historical specificity is not the only available strategy for de-fixing postmodernist theories of subjectivity, nor is it a particularly reified one; doubling, irony, the split subject itself are also available for disrupting the shattered but exclusionary sovereignty of the postmodernist Humpty Dumpty.

There seem to me to be dangers in both kinds of feminist intervention in postmodernist theories of subjectivity. Opening interpretation to historical specificity is not, as a conservative tradition in historical scholarships tells us, an automatic alignment with leftist politics. Nor does a feminist co-optation of deconstructionist strategies of reading always result in political clarity. Naomi Schor's splendid article provides an excellent example of a feminist reader deploying postmodernist strategies to displace postmodernist critical hegemony, but it also illustrates the danger of creating a reading that may be all-too recuperable by conservative ideology. Schor begins by describing the tension between a postmodernist reading "beyond difference" and a feminist reading "for difference." She goes on to suggest "reading double," a strategy aligned with "tricksterism," as a way of working through that tension. Schor's strategy offers a way to get past the point at which American feminist and postmodernist theories of language and subjectivity seem to cancel each other out. She also suggests, however, the interpretive danger in "reading double":

> To read beyond difference is inescapably to run the risk of reinforcing the canon and its founding sexual hierarchies and exclusions, while to read for difference is to risk relapsing into essentialism and its inevitable consequence, marginalization. Reading double presents, of course, its own dangers, those inherent in tricksterism: ambiguity and equivocation. But, as I hope to show, it offers a possible way out of the current impasse, by suggesting a way of reconceptualizing the problematics of sexual difference. (250)

The dangers of "ambiguity and equivocation" are also, I would add, implicit in Gallop's fashion metaphor, and these dangers may be clearest to readers at the points in discourse where criticism flirts with—instead of committing to—making a political difference. It is possible, for instance, to read Schor's "My concern here is, however, with textual and not political strategies, if the two can ever be separated" (249) as a marginalization of politics.

The Poetics of Gender opens a theoretical system potentially closed to specifically political, feminist articulations of subjectivity. But the very terms of the opposition between postmodernism and feminism, as I have laid them out, can create a claustrophobic theoretical universe, a closed system sealed off against political energy Other to its terms. Alice Jardine's essay "Opaque Texts and Transparent Contexts" suggests most strongly the self-enclosing potential of this theoretical opposition, a potential present but less obvious in essays such as Schor's. Jardine deploys a "double" reading strategy similar to Schor's, bringing together the postmodernist assumption of textual opacity and the American feminist commitment to transparency. While Jardine does not reify one side of her reading process over the other, she does, it might be fair to say, reify both—if I am allowed to use that word in a context that renders it problematic, to say the least. Perhaps it would be more accurate to say that Jardine *fixes* (is fixated by?) both, gives both a totalizing presence in her text. In speaking of modernity, Jardine states that "these discourses in France attempting to take into account the modes of transdisciplinary conceptuality attuned to modernity are the *only* contemporary Western discourses I have discovered thus far that seem able to account for the new texts and contexts of the world as it appears to us, or to imagine other worlds whether they are possible or not" (101; my emphasis). On the other hand, Jardine stresses her belief in the "ethicity" of American feminism. Jardine takes the stance of a "MORAL POSITION #3" in which she rightly refuses an easy resolution. The difficulty of her self-divided position is expressed in charged terms that indicate what Ann Rosiland Jones might call the emotional "pre-text" of the feminist duplicity suavely practiced in this volume: Jardine talks of anger, of good and bad positions with an unsettling and, to me, useful honesty (103-4). Jardine's critical voice, for all its theoretical sophistication and erudition, and its political acumen and commitment, expresses a sense of being caught within a totalizing system that excludes any possibilities for furthering her feminist project outside of the binary terms of the opposition that she herself creates.

Jardine's strategy for dealing with opposition is a sort of shuttling back and forth maneuver: "In France, I'm more 'American' Feminist—whittling away at the accepted currency of feminine metaphors. Here, I try to be more 'French'—and shake up, whenever I can, our so-called 'identities' so intent on procuring an idea named 'equality'" (104). But this strategic mobility occurs within the parameters of the theoretical opposition itself—which seems, in her essay, to define the (French or American) feminist's "only" space. Jardine does admirable work on a juncture in literary theory that may be confrontable only through self-division and the anger and claustrophobia that impasse breeds, and I am not reading her essay as a "bad" way of dealing with this juncture. But for the purposes of political agency, this rehearsing of positions possible within a closed system of binary opposition seems, while honest, debilitating, and not the only place to go.

The conjunction of academic feminism and postmodernist theory is, in the first place, an exclusive relationship between two fairly elitist modes of discourse, and I think that an awareness of this particular limitation reveals the artificiality of Jardine's binary opposition of feminism and postmodernism. Critics such as Jardine, Gallop, Schor, and Miller are, quite rightly, interested in possibilities for political exploration in the somewhat rarified atmosphere of high theory, but Jardine's anger at her dilemma might warn us that such explorations may become more smothering than enabling to feminists. The feminist strategy of masquerade seems one way of ironizing such an artificially exclusive opposition and of opening it to the reality check of other histories of ongoing struggle against patriarchal, capitalist oppression. One of the effects of this masquerade might be, for feminists such as Jardine, more distance on the critical systems that oppress her and more power over what seem to be the all-defining intellectual and moral imperatives of the current academy.

Feminism may, in turn, along with other forms of politically oriented criticism, help recuperate postmodernist theory for the left by interrupting its re-
telling, in decentered, displaced, and fragmented forms, of the same old stories
of capitalist male hegemony. There is much work to be done, however, if
deconstruction is to be put to the use of leftist politics. In a recent article,
"'Refunctioning' Reconsidered: Towards a Left Popular Culture," Laura Kipnis
astutely points out that postmodernist high theory, as it is becoming institutionalized in the academy, constitutes a politically closed system, hermetically
sealed against popular culture (except as grist for its hermeneutic mill) (28).
Feminist criticism may provide much of the subversive energy needed to work
against the erection of postmodernism as yet another phallic monument to the
academy's chronic isolation from and stupidity about popular culture. But the
subversive energy of feminism derives in part from feminists' ability to remain
open to leftist political strategies, such as Kipnis's populism, as well as to the
lure of fashionable French theory.

   Feeling a bit stifled, and borrowing Gallop's strategy, I turn to the cover of
The Poetics of Gender. It is pink, not a fashionable (or French) mauve. The
cover photograph, by Ronald Hammega, is entitled "Man or Woman" and
depicts a discreetly decorated, dark high-heeled pump, shined to a muted gloss,
kicking its toe against (or being kicked by?) a well-kept, large work boot. The
book's cover, like its contents, provokes a desire to investigate the process of
image-making implicit in theory itself. What images is feminism assuming in
its academic manifestations, and how do those images position feminism in
relation to an academic theoretical elite, on one hand, and popular feminism, on
the other? Pink seems a rather popular color for feminist books: as I write I can
see on my shelves Miller's *The Heroine's Text* and Lillian Faderman's *Surpass-
ing the Love of Men*, both covered in a pink approximately like the pink of *The
Poetics of Gender*, all several shades lighter than the mauve of *Writing and Sexual Difference*. Are publishers consciously or unconsciously trying to render the
appearance of these texts innocent? Perhaps pink signifies a feminine naivete,
a womanly innocence untouched by feminism or any kind of theory. In this
sense, the color would seem to be a red herring. Pink is also associated with the
collars of women who, by conventional division of labor in our capitalist society, work at the "feminine" equivalent of labor done by the wearer of the man's
work boot. The book's cover may, perhaps, be read in this sense as the unconscious of the book's contents: a reminder of subjectivities defined by their labor,
their class and economic positions as well as by gender and the postmodernist,
fragmented, and confusing world of "lost" subjectivity. The cover may remind
us of the political "realities" of class and race as well as gender—factors that
may provide, as they do in Gallop's essay, a healthy disruption of the tête-à-tête
between feminist and postmodernist theory.

   The opposition between the polished high heel (academic feminism?) and the male work boot also seems, like the color of the jacket, significantly—and refreshingly—out of line with the opposition between the book's covers. (Dale Bauer, my former colleague at Miami, has commented to me that feminism in confrontation with an elite, philosophical body of thought might be better represented if the masculine shoe were a Gucci loafer.) The cover suggests that other oppositions (already taking place in British and American theory and criticism) might serve to displace the binary fixity of feminism's relation to postmodernism. Gallop reminds us not to forget other women, and I would add that "other men" deserve a place in our critical and theoretical systems as well. I am not suggesting an uncritical return to the nostalgic constructs of sisterhood and brotherhood; the former can, we have learned, result in the erasure of women not culturally "equal" to their white, heterosexual, middle-class sisters. And feminist attempts to embrace a male-dominated left have too often, to our sorrow, ended in our physical, emotional, and intellectual rape.[4] Breaking out of the binary opposition such as that articulated in *The Poetics of Gender* may involve, simply, the recognition of other oppositions, equally painful and equally important.

It may not be sufficient for feminist critics in America to wear their postmodernist clothes with a certain, ironic élan, but *The Poetics of Gender* suggests, however incompletely, that feminists need not throw out their wardrobes to keep feminism politically effective. The awareness of other contexts for critical analysis—historical specificity, awareness of racial differences, differences in class, in economic power—and the translation of that awareness into the critical work of understanding and de-mystifying the construction of gender may enable feminists in the academy to have their political "ethicity," to co-opt Jardine's term, without rejecting the empowerment and strategical capacity of postmodernist theory. Learning from the "impasse" in which Jardine and others whose work is published in *The Poetics of Gender* find themselves, I would suggest that those of us who work in the juncture of feminism and deconstructive theory take a good look at the figures we cut in our postmodern, theoretical fashions. Have we bought into a style that might limit us as much as, though in different ways than, the essentialist methodology we traded in? What can we do to resist those limits while still making use of the evidently valuable strategies of deconstruction?

As a small contribution to the work that is going on in American feminism to find answers to this question, I would propose that one real advantage to reading theory as image-making, as fashion and style, a part of the process by which ideologies are made and sustained, is that it allows one to question the definitions and boundaries of many of the institutional and ideological constructions with which we live and work. The deconstructive questioning of essentialist categories and binary oppositions can itself become a trap for the feminist political project if that questioning is not carried to the disciplinary and institutional boundaries that define "postmodernist theory"—or "theory" itself, for that matter. And that questioning is, in fact, going on in the junctures between academic feminism and deconstruction, in the work, for instance, of many of the critics cited in this essay. For the purpose of illustration, it might be useful to single out Janice Doane and Devon Hodges's *Nostalgia and Sexual Difference* for its resistance to the boundaries that separate theory from politics, the academic from the popular. The book itself challenges our ideas of what an academic book should be; while it can certainly be called a collection of deconstructive close readings with a feminist political edge, it does not stake out territories in generic or disciplinary terms. Doane and Hodges analyze the "nostalgic" rhetoric of texts ranging from the novels of John Irving to the theoretical work of Harold Bloom. What is gained from this openness to different kinds of discourses, from a range of cultural contexts, is the ability to deploy deconstructive reading strategies and theoretical assumptions without allowing those assumptions to define the limits of the political project. Unlike Jardine, Doane and Hodges do not confine themselves to the ideological limits of a particular set of "contemporary Western discourses"—a freedom that allows them to challenge modes of image-making that conduce to women's oppression.

The juncture between feminism and deconstruction is, after all, only one of the many junctures between feminism and various other political and theoretical discourses—indeed, between different kinds of feminisms. It is best, perhaps, perceived in the context of feminism's multiplicity, a diversity of feminisms that is both the focus of feminist concerns about solidarity and a kind of strength. Doane and Hodges make another gesture that might be helpful to formulating the relations between different kinds of feminists (including the conflicting feminists, pragmatic strategist and postmodern theorist, within myself, as within many of us). The authors point out that the disturbing nature of feminist diversity may, in fact, carry with it, at this moment in history, a significant political edge—not pluralism, but the strength of the uncontainable: "Anyone, male or female, might be made uneasy by the collection of difference to be found under the heading of 'feminism.' What is feminism and what do women want? Even women who celebrate the heterogeneity of feminism want to embrace particular goals. But for men, the proliferation of different kinds of feminism is still more threatening" (6-7). Feminisms constitute a multiplicitous source of strength, a populist political edge—as well as the object of struggle to define political and theoretical agendas. Allowing any prevailing theory to eclipse either the struggle or the strength would be giving up more than those of us engaged in feminist political endeavors, inside and/or outside the academy, can afford to ignore.[5]

Notes

1. See Barbara Creed, Tania Modleski, Alice Jardine (*Gynesis*, "Opaque Texts"), Domna C. Stanton, and Mary Poovey.

2. For a thorough discussion of this idea, see Jardine, *Gynesis*.

3. Suleiman argues that "a feminist reading of Bataille's and other modern male writers' pornographic fictions must seek to avoid both the blindness of the textual reading which sees nothing but *ecriture*, and the blindness of the ultrathematic reading, which sees nothing but the scene and the characters."

4. For the troubled history of women and leftist, socialist movements, see Rosalind Coward.

5. I want to thank Dale Bauer, Danae Clark, and Andy Lakritz for reading and commenting on various drafts of this essay. David Downing also made many useful suggestions at a later stage of its writing.

Works Cited

Coward, Rosalind. *Patriarchal Precedents: Sexuality and Social Relations*. London: Routledge & Kegan Paul, 1983.

Creed, Barbara. "From Here to Modernity: Feminism and Postmodernism," *Screen* 28 (1987): 47-67.

Doane, Janice and Devon Hodges. *Nostalgia and Sexual Difference: The Resistance to Contemporary Feminism*. New York: Methuen, 1987.

Jardine, Alice. *Gynesis: Configurations of Woman and Modernity*. Ithaca: Cornell UP, 1985.

————. "Opaque Texts and Transparent Contexts: The Political Difference of Julia Kristeva." Miller 96-116.

Kipnis, Laura. "'Refunctioning' Reconsidered: Towards a Left Popular Culture." *High Theory/Low Culture: Analyzing Popular Television and Film*. Ed. Colin MacCabe. New York: St. Martin's P, 1986. 11-36.

Miller, Nancy K. ed. *The Poetics of Gender*. New York: Columbia UP, 1986.

Modleski, Tania. "The Terror of Pleasure: The Contemporary Horror Film and Postmodern Theory." *Studies in Entertainment: Critical Approaches to Mass Culture*. Ed. Tania Modleski. Bloomington: Indiana UP, 1986. 155-66.

Poovey, Mary. "Deconstruction and Feminism." Paper delivered at Miami University of Ohio, 8 April 1987.

Russo, Mary. "Female Grotesques: Carnival and Theory." *Feminist Studies/Critical*

Studies. Ed. Teresa de Lauretis. Bloomington: Indiana UP, 1986. 213-29.

Schor, Naomi. "Reading Double: Sand's Difference." Miller 248-69.

Showalter, Elaine. "Towards a Feminist Poetics." *The New Feminist Criticism: Essays on Women, Literature and Theory.* Ed. Elaine Showalter. New York: Pantheon, 1985. 125-43.

Silverman, Kaja. "Fragments of a Fashionable Discourse." *Studies in Entertainment: Critical Approaches to Mass Culture.* Ed. Tania Modleski. Bloomington: Indiana UP, 1986. 39-154.

Stanton, Domna C. "Difference on Trial: A Critique of the Maternal Metaphor in Cixous, Irigaray, and Kristeva." Miller 157-82.

Suleiman, Susan Rubin. "Pornography and the Avant-Garde: Bataille's *Story of the Eye.*" Miller 117-36.

Chapter 13

Interview with Jean Baudrillard

Dianne Hunter

America is radically obscene, there
everything is on show. This radicalization of the obscene is an extreme
increase in force.

—Jean Baudrillard

Dianne Hunter: To what field do you regard your work as belonging? What form did your intellectual development take?

Jean Baudrillard: I started out writing literature. I was interested particularly in poetry. I didn't start writing theory until I was 36 or 38 years old. Lately there has been a rupture in the style of my writing; I have broken with theory and began writing literature again, as in *Cool Memories* [1987], an account of my trip to America, a notebook of five years of my life, 1980 to 1985. The rhythm and style of that book breaks with my theoretical works.

By training I was a Germanist. I did studies in German philosophy, the history of philosophy, and the history of ideas as a young man; and that philosophical education, above all influenced by my study of Nietzsche, remains as a philosophical drive in my work.

Poetically, I was much impressed by Artaud, Rimbaud, and Bataille.

Psychoanalysis interests me, but not the academic discipline called psychology. I don't think I belong to any particular field. My work is outside of the disciplines or transdisciplinary. When I was appointed to teach at Nanterre, I was appointed as a sociologist, but that was in a very free era. I think my work has a transversality, a cross-disciplinarity. I am a metaphysician and a moralist. I write manifestos.

Hunter: What were the important elements in the intellectual context of your training that influenced your development as a writer?

Baudrillard: Before 1968, I was much influenced by the 1960s Situationalists, who were radical internationalists, anarchists, leftists. I was distantly Marxist, anti-media, and against the advertisement establishment. I was taken with the ideas of Marcuse.

Then, after 1968, after the Algerian war, a theoretical constellation came together for me, so I began writing theory. I wanted to transform radical politics into radical theory. Nineteen sixty-eight was a riverbank marking the end of a development that had lasted more than thirty years.

Hunter: Who are the other writers who have most influenced your work? Do you have any masters?

Baudrillard: Nietzsche, Artaud, Bataille. I read Faulkner when I was in my twenties. I was attracted by his universe, its metaphysics of abstraction, his fabulation, and his way of reading reality. More recently, in my political period, I was influenced by Sartre, Barthes especially, Benjamin, Bataille, and Borges, and of course, Marx and Freud. Among my contemporaries, Derrida and Lyotard are friends, but I don't read them. If I have a master, it is Nietzsche.

Hunter: In the United States, you are often cited as a defender of seduction. How would you explain your concept of seduction?

Baudrillard: My first books criticized the idea of production and Marxist dialectics, which I associate with death. Production is about material, value, the market, and the law; seduction is about play, the rules of the game of appearances. I am interested in a strategy which differs from the materialist emphasis on production. I prefer a strategy that slides to one that confronts.

Another game was sexual liberation. So I wanted to write a critique of the theory of desire and of the sexual liberation movement. I critiqued the imperative of the liberation movement in place of critiquing desire, which would have been too frontal an opposition. Therefore, I passed over to the theme of seduction.

I am interested in the play in the rules which are not transposable to politics or to production. I want to change the rules of what is considered "reality." Part of reality is play and the phenomenology of seduction. I am interested in the metaphysics of seduction, in what appears and disappears, not in the ordinary sense of the word seduction.

Seduction for me is the turning aside of the world, the turning aside of reality, a challenge and a duel with the world, with the law of the world, with the reality principle.

Art participates in seduction, in the power of illusion. This is something different from mass media's fascinations and manipulations. Seduction in mass media is not a seduction in the strong sense of seduction. Advertisements practice a vulgar seduction; and that is a degradation of the term seduction. I prefer to use the concept of seduction in a strong sense—as it relates to the field of dreams. This sense is outside of the idea of seduction of the senses.

My concept of seduction is a critique of production, but not a rational critique. I preferred to pass to the idea of the enchanted moment. I regard seduction as the fatal strategy—playing with death. My notion of seduction is a fatal notion. There is a fatality in it that has to do with predestination of signs and loss of identity.

I saw this as a problematic of symbolic exchange and death.

This caused cuts and ruptures in my theoretical persona, and I thus adopted a different strategy of fatality—aphorisms of a fragmented self. This is the style of *Amerique* [1986], which is marked by a disappearance of theory. In that book, writing itself becomes the fatal strategy. There is a materialization of seduction as a fatal strategy in the writing.

Hunter: Why do you regard America as an obscene desert?

Baudrillard: I love the desert, its emptiness, its total indifference. It is neither nature nor culture. It is obscene in the sense that it does not have a scene. It has no play, no seduction. America is radically obscene, there everything is on show. This radicalization of the obscene is an extreme increase in force. There is nothing hidden. All is visible, illuminated. My description of America is enthusiastic. The desert is a metaphor. My response to it is visceral.

Hunter: How do you see the relation between your valorization of appearances and the critique of the look and of representation offered in recent French philosophy, by Derrida, for example?

Baudrillard: The deconstructive critique of the 1960s and 1970s is a critical field with subtle conclusions. I don't work with that critique. I am interested in what is beyond representation, in the field of the appearances and disappearances of things. I think things are already deconstructed. I have been interested in starting something new, forgetting critiques. Simulation is an extreme of representation; it is beyond appearances. Simulation is not the same as appearances; it belongs to the order of playing. Simulation is a work of mobilization of signs. My interest in simulation has no direct relation with Derrida. Barthes influenced me, especially his ideas on marginality. My work is outside of deconstruction. For me, the fatal is the same sign as appearance and disappearance.

I am interested in the rules of the game of the symbolic. By "symbolic" I do not mean the Lacanian symbolic, but the universe of mental simulation.

Lacan's idea of the sign as a chain of signifiers chains up seduction. For me, the symbolic order is the register of desire, where ideology is fatal. The Lacanian sign is a chain of representations, but I am interested in another kind of sign, which is elliptical, as in poetry, where the sign is fatal. Poetry is a seductive duel. This is anti-semiotic analysis. Semiology was interesting in 1968, but twenty years is enough. It is time to go beyond the study of representation and semiology.

Hunter: How do you introduce the question of sexual difference into your theory of seduction? Does the question of sexual difference have a pertinence for you? What place does a reflection on power have for you here?

Baudrillard: I am interested in the power of seduction. I study the power of fascination and incarnation. I read Foucault before I wrote *De La Séduction* [1979]. Foucault's notion of power interested me. According to his analysis, power is being exerted everywhere. I decided to reverse this and say that power does not exist. My hypothesis is that masculinity does not exist, it is a gigantic story of simulation. My idea is that power is on the side of the feminine and of simulation. Liberation movements stay on the side of an exacerbation of sexual difference. There is difference when there is power. In seduction there is a provocation and a duel. In the game, there is neither equality nor difference: sexual difference is secondary. In the game, there is contamination, a loss of differences. Indeterminacy, a lack of difference, is an unhappy result of sexual liberation. I am interested in seduction apart from ideology. Seduction *plays* with sexual difference. It *plays* with desire. It plays with sexual difference, but it does not believe in it. Seduction does not make desire and sexual difference an issue except to reverse or play with it. Seduction dissolves sexual difference. It creates a scene. The power of desire is what is played with in this scene. It is a game where one plays with the power of desire and the power of desire is in play. This is a rule of the game in the symbolic. We must distinguish between virtual power and positive power. Positive power is mastery of the real world. Seduction is mastery of the symbolic world.

Hunter: What does the idea of symbolic exchange mean for you?

Baudrillard: I have passed beyond that theme. When I was interested in anthropology and production, symbolic exchange had to do with semiotic spiralling. It was connected to my reading of Mauss and the study of primitive societies. Now that idea is too nostalgic for me.

Hunter: In 1968, you were calling for a taking of the floor to speak as part of taking power. Mark Poster has pointed out that your celebration of *la parole* implies a total presence in the subject who speaks.[1] Is the divided subject an issue in your work?

Baudrillard: In 1968, *prendre la parole* was to act against those who controlled power; the word opposed the code that imposed subjectivity. I wanted a radical subjectivity to articulate itself. Now that is all passé. Desire, the subject, and *la parole* are on one side; and on the other, is the object. I am interested in what happens in the world of objects. As far as I am concerned, the subject of the subject is past. I am interested in the object, which is silent, a seductive desert. It is the object and seduction which attract me in place of the subject and desire.[2]

Notes

1. Mark Poster, translator's introduction, *The Mirror of Production*, by Jean Baudrillard, trans. Mark Poster (St. Louis: Telos, 1975) 11.

2. This interview took place on 20 October 1988, in Paris, France; my translation.

Chapter 14

Selections from *De La Séduction*

Jean Baudrillard, Translated by Dianne Hunter

An ineffaceable destiny weighs on seduction. For religion, seduction was the strategy of the devil. Whether in the form of witchcraft or of the amorous woman, seduction is always the seductive lure of evil, or worldliness. It is *the artifice* of the world. The malediction on seduction remains unchanged throughout morality and philosophy, and today, throughout psychoanalysis and the liberation of desire. It may seem paradoxical that the valuations of sex, evil, and perversion have become promotional, so that, even when all that which had been condemned now celebrates its often programmatic resurrection, seduction still, however, remains under a shadow, or has even gone definitively into disrepute. Because the eighteenth century still spoke of it; it was even, with defiance and honor, the deep preoccupation of aristocratic spheres. The bourgeois revolution put an end to this preoccupation; and the others, the later revolutions, put an end to it for good—every revolution seeks, in its beginning, to end the seduction of appearances. The bourgeois era devoted itself to nature and to production, things quite foreign and even expressly fatal to seduction. And since sexuality proceeds as well, as Michel Foucault says, from a production method (of discourse, of the spoken word, and of desire), it is not at all surprising that seduction is more occulted than before. We still hear nature being promoted; whether it was the good nature of the soul in former times, or the good material nature of things, or else again a psychic nature of desire, nature goes on being valued across all metamorphoses of the repressed, across the liberation of all energies, whether they be psychic, social, or material.

Now seduction is never of the order of nature, but always of the order of artifice; never of the order of energy, but of signs and rituals. That is why all the great systems of production and interpretation have not stopped excluding seduction from the conceptual field—fortunately for seduction, because it is from the outside, from the depths of that neglect, that seduction continues to haunt these systems and threaten them with collapse. Seduction is always on watch to destroy every godly order, whether the deity has become one of production or of desire. For all the orthodoxies, seduction continues to be an evil spell and an artifice, a black magic overturning all truths, a conjuration of signs, an exaltation of signs in their malicious uses. Every discourse is threatened with this sudden reversibility, absorption into its own signs without a trace of meaning. This is why all the disciplines, for which the coherence and finality of their discourse is axiomatic, can only exorcise seduction. Here is where seduction and femininity merge, have always merged. All masculinity has always been haunted by this sudden reversibility in the feminine. Seduction and femininity are ineluctable as the reverse of sexual difference, of sense, of power.

Today the exorcism becomes more violent and more systematic. We are entering the era of final solutions, that of the sexual revolution, for example, of the production and the administration of all liminal and subliminal pleasure, the microprocessing of desire, of which the woman producer of herself as woman and as sex is the last avatar. This is the end of seduction.

Or better, the triumph of the *weak* seduction, the diffuse and white feminization and eroticization of all relationships in an enervated social universe.

Or better still, none of that. Because nothing could be any greater than seduction itself, not even the order that destroys it.

The Ecliptic of Sex

Nothing is less certain today than sex, behind the liberation of its discourse. Nothing is less certain today than desire, behind the proliferation of its images.

In the matter of sex also, the proliferation is approaching total loss. That is the secret of this overproduction of sex, of signs of sex, hyperrealism of orgasm, particularly woman's orgasm: the uncertainty principle has extended to sexual rationale as to political rationale and economic rationale.

The stage of the liberation of sex is also that of its indeterminacy. No more lack, no more interdiction, no more limitation: it is the loss of all principle of reference. Economic reason supports itself only by penury; it disappears as it achieves its objective, the abolition of penury. Desire itself lasts also only from lack. When it passes entirely into demand, when it goes into operation without the imaginary, it is everywhere, but in a generalized simulation. The spectre of desire haunts the defunct reality of sex. Sex is everywhere, except in sexuality (Roland Barthes).

The transition toward the feminine in sexual mythology is contemporaneous with the passage from determinability to general indeterminability. The feminine is not substituting itself for the masculine as one sex in place of the other, according to a structural inversion. It is substituting itself as the end of determined representation of sex, as the fluctuation of the law that regulates sexual difference. The assumption of the feminine corresponds to the apogee of orgasm and the catastrophe of the reality principle of sex.

As in former times, femininity is fascinating in this fatal climate of hyperreal sex, but in a manner just the opposite—in irony and in seduction.

Freud was right: there is only one sexuality, one libido—the masculine. Sexuality is that strong structure, discriminant, centered on the phallus, castration, the name of the father, and repression. There is no other. It is no good dreaming of a sexuality that is not phallic, not barred, not marked. It is no good, within this structure, wanting to move the feminine over to the other side of the barrier and to mix up the terms—the structure remains the same: all the feminine is absorbed by the masculine, or the feminine collapses, and there is no longer either feminine or masculine, a zero degree structure. That is very much what is happening simultaneously today: erotic polyvalence, infinite potentiality of desire, libidinal branchings, diffractions, and intensities—all the multiple variants of a liberating alternative coming from the confines of a psychoanalysis freed from Freud, or from the confines of a desire freed from psychoanalysis. Behind the effervescence of the sexual paradigm, this all combines toward the indifferencing of the structure and its potential neutralization.[1]

The trap of the sexual revolution for the feminine is to enclose it in one sole structure where it is condemned either to negative discrimination when the structure is strong or to derisory triumph in a weakened structure.

The feminine, however, is elsewhere, it has always been elsewhere: that is the secret of its strength. Just as it is said that an object lasts because its existence is inadequate to its essence, it must be said that the feminine seduces because it is never where it thinks it is. It is thus not to be found, either, in the history of suffering and oppression imputed to it—this historical cavalry of women (it craftily hides behind it). The feminine assumes this aspect of servitude only in the structure where it is assigned and repressed, and where the sexual revolution assigns and represses it even more dramatically. But what complicitous aberration (complicitous with what, if not precisely the masculine?) wants us to believe that the history of the feminine is martyrdom? The repression is already entirely there, in the story of *the sexual* and political misery of women which excludes all other modes of power and sovereignty.

There is an alternative to sex and to power of which psychoanalysis is unaware because the axiomatic organization of psychoanalysis is sexual; and this alternative is undoubtedly indeed within the realm of the feminine, that is, outside the masculine/feminine opposition. This opposition is essentially masculine, intentionally sexual, and cannot be reversed without actually ceasing to exist.

This strength of the feminine is that of seduction.

The decline of psychoanalysis and of sexuality as strong structures, their reduction to a psychic and molecular universe that is only their ultimate liberation, allows a glimpse of another universe, parallel in the sense that these never meet. This parallel universe no longer interprets itself in terms of intrapsychic or psychological relations, or in terms of repression or the unconscious, but rather in terms of play, of defiance, of dual relationships and strategic appearances: in terms of seduction—no longer in terms of structure and distinctive oppositions, but of seductive reversibility—a universe where the feminine is not what opposes itself to the masculine, but what *seduces* the masculine.

In seduction, the feminine is neither a marked nor an unmarked term. It does not apply, either, to a lost autonomy or desire or pleasure, an autonomy of the body, of the spoken word or of writing. It does not reclaim its truth; it seduces.

Of course the sovereignty of seduction can be said to be feminine by convention, the same convention that wants sexuality to be fundamentally masculine; but the essential is that this conventional form has always existed, conceiving subsidiarily the feminine as nothing, as what never "occurs" and what is never where it occurs (thus certainly not in any "feminist" revindication). This is not from a perspective of psychic or biological *bisexuality*, but of a *transsexuality of seduction* which the whole sexual organization tends to reduce, and which psychoanalysis itself, in accord with the axiom that there is no structure other than the sexual one, is constitutionally incapable of speaking.

In their movement of contestation, what do women oppose to phallocratic structure? An autonomy, a difference, a specificity of desire and of pleasure, an other way of using their bodies, a spoken word, a specific form of writing—*never seduction*. They are ashamed of it as an artificial placing of their bodies on display, as a destiny of bondage and of prostitution. They do not understand that *seduction represents the mastery of the symbolic universe, whereas power represents only the mastery of the real universe.* The sovereignty of seduction is incommeasurable with the holding of political and sexual power.

The complicity of the feminist movement with the order of truth is strange and ferocious. Because seduction is fought against and rejected as an artificial turning away from the truth of woman, that which in the last instance one will find inscribed on her body and in her desire. This rejection effaces in one stroke the immense privilege of the feminine never to have acceded to the truth, to sense, and to have remained absolute master of the realm where appearances reign. The immanent power of seduction is to deprive everything of its truth and to make the feminine come back to the game, the pure play of appearances, and there to elude in a twinkling of an eye all the systems of sense and of power: to set appearances into motion, to play on the body. Since appearances are reversible, on this one level systems are fragile and vulnerable. Sense is vulnerable only to this magic spell. It is incredibly blind to negate this unique power equal and superior to all others when it reverses all by the simple game of the *strategy of appearances.*

Freud said anatomy is destiny.[2] One can wonder that the refusal in the woman's movement of this destiny, phallic by definition, and sealed by anatomy, opens an alternative that remains fundamentally anatomical and biological. Thus Luce Irigaray writes: "Woman's pleasure does not have to choose between clitoral activity and vaginal passivity, for example. The pleasure of the vaginal caress does not have to be substituted for that of the clitoral caress. They each contribute, irreplaceably, to woman's pleasure. Among other caresses. . . . Fondling the breasts, touching the vulva, spreading the lips, stroking the posterior wall of the vagina, brushing against the mouth of the uterus, and so on, to evoke only a few of the most specifically female pleasures."[3] Women's word? But always an anatomical word, always that of the body. The female specificity is in the diffraction of erogenous zones, in a decentered erogeneity, diffuse polyvalence of pleasures and the transfiguration of the whole body by desire: that is the leitmotif which runs everywhere through the sexual and female revolution, but also through all our culture of the body, from the Anagrams of Bellmer to the mechanical branchings of Gilles Deleuze. Always it is a question of the body, if not the anatomical, at least the organic and erogenous. The issue is the functional body, of which, even in this exploded and metamorphic form, orgasm would be the destination and desire, the natural manifestation. It must be one of two things: either the body in all this is only a metaphor (but then what is the sexual revolution talking about, and all our culture, having become that of the body?), or else we have, with this speech of the body, with this speech of woman, entered definitively into an anatomical destiny, into anatomy as destiny. Nothing at all that opposes itself radically to the formulation of Freud.

Nowhere is there a question of seduction, of the work of the body by artifice and not by desire, of the body seduced, of the body to seduce, of the body passionately separated from its truth, from the ethical truth of desire that haunts us—serious, profoundly religious truth which the body incarnates today, and for which seduction is always as baneful and deceitful as it was in yesteryear for religion—nowhere is there a question of the body surrendering to appearances.

But *only seduction radically opposes itself to anatomy as destiny*. Only seduction breaks the distinctive sexualization of the body and the ineluctable phallic economy that results from it.

All movements that believe they subvert systems through their infrastructure are naive. Seduction is more intelligent; it is intelligent as if spontaneously, and with dazzling evidence. It does not have to demonstrate its basis, it is immediately there, in the turning upside down of all the pretended profundity of the real, of all psychology, all anatomy, all truth, all power. Seduction knows, it is seduction's secret, *that there is no anatomy*, there is no psychology, that all signs are reversible. Except for appearances, nothing helps seduction—all powers slip away from it, but it reverses all signs of them. Who can oppose seduction? The only true stakes are there: in the mastery and the strategy of appearances, against the power of being and of the real. No good comes from playing being against being, truth against truth: that is the very trap of a subversion of fundamentals, whereas a *light* manipulation of appearances suffices.

Now woman is only appearance. And it is the feminine as appearance that defeats the profundity of the masculine. Instead of rising up against this "insulting" formula, women would do well to let themselves be seduced by this truth, because here is the secret of their strength which they are in the process of losing by setting up the profundity of the female against the male.

It is not even exactly the feminine as surface that opposes the masculine as depth; it is the feminine as the indistinguishability of surface and depth, as no difference between the authentic and the artificial. What Joan Riviere says in "Womanliness as a Masquerade" is a fundamental proposition locking together seduction and womanliness: Whether femininity be authentic or superficial, it is fundamentally the same thing.[4]

But this proposition that the distinction between authenticity and artifice is without foundation in femininity also strangely defines the space of simulation wherein a distinction between the real and model is no longer possible. In simulation, there is no real femininity other than that of appearances. Like femininity, simulation is insolvable. This strange coincidence returns the feminine to its ambiguity: it is at the same time a radical certification of simulation and the only possibility of passing beyond simulation—precisely into seduction.[5]

Notes

1. In an interview with Catherine Francblin, published in *Flash Art* 130 (October-November 1986): 54-55, Baudrillard argues that indifference toward cultural values is a hallmark of postmodernism, which he sees as a cultural moment registering the loss of meaning and of desire. He says, "In my opinion, we must make of indifference a stake, a strategy: dramatize it."

2. Freud was quoting Napoleon.

3. Luce Irigaray, *This Sex Which Is Not One*. Trans. Catherine Porter with Carolyn Burke (1977; Ithaca: Cornell UP, 1985) 28. I have adopted the Porter-Burke translation.

4. Joan Riviere, "Womanliness as a Masquerade," *International Journal of Psychoanalysis* 10 (1929): 306.

5. This translation is of pages 112-31 of *De La Séduction*. Paris: Galilée, 1979.

Chapter 15

The Perfect Alibi of Images

Michael Walsh

Unfortunately they [the iconoclasts] lost; God never responded to their provocation. The divinity is no fool: he sided with the iconolators, who never really believed in him, venerating only the simulacrum. After so many iconoclastic efforts, we should no doubt surrender to this logic, and no longer question a reality which has preferred (just like the God of old) to disappear behind the perfect alibi of images.

—Jean Baudrillard

I do not set my statements up "against" Baudrillard's, nor would I relegate his comments to the "incorrect" kingdom of "deadness" or "wrongness." . . . Of course I disagree with Baudrillard in his pronouncement that power and the masculine no longer exist, which strikes me merely as a hilarious idea for a 90's screwball comedy. Nothing crawls so profoundly between laughter and tragedy as power's cutely disingenuous attempts at self-effacement.

—Barbara Kruger

Reading Baudrillard, it's hard to avoid the feeling that he is the French theorist our more traditional colleagues warned us against. In *De La Séduction*, he tells us that he always prefers a paradoxical hypothesis to a received one (31), but he has so much difficulty in imagining a hypothesis which is neither paradoxical nor received that he sometimes seems to revel in the most irrational and peremptory tendencies of his intellectual generation. At times, he even seems to impute these tendencies to others as conscious strategies: "The more imperious, despotic and arbitrary Foucault became, the more his authority accrued in the intellectual milieu" (*Memories* 198). When he turns attention on himself, as he does in his recent diaristic books, he becomes capable of an idealism disarming in its very flagrancy ("As a result of talking about certain things, they begin to materialize in one's life: simulation, seduction, reversibility, indifference" [*Memories* 251]) and of an outspoken misogyny ("Certain women we can love neither as we would like nor as they would like. We prefer to rape them and lose them" [*Memories* 243]).

Yet as my title and pair of epigraphs suggest, the work of Baudrillard can also be seen as a new development in the relationship between image and ideology, even if Baudrillard is so devoted to images and so dismissive of ideology that the relationship threatens to become what Lyotard calls a "differend," "a conflict between (at least) two parties that cannot be equitably resolved for lack of a rule of judgement applicable to both arguments" (*Differend* xi). For Baudrillard, unworried by Lyotard's suspicion that "a universal rule of judgement between heterogeneous genres is lacking in general" (xi), the image is everywhere victorious; it has dissuaded, evacuated, dismantled, and replaced reality itself. Thus it becomes the merest of nostalgias to seek behind the image or the appearance for some deeper truth; we no longer have anything *but* images and appearances, which precede and secrete the hyperreal which has taken reality's place. For Baudrillard, as David Downing and Susan Bazargan mention in their introduction to this volume, the mistake of Marx, Freud, and all subsequent theorists of ideology is that they "want to restore the truth beneath the simulacrum" (*Simulations* 48). One might question the metaphysics of depth implicit in this last phrase, since Marxist and Freudian theorists of ideology have for some time denied that they seek beneath and behind things.[1] One might also question the accuracy, even the credibility, of the immediately preceding claim that "it is always the aim of ideological analysis to restore the objective process"; this may quite well describe the most routine or everyday kind of ideological analysis, but is hardly an exhaustive definition. Or one might interpret both assertions as preemptive or counterphobic; just because his work emerges quite directly from the ideological critique of Barthes (as he acknowledges in the interview with Dianne Hunter), and because Barthes had remarked as early as 1971 that "denunciation, demystification (or demythification) has itself become discourse, stock of phrases, catechistic declaration" (166), it is important for

Baudrillard to impress on us that his work ranges far beyond the imaginative compass of the mere critic of ideology.

Yet Barbara Kruger, responding to Baudrillard's 1987 catalog essay on her photographic work, chooses precisely to try to recontain his efforts as ideology; in her view, it is a typical, even predictable, ruse of power to say that it doesn't exist, or that it no longer exists, or that it has become an image which, according to Baudrillard, "bears no relation to any reality whatever" (*Simulations* 11). In other words, simulation dissimulates. It is clear from the words quoted in the epigraph that Kruger's position is not immediate or thoughtless; she has some sympathy for Baudrillard's account of advertising and seeks to criticize him "without retreating into the armed camps of oppositional warfare" (Stephanson 56), a point worth stressing since Baudrillard so completely equates political conviction with mirroring, with oppositional naivete and vulgarity. Yet it is also clear that she finally sees at least some of his ideas as symptoms, as effects of ideology: "I have always read him critically, savoring the rigor and economy of the 'good' parts and then quickly changing channels when 'His Master's Voice' hits th̲ ̲ ̲ ̲." (̲ ̲ ̲ ̲ ̲ ̲ ̲ ̲ ̲ ̲ ̲ ̲ Baudrillard, "ideology" names habits of thou̲ ̲ ̲ ̲ ̲ ̲ ̲ ̲ ̲ ̲ ̲ ̲ ̲ ̲ ̲ ̲ ̲t, Kruger implies that ideology is itself more than̲ ̲ ̲ ̲ ̲ ̲ ̲ ̲ ̲ ̲ ̲ ̲ ̲ ̲ ̲ ̲inate his writing.

̲ ̲ ̲ ̲ ̲ ̲ ̲ ̲ ̲suggested that Baudrillard's imagined reader is the well-mean̲ ̲ ̲ ̲ ̲ ̲ ̲ ̲ ̲nose shibboleths he desecrates with such verve, and have commented on the strange mix of recognition and misrecognition inevitable when the demoralized radicalism of a culture which had mass parties of the left for most of the century is received into cultures which did not. According to Douglas Kellner, readers in France have made of *Cool Memories* a kind of best-seller, and, as of this writing, representatives of Verso Books report that something similar is happening in America with *America*. Intellectuals, for their part, have reacted with a mixture of fascination and skepticism—Jane Gallop is dismayed by the hostility of *De La Séduction* to feminism, while Andrew Ross speaks of Baudrillard's lack of "an attitude toward history" and "active or willful complicity with the given" (215). Christopher Norris, echoing Baudrillard's own imperative to *Forget Foucault*, recommends that we forget Baudrillard, "though not without treating his texts to more in the way of argued critique than [he] sees fit to provide when dealing with his own precursors and rivals on the intellectual scene" (360).

However, it is the encounter between Baudrillard and Barbara Kruger, already explored to some extent by Frederick Garber, which seems most suggestive in the context of this book. I say this first of all because of Baudrillard's stress on the image as such, although it is important to recognize that what he seems most centrally to understand by the term "image" is the spectacular image, the mass-media image of advertising, cinema, and television rather than the literary or art-historical image. Even so, it is in directing attention away from language-based notions of discourse that Baudrillard differs most sharply from other postmodern theorists such as Althusser, Lacan, and Derrida. We should note, though, that Baudrillard is less sharply distinguished from Foucault, who thus becomes his most favored antagonist, and from Lyotard, whose *Discours, Figure* works to complicate the tendency to imagine discourse as language and oppose it to the image.

Yet what most dramatically distinguishes Barbara Kruger's work from that of many of her contemporaries is, of course, its emphasis on bannering images with text. The ironies here are compounded insofar as Baudrillard chose to comment on Kruger while disowning such artists as Peter Halley, Haim Steinbach, and Jeff Koons, who considered themselves "simulators" and had sometimes invoked him by name.[2] They are compounded, too, by Kruger's readiness to agree with Baudrillardian formulations which might seem, at least immediately, to militate against her kind of work. There is finally a darker irony in the fact that this is an encounter between a leading feminist artist and a theorist of seduction whose *Cool Memories* makes a calmly musing thematic of rape: "Terrorism is an intolerant reaction to the hypertolerance of our societies, just as rape may be intolerant of our limitless sexual tolerance". That Baudrillard has somehow missed the feminist point that rape is not essentially sexual becomes very clear when he adds that "the rate (of rape) has increased along with the rate of sexual liberation, which is paradoxical" (118).

Perhaps, then, it will prove instructive to turn to a narrative fragment in which Baudrillard personally encounters a feminist, finds himself caught between fascination and repulsion, and seems to be seduced by an image. This is the story in *Cool Memories* of the student who joins a Nanterre seminar on seduction in order (according to Baudrillard) to denounce the concept as a sexist ideology; while in class, she befriends another student who suffers from physical handicaps which make it difficult for him to move and to speak.[3] Baudrillard is convinced that the handicapped student detests him, and speaks frankly both of the horror the student inspires in him and of his surprise that a person he describes as "chilling the auditorium with his broken interventions" (104) should nonetheless presume to speak of seduction. He is frank too about his contempt for the feminist, calling her "ridiculous" (105) and her beliefs "crappy" (106).

Yet he is also moved to a distinct envy when the feminist begins to minister to the handicapped student, "leaning tenderly towards him to slip a lit cigarette into his mouth" (105). This is so much the case that when he runs into the woman at a party and she begins to flirt with him "unscrupulously" (once again, this is his account), he scorns her approaches and tells us that he would prefer to have been the handicapped student for the duration of "a seminar when she placed a cigarette between his lips" (105).

In its conscious defiance of progressive standards, this is *echt* Baudrillard.

In its fascination with what Barthes called the "punctum," the compelling detail within the image (in this case the cigarette between the lips, which seems to have both erotic and maternal connotations) it is also, I want to suggest, *echt* seduction. Indeed, I will spend the remainder of this discussion looking at ways in which Baudrillardean seduction begins with ideas apparently familiar to readers of theory but characteristically takes those ideas in directions which are always surprising and not always agreeable; as *De La Séduction* points out, the Latin root *se-ducere* means "to lead aside" or "to lead astray" (38).

Baudrillard is not a really systematic thinker, preferring to introduce, dismiss, and reintroduce concepts through a sequence of texts. Sometimes, the result is allusive; when the last page of *Cool Memories* asks "Where to go? Berlin, Vancouver, Samarkand?" (290) we are presumably supposed to recall the discussion in *De La Séduction* of a fable in which a soldier goes to Samarkand to keep his appointment with death. At other times, the result is more revisionist; if Baudrillard has developed a reputation for making announcements of the end of things (the real, the social, the spectacle, history), he reserves the later right to announce the end of saying "the end" (*Forget Foucault* 67-69). However, despite these complicating factors, we can roughly divide the work of Baudrillard into three phases. The first consists of books like *Le Système Des Objets*, *The Mirror of Production*, and *For A Critique of the Political Economy of the Sign*, which criticize consumer society and Marxism while advocating what Douglas Kellner calls a "radical semiurgy." The third and most recent phase consists of the two volumes of travelogue and aphorism, *America* and *Cool Memories*. Between these two lies a second phase which begins in 1976 with *L'Échange Symbolique Et La Mort* and develops the characteristically Baudrillardean themes of seduction and simulation, dissuasion and deterrence, the hyperreal and the social coma. Yet with its debts to Bataille and to Mauss, *L'Échange Symbolique Et La Mort* may be as much transitional as inaugural. In one way, then, *De La Séduction* can be considered the first purely Baudrillardean text, the first book-length elaboration of a concept which he seems to discover and confirm in the writings of others rather than assimilate or borrow from them.

The writings in question are those of Kierkegaard *(Diary of A Seducer)*, Borges ("The Lottery in Babylon"), and (in passing) Laclos, Sade, Baudelaire, and Philip K. Dick. However, it would be quite misleading to suggest that *De La Séduction* is a book of literary criticism; as much as it reads literary texts, it reads snippets of theory, snippets of journalism, current social developments, the fable mentioned above, and (as Dianne Hunter's translations make clear) notions of femininity. *De La Séduction* is sometimes amusing, as in its comparison of sexual and audio fidelity and its claim that sexual liberation has made orgasm a virtual obligation; it is sometimes incisive, as in its account of the historical coincidence of the liberation of women as subjects and their new objectification in a much more widely available pornography. At other times, however, it seems self-parodic: "the real is growing . . . one day the whole universe will be real" (53). Like many Baudrillard texts, *De La Séduction* also asks us to tolerate an inclination to fly in the face of common sense, as in "at bottom, power doesn't exist" (69) and "the feminine has never been dominated; it has always been dominant" (30). This last, however, begins to seem somewhat more plausible when Baudrillard adds that he is not speaking of the feminine as a sex, but as a form "transversal" of all sex, an idea which gives rise to a number of cognate formulations: femininity is an "uncertainty principle" (25); femininity is not "an ensemble of specific qualities . . . but the expression of an erotic indetermination" (43); femininity is not a "surface which opposes itself to the masculine as depth" but something which erodes the distinction between surface and depth (23). As a "fundamental proposition which encloses all seduction within it", Baudrillard also quotes Joan Rivière's 1929 argument that "Whether femininity is authentic or superficial is fundamentally the same thing" (23).

By making of femininity a kind of dangerous supplement and referring approvingly to an essay so often cited by feminists, *De La Séduction* thus begins to seem quite congenial to a semiotic or deconstructive feminism which would stress the symbolic aspect of femininity (see Sue-Ellen Case for an argument along this line), and not so distant from any feminism which sees femininity as a social construction. At the same time, however, Baudrillard might be criticized just *because* he sees femininity as supplementary. Moreover, as Jane Gallop remarks, when it comes to direct consideration of feminism, *De La Séduction* is unremittingly hostile, insisting that feminism is the mirror of patriarchy; according to Baudrillard, to believe that women have been oppressed is to reinforce phallocracy, while Irigaray's account of the sexual pleasures particular to women's bodies shows that feminism cannot evade Freud's dictum that anatomy is destiny. The latter assertion appears to combine a simple non sequitur with a wild generalization, but for Baudrillard the point of overriding importance is that we abandon political postures, which he sees as necessarily oppositional, and instead give ourselves over to seduction.

In *De La Séduction's* discussion of Pasolini's *Salo*, a parallel rhetorical progress may be followed:

> The film illustrates the truth that in a system of male domination, in any system of domination (which becomes by that token masculine), it is femininity which incarnates reversibility, the possibility of play and symbolic implication. *Salo* is a universe completely purged of that minimum of seduction which is at stake not only in sex, but in every relation, including that of death and the exchange of death (this is expressed in *Salo*, as in Sade, by the hegemony of sodomy). This is where it becomes clear that the feminine is not one sex opposed to another, but that which brings back to the sex without ques-

tion, the sex in full effect, the sex which holds a monopoly on sex (the masculine), the phantom of something other, of which sex is only the disenchanted
form: seduction. (37)

Once again, Baudrillard begins with an assimilation of masculinity to domination and femininity to playfulness which might prove attractive to some feminists, but he quickly passes to his horror at the unseductive imaginative universe
of *Salo*. The issue here is complicated by the particular example, since
Pasolini's use of Sade as a metaphor for the final excesses of Italian fascism is
a conscious attempt to make the position of the spectator quite unbearable; any
erotic interest we may feel is implicated with fascism, so that we are not *supposed* to be seduced. What should be clear, however, is the extent to which
Baudrillard equates seduction as such with what he finds seductive, a point
underscored by his Brigitte Bardot fantasies in *Cool Memories*. What follows
reveals the extent to which questions of femininity may be for Baudrillard no
more than an occasion; if femininity haunts masculinity, reminding the latter
that it remains implicated with and defined by what it has repressed and
excluded, this leads not to any further or fuller exploration of the construction
and imagination of sexualities, but to the announcement that sexuality as such
is only the disenchanted form of what really interests Baudrillard: seduction.
After the initial flourishes which prove, at least to Baudrillard's satisfaction, that
femininity is seductive (and suggest that he finds femininity interesting *only*
insofar as it is seductive), the rest of *De La Séduction* does in fact drift away
from direct consideration of questions of gender.

In conclusion, I would like to propose that this recurrent strategy of evac-
uating and reorienting seemingly familiar ideas is *De La Séduction's* own effort
at seduction. Thus if we are lured by what we think is Saussurean in the discussion of the seductive efficacy of the "insignificant signifier" (104), a string of
examples shows us that what really counts is not the arbitrariness of the signifier but its nullity, its status as non-sense. Or if we are intrigued by what we
think is Lacanian in the discussions of the symbolic and the real, we discover
that Baudrillard's symbolic precedes and supposedly annihilates the real, in
marked distinction from Lacan, whose efforts from *Les Psychoses* onwards can
be said to have rehabilitated the Real. Or again, when Baudrillard's citation of
Rivière and insistence on femininity as irony leads him to the claim that "there
is no other real than that secreted by the models of simulation" (23), we may
think (as readers of modernist literature and postmodernist theory) that we are
on at least relatively familiar terrain. Yet it should be clear that Baudrillard is
not (like Barthes) a voice which says that reality is an effect of discourse, nor
(like Derrida) a voice which says that there is nothing outside the text. For Baudrillard, who has recently begun speaking of his work as fiction, there is no
question of a reality which is coded or constructed or mediated or even textu-
ally contained; reality has instead disappeared, has abdicated, has been swal-

lowed up by simulacra, by images. Whether this strategy is banal or fatal, and to what extent it is recontained by ideology, I will leave up to readers to decide.

Notes

1. Among many possible examples, see Stephen Heath: "psychoanalysis is directed against any idea of there being a set of contents of the unconscious, makes of the unconscious a term of subject-division" (72). For a recent restatement, see Slavoj Zizek: "The theoretical intelligence of the form of dreams does not consist in penetrating from the manifest content to its 'hidden kernel' . . . it consists in the answer to the question: why have the latent dream-thoughts assumed such a form, why were they transposed into the form of a dream? It is the same with commodities: the real problem is not to penetrate to the 'hidden kernel' of the commodity . . . but to explain why work assumed the form of the value of a commodity" (11).

2. See Kellner 112-13 and Foster.

3. After finishing a draft of this essay, I discovered that Douglas Kellner also comments at some length on this particularly provocative anecdote. See Kellner, 182-84.

Works Cited

Barthes, Roland. "Change The Object Itself. Mythology Today." *Image-Music-Text*. Ed. and trans. Stephen Heath. New York: Hill and Wang, 1977. 165-69.

Baudrillard, Jean. *America*. New York: Verso, 1989.

―――― . *Cool Memories*. Paris: Galilée, 1987.

―――― . *De La Séduction*. Paris: Galilée, 1979.

―――― . *For a Critique of the Political Economy of the Sign*. St. Louis: Telos Press, 1981.

―――― . *Forget Foucault*. Trans. Nicole Dufresne. New York: Semiotext(e), 1987.

―――― . *L'Échange Symbolique Et La Mort*. Paris: Gallimard, 1976.

―――― . *Le Système Des Objets*. Paris: Denoël, 1968.

―――― . *The Mirror of Production*. Trans. Mark Poster. St. Louis: Telos Press, 1975.

―――― . *Seduction*. Trans. Brian Singer. New York: St. Martin's, 1990.

―――― . *Simulations*. Trans. Paul Foss, Paul Patton, and Philip Beitchman. New York: Semiotext(e), 1983.

―――― . "Untitled." Trans. Joachim Neugroschel. *Barbara Kruger*. New York: Mary Boone Gallery, 1987. N. pag.

Case, Sue-Ellen. "Towards A Butch-Femme Aesthetic." *Discourse* 11.1 (Fall-Winter 1988-89): 55-73.

Foster, Hal. "Signs Taken for Wonders." *Art in America*, (June 1986): 80-91.

Gallop, Jane. "French Theory and the Seduction of Feminism." *Men in Feminism.*" Eds. Alice Jardine and Paul Smith. New York and London: Methuen, 1987. 111-115.

Garber, Frederick. "Re Positioning: The Syntaxes of Barbara Kruger." *University of Hartford Studies in Literature* 21.1 (1989): 3-25.

Heath, Stephen. "Notes on Suture." *Screen* 18.4 (Winter 1977/78): 48-76.

Kellner, Douglas. *Jean Baudrillard. From Marxism to Postmodernism and Beyond.* Stanford: Stanford UP, 1989.

Kruger, Barbara. "Untitled." *Barbara Kruger*. New York: Mary Boone Gallery, 1987. N. pag.

Lacan, Jacques. *Le Séminaire. Livre III. Les Psychoses.* Paris: Seuil, 1981.

Lyotard, Jean-Francois. *Discours, Figure.* Paris: Klinksieck, 1971.

——— . *The Differend. Phrases in Dispute.* Trans. Georges Van Den Abbeele. Minneapolis: U of Minnesota, 1988.

Norris, Christopher. "Lost in the Funhouse: Baudrillard and the Politics of Post-Modernism." *Textual Practice* 3.3 (Winter 1989): 360-87.

Stephanson, Anders. "Barbara Kruger." *Flash Art* 136, October 1987: 55-59.

Rivière, Joan. "Womanliness As A Masquerade." *International Journal of Psycho-Analysis* 10 (1929): 303-13.

Ross, Andrew. "Baudrillard's Bad Attitude." *Seduction and Theory: Readings of Gender, Representation, and Rhetoric.* Ed. Dianne Hunter. Urbana: Illinois UP, 1989. 214-25.

Walsh, Michael. "Postmodernism Has An Intellectual History." *Quarterly Review of Film and Video* 12.1 (1990): 137-51.

——— . "Reading the Real in the Seminar on the Psychoses." *Criticism and Lacan: Essays and Dialogue on Language, Structure, and the Unconscious.* Ed. Patrick Hogan and Lalita Pandit. Athens: Georgia UP, 1990. 64-83.

Zizek, Slavoj. *The Sublime Object of Ideology.* London: Verso, 1989.

Chapter 16

Modern Iconology, Postmodern Iconologies

Timothy Erwin

The appearance of W. J. T. Mitchell's *Iconology* (1986) brings new interest to the study of the *pictura-poesis* relation for literary critics and art historians who advocate a more critically informed approach to their shared subject. Author of the well-received *Blake's Composite Art* (1978), Mitchell comes naturally to the study of the sister arts, yet little in the Blake study prepares readers for the ideological reach of *Iconology*. Apart from the occasional glance at Milton or Wordsworth the book includes no readings of ecphrastic verse or narrative images. Instead of offering the expected reflexive views of poetry and painting, it comments on the possibility of ideological critique in contemporary and traditional readings in the interdisciplinary analogy. In taking up with analytic precision a topic that typically invites the prose of soft focus, *Iconology* is determinedly theoretical (more than most studies that claim the epithet, it can be called metatheoretical). In brief, the method is to compare different approaches to the sister-arts relation in comparative commentary ranging from contemporary figures like E. H. Gombrich and Nelson Goodman back to the classic texts of Edmund Burke and G. E. Lessing in order to argue against the nineteenth-century notion, still widely held among comparatists, that there exists a single essential difference between poetry and painting.

As argumentative first moves go, the premise is little short of breathtaking. To say that the experiential difference between space and time is not at all great when compared to the cultural difference invested in these opposed categories is to argue against a commonplace of intellectual history reified by disciplinary division. Little in contemporary culture or the academy will have prepared readers to accept the argument. One useful way of taking up Mitchell's revisionism is by way of a lexical overview of the title term, a term now asked to perform interdisciplinary double duty. In art history the formidable notion of an iconological practice approaches the half-century mark even as the discipline which gave it voice enjoys its centenary. In literary studies the term is just now broached to define an evaluative approach to a new area of interest. What can we expect *iconology* in both senses to mean to the future of interartistic study? We might

begin with a narrative scene of introduction. Like the ancient histories of Dibu-
tade and Polemon, of Zeuxis and the painted grapes, Panofsky's story of the
greeting is perhaps the ur-narrative of modern visual theory, celebrating not the
beginnings of representation or ancient standards of excellence but the origin of
a totalizing mode of interpretation, the myth of modern iconology.

I

Somewhere in Europe, between the world wars, a man is strolling pensively
down a city street. From the other direction another man steps out of the crowd
and begins to perform a vague gesture. Approaching nearer, the second man
raises his hand toward his hat. Before passing by he gently lifts the brim and in
nearly the same motion returns the hat to its former position. What strikes the
first man most forcibly is that the meaning of the gesture depends upon a host
of contingencies, most of which, like the state of mind of his acquaintance, he
can never know firsthand. He recognizes that the gesture would likely become
invisible for him once it left the path of social significance, and he also senses
that the gesture registers the expression of an attitude or emotion almost as soon
as it registers a physical fact. While the man knows that the gesture is significant he is unsure of its meaning. Does the greeting express simple recognition?
like or dislike? indifference? A student of conventional signs, our observer
associates the greeting with the medieval doffing of helmets as a sign of cour-
tesy. And as he looks into the matter he makes several preliminary distinctions.
     For purposes of setting out an interpretive practice he decides to separate
the motif of the gesture (the actual lifting of the hat) from its traditional conventional meaning or theme (politeness). He calls his first impressions of the gesture primary, factual, and expressional, and distinguishes them from his second
thoughts on the matter, which he terms secondary and conventional. Borrowing
a familiar dichotomy he calls the object of his first impressions the form and the
object of his second thoughts the subject matter of the event. Neither of these,
he decides, should be considered the content of the gesture. Instead he'll understand the intrinsic meaning or content to be the historically constituted composite of all three things taken together—of formal event, of the primary and secondary aspects of the subject matter, and of the symbolic value of the gesture.
     For Panofsky, who tells the story in his famous essay on iconography and
iconology and whom art historians will recognize as its young protagonist
strolling the avenues of Freibourg, it is the last of these which almost alone
brings point to the anecdote. In taking the gesture as a metonymy for the *Kunst-
wollen*, Panofsky wants to view the artwork as the historical expression of the
symbolic human dimensions which lend art its greatest value. Where the
descriptive practice of iconography had analyzed the allegories of the settecento
in terms of emblem literature, noting with Emile Mâle, for example, how the
mysteries of Bernini's *Truth* could be decoded in Ripa, Panofsky's new science

of iconology would take formal interpretation into the more intuitive and ideal-izing sphere of the symbolic form.[1] To understand the basic principles of icono-graphic production and interpretation, Panofsky goes on to explain, "we need a mental faculty comparable to that of a diagnostician—a faculty which I cannot describe better than by the rather discredited term 'synthetic intuition'" (38).

In theory the intuited synthesis of the art historian will open onto both his-tory and politics. Ideally the all-encompassing gaze of iconology will be cor-rected by

> an insight into the manner in which, under varying historical conditions, the general and essential tendencies of the human mind were expressed by spe-cific themes and concepts. This means what may be called a history of cultural symptoms—or "symbols" in Ernst Cassirer's sense—in general. The art his-torian will have to check what he thinks is the intrinsic meaning of a work . . . against . . . the intrinsic meaning of as many other documents . . . historically related to that work . . . as he can master: of documents bearing witness to the political, poetical, religious, philosophical, and social tendencies of the per-sonality, period or country under investigation. Needless to say that, con-versely, the historian of political life . . . should make analogous use of works of art. (39)

In practice the iconology of Panofsky proves political and historical in only the broad-brush sense though, and for a couple of reasons. Generally speaking, the artwork is seen to mediate between the informing cultural epistemology brack-eted by history and some more essential tendency of the human mind, the sym-bolic form. As is often remarked, iconology thus presupposes the neo-Kantian epistemology of Panofsky's Hamburg colleague Cassirer. Panofsky wants to lead us to a truth writ large by both the objective hand of the event and by the subjective impulse to grasp it whole, and so raises early the methodological problem of distinguishing between the subjective and objective elements of the inquiry. In Michael Podro's astute account of the essay, the problem of the mind-world relation locates itself at once within and without the artwork so that the expressive features of the work are made available with other features for the emotional response of the viewer. Yet Podro also points out that for two related reasons the mind-world problem rests unresolved: for one thing, every aspect of the artwork is implausibly expected to reveal the same a priori regu-lative idea, and for another the regulative idea rejects in advance the social facts of history.[2]

As a result, modern iconology will tend to confuse the inevitable bias of the inquirer with the subjective dimension of the object of inquiry, using the for-mer as its rationale for rarely exploring the latter. Rather than assume that the two stand in reciprocal relation and that together they might be used to plot an Archimedean point of *engaged* objectivity for the inquirer, iconology keeps its distance from the ideology of cultural history, a distancing evident even at the level of the anecdote. In part because the affect latent in the story Panofsky tells is so unpromising, the narrative only separates further the local meaning of the gesture from the reaches of figurative art. As a result, the movement of the hand toward the head in greeting finally seems alien to the movement of the mind toward representational and cultural truth. Surely the mind wants to know more about the gesture than its summary implication presented in the intellectual shorthand of epistemological cipher. Other questions inevitably suggest themselves. In order to recognize the event as a gesture, the mind would first need to know when the event loses consciousness, as it were, and becomes conventional. Another moment worth knowing would be when the behavioral convention begins to be represented, since that would tell us something about the local relation of behavioral to representational convention. And as the inquiry of Panofsky turns back upon itself, it leaves us to wonder whether the lasting effect of the story of the greeting as modernist narrative is not in fact to discount gesture as a sign of the particular urgency of any historical moment. The iconology of Panofsky, it seems fair to say, is easily inserted into the modernist narrative of a sleek and immediate representation and shares a modernist potential noted by Linda Hutcheon (140), an isolationism that would separate the artwork from the world.

In Panofsky's own writings the subjective dimension of the artwork remains locked within the realm of the formal event, relatively inaccessible to historical synthesis. In "Perspective as Symbolic Form" (130-57), Panofsky contrasts the haptic, aggregate space of ancient axial perspective to the systematic Renaissance world of the central vanishing point. The central perspective of Alberti is for Panofsky largely an artificial construct, one that suppresses the curvilinear vision of the ancients at the expense of a new rectilinear vision. Since painting shares its new vision with other aspects of period epistemology—or since in the words of Michael Ann Holly, on whose excellent analysis of the essay I rely, "everything becomes symptomatic of everything else" (141)[3]—through linear perspective the Renaissance is restructured as a radically different psycho-physiological space. The essay is a uniquely complex contribution to perspective theory and offers a kaleidoscope of shifting cultural relations between a representation and the epoch that shapes it. At the same time, Panofsky excludes the hapless human procedures of trial and error that other writers treating the discovery of linear perspective have described, the struggles of Brunelleschi with mirror and compass in the parallel account of Samuel Edgerton, to take one example, as well as the differentiated aims of the artists themselves, the quattrocento formulation through perspective of the several quite different metaphysical views of time distinguished by Yves Bonnefoy, to take another. In a universe where perspective is a metaphor for reshaping the world according to symbolic form, little place will be found for ordinary men and women, no matter how extraordinarily gifted or temporally attuned.[4]

As powerful as Panofsky's critical program undeniably is, his notion of iconology turns its back on social history in a way that the deeper contextualism of Aby Warburg could never have done. Yet interesting recent work reveals how the social fact may be incorporated into the social gesture. In *Looking into Degas* Eunice Lipton foregrounds the image of the laundress in Degas to show how the sublimated eroticism of the pose reflects social conditions during the 1870s. Among the determining factors she brings to bear on Degas are these: during this decade more workers resided in Paris than ever before; workers imagined for the first time in the popular mind to exhibit not sickliness but robust animal spirits. The laundry industry employed fully a quarter of the metropolitan population, a work force predominantly female. Because of their working-class status and intimate access to the bourgeois household, these working women became associated with a careless sexuality, and their long days and short wages made alcoholism and prostitution real dangers. Perhaps most important in stressing the historical contemporaneity of the image is the fact that laundresses were available subjects for painting mainly because they bent to their tasks in overheated ground-floor shops opening onto the street. In the ephemeral popular imagery of the day the women represented a source of mild titillation, yet when we look at them in retrospect through Lipton's eyes their boredom and fatigue is almost palpable. Degas paints the laundress from a perspective more frontal than that of the ballerina and without the diminuendo of recessional space the dancer enjoys as class privilege, though the two women are otherwise filtered through much the same minor-key palette. Drawn from the substrata of the social discourse, the conditions of the laundress invest her casual portrait with an air so highly charged and ambiguous that until Degas she seems invisible as a social being. It is by stooping to detail in this way, Keith Moxey suggests, that iconology will become as flexible as the other master theories of *Kunstgeschichte*. By way of introducing a groundbreaking recent study of popular late medieval German woodcuts, *Peasants, Warriors, and Wives*, Moxey says that a critic may rely on Panofsky and at the same time study the artwork as an ideological construct or system of cultural semiotics. "If ideology is equated with cultural sign systems," Moxey writes, "and sign systems are regarded as projections of consciousness that are intended to make the world of phenomena intelligible, then it follows that all aspects of social life are ideologically meaningful" (8). So it may be that the legacy of Panofsky is only in its purest state indifferent to ideological analysis, and that the idealizing abstraction which Hans Belting identifies as its major limitation has already found its practical transformation. Iconology failed to construct an adequate synthetic method, according to Belting, because it never came to grips with its historical subject. Only against its will, he writes, would iconology have been able to "lift the restrictions on the classical genres of 'high art' and to broaden the field of questioning to other sorts of images and texts" (19). His diagnosis is also a prognosis, of course. It looks forward to a postmodernism that would maintain the innovative rigor of modernism, though not its austerity, and at the same time allow history its full range of different voices.

II

Where Mitchell broadens the inquiry is in asking us to reimagine the study of iconology from a thoroughly interdisciplinary perspective, a critical stance that would take the narrative force of the story of the greeting into full account. Gesture is the archetypal action for the art historian, of course, comparable to both the trope and the event of the literary critic; academic tradition likens gesture in history painting to the spoken monologue of drama and, less directly, to the suspenseful sequencing of narrative episode. Unlike Panofsky, Mitchell is not concerned to sketch out a working method based in a central trope or narrative moment, and rather than construct a grammar of the written gesture, Mitchell means to point to some problems in the history of pictorial theory and in their possible solution to the inevitability of ideological critique. If we can speak with Jean Starobinski of the fundamental theoretical gesture—of the evaluative, philological, allegorical, and canonizing movements that a pluralistic criticism makes toward the object of study and that an everpresent "polyvalence of meaning" (514) answers—we can trace in *Iconology* a basic gesture of three main movements. We should imagine an ongoing conversation between Urania and Calliope, muses of painting and poetry. For the sake of sorting out various local interests, let's imagine that the colloquy takes place in an ideal superlunary domain where earthly disputes are adjudicated, and that below the conversation is usually monitored by misunderstanding.

Although the muses discourse easily in the way of loving sisters, one in 'natural' images and the other in a 'conventional' language, their dialogue is often taken to be contentious. Throughout the centuries (particularly during the ninth and seventeenth) there are several occasions when the somewhat opposed accents of the sister arts are misconstrued as different aesthetic dialects. In the mid-nineteenth century G. E. Lessing goes so far as to hear in their differing vocabularies of time and space reason enough to suspend the interdisciplinary dialogue altogether. A first theoretical movement on the part of *Iconology* is professional. Mitchell wants to bring the figure and ground of word and image into a more equivalent relation for art historians and literary critics, despite the long romantic wake that threatens still to keep them apart. Mitchell prefers that the discussion remain contestatory enough to be kept alive as conversation but no more quarrelsome than need be, especially since what is at stake is extrinsic to the basic terms of the analogy. Most of all, his study asks students of both disciplines to return to their images and texts with a more thoughtful sense of the various pressures, many of them political, which have determined historical relations among the arts. The aesthetic separation of the temporal from the spatial, he reminds us, is at best an unexamined assumption. What we tend to regard as a solid theoretical distinction was for centuries unheard of and is probably better understood as the result of a series of passing ideological differences. On the whole, the affect of the study tends for the sake of an ongoing dialogue toward the reduction of critical conflict, and the corollary hope is that other, more hidden sorts of conflict may emerge. If our critical quarrels are not those of the muses, then how do they arise?

A second, related movement of *Iconology* is to redefine the terms of the analogy. Mitchell remarks how thoroughly temporal and spatial discourse have come to permeate each other, so that it's nearly impossible to imagine one dimension without thinking in terms of the other. When we speak of a *long time* or an *early arrival* our very language affirms the illusionary character of any basic dimensional difference. Since his first concern is to clarify "the *idea* of imagery" (1), Mitchell grants mental imagery foundational status by turning to the philosophical tradition of the younger Wittgenstein, who occupies a position in Mitchell roughly comparable to that of Cassirer in Panofsky. The Wittgenstein of the *Tractatus* developed a picture theory of meaning where mental imagery plays a large role; in brief, he argued that reality consists of simple objects that can be named, and that their names can then be combined to form elementary propositions. Each proposition is logically independent and positive and depicts what Wittgenstein calls "states of affairs." As A. J. Ayer describes the situation, "These pictures themselves are facts and share a logical and pictorial form with what they represent" (17). Reality, in other words, is made up of the truth or falsity of the sum total of all pictured states of affairs. After the manner of ordinary language philosophy, Mitchell next asks how we think of a concept so central to reality as the image in consciousness. His answer is literally more images: two schematic diagrams of the taxonomic scale of the image as discursive practice, a sliding scale not so much perceptual as professional (10), and of the material object reflected in the mind (16). The preliminary discussion is lexical in the usual way of clearing argumentative space, and also by way of calling into question aspects of the traditional theory of representation. To clarify the difference between the mental image and verbal imagery, Mitchell rehearses the status of the image during the eighteenth century, since it is the discussions of Hobbes and Locke, of Hume and Reid, which even today determine the intellectual and affective contours of the phrase *verbal imagery* in its professional sense. After the verbal image is joined to the visual image in a third diagram where the ideogram "man" joins the trio of *picture*, *pictogram*, and *phonetic sign* (27)—the point is to inscribe within different notational systems a cultural development that maintains the visual dimension of language in the very practice of being human—the argument is off and running.

The larger formal movement of the study is to structure itself as a dual dialectic in which several theoreticians of the *pictura-poesis* debate, each with his own internal *paragone* or contest, are paired off in successive consideration of individual argument and undisclosed interest. In the course of a chapter-by-chapter regress readers are asked to recognize in the preconceptions of current theory unresolved historical debates. The verbal-visual distinctions of Nelson Goodman may look like a semiotic system, for instance, but turn on the notational matter of density, not on the slippery difference of sign and signified. And though he steers clear of them himself, Goodman allows us to ask, and to answer, cultural questions of interartistic value. The unstable mixture of the natural and the conventional in Gombrich's notion of representation, on the other hand, prevents a strong ideological critique. Internal and external oppositions like these chart the history of the division of word and image and at the same time query its logic. The logic of *Iconology* itself, it should be said, is not the negative logic of division. It is not the essentialist Panofsky who is set against the nominalist Goodman, for instance. Instead, Gombrich and Lessing, proponents of a natural visual purity, are engaged by Goodman and Burke, spokespersons for the primacy of the verbal. Although the argument shares with deconstruction a binary opposition, what is revealed by the dual structure of collapsing oppositions is not merely a verbal bias against the visual but the relative unity of word and image within the various historical interests which kept them apart—a deconstruction, if you like, of representational difference itself. A last chapter looks at subjective distortions of the visual model in the greatest modern proponent of ideology, a proponent no less ideological for all that, Marx. Even the best of dialecticians, Mitchell suggests, may have some hidden personal stake in misreading the dialectic of the muses.

III

When the lines of iconological difference are drawn, the more novel aspect of Mitchell's approach, I think, is the concern for the affect of the image, for retrieving the subjective dimension in image-text relations. Where Panofsky inscribes a powerful myth of cultural unity in a banal narrative, Mitchell charges that contemporary ideologies of sexism, insularity, and conservative thought are implicated in the long-standing separation of aesthetic spheres. Panofsky recommends an idealist praxis that is open to other disciplines but not to social history, not at least without some serious tinkering. Mitchell suggests ways in which a partial, pragmatic treatment of the *pictura-poesis* analogy discloses ideology both as the false consciousness of the other and as the inevitable investment of the writing self. More important, he quite persuasively indicts professional literary study for an unfeeling blindness. While the New Critics were able and enabling pioneers in the technique of metaphysical and romantic poetry, their loose talk of *verbal imagery* now seems almost wilfully imprecise. To discuss Donne's famous metaphor of affection leaning like the arm of a compass across distance in the same interpretive terms as the urn we walk

around in Keats's ode, for instance, is to elide the development of pictorial difference in English literature. To name all figurative language *imagery*, as practical criticism does, is to deny poetry a specifically visual interest and to
obscure the politics of the visual metaphor. These politics emerge in the seventeenth-century loss of a local, figurative rhetoric, the eighteenth-century appropriation of the visual dimension to a masculine *enargeia* in language, and the
complete separation of the basic terms of analysis during the nineteenth century.
Hence for Mitchell the importance of defining what *image* actually means:
undefined, the term condemns us to wander aimlessly, beyond sight of the historical interests of a visual rhetoric. In its totalizing ambition *verbal imagery*
blinds us to the fearful iconoclasm of such ostensibly visual poems as Marvell's
"Gallery" or Browning's "Last Duchess." Where art history could benefit well
before the war from Rensselaer Lee's groundbreaking *Ut Pictura Poesis*, it
wasn't until 1958 that Jean Hagstrum sketched out the historical relations of
painting and poetry for literary criticism. Only by the time of Mario Praz's 1970
Mnemosyne was a field of study charted, if one with very diffuse borders still.
And although Mitchell remarks that the seventies and eighties have brought
interesting new perspectives, the pictorial analogy is probably still most often
discussed in impressionistic touchstone fashion. Yet there are signs that interdisciplinary criticism is coming to its senses.

A lasting influence of *Iconology*, I suspect, will be to make it more difficult
to speak in an unexamined way about figures and images, as if theory already
understood all that imagery entails and were somehow beyond the deceptive
workings of culture. When Mitchell encourages us to listen for the distinct feeling each poem brings to its visual imagery, most readers will want to catch the
interested inflection. Another will be to reveal how the English ideology structures within literary history rival canons for the iconoclast and iconophile in
every reader, and here each critic will play the game a little differently, forcing
a change in the rules only gradually. Until the pictorial aspect of English verse is
fully acknowledged it will still be Milton, Collins, Wordsworth, and Wallace
Stevens who form the winning roster, the one that shapes visual tradition. Dryden, Pope, Byron, Marianne Moore, and Auden will form the second team.
Eventually, with his allies the feminist critic and the political critic proper, the
pictorialist critic will help to reshape the canon, and the general reader that forms
the larger part of the critical audience will be moved to recognize another sphere
of interest. It is in this sense that the aims of *Iconology*, so strikingly original,
might also be aligned with the oppositional postmodernism of the *October*
group, with what Hal Foster has called "a postmodernism of resistance" (xii).

My questions are asked on behalf of the smaller audience already engaged
in political and pictorial critique. It is only with the recent work of semiotic critics and of critics of spatial form in literature that one can say that the powers
and limits of the pictorial analogy have been tested by theory.[5] While *Iconology*

takes these recent gains into account and makes its own advances, it also envisions three different kinds of further study: (1) more investigation into the roots of resistance to the interartistic analogy, particularly in mixed media where the arts have already joined forces, as in film and theater; (2) more sociohistorical work aimed at the local context of the *paragone*, quite possibly irrespective of any master theory adduced to explain the relation; and (3) a theoretical probing of the emotional and psychological determinants of ecphrastic fear (156-58). I would end my survey by asking Tom Mitchell whether he would care to say more about any of these approaches, perhaps by pointing to recent examples. Secondly, other theoretical voices either discount the contemporary importance of the analogy or else view the two sorts of practice which a sociohistorical approach might adopt, historical scholarship and a theoretically informed intuition, as embodying antipodal interests. What would you say in response to the postmodern claim of Baudrillard that in the multiplicity of simulacra the opposing ideologies of iconoclast and iconophile amount to the same thing, the disappearance of God?[6] Or to the claim of Derrida that in the *parergone* between Meyer Schapiro and Heidegger on Van Gogh's painting of peasant shoes, the scholarly lacing up of the reference to Van Gogh, on one hand, and putting the truth of the painting to work on the other, are two very different things? What sorts of felt critical investments initially made it important to write a book like *Iconology*? And does iconological practice necessarily lead one down a path wholly divergent from parallel disciplinary routes, or is it more a matter of pointing out ideological pitfalls along the way?

Notes

For inspiring conversation and sustaining friendships I'm grateful to NEH Summer Institutes on Theory and Interpretation in the Visual Arts held at Hobart and William Smith Colleges and the University of Rochester in 1987 and 1989.

1. Panofsky's "Iconography and Iconology: An Introduction to the Study of Renaissance Art" first appeared as the introduction to *Studies in Iconology: Humanistic Themes in the Art of the Renaissance* (1939), and offered a sharp departure from the *Stilfragen* of Alois Reigl and the binary categories of Heinrich Wolfflin.

The sharp distinction Panofsky draws between iconography and iconology would seem to owe something to the iconographic work of Emile Mâle on post-tridentine Europe. When Mâle tells us that the allegories of Versailles represent an aspect of the French mind of the seventeenth century, or that the allegories of the middle ages are more profound than those of Ripa for freezing medieval thought in stone, iconography already takes on iconological proportions. Mâle more than anyone, moreover, made iconography widely available for theoretical analysis. As D. J. Gordon puts it, "it was Mâle who . . . made Ripa inescapable for anyone concerned with the art of the Renaissance" (54). As Michael Ann Holly points out (200 n. 48), Panofsky doesn't use the term *iconology* in the first version of his essay but speaks instead of levels of iconographical analysis. The point is to diminish neither the achievement of Panofsky nor the importance of his break with formalism but simply to note that the emphasis on the symbolic as an inevitably subjective realm turns away from the prior historical and thematic iconography of Mâle.

2. Podro argues that Panofsky actually follows Riegl rather than Cassirer in his understanding of the subjective and objective basis of the mind-world relation (182).

3. Holly's discussion of the perspective essay (130-57) is authoritative. Her admiration for Panofsky stems from a belief that the most promising aspects of the iconological legacy are already well-founded in his work.

4. Ernst Gombrich remarks that Panofsky "never renounced the desire to demonstrate the organic unity of all aspects of a period" (28) and situates him in the Hegelian tradition of Jacob Burckhardt. In noting that "no culture can be mapped out in its entirety" but that at the same time "no element . . . can be understood in isolation" (41), Gombrich demurs from the iconological project, preferring to reduce the cultural symptom to the scale of the aberrant syndrome offering the individual multiple roles rather than a single unique one. (Interestingly, the aberrant syndrome that informs his demurral is the sixties counterculture; his example of a time offering the individual multiple roles is 1968; and these phenomena are often cited as midwives of postmodernism.)

5. Several poststructuralist theories of the sister-arts relation compare the visual image to verbal coloring in the tradition of rhetorical *elocutio*, the semiotic work of Norman Bryson and Wendy Steiner probably being best known. Spatial form is a quasi-visual approach to narrative first developed in response to the simultaneous topography of high modernism. The theory tracks the temporal movement of narrative through representational space and may itself be traced in art theory back to the analogy of *dispositio* to fable. In "Spatial Form in Literature: Towards a General Theory" Mitchell extends the theory beyond modernist boundaries and offers a fourfold definition of narrative space.

6. "It can be seen that the iconoclasts," writes Baudrillard of the seventeenth-century version of the dispute, "who are often accused of denying and despising images, were in fact the ones who accorded them their actual worth" as signs of a divine absence. "But the converse can also be said," he goes on, that it was the iconophiles who through the making of images ritually enacted the death of God (256).

Works Cited

Ayer, A. J. *Wittgenstein*. New York: Random House, 1985.

Baudrillard, Jean. "The Precession of Simulacra." *Art After Modernism: Rethinking Representation*. Ed. Brian Wallis. New York: New Museum of Contemporary Art, 1984. 253-81.

Belting, Hans. *The End of the History of Art*. Chicago: U of Chicago P, 1987.

Bonnefoy, Yves. "Time and the Timeless in the Quattrocento." *Calligram: Essays in the*

New Art History from France. Ed. Norman Bryson. Cambridge: Cambridge UP, 1988. 8-26.

Bryson, Norman. *Vision and Painting: The Logic of the Gaze.* New Haven: Yale UP, 1983.

Derrida, Jacques. *The Truth in Painting.* Chicago: U of Chicago P, 1987.

Edgerton, Samuel Y. *The Renaissance Rediscovery of Linear Perspective.* New York: Basic Books, 1975.

Foster, Hal, ed. *The Anti-Aesthetic: Essays on Postmodern Culture.* Port Townsend, Washington: Bay P, 1983.

Gombrich, E. H. *In Search of Cultural History.* Oxford: Clarendon P, 1969.

Gordon, D. J. "Ripa's Fate." *The Renaissance Imagination: Essays and Lectures by D. J. Gordon.* Ed. Stephen Orgel. Berkeley: U of California P, 1975. 51-74.

Hagstrum, Jean. *The Sister Arts: The Tradition of Literary Pictorialism and English Poetry from Dryden to Gray.* Chicago: U of Chicago P, 1958.

Holly, Michael Ann. *Panofsky and the Foundations of Art History.* Ithaca: Cornell UP, 1984.

Hutcheon, Linda. *A Poetics of Postmodernism: History, Theory, Fiction.* New York: Routledge, 1988.

Lee, Rensselaer W. *Ut Pictura Poesis: The Humanistic Theory of Painting.* 1940, New York: Norton, 1967.

Lipton, Eunice. *Looking Into Degas: Uneasy Images of Woman and Modern Life.* Berkeley: U of California P, 1986.

Mâle, Emile. *L'Art Religieux après le Concile de Trente.* Paris: A. Colin, 1932.

Mitchell, W. J. T. *Iconology: Image, Text, Ideology.* Chicago: U of Chicago P, 1986.

———. "Spatial Form in Literature: Towards a General Theory." *The Language of Images.* Ed. W. J. T. Mitchell. Chicago: U of Chicago P, 1980. 271-99.

Moxey, Keith. *Peasants, Warriors, and Wives: Popular Imagery in the Reformation.* Chicago: U of Chicago P, 1989.

Panofsky, Erwin. *Meaning in the Visual Arts.* 1955, Chicago: U of Chicago P, 1982.

Podro, Michael. *The Critical Historians of Art.* New Haven: Yale UP, 1982.

Praz, Mario. *Mnemosyne: The Parallel Between Literature and the Visual Arts.* Princeton: Princeton UP, 1970.

Starobinski, Jean. "On the Fundamental Gestures of Criticism." *New Literary History* 5 (1974): 491-514.

Steiner, Wendy. *The Colors of Rhetoric: Problems in the Relation between Modern Literature and Painting.* Chicago: U of Chicago P, 1982.

Chapter 17

Iconology and Ideology:
Panofsky, Althusser, and the Scene of Recognition

W. J. T. Mitchell

I

It would be difficult to comply with Tim Erwin's request for a fuller discussion of recent work on the interartistic analogy, mixed media, the *paragone*, and ecphrastic fear without writing a lengthy bibliographical essay, or simply summarizing three years of work since *Iconology* was published. For anyone who is interested in the "payoff" of *Iconology* for practical criticism in the arts, I might just mention two recent pieces: (1) "The Ethics of Form in the Photographic Essay," a discussion of the relation of photography and writing; and (2) "*Ut Pictura Theoria*: The Repression of Language in Abstract Painting," an account of the purification of linguistic elements in Modernist painting.[1]

The invitation to comment on Baudrillard and Derrida is a temptation I must also resist for now, except to say that both writers figure strongly in the cultural situation that provoked a book like *Iconology*. In certain ambitious moments it has occurred to me to think of *Iconology* as modeled on *Of Grammatology*, attempting a historical/philosophical reflection on the general problem of the "image" and "similitude" that would answer to Derrida's critique of the "text" and "difference." Some reviewers have made this comparison, not always to my advantage, and I think it may have an element of truth. But my sense is that *Iconology* is not really a philosopher's book so much as it is a text for writers, artists, and critics. It doesn't offer a powerful new theory of imagery or a new way of writing so much as a series of scholarly and critical reflections aimed at freeing us from some deeply entrenched habits of thinking about imagery, allowing us to see it afresh and perhaps even use it with a more critically alert sensibility. As for Baudrillard, I became aware of his work rather late and felt a kindred spirit in his critique of the simulacrum. His argument for the intertwining of iconoclasm and idolatry struck me immediately as very close to my own work on the Marxist discourse of fetishism and ideology. (Since publishing *Iconology* I should add that the important work of J. J. Goux, especially

Les Iconoclastes, has also come to my attention.) In retrospect, it's hardly surprising to find a book like *Iconology* emerging in a period that seems so immersed in visual and pictorial signs, and yet I didn't write it with any conscious attempt to be "contemporary" or "postmodern." The aim was simply to see how far one could go with the problem of the image and, more specifically, of text-image relationships, to find out why these issues are distinct historical and theoretical problems that might not be simply reducible to something else. I don't feel that I've gotten to the bottom of these problems yet, and so the topic remains of central interest to me.

If I were to differentiate my work from other "postmodern" critics of the image like Baudrillard and (say) writers of the *October* group such as Rosalind Krauss, Hal Foster, Douglas Crimp, and Craig Owens, I would focus on the relative absence of polemic in *Iconology*. I think of Baudrillard as a radical iconoclast, exorcising "The Evil Demon of Images" (to cite the title of one of his essays). I always think of my work as dialectical, built on the possibility of dialogue—even identification—between iconoclast and idolater. This sense of criticism as mediation (understood as the staging of confrontation and crisis) grows out of my work with Blake, and it applies to political positioning ("liberal" and "radical") as well as to professional discourse. I take very seriously the difficulty (and thus the importance) of bringing together the (at least) "two very different things" that can be brought to/sought from images: philosophical reflections (Heideggerean/Derridean) that work through, perhaps interminably, the "truth in painting," and the finite historical explanations provided by scholarship like that of Meyer Schapiro. Derrida notes that "the moment when Schapiro seems to oppose Heidegger most radically is also the moment when his procedure most resembles that of his opposite number" (370).

If *Iconology* provides any model for others, then, it won't be "a path wholly divergent from the traditional scholarly route" (Erwin), but perhaps a new synthesis of theoretical reflection and scholarly inquiry. I'm sure of one thing: "pointing out ideological pitfalls" is not the main agenda, for that would assume that we know "ideology" when we see it, or have the appropriate instruments to point it out. I'm really more interested in the iconological analysis of ideology, the excavation of the archaic figures and image-fragments that constitute the whole discourse we call "ideology."

At the same time, I know that something called "iconology" is not simply delivered to us as an unproblematic method either. It has a long and complex history, particularly in the modern period, and I hope that I can contribute to its reconstruction. The key move, in my view, is to stage an encounter between the two parts of icon/ology—the "icon" and the "logos"—which is why the "sister arts" tradition and the *paragone* of painting and literature strike me as central. If these traditional subjects provide a center, however, Erwin's remarks remind us that the circumference of iconology goes well beyond the comparative study of visual and verbal art and into the basic construction of the human subject as a mixed linguistic and imagistic being. Is this subject primarily constituted by language or imaging? by invisible, spiritual, inward signs, or by visible, tangible, outward gestures? The traditional answer to these very traditional questions has been to privilege the linguistic: man is the speaking animal. The image is the medium of the subhuman, the savage, the "dumb" animal, the child, the woman. These associations are too familiar to belabor. But how, we must ask, does the traditional dominance of word over image enter into the structure of a "science" of images, an iconology? What has iconology been? What purpose might there be in reviving and revising it now? What might it become?

The other key move for a revived iconology is, as I've suggested, a mutually critical encounter with the discourse of ideology. I attempted to stage such an encounter in the final chapter of *Iconology* by working through the constitutive figures (*camera obscura* and fetish) in Marx's account of ideology and commodity. I'd like to extend that discussion here by shifting from what might be called the figurative "apparatus" of ideology (especially its optical, epistemological metaphors) to its *theatrical* figures, what Geoffrey Hartman has called "The Recognition Scene of Criticism" (253-64).

II

Erwin recalls us to the "primal scene" of iconology in Panofsky's influential introduction to *Studies in Iconology:* "When an acquaintance greets me on the street by removing his hat, what I see from a *formal* point of view is nothing but the change of certain details within a configuration forming part of the general pattern of colour, lines and volumes which constitutes my world of vision" (3). Panofsky's subsequent elaboration of this scene as a hierarchy of ever more complex and refined perceptions is familiar to all art historians: the "formal" perception gives way (is "overstepped") to a "sphere of subject matter or meaning," the "factual" identification of the formal pattern as an "*object* (gentleman)"—that is, a thing that has a *name*. This level of "Natural" or "practical experience" Panofsky associates anthropologically with savages (the Australian bushman), and it gives way, in turn, to a secondary level of "conventional subject matter," or meaning. The "realization that the lifting of the hat stands for a greeting belongs in an altogether different realm of interpretation." Finally, the greeting reaches the level of global cultural symbol: "besides constituting a natural event in space and time, besides naturally indicating moods or feelings, besides conveying a conventional greeting, the action of my acquaintance can reveal to an experienced observer all that goes to make up his 'personality,'" a reading that takes this gesture as "symptomatic" of a "philosophy," a "national, social, and educational background."

These four terms—form, motif, image, and symbol—are overlapped to construct a three-dimensional model of interpretation that moves from "pre-

iconographical description" of "primary or natural subject matter," to "iconographical analysis" of "secondary or conventional subject matter," to "iconographical interpretation" of the "intrinsic meaning or content," the (iconological) world of "symbolical values" (14). The movement is from surface to depth,
from sensations to ideas, from immediate particulars to an insight into the way
"essential tendencies of the human mind" were expressed by specific *themes* and
concepts" (15; emphasis Panofsky's).

There are, as Erwin notes, plenty of reasons to accept the naturalness of the
scene of greeting as a starting place for the explanation of painting. The silent,
visual encounter, the gesture of raising the hat, the motif of "gesturality" as
such, may seem simply inevitable as a basic example, since it captures one of
the central features of Western history painting, the language of the human body
as a vehicle for narrative, dramatic, and allegorical signification. We might also
look forward to Michael Fried's accounts of "gesturality" in modernist painting
and sculpture to reinforce a sense of Panofsky's scene as inevitable and natural.
But suppose we resisted these natural inevitabilities, and questioned the scene
itself. What might we notice?

1. The banality and minimal interest of the scene, its empty typicality as
an emblem of something like "bourgeois civility," the mutually *passing* recognition of subjects who take no interest in one another, *say nothing* to one
another, and go on with their business. The example is not important, of course;
it *exemplifies*, stages, even flaunts its insignificance, lack of importance. It does
not deserve harsh, picky scrutiny or judgment. It is not dignified enough to be
the subject of a painting—no great history, epic, or allegory is being enacted. It
is just there to exemplify the *minimal* features of visual communication and representation; it provides a baseline from which to measure more complex, more
important forms of visual representation.

2. The transformation of this simple, social encounter (the men passing in
the street) into the encounter between a subject and an object (the perception
and "reading" of an image, a painting), and finally into the encounter between
two "objects" of representation (the two passing figures—"gentlemen"—staged
for us in Panofsky's own "theoretical scene"). "Transferring the results of this
analysis from every-day life to a work of art" (5) we find the "same three
strata"—forms as objects; objects as images; and images as symbols. Panofsky
on the street greeting an acquaintance becomes a figure for his encounter with
the individual painting; the "scene" of greeting between iconologist and icon
becomes the paradigm for a science of iconology.

3. The construction of a hierarchical structure deployed as a narrative
sequence from simple to complex, trivial to important, natural to conventional,
"practical" to "literary" or "philosophical" knowledge, analytic to synthetic
understanding, primitive, savage confrontation to civilized intersubjective

encounter. Early stages are "automatic" (3), later ones are reflective, delibera-tive. In our inability to recognize the subject of a painting "all of us are Aus-tralian bushmen."

4. The opposition between "iconography" and "iconology" deployed as a reverse narrative, in which the higher level precedes the lower in a hierarchy of control. Thus, "our practical experience had to be controlled by an insight into the manner in which objects and events were expressed by forms" (15); the fact "that we grasp these qualities in the fraction of a second and almost automati-cally, must not induce us to believe that we could ever give a correct pre-icono-graphical description of a work of art without having divined, as it were, its his-torical '*locus*'" (11).

5. The privileging of literary painting in which "Images" of the human body and its gestures are the principal bearers of meaning, and the marginaliz-ing of nonliterary forms ("landscape painting, still-life, and genre") as "excep-tional phenomena, which mark the later, oversophisticated phases of a long development" (8). No mention of abstract art or other forms "in which the whole sphere of secondary or conventional subject matter" (i.e., literary images) is "eliminated." No mention of pictorial traditions that impose severe con-straints (including prohibitions) on the representation of the human form.

6. A homogenizing of these oppositions and hierarchies into an "organic whole"—the "essential tendencies of the human mind" accessible to the "synthetic intuition" of the iconologist.

Simply to list these features is probably sufficient to demarcate the outlines of a critique which would question the homogeneity of the iconological pro-cess. The "control" of lower levels of perception by higher levels immediately suggests the possibility of resistance; modernism becomes intelligible, for instance, precisely as a resistance to Panofsky's iconology and its romantic hermeneutic, its literary/figural basis, and its familiar array of analytic/synthetic oppositions. Panofsky's is an iconology in which the "icon" is thoroughly absorbed by the "logos," understood as a rhetorical, literary, or even (less con-vincingly) a scientific discourse.

But there is more to do here than simply to note the way Panofsky's method reproduces nineteenth-century conventions or undermines its own logic in the play of its figurative language. We need to ask: (1) what stands between this scene, its extrapolation, and the hoped for "science" of iconology; why is this scene inconvenient for that goal, and what other scenes might serve it bet-ter? This question will take us ultimately to Panofsky's essay on perspective; (2) what can we learn from Panofsky's canny choice of the primal scene of greeting? How might this scene be revisited by a postmodern iconology, or (as I should prefer to label it) a *critical* iconology?

One thing a critical iconology would surely note is the resistance of the icon to the logos. Indeed, the cliché of postmodernism is that it is an epoch of the absorption of all language into images and "simulacra," a semiotic hall of mirrors. If traditional iconology repressed the image, postmodern represses language. This is not so much a "history" as a kernel narrative embedded in the very grammar of "iconology" as a fractured concept, a suturing of image and text. One must precede the other, dominate, resist, supplement the other. This otherness or alterity of image and text is not just a matter of analogous structure, as if images just happened to be the Other to texts. It is, as Daniel Tiffany has shown, the very terms in which alterity *as such* is expressed in phenomenological reflection, especially in the relation of speaking Self and seen Other.

Critical iconology, then, is what brings us back to the men greeting one another silently in the street, the constitutive figure or "theoretical scene" of the science of iconology—what I have called the "hypericon." It would be all too easy to subject this scene (as I have partly done) to ideological analysis, to treat it as an allegory of bourgeois civility built, as Panofsky reminds us, upon a "residue of medieval chivalry; armed men used to remove their helmets to make clear their peaceful intentions" (4). Instead, let us subject a different scene—an explicitly ideological one—to an iconological analysis.

III

The scene is Althusser's description of ideology as a process which "hails or interpellates concrete individuals as concrete subjects" (174). Ideology is a *"(mis)recognition* function" exemplified by several of what Althusser calls "theoretical scenes" (174). The first scene:

> To take a highly "concrete" example, we all have friends who, when they knock on our door and we ask, through the door, the question "Who's there?", answer (since "it's obvious") "It's me." And we recognize that "it is him," or "her." We open the door, and "it's true, it really was she who was there." (172)

This scene immediately coupled with another—a move into the street:

> To take another example, when we recognize somebody of our (previous) acquaintance ((re)-connaissance) in the street, we show him that we have recognized him (and have recognized that he has recognized us) by saying to him "Hello, my friend," and shaking his hand (a material ritual practice of ideological recognition in everyday life—in France, at least; elsewhere there are other rituals). (172)

How do we "read" these scenes of greeting in comparison with Panofsky's? First, they are slightly more detailed, more "concrete," as Althusser puts it—in quotation marks. The social encounter, similarly, is slightly more intimate and consequential—a mutual greeting of acquaintances, friends, gendered persons, not a one-way token of civility that could as well pass between anonymous strangers. Althusser's scene is a prelude to a narrative or dramatic encounter, a dialogue of which these are the opening words; it brackets the visual and privileges the blind, oral exchange—the greeting through the closed door, the "Hey, you there!" of an unseen caller in the street—"the most commonplace everyday police (or other) hailing" (174). Panofsky's is a purely visual scene; no words are exchanged, only gestures, and we are led to expect nothing further from the passing acquaintances. Panofsky never tips his hat in return; he withdraws into an anatomy of his own perceptual and interpretive activity, the three dimensional interpretation of an object in visual/hermeneutic space.

These are the constitutive "theoretical scenes" of two sciences, Panofsky's science of images (iconology) and Althusser's science of (false) consciousness (ideology). The symmetry is imperfect, of course. Iconology is the science; ideology is supposed to be the object of a science. Ideology is a theoretical object, not a theory; it is the bad symptom that has to be diagnosed. Iconology is the "diagnostician" (15) according to Panofsky; the (good) "symptoms" are the cultural symbols he interprets with his "synthetic intuition"—those theoretical objects (other men) encountered in the primal scene of visual recognition and greeting.

Let us now stage a recognition scene (as opposed to a mere comparison) between Panofsky's iconology and Althusser's ideology by asking each to recognize and "greet" itself in the other. Iconology recognizes itself as an ideology, that is, as a system of naturalization, a homogenizing discourse that effaces conflict and difference with figures of "organic unity" and "synthetic intuition." Ideology recognizes itself as an iconology, a putative science, not just the object of a science. It makes this discovery most simply by re-cognizing and acknowledging its origins (etymological and historical) as a "science of ideas" in which "ideas" are understood as images—the "science" of Destutt de Tracy and the original "ideologues" of the French Revolution.[2]

The point of this greeting, then, is not simply to make iconology "ideologically aware" or self-critical, but to make the ideological critique iconologically aware. Ideological critique cannot simply enter the discussion of the image, or the text-image difference, as a super-method. It intervenes, and is itself subjected to intervention by its object. That is why I've called this notion of iconology critical and dialectical. It does not rest in a master-code, an ultimate horizon of History, Language, Mind, Nature, Being or any other abstract principle, but asks us to return to the scene of the crime, the scene of greeting between Subjects—between the speaking and the seeing Subject, the ideologist and the iconologist.

What we learn from this greeting is that the *temptation to science*, to a panoptic surveillance and mastery of the other (individual or art object) is the "crime" embedded in these scenes. It is not staged directly for us; the figures merely engage in more or less conventional social greetings. To "see" the crime, we need to remove the figures from the stage and examine the stage itself, the space of vision and recognition, the very ground which allows the figures to appear.

Panofsky presents us with this empty stage in his celebrated essay, "Die Perspective als 'symbolische Form'" (1927). This paper, as Michael Podro has shown, makes a double (and contradictory) argument about Renaissance perspective: first, that "it has no unique authority as a way of organizing the depiction of spatial relations, that it is simply part of one particular culture and has the same status as other modes of spatial depiction developed within other cultures"; second, that it "provides an absolute viewpoint for interpreting other constructions" (Podro 186). Perspective is a figure for what we would call ideology—a historical, cultural formation that masquerades as a universal, natural code. The continuum of "homogeneous infinite space" (187) and the bipolar reduction to a single viewpoint/vanishing point at the "subjective" and "objective" ends of visual/pictorial space provide the structure or space in which Panofsky's three dimensional iconology makes sense. Perspective is thus both a mere symptom, and the diagnostic synthesis which allows interpretation to be scientific.[3]

The equivalent stage in Althusser's notion of ideology is unveiled when he moves to "the formal structure of ideology" which, he informs us, "is always the same" (177). Althusser's example for the universal structure of ideology (which he says could be replaced by any number of others, "ethical, legal, political, aesthetic ideology, etc.") is "Christian religious ideology." Specifically, he invokes the theological greeting or "interpellation of individuals as subjects" by a "Unique and central Other Subject" (178), that is, God. The relation established in this greeting is one of mirroring the subjection or dominance: "God is thus the Subject, and Moses and the innumerable subjects of God's people, the Subject's interlocutor-interpellates: his *mirrors*, his *reflections*. Were not men made *in the image* of God?" (179). The stage on which the ideological greetings of individuals occurs, then, is something like a hall of mirrors:

> We observe that the structure of all ideology, interpellating individuals as subjects in the name of a Unique and Absolute Subject is *speculary*, i.e., a mirror-structure, and *doubly* speculary: this mirror duplication is constitutive of ideology and ensures its functioning. Which means that all ideology is *centred*, that the Absolute Subject occupies the unique place of the Centre, and interpellates around it the infinity of individuals into subjects in a double mirror-connexion such that it *subjects* the subjects to the Subject, while giving them in the Subject in which each subject can contemplate its own image . . . the guarantee that this really concerns them and Him. (180)

It should be noted that this is the moment when Althusser's ideological "scenes" give way to the possibility of a "science," a general account of "the formal structure of all ideology." It is hard to ignore the irony, however, in grounding a scientific theory of ideology in a model drawn from theology. Of course Althusser stands outside this model; he views it from afar, puts it, as Panofsky might say, "in perspective" for us. If we can see that ideology is a hall of mirrors, perhaps we can smash the mirrors and rescue the oppressed subjects from the all-powerful Subject. Or can we? Is this "formal structure of all ideology," like Panofsky's perspective, a peculiar historical formation which will pass when relations of production, reproduction, and the social relations deriving from them are transformed? Or is it (also like Panofsky's perspective) a universal, natural structure which absorbs social forms, all historical epochs in its purview? If Althusser takes the first alternative (the model as specific historical formation) he forsakes his claim to science and universality; the structure of Christian religious ideology might *not* be replicated exactly in "ethical, legal political, aesthetic ideology, etc." The "etc." might include formations quite different from the religious, and religious ideology itself might vary with history and culture. If Althusser takes the second alternative, and insists on the universal, scientific generality of the specular model, he becomes, like Panofsky, an iconologist who has an ideology and doesn't know it.

How can we stage a greeting of Panofsky and Althusser that is anything more than an impasse between science and history, a fatal mirroring of ideology and iconology? What can the French communist philosopher and the German Kantian art historian do for each other besides tip their hats in the street? Can they "hail" each other, as Althusser dramatizes it, from the opposite sides of a closed door, and expect any recognition, any acknowledgment other than the misrecognition of the "everyday police" suspect? Perhaps not, except insofar as we map out the common space they occupy, which is simply the placement of the recognition scene at the center of their reflections. The main importance of *recognition* as the link between ideology and iconology is that it shifts both "sciences" from an epistemological "cognitive" ground (the knowledge of objects by subjects) to an ethical, political, and hermeneutic ground (the knowledge of subjects by subjects, perhaps even Subjects by Subjects). The categories of judgment shift from terms of cognition to terms of re-cognition, from epistemological categories of knowledge to social categories like "acknowledgment." Althusser reminds us that Panofsky's relation to painting begins with a social encounter with an Other, and that iconology is a science for the absorption of that other into a homogeneous, unified "perspective." Panofsky reminds us that Althusser's local instances of ideology, the greeting of subject with subject (s/s), are all staged within a hall of mirrors constructed by the sovereign Subject (S/s), and that the ideological critique is in danger of being nothing more than another iconology. These reminders do not get us out of the problem, but they may help us to recognize it when we see it.

Notes

1. W. J. T. Mitchell. "The Ethics of Form in the Photographic Essay," *AfterImage* January 1989 8-13. "*Ut Pictura Theoria*: The Repression of Language in Abstract Painting," *Critical Inquiry* 15.2 (Winter 1989) 348-371.

2. See my discussion of the French ideologues and the history of ideology in *Iconology.*

3. Joel Snyder urges caution on this point, arguing that Podro "misunderstands an implicit inner/outer distinction made by Panofsky." "The painters," claims Snyder, "believed that perspective provided an 'absolute standpoint.' But the understanding of perspective from the standpoint of a neo-Kantian, twentieth century art historian shows that it does not have a special privileged, natural claim upon us. Panofsky takes the latter to be his contribution to the study of perspective and the inner view to be the prevailing, uninformed position" (correspondence with author). I agree that Panofsky believes in such distinction between the painter's and the iconologist's "perspective," but I think Panofsky's practice, choice of examples, and model of analysis undermine it. It isn't that Panofsky believes that pictorial perspective, literally understood, is a universal, ahistorical norm, but that this model, with all its figural and conceptual furniture (surface-depth, three dimensionality, the "subject/object" paradigm for the relation of beholder and beheld) is embedded in the rhetoric of Kantian epistemology.

Works Cited

Althusser, Louis. "Ideology and Ideological State Apparatuses (Notes Toward an Investigation)." *Lenin and Philosophy*. Trans. Ben Brewster. New York: Monthly Review P, 1971. 127-86.

Derrida, Jacques. *The Truth in Painting*. Trans. Geoff Bennington and Ian McLeod. Chicago: U of Chicago P, 1987.

Hartman, Geoffrey. *Criticism in the Wilderness*. New Haven: Yale UP, 1980.

Mitchell, W. J. T. *Iconology: Image, Text, Ideology*. Chicago: U of Chicago P, 1986.

Panofsky, Erwin. "Die Perspective als 'symbolische Form'" in *Aufsatze*. 1927.

––––––– . *Studies in Iconology. Humanistic Themes in the Art of the Renaissance*. New York: Harper and Row, 1962.

Podro, Michael. *The Critical Historians of Art*. New Haven: Yale UP, 1982.

Tiffany, Daniel. "Cryptesthesia: Visions of the Other," *American Journal of Semiotics*. (Forthcoming.)

Contributors

Gian Balsamo received his Doctorate in Political Science from the University of Turin, Italy, and his M.F.A. in English from the University of Massachusetts at Amherst. Presently he is a Mellon Scholar at Vanderbilt University. His recent publications include "The Peripheral Man—A Hermeneutic Discourse" in *Massachusetts Studies in English*, and "Poetica della citta invisibili," *Astragalo*. His fiction is also published by *Astragalo*.

Jean Baudrillard has taught at the University of Paris X (Nanterre) and at the University of California, San Diego. He is the author of numerous books, among them: *For a Critique of the Political Economy of the Sign* (1972), *The Mirror of Production* (1973), *In the Shadow of the Silent Majorities* (1983), *Simulations* (1983), *Oublier Foucault* (1977), and *De La Séduction* (1979), from which the translation in this issue is taken.

Susan Bazargan teaches English at Eastern Illinois University. She is an associate editor of the journal *Works and Days: Essays in the Socio-Historical Dimensions of Literature and the Arts*. She has published articles on James Joyce, and is currently working on *Joyce and Vico: Narrative and History in Ulysses*.

Margie Burns teaches at the American University, Washington, D.C. She is currently working on two books, one of which concerns images of the South in the American national consciousness—literature, media, advertising, etc. The other is about Shakespeare's romances, set in contexts provided by social history such as women in seventeenth century England.

James M. Buzard is a member of the Society of Fellows at Harvard University and an editor of the journal *Critical Texts*. His major areas of interest include Modern and Victorian British Literature, Marxism, and Cultural Theory and Criticism. He is currently at work on a study of literature and tourism in Europe from 1800 to 1918.

Brian G. Caraher is Associate Professor of English at Indiana University. He is the author of a forthcoming book, *Wordsworth's "Slumber" and the Problematics of Reading*, and the editor of *Intimate Conflict: Contradictions in Literary and Philosophical Discourse*. He has published numerous essays in critical theory and modern literature in such journals as *ELH*, *Philosophy and Rhetoric*, *Pre/Text*, *The Journal of Mind and Behavior*, *The*

Wordsworth Circle, and many others. He is an associate editor of the journal *Works and Days.*

David B. Downing teaches critical theory and cultural studies in the English Department of Indiana University of Pennsylvania. He is the editor of the journal *Works and Days: Essays in the Socio-Historical Dimensions of Literature and the Arts,* and he has co-edited, with James M. Cahalan, *Practicing Theory in Introductory College Literature Courses.* He has published essays in critical theory and American literature in such journals as *Diacritics, American Literature, Pre/Text, Critical Exchange, Literature and Psychology,* and others.

Timothy Erwin teaches sister arts theory and the eighteenth century at the University of Nevada at Las Vegas. A related essay, "Poussin and the Rhetoric of Depiction: A Response to Michael Podro" appears in *Visual Theory: Painting and Interpretation* edited by Norman Bryson, Michael Ann Holly, and Keith Moxey.

Dianne Hunter teaches English at Trinity College, Connecticut. She is coauthor of *Dr. Charcot's Hysteria Shows,* and the editor of *Seduction and Theory: Readings of Gender, Representation, and Rhetoric* (1987), and the author of numerous essays in feminist and psychoanalytic literary theory. She is currently editing *Hysteria Aesthetics and Politics* and *Theater of the Female Body.*

Brian Macaskill is an Assistant Professor of English at John Carroll University where he teaches courses in literary theory and twentieth century narrative. He has published in *Sub-Stance* and *Novel,* and he is presently working on a book-length study of framing in literature.

Michael Messmer is Associate Professor of History at Virginia Commonwealth University, specializing in the intellectual history of modern Europe. He has published articles recently on E. M. Cioran, on modernism and postmodernism, and on the criticism of nuclear culture.

W. J. T. Mitchell teaches English and Design at the University of Chicago where he edits *Critical Inquiry.* He is the author of *Iconology: Image, Text, Ideology,* and he has edited *The Politics of Interpretation, The Languages of Images,* and many other collections. He has published many articles in the areas of iconology and ideology.

Richard Pearce teaches Modern British and American literature in the English Department at Wheaton College. He is the author of *Stages of the Clown: Perspectives on Modern Fiction from Dostoevsky to Beckett* (1971) and *The Novel in Motion: An Approach to Modern Fiction* (1983). He has recently completed *The Politics of Narration: James Joyce, William Faulkner, Virginia Woolf,* forthcoming from Rutgers UP.

Harry Polkinhorn is Associate Dean for Academic Affairs at San Diego State University, Imperial Valley Campus. He has published articles focusing on the interdisciplinary implications of mixed media art forms in *American Book Review, American Imago, Poetics Journal, Afterimage, PhotoStatic, Smile,* and elsewhere. His poems, photographs, and graphics have appeared in journals and exhibitions throughout the world. Plutonium Press will soon be publishing his long poem, *Bleeding,* and *Corrisive Signs* (translation from the Spanish of critical essays on alternative art forms in Latin America) is being published by Maisonneuve Press.

Azade Seyhan teaches German literature and literary theory at Bryn Mawr College. She has published articles on German Romanticism, Heine, and cultural theory in *The German Quarterly, Pacific Coast Philology,* and *Deutsche Vierteljahrsschrift.* She is completing a book manuscript on the critical legacy of German Romanticism.

Kristina Straub is an Assistant Professor of English in the program for Literary and Cultural Studies at Carnegie Mellon University. She has published a book on Fanny Burney and numerous articles on issues of gender in eighteenth-century texts and on feminist criticism and theory.

Norman Wacker is an Assistant Professor of English at the University of Washington. His work includes a study of representations of national culture in Virgil, Blake, and Pound and an analysis of an emerging performative ethos as the grounds of textual and ideological construction in Pound's *Cantos.* He is presently working on provocations to intersubjective forms of reader response in the works of Walter Abish, Raymond Carver, and Don DeLillo.

Michael Walsh is an assistant professor of English at the University of Hartford where he teaches film and edits *University of Hartford Studies in Literature.* He has recently published on Jacques Lacan in *Criticism and Lacan* (Georgia UP, 1990), on Chris Marker in *Cineaction,* on William Burroughs in *Motion Picture,* and on postmodernism in *Quarterly Review of Film and Video.*

Index

A

ABC of Reading (Pound): and *logopoeia, melopoeia, phanopoeia*, 88

About Looking (Berger), 203

Abstractionism: Osborne on, 89; and Pound 89, 93, 102

Act and Quality (Altieri), 89-90

"Addressed to Survivors" (Berger, *Pig Earth*), 204

Ad Imaginem Dei. See Ladner

Adventure tales: and imperialism, racism, and sexism, 74

After the Great Divide (Huyssen), 224n.10

After the Last Sky: Palestinian Lives (Said and Mohr), 35n.19, 213-14, 216

Agee, James and Walker Evans, *Let Us Now Praise Famous Men*, 216

Alberti, Rafael, 312

Allegory, 7, 9, 12, 64, 85, 242, 324, 326; as "armor of modernity," 243; baroque, 239; and Baudelaire, 243; and Benjamin, 26, 232, 237-40, 242-43, 245-46; Bürger on, 240; and *flâneur*, 241; Holz on, 239-40; and mimesis, 244, 246; modern, 239-41; political, 155-57; and simulacra, 243, 245; symbol/allegory opposition, 237-38, 246n.4; Wolin on, 238. Works on: "Catastrophic Utopia: The Feminine as Allegory of the Modern," (Buci-Glucksmann), 244

Allegory of narration, 48, 51-53, 59, 64; and Conrad, 64

Allen, Walter: on Marlow in Conrad's "Youth," 55

Althusser, Louis, 23, 158, 117n.15, 326-29; and art and ideology, 177 n.16; definition of subject applied to le Carré's works, 157; on ideology, 157; and interpellation, 172; and subject definition, 168; and subjectivity in le Carré, 174

Altieri, Charles, *Act and Quality*, 89-90; "First Cantos," 92, 103n.1

America (Baudrillard), 245, 289, 301

Animal Farm (Orwell), 258

"Annie Leclerc Writing a Letter, with Vermeer" (Gallop), 275-76

Another Way of Telling (Berger and Mohr), 199-201, 202, 204-205, 211-14, 223n.8, 224n.9

"Another Way of Telling" (Berger), 210-212

Anti-foundationalism, 16

Arac, Jonathan, 38n.26; on the postmodern, 38n.26

"Arachnologies" (Miller), 278

"Arrested unrest" (Benjamin), 240

Aretino, Pietro, 133

Aristos, The (Fowles), 135-36

Aristotle, 9, 33nn.11, 12; and metaphor, 189-90; *Poetics*, 10, 33nn. 11, 12

Arnold, Matthew, *Notebooks* 137

"Arte latinoamericano, El" (Padín), 184

Auerbach, Erich, 31n.1

Avant-garde, 24, 27, 87; in Chicano art, 187; and postmodernism, 187-88

Ayer, A. J., 315

B

Bakhtin, Mikhail, 22, 81, 85, 92, 257; and "carnival," 80; distinction between monologic and polylogic

Conservationist, The (Gordimer), 262-
67, 268n.15; Calloway quotations in,
264; as hypertext, 263
Cool Memories (Baudrillard), 287, 300-
303, 305; Kellner on, 301
Constantine V, 11
Cowan, Bainard, 236
Cratylus (Plato), 252
Creed, Barbara, 274
Criticism by Composition (Pound), 91

D

Daniel Martin (Fowles), 142
*Darstellung der Freiheit: Schillers
transzendentale Frage nach der
Kunst* (Heuer), 246n.2
Darstellung, 246n.2; Benjamin and, 236,
239; discussion of, 235
"Dateline" (Pound), 91
Da Vinci, Leonardo: and *paragone*, 250-
51
Débordement, 253, 261
Decameron (Boccaccio) 267n.6
Deceptive Text (Watts), 51
Deconstruction: Baudrillard on, 289
Dedalus, Stephen, 165, 176n.9
De la séduction (Baudrillard), 29-30,
290, 300-301, 303, 304-305
Deleuze, Gilles, 297
De Man, Paul, 194
Derrida, Jacques, 247n.6, 321-22;
concept of "primariness," 100; and
metaphor, 190; *Of Grammatology*,
321; and *parergon*, 35n.19, 251, 318;
on Plato's *pharmakon*, 9; and "trace,"
101
De Tracy, Destutt, 3, 327
Deuteronomic Reformation. *See*
Gutmann
Differend (Lyotard), 300
Discipline and Punish (Foucault), 99
Discours, Figure (Lyotard), 302
Dittmar, Linda, 260
"Dominant, Residual, and Emergent"

(Williams, *Marxism*), 224n.12
Doane, Janice and Devon Hodges, 274;
Nostalgia and Sexual Difference, 29,
284
Donne, John, 316
Doxa: and Plato, 32
Draft of Thirty Cantos, A (Pound), 92,
94
Du Plessis, Rachael Blau: on *To the
Lighthouse*, 75
Duras, Marguerite: and *Hiroshima mon
amour*, 259-62
Dworkin, Andrea, 279

E

Eagleton, Terry, 235, 240-42, 244-46; on
Conrad's "Youth," 52; *physis* and
psyche in "Youth," 53
Earl, James, W., 12-14, 35n.18, 36n.22
Ebony Tower, The (Fowles) 141, 143
"Ebony Tower, The" (Fowles), 144
Eco, Umberto, 155-56; and objective
structure strategy, 155; *Name of the
Rose, The*, 237
Eddins, Dwight: on *French Lieutenant's
Woman, The*, 141
Edgerton, Samuel, 312
Electra complex: in *A Rose for Emily*,
118
Electric Kool-Aid Acid Test, The
(Wolfe), 251
Elements d'Ideologie. See de Tracy
Eliot, T. S.: and Pound, 89, 91-92;
"Tradition and the Individual Talent,"
89; tradition as ideal order, 91
Eliduc: and Fowles, 143, 149n.7; and
Marie de France, 143
Enargeia, 317
Engels, Friedrick: and false
consciousness, 31n.3
"Epistemo-Critical Prologue"
(Benjamin, *Origin of German Tragic
Drama*), 235
Ethical collectivity, 17

Maggot, A (Fowles), 22, 128-41, 142-45, 148; heteroglossia in, 134, 140-41, 148-49; and *Historical Chronicle, The*, 130-33; and Lee, Ann, 135; Lee as character in, 140; as tribute to Lee, 142

Magic realism: in Berger, 206-207, 221; Jameson on, 206-207

Mâle, Emile, 306, 318n.1

"Male sentence": Gilbert and Gubar on, 70; Woolf and, 70-71

"Man or Woman" (photo) [Hammega], 282

Mandel, Ernest, *Late Capitalism*, 15

Mantissa (Fowles), 141

"Mapping the Postmodern" (Huyssen), 22n.10

Marcus, George E., 207-208; *Writing Culture: The Poetics and Politics of Ethnography*, 207-208; *Writing Culture*: "Contemporary Problems of Ethnography in the Modern World System," 207

Marcus, Jane: on *Orlando*, 80

Marcuse, Herbert, *Negations*, 33n.12

Marie de France, *Eliduc*, 143

Martin, E. J., 35n.18

Marvell, Andrew, 111; "Gallery," 317

Marx, Karl, 3, 316, 323; and Fowles, 137

Marxian existentialism: as *master trope*, 137

Marxism and Literature (Williams) 224n.12

Melopoeia (Pound), 88

Memories (Cassanova), 130

Memory, 7, 210, 213, 216, 219, 246; and Benjamin, 234, 242; and Berger, 25; as "key figure in modern allegory," 241

Men In Feminism. See Smith and Jardine

Meniñas, Las (Velasquez), 138

Metaphor: Aristotle and, 189-90; and Derrida, 190; discussion of, 189; and Wittgenstein, 190

Method of reduction (Havelock), 5

"Michel Foucault, 1927-1984" (Said), 218

Mikado, The, 117

Miles, Margaret, 34n.16

Miller, Nancy K., 278; "Arachnologies," 278; *Heroine's Text, The*, 282; on "erotic text," 77; and "over-reading," 279

Millet, Jean Francois: Berger on, 203

Mimesis, 6, 8, 10, 32n.5; and allegory, 244, 246

Mrs. Dalloway, 19, 71-74; on subversion of male sentence in, 71. *See also* Woolf

Mitchell, W. J. T., 253-54, 314, 317; on Althusser, 326-29; on Baudrillard, 321; discussion of Panofsky's "greeting," 323-24; and "hypericon," 326; *Pictura-poesis* and, 309, 316; on Panofsky, 323-29; on postmodern iconology, 30-31. Works: *Blake's Composite Art*, 309; "Ethics of Form in the Photographic Essay, The," 216, 321; *Iconology and Ideology*, 3, 30, 31n.1, 38n.27, 41, 309, 314-318, 321-23; *Iconology*: "Iconology and Ideology," 15; "Spatial Form in Literature: Towards a General Theory," 319n.5; "*Ut Pictura Theoria*: The Repression of Language in Abstract Painting," 321

Mnemosyne (Praz), 317

Modleski, Tania, 274

Modern Discovery of Primary Oral Cultures. See Ong

"Modern Fiction" (Woolf), 81

Modern Marriage Market, The: Blackwood on, in relation to Conrad's ideals, 59-60

Modernism, 14-16, 18, 20, 38n.26, 48, 63, 69, 187, 194, 252, 319n.5, 325; and Benjamin, 26; and Berger, 25, 216; Jameson on, 257; and *physis* and *psyche*, 52; contrasted with postmodernism, 14-16, 63; relation to postmodern discourse, 62-63. Works